Case Problems in Management

THIRD EDITION

Case Problems in Management

THIRD EDITION

Randall S. Schuler
New York University

Dan R. Dalton
Indiana University

West Publishing Company
St. Paul   New York   Los Angeles   San Francisco

Production Credits

Cover Design: Alice B. Thiede

Copyediting: Rosalie Koskenmaki

Composition: Cumberland Valley Offset

Library of Congress Cataloging in Publication Data

Schuler, Randall S.
  Case problems in management.

  Includes bibliographical references.
  1. Management—Case studies. I. Dalton, Dan R.
II. Title.
HD31.S34155 1986   658.4   85-13620
ISBN 0-314-93507-X

To the faculty and students who will use this information to make organizations places where individuals can work more happily and productively.

Contents

Preface

Case Problems in Management, Third Edition, was written to provide a single, comprehensive source of several types of cases that have proven useful in many management and organizational behavior courses. As with the second edition, this casebook contains several classic cases such as "Hovey and Beard," "Chandler's Restaurant," "The Case of the Missing Time," and "The Case of the Changing Cage." It also contains several new cases such as "Northeast Data Resources," "The National Insurance Company," "The Reporter," and "Peoples Trust." In total, it contains forty-nine cases that we think provoke student interest and that you may find appropriate to use as a single text in a management or organizational behavior course taught entirely by the case method or as a supplement to a management or organizational behavior textbook.

The cases depict several organizational settings, from hospitals to manufacturing companies, from relatively small companies to rather large companies, the largest being General Motors in the Lordstown case. Although we have categorized each case into a major section of management and organization by topic, many of the cases could have been as appropriately placed in another section. Thus each case offers a great variety of management and organization topics that can be analyzed and discussed. The cases included in this book can be analyzed by students having relatively no background in management and organization to those having extensive background in management and organization either from previous course work or from personal work experience. Therefore, this casebook should be appropriate for all levels of management and organizational behavior courses, not just in business administration but also in hospital administration, social work administration, and any other area of administrative science. Because the cases in this book are taken from copyrighted material, it is not possible to change their wording, and readers will notice some sexist language. However, these cases have been included here because they are significant and valid even if some of their language is not.

This third edition of *Case Problems in Management* differs from the second edition in several respects. First, we have included new cases not in the second edition. Second, cases have been deleted in order to keep this casebook at a reasonable length. None of the classics introduced in the second edition, however, has been deleted. Third, the casebook has a new organization to better reflect and emphasize the structure, functions, and processes of management and behavior in organizations. Thus this edition has a much more tightly organized set of cases that topically flow with many of the current textbooks in management and organizational behavior. Fourth, the instructor's manual has been expanded by including more discussion topics for several of the cases.

A great many colleagues have been especially helpful to us in the preparation of this casebook. Several sent us some of their favorite cases and others made invaluable suggestions about the content of the book and the instructor's manual. Based upon the majority of the suggestions, we decided to incorporate all objectives, questions, and comments for each case in the instructor's manual.

Many colleagues indicated this would give them the greatest latitude in using the cases in the book. In addition, where possible, solutions or follow-ups to cases were included in the instructor's manual. Several authors of the cases used graciously provided us with these solutions or follow-ups. We are grateful to them.

We would like to thank those individuals who provided us with their cases: Susan E. Jackson, The University of Michigan; Steve Stumpf, Tom Mullen, Hrach Bedrosian, and Joe Martocchio, New York University; Jim Barnes (deceased), Tim W. Collins, and Brenda J. Moscove, California State University, Bakersfield; Martin R. Moser, Lawrence Ondovic, and William Naumes, Clark University; D. Jeffrey Lenn, The George Washington University; Floyd G. Willoughby, Oakland University; Peter G. and Lynda L. Goulet, University of Northern Iowa; Molly Bateson and Nancy Sherman, Tulane University; Jan P. Muczyk, Donald Scotton, and Jeffrey Susbauer, The Cleveland State University; Ed Christensen, Southwestern Publishing Company; Theodore Herbert, Rollins College; Margaret Fenn and Harry Knudson, University of Washington; W.F. Whyte, Cornell; Hank Sims, Jr., The Pennsylvania State University; Richard T. Mowday, University of Oregon; Andrew D. Szilagyi, Jr., University of Houston; Antone F. Alber, Bradley University; Jack Rettig, Oregon State University; Hak-Chong Lee, Yonsei University; James C. Conant, California State University; Terry Beehr, Central Michigan University; Robert J. House, University of Toronto; John R. Rizzo, Western Michigan University; Herb Shepard, Albert Rubinstein, Northwestern University; Alex Bavelas, Stanford Research Institute; Donald D. White, University of Arkansas; H. William Vroman, Tennessee Technological University.

The cooperation and assistance by several publishers were also greatly appreciated. The publishers are: Macmillan Publishing Co., Inc.; Prentice-Hall, Inc.; The Board of Trustees of the Leland Stanford Junior University; The Board of Trustees of the University of Wichita; Southwestern Publishing Company, Inc.; Holbrook Press Inc.; McGraw-Hill Book Company; Business Week; Northwestern University; Winthrop Publishing Co.; Society for Applied Anthropology; Doubleday & Company, Inc.; The Fellows and President of Harvard College; Intercollegiate News and Views; Houghton Miffin Company; and the American Council on Education.

In the instructor's manual we have included several articles on the use, teaching evaluation, and application of cases. Several colleagues indicated they had never used cases before, and would appreciate some basic guidelines to get them started in the right direction in using cases. It was a combination of this feedback and the suggestion of Kay Bartol, University of Maryland, that resulted in the inclusion of the articles on using cases.

Finally we wish to thank those with whom we worked most closely during this project and who provided us with invaluable encouragement and support. Our editors at West, Lisa Palmisano, Esther Craig and Dick Fenton, and John W. Slocum, Jr. at Southern Methodist University all provided important assistance from the very beginning to the very end. We thank Eddie Roberts for typing the Instructor's Manual and for the fine secretarial support provided by the staffs at New York University and Indiana University.

RANDALL S. SCHULER
DAN R. DALTON

Case Problems in Management

THIRD EDITION

Part I

Managerial Functions and Activities

Cases Outline

- The Industrial Controls, Incorporated (A)
- The Case of the Missing Time
- Dick Spencer
- Chrysler Corporation
- Tale of Three Tales
- Work Group Ownership of an Improved Tool
- Far-West Water District: Policy, Strategy, and Functional Problems

1. The Industrial Controls, Incorporated (A)*

Background and Philosophy of the Founder

Mr. Bauer had been a respected executive in one of the larger and most successful conglomerates. He rose to the position of Group Vice-President, and his career in the company appeared promising. After all, he had an undergraduate degree in mathematics, a Harvard MBA, a good deal of experience in a large firm, and a history of success. Yet, approximately twelve years ago, Mr. Bauer elected to acquire a small firm engaged in manufacturing controls for a wide range of industrial machines, doing about $200,000 worth of business annually.

Mr. Bauer intended from the very beginning to expand his firm from a small company to a medium-size enterprise. This he wanted to accomplish through retained earnings and occasional loans in order not to dilute his ownership and control. In fact, Industrial Controls, Incorporated, did grow at an average rate of 20 percent per year until 1984, when the company had sales in excess of $5,000,000 and employed eighty-nine people (seventy-nine full-time and ten part-time).

Evolution of the Firm

Stage 1. After acquiring Industrial Controls, Incorporated, Mr. Bauer hired a production manager. He selected a Mr. Dooley who had been a foreman in Mr. Bauer's former division at the conglomerate and was known to him as a hard worker. Dooley did not have a college degree but had some electronic training in the Navy and took several evening courses at a local university.

Four years after acquiring Industrial Controls, Incorporated, Mr. Bauer availed himself of the opportunity to acquire another small firm (a four-man operation) owned and operated by a Mr. Cotton, an engineer who held several patents on equipment similar to that manufactured by Industrial Controls, Incorporated, but more sophisticated. Prior to forming his own company, Mr. Cotton had been

*This case was prepared by Donald W. Scotton, Chairman, Departments of Marketing and General Administration, and Jan P. Muczyk, Department of Management and Labor, The Cleveland State University, and is used here with their permission. Copyright © Donald W. Scotton and Jan P. Muczyk.

employed as a sales engineer in a large firm in a similar line of business. Mr. Bauer also hired Mr. Cotton as the Chief Engineer and salesman. Mr. Cotton was given the opportunity to purchase a small interest in the firm and took advantage of it.

As long as the firm was small, these three individuals and the Sales Manager were able to manage the operations quite well. They worked out of the same office in a small building, saw each other frequently, remembered important matters without writing them down, and informally coordinated all of the details of day-to-day operations with minimum of policy, procedures, and paper work. There was even no need for an organizational chart or formal job descriptions.

Stage 2. There was nothing so unique in what Industrial Controls, Incorporated, was making and doing that could not be provided by any of a number of large corporations in the machine controls field. In fact, Industrial Controls, Incorporated, was in competition with the larger companies when it came to producing and selling machine controls that had standard applications. Consequently, Industrial Controls, Incorporated, had elected to carve out for itself a niche, viz., machine controls custom made to the specifications of a client and personalized service that the larger suppliers of more standardized equipment were not interested in providing.

Business continued to expand as the result of development of new and more complex lines of machine controls, and the operation was moved to a new and larger facility with individual offices for all corporate officers. Growth was further accelerated by the acquisition of several additional lines of related machine controls.

Up to this time, Mr. Bauer had been able to orchestrate the entire operation, i.e., he was the glue that held everything together and gave it direction. It just happened that at this juncture of the company's evolution, Mr. Bauer became involved in a number of community affairs which took more and more of his time.

When the Sales Manager resigned, Mr. Cotton, because he liked selling above all else, was made the Vice-President of Sales and Marketing. Mr. Daren, the Chief Development Engineer who had reported to Mr. Cotton, was elevated to the position of Chief Engineer in charge of research and development as well as application engineering. Mr. Daren earned this promotion primarily on the basis of being a brilliant circuit designer. He also sought the position, and may have left the organization if it were denied him. Mr. Daren continued to do a considerable amount of R & D and application engineering after his promotion. Mr. Dooley remained as the Production Manager but had a much larger operation.

It must be kept in mind that in a company producing sophisticated industrial equipment to customer specifications which are at times incomplete because the customer isn't certain about what he wants, the interdependence between Sales, Production, and Engineering is considerable.

At this point of the company's evolution, a number of problem areas required attention. The inventory of components increased from $400,000 to $1,200,000 in one year. Although some of the increase was justified by greater volume of business, the latter figure was deemed excessive. Engineering complained that it was not receiving accurate customer specifications from Sales as well as receiving late modifications of the specifications. Production was complaining that it was receiving inadequate engineering releases and not enough lead time for assembling and testing the equipment. Furthermore, Mr. Dooley argued that since most orders were customized, production inefficiencies and delays were inevitable. Mr. Dooley and Mr. Daren felt that Sales was not developing markets for more standardized items in larger quantities which in turn would ease the workload for Engineering and Production alike. Sales and Production felt that engineering was not giving them the support that was essential in this type of operation. When the Customer Service personnel needed assistance on a major equipment problem in the field, Engineering was reluctant to drop development and application work to assist with the problem. Customer Service personnel complained that Engineering was designing equipment that was difficult to service in the field. Sales believed that Engineering preferred to develop new product lines rather than perfect existing equipment. Manufacturing personnel complained that they were not getting the amount of assistance from Engineering required to assemble a product either designed or modified by the Engineering Department. Customer complaints also started arriving at an increasing rate.

Stage 3.   In light of rapid growth and increased complexity of the product lines, Mr. Bauer decided to reorganize. As a first step, he hired Mr. Cline as an assistant to the president in order to augment his time. Mr. Cline had considerable experience in several manufacturing plants, in a consulting firm, and taught marketing courses part-time at a local university. Soon after, Mr. Bauer assigned Mr. Cline the responsibility for corporate planning. He also separated the marketing functions from Sales and put Mr. Cline in charge of the former.

Mr. Bauer then hired a controller to assist in managing the accounting and financial aspects of the firm. Although Mr. Paves was a C.P.A. and had accounting experience, he was new to financial planning and control. Consequently, Mr. Bauer retained these responsibilities.

Since the product line had become more sophisticated and because the work load was now greater, Mr. Bauer appointed Mr. Hinds, who had formerly worked in the Engineering Department and had half-time responsibility for quality control, as a full-time Quality Control Manager reporting directly to him. Mr. Affermon was hired as a part-time Personnel Manager to establish personnel policy and handle personnel problems which had increased to the point that they were consuming a considerable amount of time of the operating personnel, including Mr. Bauer. Although Mr. Affermon had personnel administration experience in a larger firm, he was out of a job at the time he was hired by Industrial Controls, Incorporated. Mr. Dooley was given the title of Vice-President of Manufacturing. Figure 1 reflects the current organization.

After a brief experience with the reorganization, Mr. Bauer concluded that something more fundamental had to be done in order to prepare his organization for future growth and to deal with the problems that were occupying his time.

Mr. Bauer believed, as did his fellow corporate officers, that a computer would aid them in a number of areas, such as processing sales orders, compiling an accurate bill of materials, controlling inventory, billing customers accurately, etc. The responsibility of integrating the new computer into company operations was given to Mr. Cline.

Mr. Bauer contemplated his future and that of the company. He concluded that he had the following choices:

1.   He could sell his firm to one of the companies which in the past expressed an interest in buying Industrial Controls, Incorporated.
2.   He could become a chairman of the board and leave the operating decisions to someone else. But who?

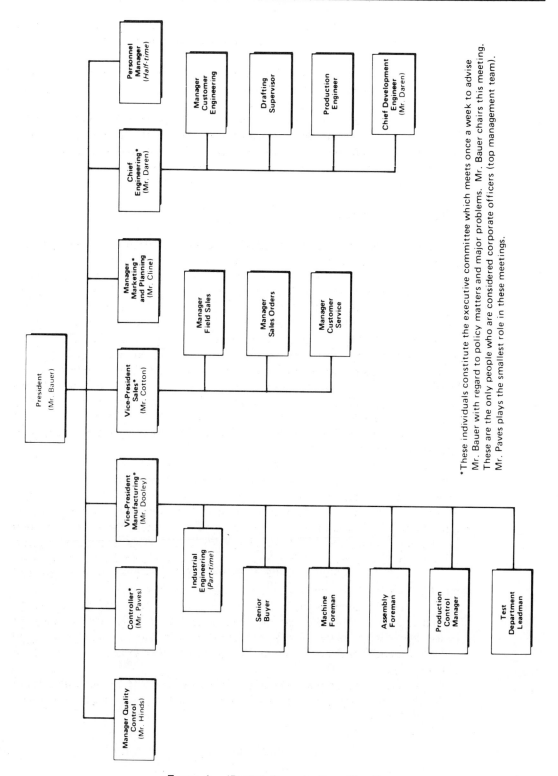

FIGURE 1. (Partial Organization Chart)

3. He could stay with the same management team and get more personally involved in the operations of the firm by divesting himself of his outside interests.
4. He could hire a new cadre of managers and remain as chief executive officer or become chairman of the board.

Mr. Bauer had a strong sense of loyalty to his present key personnel who played a large role in building the company. Consequently, he opted for the third alternative but decided to seek outside help to aid him in overcoming the present problems and preparing the company for future growth.

Bring in Consultants

Mr. Bauer contacted two consultants who suggested performing a needs analysis first and a general approach to solving the firm's problems which would be made more specific after the needs analysis was completed. Messrs. Muzak and Ragu accepted the assignment and found that the motivation level of the managers and supervisors was very high. They worked long hours (including Saturdays and Sundays), but they were still getting behind. These men were seldom in their offices because of the day-to-day crises that came up. Cotton was on the phone with customers, manufacturer's representatives, and factory salesmen. Daren was designing and testing several pieces of equipment in order to make delivery dates. Dooley was on the shop floor helping the production people with their problems and expediting rush orders. Cline instead of Affermon was dealing with a number of personnel problems in addition to his other duties. Nobody had time to train his subordinates. Few people understood fully what Mr. Cline was doing, and no one knew what Mr. Affermon was doing.

Meetings were held frequently, but the consensus was that they were too long and at times unproductive. Personal conflicts were apparent between some people in Sales, Engineering, and Production who needed to interact in order to get the job done. A number of procedures that Mr. Bauer initiated were frequently ignored. In addition, some procedures that could have been routinized remained unnecessarily complex. Mr. Hinds proved to be an irritant to Engineering and Production, and even his subordinate questioned his competence in the job.

In spite of the problems that have been identified, the company experienced rapid growth and was profitable every year of its existence.

During the needs analysis, two things left a special impression on the consultants. First, when the managers were asked by Mr. Bauer some time earlier to formulate action plans for next year, most of them had trouble beginning and completing them. Second, all of the managers genuinely wanted to improve their effectiveness.

The consultants concluded that they should present Mr. Bauer with a list of major problems, their priorities, and a concrete action program for dealing with these problems.

2. The Case of the Missing Time*

It was 7:30 Tuesday morning when Chet Craig, General Manager of the Norris Company's Central Plant, swung his car out of the driveway of his suburban home and headed to the plant in Midvale, six miles away. The trip to the plant took about twenty minutes and gave Chet an opportunity to think about plant problems without interruption.

The Norris Company operated three printing plants and did a nationwide business in quality color work. It had about 350 employees, nearly half of whom were employed at the Central Plant. The company's headquarters offices were also located in the Central Plant building.

Chet had started with the Norris Company as an expeditor in its Eastern Plant ten years ago, after his graduation from Ohio State. After three years he was promoted to Production Supervisor, and two years later was made assistant to the manager of the Eastern Plant. A year and a half ago he had been transferred to the Central Plant as assistant to the Plant Manager and one month later, when the manager retired, Chet was promoted to General Plant Manager.

Chet was in good spirits this morning. Various thoughts occurred to him as he said to himself, "This is going to be the day to really get things done." He thought of the day's work, first one project, then another, trying to establish priorities. He decided that the open-end unit scheduling was probably the most important; certainly the most urgent. He recalled that on Friday the Vice-President had casually asked him if he had given the project any further thought. Chet realized that he had not been giving it any attention lately. He had been meaning to get to work on his idea for over three months, but something else always seemed to crop up.

"I haven't had time to really work it out," he said to himself. "I'd better get going and finish it off one of these days." He then began to break down the objectives, procedures, and installation steps in the project. It gave him a feeling of satisfaction as he calculated the anticipated cost savings. "It's high time," he told himself. "This idea should have been completed a long time ago."

Chet had first conceived the open-end unit scheduling idea almost two years ago just prior to leaving the Eastern Plant. He had talked it over with the General Manager of the Eastern Plant, and both agreed that it was a good idea and worth developing. The idea was temporarily shelved when Chet had been transferred to the Central Plant a month later.

His thoughts returned to other plant projects he was determined to get under way. He started to think through a procedure for the simpler transport of dies to and from the Eastern Plant. He thought of the notes on his desk: the inventory analysis he needed to identify and eliminate some of the slow-moving stock items; the packing controls which needed revision; and the need to design a new

*Copyright 1971, Northwestern University. Reprinted by permission.

All names and organizational designations have been disguised. Northwestern University cases are reports of concrete events and behavior prepared for class discussion. They are not intended as examples of good or bad administrative or technical practices.

special order form. He also decided that this was the day to settle on a job printer to do the outside printing of simple office forms. There were a few other projects he could not recall offhand, but he felt sure that he could tend to them some time during the day. Again he said to himself, "This is the day to really get rolling."

When he entered the plant, Chet was met by Al Noren, the stockroom foreman, who appeared troubled. "A great morning, Al," said Chet, cheerfully.

"Well, I don't know, Chet: my new man isn't in this morning," said Noren morosely.

"Have you heard from him?" asked Chet.

"No, I haven't."

"These stock handlers take it for granted that if they're not here, they don't have to call in and report. Better ask Personnel to call him."

Al hesitated a moment. "Okay, Chet," he said, "but can you find me a man? I have two cars to unload today."

Making a note of the incident, Chet headed for his office. He greeted some workers discussing the day's work with Marilyn, the Office Manager. As the meeting broke up Marilyn took some samples from a clasper and showed them to Chet and asked if they should be shipped that way, or if it would be necessary to inspect them. Before he could answer Marilyn went on to ask if he could suggest another clerical operator for the sealing machine to replace the regular operator, who was home ill. She also told him that Gene, the Industrial Engineer, had called and was waiting to hear from Chet.

Chet told Marilyn to ship the samples and made a note of the need for a sealer operator and then called Gene. He agreed to stop by Gene's office before lunch, and started on his routine morning tour of the plant. He asked each foreman the volumes and types of orders they were running, the number of people present, how the schedules were coming along, and the orders to be run next; he helped the folding room foreman find temporary storage space for consolidating a carload shipment; discussed quality control with a pressman who had been running poor work; arranged to transfer four people temporarily to different departments, including two for Al in the stockroom; talked to the shipping foreman about pickups and special orders to be delivered that day. As he continued through the plant, he saw to it that reserve stock was moved out of the forward stock area; talked to another pressman about his requested change of vacation schedule; had a "heart-to-heart" talk with a press helper who seemed to need frequent assurance; approved two type and one color okays for different pressmen.

Returning to his office, Chet reviewed the production reports on the larger orders against his initial projections and found that the plant was running slightly behind schedule. He called in the folding room foreman and together they went over the line-up of machines and made several changes.

During this discussion the composing room foreman stopped in to cover several type changes and the routing foreman telephoned for approval of a revised printing schedule. The stockroom foreman called twice—first to inform him that two standard, fast-moving stock items were dangerously low; later to advise him that the paper stock for the urgent Dillon job had finally arrived. Chet telephoned this information to the people concerned.

He then began to put delivery dates on important inquiries received from customers and salesmen. (The routine inquiries were handled by Marilyn.) While he was doing this he was interrupted twice—once by a sales correspondent calling from the West Coast to ask for a better delivery date than originally scheduled; once by the Vice-President, Personnel, asking Chet to set a time when he could hold an initial induction interview with a new employee.

After dating the customer and salesmen inquiries, Chet headed for his morning conference in the executive office. At this meeting he answered the Vice-President, Sales's questions in connections with "hot" orders, complaints, the status of large-volume orders and potential new orders. Then he met with the Vice-President and General Production Manager to answer "the old man's" questions on several production and personnel problems. Before leaving the executive offices, he stopped at the office of the Purchasing Agent to inquire about the delivery of some cartons, paper, and boxes, and to place an order for some new paper.

On the way back to his own office Chet conferred with Gene about two current engineering projects. When he reached his desk, he lit a cigarette, and looked at his watch. It was ten minutes before lunch—just time enough to make a few notes of the details he needed to check in order to answer knotty questions raised by the Vice-President, Sales, that morning.

After lunch Chet started again. He began by checking the previous day's production reports; did some rescheduling to get out urgent orders; placed delivery dates on new orders and inquiries received that morning; consulted with a foreman on a personal problem. He spent about twenty minutes at the TWX[1] going over mutual problems with the Eastern Plant.

By midafternoon Chet had made another tour of the plant, after which he met with the Vice-President, Personnel, to review with him a touchy personal problem raised by one of the clerical employees, the vacation schedules submitted by his foreman, the pending job evaluation program. Following this conference, Chet hurried back to his office to complete the special statistical report for Universal Waxing Corporation, one of Norris's biggest customers. When he finished the report he discovered that it was ten after six and he was the only one left in the office. Chet was tired. He put on his coat and headed for the parking lot. On the way out he was stopped by the night supervisor and the night layout foreman for approval of type and layout changes.

As he drove home Chet reviewed the day he had just completed. "Busy?" he asked himself, "Too much so—but did I accomplish anything?" The answer seemed to be "Yes, and no—there was the usual routine, the same as any other day. The plant kept going and it was a good production day. Any creative or special work done?" Chet winced. "I guess not."

With a feeling of guilt Chet asked himself, "Am I an executive?" I'm paid like one, and I have a responsible assignment, and the authority to carry it out. My supervisors at headquarters think I'm a good manager. Yet one of the greatest returns a company gets from an executive is his innovative thinking and accomplishments. What have I done about that? Today was just like other days, and I didn't do any creative work. The projects that I was so eager to work on this morning are no further ahead than they were yesterday. What's more, I can't say that tomorrow night or the next night they'll be any closer to completion. This is a real problem, and there must be some answer to it."

---

1. Leased private telegram communication system using a teletypewriter.

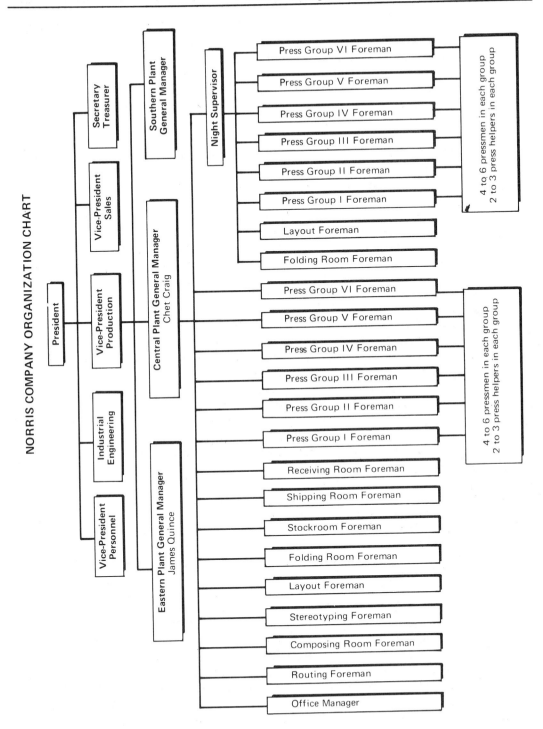

NORRIS COMPANY ORGANIZATION CHART

- President
  - Vice-President Personnel
  - Industrial Engineering
  - Vice-President Production
    - Southern Plant General Manager
    - Central Plant General Manager
      Chet Craig
      - Night Supervisor
        - Press Group VI Foreman
        - Press Group V Foreman
        - Press Group IV Foreman
        - Press Group III Foreman
        - Press Group II Foreman
        - Press Group I Foreman
        - Layout Foreman
        - Folding Room Foreman

        4 to 6 pressmen in each group
        2 to 3 press helpers in each group

      - Press Group VI Foreman
      - Press Group V Foreman
      - Press Group IV Foreman
      - Press Group III Foreman
      - Press Group II Foreman
      - Press Group I Foreman

        4 to 6 pressmen in each group
        2 to 3 press helpers in each group

    - Eastern Plant General Manager
      James Quince
      - Receiving Room Foreman
      - Shipping Room Foreman
      - Stockroom Foreman
      - Folding Room Foreman
      - Layout Foreman
      - Stereotyping Foreman
      - Composing Room Foreman
      - Routing Foreman
      - Office Manager
  - Vice-President Sales
  - Secretary Treasurer

FIGURE 1

"Night work? Yes, sometimes. This is understood. But I've been doing too much night work lately. My wife and family deserve some of my time. After all, they are the people for whom I'm really working. If I spend much more time away from them, I'm not meeting my own personal objectives. I spend a lot of time on church work. Should I eliminate that? I feel I owe that as an obligation. Besides, I feel I'm making a worthwhile contribution in this work. Maybe I can squeeze a little time from my fraternal activities. But where does recreation fit in?"

Chet groped for the solution. "Maybe I'm just rationalizing because I schedule my own work poorly. But I don't think so. I've studied my work habits and I think I plan intelligently and delegate authority. Do I need an assistant? Possibly, but that's a long-time project and I don't believe I could justify the additional overhead expense. Anyway, I doubt whether it would solve the problem.

By this time Chet had turned off the highway into the side street leading to his home. "I guess I really don't know the answer," he said to himself as he pulled into his driveway. "This morning everything seemed so simple, but now. . . ."

3.   Dick Spencer*

After the usual banter when old friends meet for cocktails, the conversation between a couple of University professors and Dick Spencer, a former student who was now a successful businessman, turned to Dick's life as a vice-president of a large manufacturing firm.

"I've made a lot of mistakes, most of which I could live with, but this one series of incidents was so frustrating that I could have cried at the time," Dick said in response to a question. "I really have to laugh at how ridiculous it is now, but at the time I blew my cork."

Spencer was plant manager of Modrow Company, a Canadian branch of the Tri-American Corporation. Tri-American was a major producer of primary aluminum with integrated operations ranging from the mining of bauxite through the processing to fabrication of aluminum into a variety of products. The company also made and sold refractories and industrial chemicals. The parent company had wholly-owned subsidiaries in five separate United States locations and had foreign affiliates in fifteen different countries.

Tri-American mined bauxite in the Jamaican West Indies and shipped the raw material by commercial vessels to two plants in Louisiana where it was processed into alumina. The alumina was then shipped to reduction plants in one of three locations for conversion into primary aluminum. Most of the primary aluminum was then moved to the companies' fabricating plants for further processing.

---

*This case was developed and prepared by Professor Margaret E. Fenn, Graduate School of Business Administration, University of Washington. Reprinted by permission.

Fabricated aluminum items included sheet, flat, coil, and corrugated products; siding; and roofing.

Tri-American employed approximately 22,000 employees in the total organization. The company was governed by a board of directors which included the chairman, vice-chairman, president, and twelve vice-presidents. However, each of the subsidiaries and branches functioned as independent units. The board set general policy, which was then interpreted ad applied by the various plant managers. In a sense, the various plants competed with one another as though they were independent companies. This decentralization in organizational structure increased the freedom and authority of the plant managers, but increased the pressure for profitability.

The Modrow branch was located in a border town in Canada. The total work force in Modrow was 1,000. This Canadian subsidiary was primarily a fabricating unit. Its main products were foil and building products such as roofing and siding. Aluminum products were gaining in importance in architectural plans, and increased sales were predicted for this branch. Its location and its stable work force were the most important advantages it possessed.

In anticipation of estimated increases in building product sales, Modrow had recently completed a modernization and expansion project. At the same time, their research and art departments combined talents in developing a series of twelve new patterns of siding which were being introduced to the market. Modernization and pattern development had been costly undertakings, but the expected return on investment made the project feasible. However, the plant manager, who was a Tri-American vice-president, had instituted a campaign to cut expenses wherever possible. In this introductory notice of the campaign, he emphasized that cost reduction would be the personal aim of every employee at Modrow.

Salesman

The plant manager of Modrow, Dick Spencer, was an American who had been transferred to this Canadian branch two years previously, after the start of the modernization plan. Dick had been with the Tri-American Company for fourteen years, and his progress within the organization was considered spectacular by those who knew him well. Dick had received a Master's degree in Business Administration from a well-known university at the age of twenty-two. Upon graduation he had accepted a job as salesman for Tri-American. During his first year as a salesman, he succeeded in landing a single, large contract which put him near the top of the sales-volume leaders. In discussing his phenomenal rise in the sales volume, several of his fellow salesmen concluded that his looks, charm, and ability on the golf course contributed as much to his success as his knowledge of the business or his ability to sell the products.

The second year of his sales career, he continued to set a fast pace. Although his record set difficult goals for the other salesmen, he was considered a "regular guy" by them, and both he and they seemed to enjoy the few occasions when they socialized. However, by the end of the second year of constant traveling and selling, Dick began to experience some doubt about his future.

His constant involvement in business affairs disrupted his marital life, and his wife divorced him during the second year with Tri-American. Dick resented her action at first, but gradually seemed to recognize that his career at present depended on his freedom to travel unencumbered. During that second year, he ranged far and wide in his sales territory, and successfully closed several large contracts. None of them was as large as his first year's major sale, but in total volume he again was well up near the top of salesmen for the year. Dick's name became well known in the corporate headquarters, and he was spoken of as "the boy to watch."

Dick had met the president of Tri-American during his first year as a salesman at a company conference. After three days of golfing and socializing they developed a relaxed camaraderie considered unusual by those who observed the developing friendship. Although their contacts were infrequent after the conference, their easy relationship seemed to blossom the few times they did meet. Dick's friends kidded him about his ability to make use of his new friendship to promote himself in the company, but Dick brushed aside their jibes and insisted that he'd make it on his own abilities, not someone's coattail.

By the time he was twenty-five, Dick began to suspect that he did not look forward to a life as a salesman for the rest of his career. He talked about his unrest with his friends, and they suggested that he groom himself for sales manager. "You won't make the kind of money you're making from commissions," he was told, "but you will have a foot in the door from an administrative standpoint, and you won't have to travel quite as much as you do now." Dick took their suggestions lightly, and continued to sell the product, but was aware that he felt dissatisfied and did not seem to get the satisfaction out of his job that he had once enjoyed.

By the end of his third year with the company Dick was convinced that he wanted a change in direction. As usual, he and the president spent quite a bit of time on the golf course during the annual company sales conference. After their match one day, the president kidded Dick about his game. The conversation drifted back to business, and the president, who seemed to be in a jovial mood, started to kid Dick about his sales ability. In a joking way, he implied that anyone could sell a product as good as Tri-American's, but that it took real "guts and know-how" to make the products. The conversation drifted to other things, but this remark stuck with Dick.

Sometime later, Dick approached the president formally with a request for a transfer out of the sales division. The president was surprised and hesitant about this change in career direction for Dick. He recognized the superior sales ability that Dick seemed to possess, but was unsure that Dick was willing or able to assume responsibilities in any other division of the organization. Dick sensed the hesitancy, but continued to push his request. He later remarked that it seemed that the initial hesitancy of the president convinced Dick that he needed an opportunity to prove himself in a field other than sales.

Trouble Shooter

Dick was finally transferred back to the home office of the organization and indoctrinated into productive and administrative roles in the company as a special assistant to the senior vice-president of production. As a special assistant, Dick was assigned several trouble-shooting jobs. He acquitted himself well in this role, but in the process succeeded in gaining a reputation as a ruthless head hunter among the branches where he had performed a series of amputations. His reputation as an amiable, genial, easygoing guy from the sales department was the antithesis of the reputation of a cold, calculating head hunter which he earned in his trouble-shooting role. The vice-president, who was Dick's boss, was aware of the reputation which Dick had earned but was pleased with the results that were obtained. The faltering departments that Dick had worked in seemed to bloom with new life and energy after Dick's recommended amputations. As a result, the vice-president began to sing Dick's praises, and the president began to accept Dick in his new role in the company.

Management Responsibility

About three years after Dick's switch from sales, he was given an assignment as assistant plant manager of an English branch of the company. Dick, who had remarried, moved his wife and family to London, and they attempted to adapt to their new routine. The plant manager was English, as were most of the other employees. Dick and his family were accepted with reservations into the community life as well as into the plant life. The difference between British and American philosophy and performance within the plant was marked for Dick who was imbued with modern managerial concepts and methods. Dick's directives from headquarters were to update and upgrade performance in this branch. However, his power and authority were less than those of his superior, so he constantly found himself in the position of having to soft pedal or withhold suggestions that he would have liked to make, or innovations that he would have liked to introduce. After a frustrating year and a half, Dick was suddenly made plant manager of an old British company which had just been purchased by Tri-American. He left his first English assignment with mixed feelings and moved from London to Birmingham.

As the new plant manager, Dick operated much as he had in his trouble-shooting job for the first couple of years of his change from sales to administration. Training and reeducation programs were instituted for all supervisors and managers who survived the initial purge. Methods were studied and simplified or redesigned whenever possible, and new attention was directed toward production which better met the needs of the sales organization. A strong controller helped to straighten out the profit picture through stringent cost control: and, by the end of the third year, the company showed a small profit for the first time in many years. Because he felt that this battle was won, Dick requested transfer back to the United States. This request was partially granted when nine months later he was awarded a junior vice-president title, and was made manager of a subsidiary Canadian plant, Modrow.

Modrow Manager

Prior to Dick's appointment as plant manager at Modrow, extensive plans for plant expansion and improvement had been approved and started. Although he had not been in on the original discussions and plans, he inherited all the problems that accompany large-scale changes in any organization. Construction was slower in completion than originally planned, equipment arrived before the building was finished, employees were upset about the extent of change expected in their work routines with the installation of additional machinery, and, in general, morale was at a low ebb.

Various versions of Dick's former activities had preceded him, and on his arrival he was viewed with dubious eyes. The first few months after his arrival were spent in a frenzy of catching up. This entailed constant conferences and meetings, volumes of reading of past reports, becoming acquainted with the civic leaders of the area, and a plethora of dispatches to and from the home office. Costs continued to climb unabated.

By the end of his first year at Modrow, the building program had been completed, although behind schedule, the new equipment had been installed, and some revamping of cost procedures had been incorporated. The financial picture at this time showed a substantial loss, but since it had been budgeted as a loss, this was not surprising. All managers of the various divisions had worked closely with their supervisors and accountants in planning the budget for the following year, and Dick began to emphasize his personal interest in cost reduction.

As he worked through his first year as plant manager, Dick developed the habit of strolling around the organization. He was apt to leave his office and appear anywhere on the plant floor, in the design offices, at the desk of a purchasing agent or accountant, in the plant cafeteria rather than the executive dining room, or wherever there was activity concerned with Modrow. During his strolls he looked, listened, and became acquainted. If he observed activities which he wanted to talk about, or heard remarks that gave him clues to future action, he did not reveal these at the time. Rather he had a nod, a wave, a smile, for the people near him, but a mental note to talk to his supervisors, managers, and foremen in the future. At first his presence disturbed those who noted him coming and going, but after several exposures to him without any noticeable effect, the workers came to accept his presence and continue their usual activities. Supervisors, managers, and foremen, however, did not feel as comfortable when they saw him in the area.

Their feelings were aptly expressed by the manager of the siding department one day when he was talking to one of his foremen: "I wish to hell he'd stay up in the front office where he belongs. Whoever heard of a plant manager who had time to wander around the plant all the time? Why doesn't he tend to his paper work and let us tend to our business?"

"Don't let him get you down, " joked the foreman. "Nothing ever comes of his visits. Maybe he's just lonesome and looking for a friend. You know how these Americans are."

"Well, you may feel that nothing ever comes of his visits, but I don't. I've been called into his office three separate times within the last two months. The heat must really be on from the head office. You know these conferences we have every month where he reviews our financial progress, our building progress, our design progress, etc.? Well, we're not really progressing as fast as we should be. If you ask me we're in for continuing trouble."

In recalling his first year at Modrow, Dick had felt constantly pressured and badgered. He always sensed that the Canadians he worked with resented his presence since he was brought in over the heads of the operating staff. At the same time he felt this subtle resistance from his Canadian work force, he believed that the president and his friends in the home office were constantly on the alert, waiting for Dick to prove himself or fall flat on his face. Because of the constant pressures and demands of the work, he had literally dumped his family into a new community and had withdrawn into the plant. In the process, he built up a wall of resistance toward the demands of his wife and children who, in turn, felt as though he was abandoning them.

During the course of the conversation with his University friends, he began to recall a series of incidents that probably had resulted from the conflicting pressures. When describing some of these incidents, he continued to emphasize the fact that his attempt to be relaxed and casual had backfired. Laughingly, Dick said, "As you know, both human relations and accounting were my weakest subjects during the Master's program, and yet they are two fields I felt I needed the most at Modrow at this time." He described some of the cost procedures that he would have liked to incorporate. However, without the support and knowledge furnished by his former controller, he busied himself with details that were unnecessary. One day, as he describes it, he overhead a conversation between two of the accounting staff members with whom he had been working very closely. One of them commented to the other, "For a guy who's a vice-president, he sure spends a lot of time breathing down our necks. Why doesn't he simply tell us the kind of systems he would like to try, and let us do the experimenting and work out the budget?" Without commenting on the conversation he overheard, Dick then described himself as attempting to spend less time and be less directive in the accounting department.

Another incident he described which apparently had real meaning for him was one in which he had called a staff conference with his top-level managers. They had been going "hammer and tongs" for better than an hour in his private office, and in the process of heated conversation had loosened ties, taken off coats, and really rolled up their sleeves. Dick himself had slipped out of his shoes. In the midst of this, his secretary reminded him of an appointment with public officials. Dick had rapidly finished up his conference with his managers, straightened his tie, donned his coat, and had wandered out into the main office in his stocking feet.

Dick fully described several incidents when he had disappointed, frustrated, or confused his wife and family by forgetting birthdays, appointments, dinner engagements, etc. He seemed to be describing a pattern of behavior which resulted from continuing pressure and frustration. He was setting the scene to describe his baffling and humiliating position in the siding department. In looking back and recalling his activities during this first year, Dick commented on the fact that his frequent wanderings throughout the plant had resulted in a nodding acquaintance with the workers, but probably had also resulted in foremen and supervisors spending more time getting ready for his visits and reading meaning into them afterwards than attending to their specific duties. His attempts to know in detail the accounting procedures being used required long hours of concentration and detailed conversations with the accounting staff, which were time-consuming and very frustrating for him, as well as for them. His lack of attention to his family life resulted in continued pressure from both wife and family.

The Siding Department Incident

Siding was the product which had been budgeted as a large profit item of Modrow. Aluminum siding was gaining in popularity among both architects and builders, because of its possibilities in both decorative and practical uses. Panel sheets of siding were shipped in standard sizes on order; large sheets of the coated siding were cut to specifications in the trim department, packed, and shipped. The trim shop was located near the loading platforms, and Dick often cut through the trim shop on his wanderings through the plant. On one of his frequent trips through the area, he suddenly became aware of the fact that several workers responsible for the disposal function were spending countless hours at high-speed saws cutting scraps into specified lengths to fit into scrap barrels. The narrow bands of scrap which resulted from the trim process varied in length from seven to twenty-seven feet and had to be reduced in size to fit into disposal barrels. Dick, in his concentration of cost reduction, picked up one of the thin strips, bent it several times and fitted it into the barrel. He tried this with another piece, and it bent very easily. After assuring himself that bending was possible, he walked over to a worker at the saw and asked why he was using the saw when material could easily be bent and fitted into the barrels, resulting in saving time and equipment. The worker's response was, "We've never done it that way, sir. We've always cut it."

Following his plan of not commenting or discussing matters on the floor, but distressed by the reply, Dick returned to his office and asked the manager of the siding department if he could speak to the foreman of the scrap division. The manager said, "Of course, I'll send him up to you in just a minute."

After a short time, the foreman, very agitated at being called to the plant manager's office, appeared. Dick began questioning him about the scrap disposal process and received the standard answer: "We've always done it that way." Dick then proceeded to review cost-cutting objectives. He talked about the pliability of the strips of scrap. He called for a few pieces of scrap to demonstrate the ease with which it could be bent, and ended what he thought was a satisfactory conversation by requesting the foreman to order heavy duty gloves for his workers and use the bending process for a trial period of two weeks to check the cost savings possible.

The foreman listened throughout most of this hour's conference, offered several reasons why it wouldn't work, raised some questions about the record-keeping process for cost purposes, and finally left the office with the forced agreement to try the suggested new method of bending, rather than cutting, for disposal. Although he was immersed in many other problems, his request was forcibly brought home one day as he cut through the scrap area. The workers were using power saws to cut scraps. He called the manager of the siding department and questioned him about the process. The manager explained that each foreman was responsible for his own processes, and since Dick had already talked to the foreman, perhaps he had better talk to him again. When the foreman arrived, Dick began to question him. He received a series of excuses, and some explanations of the kinds of problems they were meeting by attempting to bend the scrap material. "I don't care what the problems are," Dick nearly shouted, "when I request a cost-reduction program instituted, I want to see it carried through."

Dick was furious. When the foreman left, he phoned the maintenance department and ordered the removal of the power saws from the scrap area immediately. A short time later the foreman of the scrap department knocked on Dick's door reporting his astonishment at having maintenance men step into his area and physically remove the saws. Dick reminded the foreman of his request for a trial at cost reduction to no avail, and ended the conversation by saying that the power saws were gone and would not be returned, and the foreman had damned well better learn to get along without them. After a stormy exit by the foreman, Dick congratulated himself on having solved a problem and turned his attention to other matters.

A few days later Dick cut through the trim department and literally stopped to stare. As he described it, he was completely nonplussed to discover gloved workmen using hand shears to cut each piece of scrap.

4. Chrysler Corporation*

On September 20, 1979, an era ended for the Chrysler Corporation. Chrysler's chairman, John J. Ricardo, took an early retirement and turned the reins of power to President Lee A. Iacocca. Lee Iacocca had been hired to fill the vacancy created when Eugene Cafiero was given the post of executive vice-chairman. Lee had become available after his brilliant career at Ford had been ended by a dispute with Henry Ford, then the chairman. Ricardo retired not only for health reasons, but also to clear the company of the last ties with a management team that is often blamed for many of the problems with Chrysler.[1]

Chrysler's 1981 position was not one that would evoke feelings of envy for Iacocca's task. The company was cash poor, had suffered huge operating losses in the model year, and faced the prospect of rebuilding its product line in the face of both governmental and market pressures. One must look into the company's history to understand just how a large manufacturer could be backed into such a tight corner. When thinking about a company of this size, one could easily assume that it would be immune to the machinations of any one individual. A review of Chrysler Corporation's history indicates that the reverse may be true.

When one looks at the founder of this company, one sees in Walter Chrysler a strong tough-minded individual. He led the company with a firm hand. He believed that strong engineering was the most important aspect of the company. His company was constantly at the leading edge of the fledgling automobile industry. Many advancements were a bit too advanced. They did not always sell, as can be illustrated by the famous air-flow design of the later 1930s. But he felt that the technological sophistication was necessary and that because of it his product could command a premium price.

*A. J. Strickland III and Arthur A. Thompson, Jr., *Cases in Strategic Management* (Homewood, Ill.: Richard D. Irwin, Business Publications, Inc., 1982). Prepared by Lawrence Ondovic under the supervision of William Naumes of Clark University. Reprinted by permission.
    1. *Business Week,* October 1, 1979, p. 45.

The first manager to run the company was L. L. ("Tex") Colbert. It is with his administration that we will begin the review.

L. L. Colbert, 1950–1961

L. L. "Tex" Colbert became involved in the automobile industry in the early 1930s. A lawyer by training, he was on a committee that wrote the automobile industry's code under the National Recovery Administration. At the age of thirty, he became a vice-president of Dodge. He was a man who, when judged by the executives of the other car companies, had no special talents. His image in Detroit was that of "a man who at times conducts himself with the bacl -slapping joviality of a small-town politician, who occasionally enjoys himself too well at a party."[2] His approach to management is summarized by the following quote:

> Management is a business of men and of giving the men the job. You have to analyze the job to be done, get the manpower, and follow up to see that the job gets done. That's the most important—the follow up.[3]

The performance of the company under his leadership was erratic. Chrysler's market share peaked in 1953 at about 20 percent of the domestic market. The rules of the game changed in the 1954 model year. While the public was being wooed by the longer, lower, wider cars of competitors, Chrysler maintained its conservative designs. Ironically, its advertising slogan for 1954 was, "Bigger on the inside, smaller on the outside."[4]

Virgil Exner was given the task of redesigning Chrysler products. His automobiles became the longest, widest, and lowest and had the highest fins of any car on the road. To accomplish this extreme redesign, it was necessary to use a two-year model cycle, instead of the traditional three-year cycle. When the 1957 models were introduced, they were well received. The company earned a substantial profit. However, Chrysler's management expected the acceptance to continue for the next two years, so they amortized most of the tooling costs in 1957. They did not plan any major revisions for either 1958 or 1959. But the lukewarm reception of the warmed-over 1958 models coupled with the recession of that year put Chrysler in a precarious position. Although Chrysler's balance sheet still looked respectable, it was now out of sync with the other carmakers. Not only would the other carmakers be marketing restyled models in 1959, but strong rumors indicated that both General Motors and Ford would be introducing new compact models in 1960.

In 1960 Chrysler not only brought out the Dodge Dart and the Plymouth Valiant but also led the industry in converting to unitized body construction, moves which cost the company around $350 million. The Dart was very successful for Chrysler in 1960, helping push total sales 80 percent ahead of 1959. But strikes by a glass supplier and the steel industry severely depressed Chrysler's overall

2. *Business Week,* April 30, 1960, p. 137.
3. Ibid.
4. *Fortune,* June, 1958, p. 130

performance. This, combined with the heavy write-off on tooling for the new models, kept earnings to around $1 per share.[5]

Colbert had another problem in the summer of 1960. He had carefully built his management team, only to have it ripped apart by a conflict-of-interest scandal. William Newberg was forced to resign as president after only nine weeks on the job. Another vice-president was also directly implicated. Because of subsequent investigations, morale in the company dropped. Others on the team either resigned or were fired.

In 1961 George Love took over as chairman of the board. He selected Lynn Townsend, who had been vice-president in charge of operations, to be the president.

George Love/Lynn Townsend, 1961–1966

George Love, who was also chairman of Consolidated Coal Company, was a businessman with a wide range of experience. He was responsible for corporate-level marketing and management. Lynn Townsend was given responsibility for day-to-day operations.

Townsend had been with Chrysler for only four years. He had worked for ten years on Chrysler's account when he was a full partner at Touche, Ross and Company. He was asked to join Chrysler to set up a profit control system so that the company could compete more effectively.[6]

The main points of his management philosophy were:

1. Make a profit on auto sales being written now, not on those that might occur in the future.
2. Institute tight cost-control procedures, with no room given for sentiment or tradition if these mean lower earnings.
3. Use scientific management methods, not seat of the pants intuition.
4. Executives either perform or they are gone.

The situation that he inherited in 1961 could at the same time be construed as a disaster and an opportunity. With morale in the company hitting rock bottom, he met little resistance with his reorganization efforts. He began building his team of modern managers. He was a firm believer in having the right man do a job. He was able to select a team in 1961 and keep it in place into 1963. At this point he made another sweeping reorganization, cutting back from fourteen to six vice-presidents.[7]

Townsend's primary objective in 1961 was to fit all the pieces together so that they would mesh into a consistently profitable whole. He wanted to create a balanced, flexible system that could expand or contract according to the market pressure. But his bottom-line concern was to sell more cars and make a larger profit from each one.

---

5. *Business Week,* April 30, 1960, p. 131.
6. *Business Week,* October 6, 1962, p. 46.
7. *Business Week,* January 19, 1963, p. 32.

In order to revitalize the company, Townsend instituted three strategic changes: (1) The dealer network was expanded and strengthened at a cost of nearly $100 million. (2) The entire line of car models was restyled to appeal to contemporary tastes and quality was improved to the point that Chrysler could offer the first extended warranty in the industry. (3) The number of models offered was expanded so that Chrysler could compete in every segment of the domestic market.

For at least two of these areas, outsiders were brought into the company to head up the tasks. Virgil Boyd was made the vice-president and general sales manager. He had been with AMC before coming to Chrysler. He took the assignment of creating new dealerships and improving the existing ones. He began to monitor the dealers' performance more closely so that deviations from sales targets could be quickly identified. By the middle of 1962 his efforts began to pay off and Chrysler's sales in the 1963 model year improved.

The other key person Townsend hired was Elwood Engel, who had been a stylist at Ford. The radical designs of Exner were dumped in favor of simpler and smoother lines like the cars at GM and Ford. He attempted to build an evolutionary concept so that each year's models were natural extensions of the previous year.

Townsend centralized many functions. The line operations were weakened so that he could maintain tighter control. One area, in particular, that was centralized was production scheduling. The product planning staff analyzed what styles, colors, and models were selling by region, then used computers to create the production schedules for each variety for each plant. Unlike GM or Ford, who built cars in response to orders from their dealers, Chrysler scheduled its production based on the results of its computer modeling. This practice was later to be named the "sales bank." This method allowed for an even schedule for production, but at times, especially when the mix was wrong or sales dropped, the company would be burdened with large inventories of finished automobiles. During the period of booming sales, Chrysler was able to maximize the use of its production capacity.

Townsend was a great believer in scientific management and felt very strongly about using computers in the company. By the middle 1960s he had the largest computer operation in Detroit. He used his computers to simulate future demand based on historical data, to schedule production, and to provide huge volumes of reports on daily operations. In at least one instance, he used the simulations to enhance his reputation with the board of directors. The board was contemplating a more aggressive expansion policy. However, one of Townsend's computer models indicated a slight downturn in business. On his recommendation the expansion was curtailed. As it turned out, he called the turn perfectly.

In 1962 Townsend instituted the Pentastar as the corporate logo. Every facet of the company's operations was emblazoned with the design. It was a small tactic that enabled the corporation to project a better picture of the scope of its operations.

From 1964 to 1967 Chrysler allocated $1.7 billion to capital expenditures. Chrysler increased its ownership of Simca and bought Rootes of Great Britain. Townsend wanted to compete with GM and Ford on an equal basis. In order to capitalize on the expanding world market, he was forced to buy into operations that often had serious problems. Approximately $500 million of the $1.7 billion was spent on these overseas operations.

Chrysler's performance, despite all of the reorganizations and other turmoil, was quite good. In fact, many of Townsend's programs were effective cost-cutting mechanisms. In addition to firing employees, which quickly reduced costs, his use of computer systems cut $60 million from Chrysler's average inventory. Another system reduced obsolete material from the end of model runs by 70 percent.

Chrysler's sales were up. Its market share was also up. But its profits, as a percentage of sales, remained low. The tooling of new models was expensive, in the neighborhood of $300 million per year. Chrysler was in the habit of writing off these expenditures rapidly, which put a large burden on the current year's profits.

With the 1965 model year, Chrysler entered phase two of its recovery. It covered 90 percent of the domestic market segments. A young, energetic management team was in place. However, it was looking at a market place where the traditional segments were beginning to blur. There was a proliferation of models with a corresponding increase in segments. Ford had introduced the Mustang. At this point in time, Townsend was not overly concerned. His goal was to have a balanced product line rather than one hot car.[8] He had every intention of continuing the expansion of both the domestic and foreign operations. Chrysler's diversification programs included recreation vehicles, air conditioning, real estate, and consumer finance.

In 1966 George Love resigned as chairman. Lynn Townsend was elected chief executive officer and chairman of the board. Virgil Boyd was elected to the office of president.

Lynn Townsend/Virgil Boyd, 1966–1970

Boyd was able to continue the momentum generated by the excellent sales year in 1965. Chrysler's sales and market share increased through the 1968 model year. However, a few disappointments clouded the otherwise rosy picture. The European operations continued to be a drag on profits. In 1968 operations abroad yielded less than one eighth of Chrysler's pretax profits, although they accounted for one quarter of all Chrysler cars built and one-fifth of its sales.[9] A second soft spot was the lack of any serious challenge to Ford's Mustang. The Plymouth Barracuda was only a reworked Valiant and was never a serious challenge.

Chrysler's management was a unified team that had been together for more than five years. Many of them had occupied various positions during this time to broaden their experience. In addition, Chrysler's compacts had been selling well. All of the key barometers of the company had improved tremendously from the rock-bottom days of 1961. Chrysler was planning to increase its production capacity in 1968, which would be used to further its market penetration in the 1970s.

Chrysler had moved aggressively in the leasing and fleet sales areas by offering discounts and cash rebates. Its price cutting reached the break-even point in many cases. Its market share in these areas had increased almost totally at GM's expense.

---

8. *Forbes*, September 15, 1965, p. 19.
9. *Economist*, September 20, 1969, p. 69.

Chrysler had not achieved parity with Ford or GM, but it had narrowed the gap significantly—the Chrysler Imperial was the only product that did not make any serious gains in its market segment. In 1968 Chrysler entered the "sporty" or "muscle" car segment. The public acceptance of the Charger far exceeded anyone's expectations.

In 1968 Chrysler's market share climbed to 16.6 percent. Boyd hinted that the corporation was aiming at 20 percent by 1970. This had been and would continue to be one of the company's goals because 20 percent was the highest that its domestic market share had been since 1953. But even with an expanding share of the domestic market, its earnings hovered between 3 and 4 percent of sales.

The 1969 model year exposed some of the increasing vulnerability of the company. Chrysler had become a "me-too" company that followed the market. It anticipated that GM would continue with the rounded look. So for 1969 Chrysler styled its cars accordingly. However, GM's 1969 models were considerably different. Unfortunately for Chrysler, the new GM look was very popular. As a result of this, Chrysler's full-sized cars were out of vogue again. Earnings and earnings per share fell almost 70 percent to their lowest levels since 1962. Chrysler was forced to restyle for the 1970 model year, an expense that had not been anticipated. Chrysler entered the 1970 model year with a huge backlog of 1969 automobiles creating a drag on 1970 sales.

Another problem that continued to plague Chrysler was the lack of a subcompact car. There had been rumors of a prototype named "25," but it never materialized. Ford introduced the Maverick and continued development on the Phoenix; GM had the Chevy II and the XP887. But Townsend continued to reject the idea. He had said, "The American automobile industry will never take most of the minicar import market. A foreign car sells because it is foreign." [10] He was not convinced that there was as much of a market for the under-$2,000 car as GM and Ford thought.

Chrysler did enter an agreement with Mitsubishi of Japan in which it would get to assemble Valiants in Japan while Chrysler would start importing the Colt. Chrysler also had Simca's models which it could import. But neither of these cars was very well received by the buying public.

The lack of a small car was only the tip of the iceberg that was threatening Chrysler. The conditions of the early 1960s, when Chrysler staged its recovery, had changed dramatically. At that time competition consisted of giving longer warranty terms, aggressive selling to taxi, leasing, and car-hire fleets, price competition, choosing better dealers, and a vast upgrading of quality, after the shoddiness of the late 1950s. Chrysler did well in all of these areas. The hard sell of a few models in a fast-growing market suited a tightly knit company like Chrysler. But by 1969 the traditional market segmentation was evolving into a very large middle-price range, which accounted for 69 percent of all domestic automobile sales. The market was becoming a battleground of options and multiple models. Although the base price of a new car had dropped by 2 percent over the decade, the average price of a new car was up by 34 percent in the same period.

So once again, Townsend began cutting costs. In October 1969 he indefinitely laid off 12,000 of the 140,000 U.S. employees, both white- and blue-

_____
10. *Business Week,* July 5, 1969, p. 48.

collar workers. Chrysler delayed its expansion plans at New Stanton, Pennsylvania, and all general and administration budgets were cut back to their 1968 levels. As the 1970 model year developed, the other automakers saw their sales drop off. But for Chrysler, the slack year in 1970, following as it did the poor year they had in 1969, spelled big trouble. The company spent about $450 million on the 1970 models, only to see them sit in the showrooms.

It was with this set of conditions that John J. Ricardo was named as president. Virgil Boyd was appointed to the nominal post of vice-chairman of the board of directors.

Lynn Townsend/John J. Ricardo, 1970–1975

Ricardo has been described as a brusque but articulate, hard-nosed, demanding manager. A minority of the board believed that he was good at executing plans but that his interpersonal skills were weak. They thought he might alienate the dealers who had become accustomed to Boyd's style.[11]

At the same time, Eugene Cafiero was promoted to fill Ricardo's position as group vice-president for U.S. and Canadian operations.

The new management team faced many of the same problems that Townsend had faced in 1961: (1) sales had declined for the previous three quarters; (2) Chrysler's products had become too conservative and its range of products too limited; (3) the demand for full-size cars, which had been Chrysler's bread and butter, had declined 8 percent in two years to about 17 percent of the domestic market; (4) its aging compacts were selling well, but it had nothing to offer the subcompact buyer except the captive imports.

There were also differences in the 1970 situation, not all of which were positive. Chrysler's cash reserve position was stronger, and it also had substantial lines of open credit. However, its foreign operations, which had been acquired during the 1960s, continued to be a financial burden. The total investment was in the neighborhood of $5.8 billion. The long boom in auto sales was over. The market was volatile and was complicated by the increased penetration by the imports. The buying public was more finicky. The range of models now included minicars, sporty cars, and specialty cars. The days of the simple, low-, medium-, and high-priced cars were over.

Ricardo moved quickly in 1970 to cut costs. By September 1970 he had lopped off $150 million from Chrysler's operating costs. This included layoffs, terminations, and reorganized functions. He considered switching to common parts and common subassemblies for greater economy.

Throughout the 1970 model year, the fiasco of the previous year continued to haunt Chrysler. The high inventory levels of 1969 models at the beginning of the 1970 model year severely dampened the year's sales performance. The situation was further aggravated by a general slump in the automobile industry in 1970.

Chrysler invested $350 million in its 1970 models. It offered the Satellite and two low-priced compacts. But it still did not offer a subcompact model. Although this did not affect 1970 profitability, the delay was definitely risky. If the subcompact market really materialized, Chrysler would be left far behind.

---

11. *Fortune,* April, 1970, p. 146.

Townsend still contented that the buying public was not ready to give up their comfortable, large cars for the small ones.

Chrysler did expand its imported offerings. It negotiated an agreement with Mitsubishi of Japan which essentially traded the Valiant for the Colt. Chrysler also imported the Cricket from England, but the reception was luke-warm. In addition, the volume of the imports was limited. While Chrysler imported 54,000 Crickets per year. Ford was building 47,000 Pintos per month.

In 1971 the company returned to profitability, due in large part to the upswing in the market. These swings in volume graphically pointed out Chrysler's condition. Since the company's margins were thin, small reductions in unit sales translated into large losses on the profit and loss statement. Conversely, increases in sales generated very little additional profit. Chrysler netted two cents on every sales dollar; GM was netting seven cents, and Ford averaged five cents. Chrysler was a scaled-down imitation of the operations at Ford and GM. It did not have the sales volume to take full advantage of its production capacity.

There were many concerns expressed about the company in the early 1970s. Chrysler's reluctance to lead into new markets was highlighted. It was clearly a "me too" company that was forced to react to the pressures of the market place. Many observers thought that the cost reductions in 1971 may have cut too deeply into the company, and resources in the engineering and product-planning departments would have been absolutely necessary for Chrysler to adequately restructure its product lines. By 1973 the sentiment was expressed that Chrysler had lost its identity—it was no longer a full-line producer. Its biggest strength was its compacts which accounted for 42 percent of its sales. Meanwhile, subcompact cars were accounting for 16 percent of all new cars sold in the domestic market.

Timing, bad luck, and other factors were all working against Chrysler in the early 1970s. Beginning in 1971, it had invested $350 million to restyle the 1974 full-size cars. Shortly after the 1974 models were introduced, the Arabs began the oil embargo. Late in the 1974 model year, Chrysler was forced to offer rebates to move its huge inventory.

Chrysler's position in the 1975 model year continued to erode. Its market share dropped to 13.5 percent, and its sales were down by 41.7 percent, as compared with declines of 34.3 percent at GM and 31.3 percent at Ford. Chrysler's plans for a subcompact were delayed because $171 million in long-term debt coming due had to be rolled over at a much higher rate of interest. Capital expenditures were trimmed by $75 million.[12] The compact cars, which had long been the stalwarts of the company, were facing stiff competition from the Ford Granada.

In the summer of 1975 Lynn Townsend resigned effective as of October 1, 1975. He had been with the company both in the good and bad times and felt that it was time to turn the company over to younger management. Ricardo was promoted to chairman of the board, and Cafiero was elected president.

John J. Ricardo/Eugene Cafiero, 1975–1978

For Ricardo and Cafiero, dubbed the "crisis team," the usual round of congratulatory cocktail parties was bypassed. Chrysler was expected to lose $100 million or more in 1975, which would have been its second straight year of losses.

---

12. *Financial World,* December 25, 1975, pp. 11–12.

The company faced the same set of problems that had plagued it for the previous fifteen years. Chrysler's basic problem seemed to be that it did not have the products the buying public wanted when they wanted them. Chrysler made a crucial decision to spend more than $700 million to revamp its full-size and intermediate-size cars in 1974 and 1975, but the oil crisis sent whatever buyers there were to smaller cars. The implication of the investment decision was that the company did not have the resources to build a subcompact car. Now it had no product to compete with the Vegas, Pintos, and Gremlins.[13]

The Dart and Valiant had gone several years without any major changes. In 1976 Chrysler introduced two luxury compacts, the Aspen and Volaré, to help broaden the small-car line.

Chrysler was suffering from its rebate program. Although the program helped to sell cars, it often reduced the profit margins to almost nothing.

In 1976 business improved again. Chrysler's earnings were about $390 million, and short-term borrowing had been eliminated, at least for the time being. Ironically, the huge losses of the previous two years helped to increase the profits further (because of the tax loss carryforwards).

But Chrysler had become a $12 billion marginal producer. Because of its high leverage and low profit margins, due both to its dependence on compact cars and high unit-production costs, Chrysler fell fast and hard whenever the market for its cars softened.

Ricardo's goal was to stop the roller coaster ride. He began by eliminating some of the losing operations that Chrysler was involved with around the world. Rootes lost $150 million between 1975 and 1976. Although the British government helped in 1976 with financial aid, the operation still had many problems. Ricardo sold Chrysler Airtemp for $58 million, sold its empty plant in New Stanton, Pennsylvania, to Volkswagen, and liquidated the Big Sky resort in Montana. In a corporate-wide move, he also reinstituted the project to increase standardization of parts. His goal was to reduce Chrysler's parts list from 75,000 to 50,000.

The economic pickup of 1975–1976 definitely helped Chrysler. The Volaré and Aspen models sold quite well in that year, as did the Cordoba. Typically, the major product revisions were aimed at the full-size cars. The introduction of a subcompact model was now targeted for the 1978 model year. However, the full impact of the extensive personnel cuts of 1971 and 1974 was now being felt. Having lost so many engineers and designers, it was becoming extremely difficult to make the necessary revisions to Chrysler products. Many products were being delivered late to the market, and the first models to be built were plagued with problems, ranging from poorly fitting parts to severe mechanical problems.

In some respects Chrysler was confronted by bona fide opportunities in late 1976. Cars, in general, were getting smaller. Chrysler led the compact-car segment with more than a 40 percent share. But to effectively compete, even in 1976, the price tag was $3 billion. If the economy and sales held up, a good portion of the $3 billion could have been generated from internal cash flows.

Unfortunately, Chrysler's sales stumbled again in 1977. Its market share fell to 12.1 percent. In the first quarter of 1978, the losses totaled more than $120 million. This level of losses was eliminating any hope for internally financing the new models, and many other forms of credit were also closed to the company.

---

13. *Business Week,* July 21, 1975, p. 16.

Having $1.3 billion in long-term debt, the company's reputation was poor on Wall Street—its bonds were dropped to BBB by Standard & Poor's Corp.[14]

While bright spots were few, the sales performance on the Omni/Horizon subcompacts, which were introduced in January 1978, was excellent. These cars quickly jumped to command 18 percent of the subcompact market. In a move to turn the company around in the long run, it was decided to rebuild each plant as the cars it produced were restyled. The Omni/Horizon plant was running 55 percent ahead of its former capacity, and dealers had a two-month backlog of orders for the new subcompacts.

In 1977 GM had changed the rules of the game with the "down-sizing" of its full-size cars. This further burdened Chrysler because the new GM products were selling very well and Chrysler did not have the capital to follow GM's lead. Chrysler's products were sliding farther from the kind that the public was buying.

The losses continued. Production and engineering problems only aggravated a bad situation. In the summer of 1978, Cafiero was given the nominal post of vice-chairman of the board. Iacocca was brought in to be the president.

John J. Ricardo/Lee A. Iacocca, 1978–1979

Iacocca was regarded as the "savior" when he came to Chrysler. He had a solid reputation for performance at Ford. His mere presence seemed to boost morale in the organization and bolster confidence in the financial community.

Iacocca's short-term objective was to keep the company afloat until major design changes could be made in the product lines. Because of the long lead time (the period between new design of a model and production), Iacocca could not make any major changes in wheelbase size and mechanical features (especially fuel economy) until the 1982 model year.

For the 1979 model year, purely cosmetic changes were planned for most of the products. The full-size cars were restyled. It was hoped that the New Yorker and the St. Regis would begin to raise their market share to the 15 percent of the full-size market segment that Chrysler had once held. However, a series of foul-ups early in the model year, such as supply hang-ups and assembly-line snags, shut off the supply of full-size cars until November. Chrysler prepared for the introduction of the new cars with a full-scale media blitz. But for the buyers who came to look at the cars, there was little new to look at.[15]

As the year continued, it was clear that, except for the Omni/Horizon, Chrysler's product line was in trouble. Sales of the compact Volaré and Aspen models were down by more than 24 percent. Both GM and Ford were now offering either down-sized or newly designed, fuel-efficient compact cars. Chrysler's overall market share slipped to 12.4 percent.

In March 1979 Harold K. Sperlich took over the manufacturing responsibilities from Richard K. Brown. When Brown announced his early retirement, he was promptly replaced by Gar Laux. Both Sperlich and Laux had worked with Iacocca at Ford.

Chrysler's inventory, or sales bank as it was called, was completely out of

---

14. *Business Week,* May 15, 1978, p. 23.
15. *Business Week,* March 12, 1979, p. 18.

balance with demand. In the early spring of 1979, Chrysler had more than a 100-day supply of unsold cars. The company began offering free inventory financing and other incentives to the dealers, along with a cash rebate to the consumer. By June the supply was down to 79 days—unacceptable, but a definite improvement.

Another problem surfaced in the spring of 1979 that was indicative of Chrysler's lack of vertical integration. The company had only ordered 300,000 engines from VW for the Omni/Horizon subcompacts. As the model year progressed, it was clear that the demand would be higher, but VW needed its extra capacity for its own production.

Losses from operations continued to mount. Chrysler lost $204 million in the second quarter of 1979. Because it was obvious that the financing for the needed expansion could never be generated internally, Chrysler turned to the federal government for assistance. The initial petition to the government was for aid in the form of either tax refunds or immediate relief from having to meet the costly safety, environmental, and mileage standards on new cars. Chrysler's proposal was rejected, but G. William Miller, the secretary to the treasury, indicated that the government might be willing to support loan guarantees. With these Chrysler could then borrow from private sources who would not consider loaning them money because of the high risk.

Early in September Ricardo and Iacocca returned to Washington with their request for $1.2 billion in loan guarantees over the next five years. They were asking for $500 million immediately and $700 million in additional loans, if needed.[16] Miller rejected this plan also. He told them to revise the plan to ask for less than $1 billion and to satisfy the Treasury Department that they would transform the company into a profitable enterprise.

Chrysler's management had rejected several options that Treasury officials had urged them to consider instead of federal aid. One option was to reduce the scope of their operations and thereby to become something less than a full-line company. A second was to merge with another firm. The third was to file for bankruptcy.[17] Chrysler management rejected the proposals for the following reasons: (1) reducing the range of automobile and truck products would be unprofitable; (2) the company's financial position made it an unlikely candidate for a merger; (3) bankruptcy would have a widespread effect on the economy and its 30,000 suppliers.

Chrysler's plan said that of the needed $2.1 billion it could probably raise $900 million by selling assets and from unspecified assistance fro the UAW and from state and local governments where Chrysler's facilities were located. The plan projected that Chrysler would become profitable by 1981 and repay the loans by 1985. It was to be assumed that the firm's suppliers would continue to accept payments the month after delivery, and that various U.S. and foreign banks would continue their existing agreements.

Miller told the company officials to rework the plan because it did not call for enough sacrificing by those with the largest stake in the company—employees, management, shareholders, and the union.

Shortly after this meeting, Ricardo announced his retirement, effective September 20, 1979. Iacocca became the company's chief executive officer.

---

16. *The Boston Globe,* September 16, 1979, p. 67.
17. Ibid.

Exhibit 1. Chrysler Corporation—Consolidated Profit and Loss Statement For 1970–1978 ($ Millions)

	1978	1977	1976	1975	1974	1973	1972	1971	1970
Sales................	$13,618	$13,059	$15,538	$11,598	$10,860	$11,667	$9,641	$7,893	$7,000
Cost of goods sold ..	12,640	11,726	13,625	10,618	9,953	10,314	8,407	6,971	6,276
GS&A expense	572	453	566	466	485	466	416	370	386
Net sundry expense .	262	280	295	233	254	216	191	149	121
Depreciation/ special amortization	352	320	402	294	321	371	366	174	177
Interest expense (net)	129	75	130	168	108	32	56	71	47
Taxes on income and property	(81)	73	212	26	(78)	203	193	66	(22)
Net income	$ (256)	$ 132	$ 308	$ (207)	$ (183)	$ 65	$ 12	$ 92	$ 15
Dividends	$ 52	$ 54	$ 18	—	$ 79	$ 69	$ 47	$ 30	$ 29

Exhibit 2. Chrysler Corporation—Consolidated Profit and Loss Statement For 1960–1969 ($ Millions)

	1969	1968	1967	1966	1965	1964	1963	1962	1961	1960
Sales										
Cost of goods sold	$7,052	$7,445	$6,213	$5,650	$5,300	$4,287	$3,505	$2,378	$2,127	$3,007
GS&A expense	6,138	6,122	5,190	4,621	4,269	3,404	2,780	1,927	1,797	2,598
Net sundry expense........	449	429	384	422	372	337	291	229	203	229
Depreciation	170	162	153	30	102	74	60	56	67	73
Interest expense (net)	32	26	13	9	9	9	10	9	9	9
Taxes on income and property	80	272	166	155	104	185	164	61	10	34
Net income	$ 69	$ 290	$ 186	$ 297	$ 338	$ 206	$ 149	$ 57	$ 8	$ 29
Dividends	$ 95	$ 93	$ 92	$ 91	$ 55	$ 28	$ 25	$ 9	$ 9	$ 13

Exhibit 3. Chrysler Corporation—Consolidated Profit and Loss Statement For 1951–1959 ($ Millions)

	1959	1958	1957	1956	1955	1954	1953	1952	1951
Sales................	$2,643	$2,165	$3,565	$2,676	$3,466	$2,072	$3,348	$2,601	$2,547
Cost of goods sold ..	2,298	1,857	2,910	2,318	2,938	1,826	2,936	2,195	2,256
GS&A expense	238	264	276	217	219	159	144	106	103
Net sundry expense .	40	34	46	30	30	23	27	23	20
Depreciation	72	80	89	68	55	50	47	37	26
Interest expense (net)	9	9	8	6	4	1	—	—	—
Taxes on income and property	(5)	(39)	132	23	126	3	125	169	79
Net income..........	$ (9)	$ (40)	$ 104	$ 14	$ 94	$ 10	$ 69	$ 71	$ 63
Dividends	$ 9	$ 13	$ 35	$ 26	$ 35	$ 39	$ 52	$ 52	$ 65

Exhibit 4. Chrysler Corporation—Consolidated Balance Sheet For 1970–1978 ($ Millions)

	1978	1977	1976	1975	1974	1973	1972	1971	1970
Assets:									
Current assets	$3,561	$4,153	$3,878	$3,117	$3,697	$3,238	$2,896	$2,411	$2,167
Fixed assets	3,420	3,515	3,196	3,150	3,036	2,867	2,601	2,588	2,649
Total assets	$6,981	$7,668	$7,074	$6,267	$6,733	$6,105	$5,497	$4,999	$4,816
Liabilities:									
Current Liabilities	$2,486	$3,090	$2,826	$2,462	$2,709	$2,094	$1,940	$1,648	$1,549
Long-term liabilities ...	1,083	1,120	928	947	875	836	670	698	791
Other	3,412	3,458	3,320	2,858	3,149	3,175	2,887	2,653	2,476
Total liabilities	$6,981	$7,668	$7,074	$6,267	$6,733	$6,105	$5,497	$4,999	$4,816

Exhibit 5. Chrysler Corporation—Consolidated Balance Sheet For 1960–1969 ($ Millions)

	1969	1968	1967	1966	1965	1964	1963	1962	1961	1960
Assets:										
Current assets	$2,176	$2,210	$1,880	$1,467	$1,480	$1,286	$1,374	$1,007	$ 893	$ 802
Fixed assets	2,512	2,188	1,975	1,682	1,454	1,135	750	518	507	567
Total assets	$4,688	$4,398	$3,855	$3,149	$2,934	$2,421	$2,124	$1,525	$1,400	$1,369
Liabilities:										
Current liabilities	$1,644	$1,428	$1,340	$1,022	$ 961	$ 901	$ 818	$ 445	$ 386	$ 371
Long-term liabilities	587	535	360	216	224	242	256	238	250	250
Other	2,457	2,435	2,155	1,911	1,749	1,278	1,050	842	764	748
Total liabilities	$4,688	$4,398	$3,855	$3,149	$2,934	$2,421	$2,124	$1,525	$1,400	$1,369

Exhibit 6. Chrysler Corporation—Consolidated Balance Sheet For 1951–1959 ($ Millions)

	1959	1958	1957	1956	1955	1954	1953	1952	1951
Assets:									
Current assets	$ 690	$ 756	$ 940	$ 669	$ 891	$ 592	$527	$590	$487
Fixed assets	685	582	557	626	472	443	371	324	271
Total assets	$1,375	$1,338	$1,497	$1,295	$1,363	$$,035	$898	$914	$758
Liabilities:									
Current Liabilities	$ 415	$ 392	$ 514	$ 461	$ 586	$ 386	$328	$366	$237
Long-term liabilities ...	250	250	250	188	125	63	—	—	—
Other	710	696	733	646	652	586	570	551	521
Total liabilities	$1,375	$1,338	$1,497	$1,295	$1,363	$1,035	$898	$914	$758

5. Tale of Three Tales

Background

Elliott Manufacturing produces a line of clothing principally directed at the young adult market. Their clothes are marketed under the title "Elliott's Elite." This company has been producing clothes for some twenty years and has enjoyed modest gains year by year until recently. It began with sales in the 300–400 thousand dollar range per year and currently enjoys annual sales of over 50 million dollars.

In its early years, it manufactured clothing for children only. They targeted their line primarily towards school age children from six years of age to eleven or twelve. This was a relatively lucrative market at the time. However, changes in the demographics of the market began to hurt sales. It was a simple matter: there were just fewer young people in this market. The so-called baby boom had passed and there were fewer children in this age bracket than ever before. There was no hope that this trend would be reversed. In fact, the evidence hinted strongly otherwise. The birthrate in the United States (domestic sales accounted for 95 percent of Elliott sales; the remainder were in Canada) indicated that there would be no increase in the number of children in Elliott's targeted range.

At this time, a relatively large change was made in the sales and manufacturing strategy at Elliott Manufacturing. A series of meetings was called and the top-level management of the company decided to make several rather major changes in the way business was to be conducted. First, the young person (6–11/12 years of age) market was to be abandoned completely. In its place, their products would be marketed towards the teenage and young adult market. There were two principal reasons for this move.

First, Elliott could pick up the same people who had passed out of their original market and hope to follow them through their teenage years into young adulthood. This could conceivably add some ten years of new market life to their products.

Second, it was rightfully decided that there was little movement in the original market. Children from ages six to eleven or twelve simply were not "clothes conscious." They are insensitive to changes in style. The major selling point to mothers of children in these brackets was not style but durability. Children would grow out of their clothes before they became "out of style." Elliott was able to capitalize on replacement clothes when children did grow out of their present clothing. This was good. Not so good was that they did not have the luxury, as many other manufacturers serving different markets, to introduce new lines of clothes which might appeal to different markets where there is a certain clothes consciousness.

With these factors in mind, the top management at Elliott Manufacturing decided to forego the children's market inasmuch as it had very little growth potential and to attack the teenage and young adult market where clothes consciousness was practically a way of life. This strategy was very successful until the last two years. Sales are now stagnant. Their market share is not increasing. In fact, it has dipped precipitously. The major reason for this decline is the tremendous increase in competition in designer-type clothing. The only reason that Elliott's sales receipts have been steady is because of inflation. Their losses in sales units have been taken up by increases in the price of their product. Of course, this is very misleading. If inflation were taken into account, Elliott Manufacturing could be shown to have slipped in its earnings.

The Present

As you would expect, Peter Elliott, chief executive officer and namesake of the company, is somewhat less than pleased with the turn of events. He ordered all divisions of his company to streamline their operations—cut back hiring except for absolutely necessary replacements, reduce inventories, make any and every move to increase efficiency and save money. Sadly, while these belt-tightening measures have helped Elliott Manufacturing's financial condition, they have proven to be far short of the improvements that Peter Elliott had demanded.

As a result, Mr. Elliott called together the heads of his functional areas and impressed upon them that the plight of Elliott Manufacturing has progressed from uncomfortable to critical. Unless some significant improvements were made in the very near future, widespread layoffs in both per diem workers and management would be Elliott Manufacturing's only course.

Elliott Manufacturing is structured similarly to many manufacturing concerns. There are three main functional areas: production, marketing, and finance. Very simply, each manager of these functional areas was ordered by Elliott to return to work, consult with other Elliott managers and employees, and submit recommendations for how each functional area could cut costs, improve productivity—in general, do a better job. Each functional manager did as he was requested. The following are the highlights of their reports to Peter Elliott.

Production

The production department spends a great deal of time in set-ups. It turns out that clothing comes in many sizes and, of course, in many colors. Beyond that, some of the fashions are essentially the same except that one is long sleeve, for example, and the other short. One may have a slightly different collar than another but otherwise they are the same. The problem for production is that there are far too many combinations. You may, for instance, need fifty dozen size 10, blue, short sleeve, with a standard collar. Then you may need the same, only in yellow, then in green, and so on. Now all of these have to be made with long sleeves, some with button-down collars. The point is that half of the time is spent not making clothes but in switching from one combination to another.

In short, production has recommended that the combinations in the clothing be reduced. Limit the number of colors, sizes, and special options. The effect of this change will be to greatly increase the efficiency and productivity of the production department. They will be able to make more units at less cost.

Marketing

The marketing department has submitted a recommendation to Peter Elliott as well. Naturally, the marketing department is interested in changes that will enhance its ability to sell the products made by Elliott Manufacturing. Their suggestions can be summarized in two parts.

First, they have recommended a change in the terms of sales to buyers of the merchandise. Essentially, marketing wants to be able to make sales to customers with relatively little money down. Marketing believes that they can sell many more units of the products if they can make relatively liberal terms available to buyers. All buyers, but especially new buyers, are much more like to make the initial decision to buy the Elliott Elite line of clothes if their out-of-pocket costs can be reduced. Also, marketing has asked that the pay-back period be extended. In other words, the total amount due will not have to be paid in 60 or 90 days, for example, but 120 or 150 days. This, of course, will allow the buyer an opportunity to sell the merchandise and then pay Elliott Manufacturing. In sum, marketing has requested that the policy on sales be changed to reflect smaller down payments and an extended pay-back period.

Second, marketing has asked that more sizes, colors, and options be made available. Marketing feels that the greater number of combinations that they can offer, the more likely they can sell the line. Most retail outlets want to be able to offer their customers the most complete line possible.

Finance

The finance department, among other things, has the charter of collecting the money which is due to Elliott Manufacturing. One of their major problems in recent years, and one which is getting worse, not better, is the time it takes to collect their receivables. In other words, Elliott Manufacturing provides credit to a buyer of its line of clothes. That amount of money is due in 30 or 60 days. The problem is that the money may not come in for 90 days or even 120 or sometimes 150 days. In the meantime, Elliott Manufacturing obviously cannot use this money for other purposes. Also, interest must be paid by Elliott on its funds.

Times are generally bad in the industry. People simple have less money to spend. This includes money that they might have spent for clothes. If the amount of new clothes that people can afford is reduced, it is clear that the sales of retail clothes outlets will be off. If those sales are off, payments to Elliott Manufacturing are likely to be made late, if at all. This is the case for Elliott Manufacturing. Bad debts (receivables that are never collected) are increasing along with the increasing pay-back periods.

Finance, therefore, has recommended that the down payment for all buyers be increased and the pay-back period reduced. It is a well known fact that larger down payments reduce bad debts. It is also well known that there is a very strong relationship between the time elapsed on money due and its eventual recovery. Simply, as a debt becomes older and older, the chances of recovering the funds get less and less.

What Now?

Peter Elliott has reviewed the recommendations from all three functional departments: production, marketing, and finance. It is perfectly obvious that the recommendations of the departments are mutually exclusive. In other words, if the recommendations of one department are accepted, then the recommendations of the other departments cannot be accepted.

Production wants fewer colors, sizes and options; marketing wants more. Marketing wants less down payment and more liberal terms; finance wants greater down payments and more stringent terms.

All three departments have done exactly what Peter Elliott requested. They have recommended those changes that will increase their efficiency and productivity. There is little question that if the individual recommendations of the departments were accepted each would be more efficient. The production department would make more clothes for less money; marketing would, no doubt, sell more clothes; finance would improve its collections. It is also obvious that all these recommendations cannot be accepted.

6. Work Group Ownership of an Improved Tool*

The Whirlwind Aircraft Corporation was a leader in its field and especially noted for its development of the modern supercharger. Work in connection with the latter mechanism called for special skill and ability. Every detail of the supercharger had to be perfect to satisfy the exacting requirements of the aircraft industry.

In 1941 (before Pearl Harbor), Lathe Department 15-D was turning out three types of impeller, each contoured to within 0.002 inch and machined to a mirrorlike finish. The impellers were made from an aluminum alloy and finished on a cam-back lathe.

The work was carried on in four shifts, two men on each. The personnel in the finishing section were as follows:

1. *First Shift*—7 A.M. to 3 P.M. Sunday and Monday off.
   a. Jean Latour, master mechanic, French Canadian, forty-five years of age. Latour had set up the job and trained the men who worked with him on the first shift.

---

*From *Personnel Administration: A Point of View and a Method,* 1956 ed. by Paul Pigors & Charles A. Myers. Copyright © McGraw-Hill Book Company, 1956. Used with permission of McGraw-Hill Book Company.

     b. Pierre DuFresne, master mechanic, French Canadian, thirty-six years of age. Both these men had trained the workers needed for the other shifts.

2. *Second Shift*—3 P.M. to 11 P.M. Friday and Saturday off.
     a. Albert Durand, master mechanic, French Canadian, thirty-two years of age; trained by Latour and using his lathe.
     b. Robert Benet, master mechanic, French Canadian, thirty-one years of age; trained by DuFresne and using his lathe.

3. *Third Shift*—11 P.M. to 7 A.M. Tuesday and Wednesday off.
     a. Philippe Doret, master mechanic, French Canadian, thirty-one years of age; trained by Latour and using his lathe.
     b. Henri Barbet, master mechanic, French Canadian, thirty years of age; trained by DuFresne and using his lathe.

4. *Stagger Shift*—Monday, 7 A.M. to 3 P.M.; Tuesday, 11 P.M. to 7 A.M.; Wednesday, 11 P.M. to 7 A.M.; Thursday, off; Friday, 3 P.M. to 11 P.M.; Saturday, 3 P.M. to 11 P.M.; Sunday, off.
     a. George MacNair, master mechanic, Scotch, thirty-two years of age; trained by Latour and using his lathe.
     b. William Reader, master mechanic, English, thirty years of age; trained by DuFresne and using his lathe.

    Owing to various factors (such as the small number of workers involved, the preponderance of one nationality, and the fact that Latour and DuFresne had trained the other workers), these eight men considered themselves as members of one work group. Such a feeling of solidarity is unusual among workers on different shifts, despite the fact that they use the same machines.

    The men received a base rate of $1.03 an hour and worked on incentive. Each man usually turned out twenty-two units a shift, thus earning an average of $1.19 an hour. Management supplied Rex 95 High-Speed Tool-Bits, which workers ground to suit themselves. Two tools were used: one square bit with a slight radius for recess cutting, the other bit with a 45-degree angle for chamfering and smooth finish. When used, both tools were set close together, they worker adjusting the lathe from one operation to the other. The difficulty with this setup was that during the rotation of the lathe, the aluminum waste would melt and fuse between the two toolbits. Periodically the lathe had to be stopped so that the toolbits could be freed from the welded aluminum and reground.

    At the request of the supervisor of Lathe Department 15-D, the methods department had been working on his tool problem. Up to the time of this case, no solution had been found. To make a firsthand study of the difficulty, the methods department had recently assigned one of its staff, Mr. MacBride, to investigate the problem in the lathe department itself. Mr. MacBride's working hours covered parts of both the first and second shifts. MacBride was a young man, twenty-six years of age, and a newcomer to the methods department. For the three months prior to this assignment, he had held the post of "suggestion man," a position which enabled newcomers to the methods department to familiarize themselves with the plant setup. The job consisted in collecting, from boxes in departments throughout the plant, suggestions submitted by employees and making a preliminary evaluation of these ideas. The current assignment of studying the tool situation in Lathe Department 15-D, with a view to cutting costs, was his first special task. He devoted himself to this problem with great zeal but did not succeed in winning the confidence of the workers. In pursuance of their usual philosophy, "Keep your mouth shut if you see anyone with a suit on," they volunteered no information and took the stand that, since the methods man had been given this assignment, it was up to him to carry it out.

While MacBride was working on this problem, Pierre DuFresne hit upon a solution. One day he successfully contrived a tool which combined the two bits into one. This eliminated the space between the two toolbits which in the past had caught the molten aluminum waste and allowed it to become welded to the cutting edges. The new toolbit had two advantages: it eliminated the frequent machine stoppage for cleaning and regrinding the old-type tools; and it enabled the operator to run the lathe at a higher speed. These advantages made it possible for the operator to increase his efficiency 50%.

DuFresne tried to make copies of the new tool, but was unable to do so. Apparently the new development had been a "luck accident" during grinding which he could not duplicate. After several unsuccessful attempts, he took the new tool to his former teacher, Jean Latour. The latter succeeded in making a drawing and turning out duplicate toolbits on a small grinding wheel in the shop. At first the two men decided to keep the new tool to themselves. Later, however, they shared the improvement with their fellow workers on the second shift. Similarly it was passed on to the other shifts. But all these men kept the new development a closely guarded secret as far as "outsiders" were concerned. At the end of the shift, each locked the improved toolbit securely in his toolchest.

Both DuFresne, the originator of the new tool, and Latour, its draftsman and designer, decided not to submit the idea as a suggestion but to keep it as the property of their group. Why was this decision made? The answer lies partly in the suggestion system and partly in the attitude of Latour and DuFresne toward other features of company work life and toward their group.

According to an information bulletin issued by the company, the purpose of the suggestion system was to "provide an orderly method of submitting and considering ideas and recommendations of employees to management; to provide a means for recognizing and rewarding individual ingenuity; and to promote cooperation." Awards for accepted suggestions were made in the following manner: "After checking the savings and expense involved in an adopted suggestion [the suggestion committee] determined the amount of the award to be paid, based upon the savings predicted upon a year's use of the suggestion. . . . It is the intention of the committee . . . to be liberal in the awards, which are expected to adequately compensate for the interest shown in presenting suggestions." In pursuance of this policy, it was customary to grant the suggestor an award equivalent to the savings of an entire month.

As a monetary return, both DuFresne and Latour considered an award based on one months's saving as inadequate. They also argued that such awards were really taken out of the workers' pockets. Their reasoning was as follows: All awards for adopted suggestions were paid out of undistributed profits. Since the company also had a profit-sharing plan, the money was taken from a fund that would be given to the workers anyway, which merely meant robbing Peter to pay Paul. In any case, the payment was not likely to be large and probably would be less than they could accumulate if increased incentive payments could be maintained over an extended period without discovery. Thus there was little in favor of submitting the new tool as a suggestion.

Latour and DuFresne also felt that there were definite hazards to the group if their secret were disclosed. They feared that once the tool became company property, its efficiency might lead to layoff of some members in their group, or at least make work less tolerable by leading to an increased quota at a lower price per unit. They also feared that there might be a change in scheduled work assignments. For instance, the lathe department worked on three different types of impeller. One type was a routine job and aside from the difficulty caused by the old-type tool, presented no problem. For certain technical reasons, the other two types were more difficult to make. Even Latour, an exceptionally skilled craftsman, had sometimes found it hard to make the expected quota before the new tool was developed. Unless the work load was carefully balanced by scheduling easier and more difficult types, some of the operators were unable to make standard time.

The decision to keep the tool for their own group was in keeping with Latour's work philosophy. He had a strong feeling of loyalty to his own group and had demonstrated this in the past by offering for their use several improvements of his own. For example, he made available to all workers in his group a set of special gauge blocks which were used in aligning work on lathes. To protect himself in case mistakes were traced to these gauges, he wrote on them: "Personnel [sic] Property—Do not use. Jean Latour."

Through informal agreement with their fellow workers, Latour and DuFresne "pegged production" at an efficiency rate that in their opinion would not arouse management's suspicion or lead to a restudy of the job, with possible cutting of the rate. This enabled them to earn an extra 10 percent incentive earnings. The other 40 percent in additional efficiency was used as follows: The operators established a reputation for a high degree of accuracy and finish. They set a record for no spoilage and were able to apply the time gained on the easier type of impeller to work on the other types which required greater care and more expert workmanship.

The foreman of the lathe department learned about the new tool soon after it was put into use but was satisfied to let the men handle the situation in their own way. He reasoned that at little expense he was able to get out production of high quality. There was no defective work, and the men were contented.

Mr. MacBride was left in a very unsatisfactory position. He had not succeeded in working out a solution of his own. Like the foreman, he got wind of the fact that the men had devised a new tool. He urged them to submit a drawing of it through the suggestion system, but this advice was not taken, and the men made it plain that they did not care to discuss with him the reasons for this position.

Having no success in his direct contact with the workers, Mr. MacBride appealed to the foreman, asking him to secure a copy of the new tool. The foreman replied that the men would certainly decline to give him a copy and would resent as an injustice any effort on his part to force them to submit a drawing. Instead he suggested that MacBride should persuade DuFresne to show him the tool. This MacBride attempted to do, but met with no success in his efforts to ingratiate himself with DuFresne. When he persisted in his attempts, DuFresne decided to throw him off the track. He left in his lathe a toolbit which was an unsuccessful copy of the original discovery. At shift change, MacBride was delighted to find what he supposed to be the improved tool. He hastily copied it and submitted a drawing to the tool department. When a tool was made up according to these specifications it naturally failed to do what was expected of it. The workers, when they heard of this through the "grapevine," were delighted.

DuFresne did not hesitate to crow over MacBride, pointing out that his underhanded methods had met with their just reward.

The foreman did not take any official notice of the conflict between DuFresne and MacBride. Then MacBride complained to the foreman that DuFresne was openly boasting of his trick and ridiculing him before other workers. Thereupon, the foreman talked to DuFresne, but the latter insisted that his ruse had been justified as a means of self-protection.

When he was rebuffed by DuFresne, the foreman felt that he had lost control of the situation. He could no longer conceal from himself that he was confronted by a more complex situation than what initially he had defined as a "tool problem." His attention was drawn to the fact that the state of affairs in his department was a tangle of several interrelated problems. Each problem urgently called for a decision that involved understanding and practical judgment. But having for so long failed to see the situation as a whole, he now found himself in a dilemma.

He wished to keep the goodwill of the work group, but he could not countenance the continued friction between DuFresne and MacBride. Certainly, he could not openly abet his operators in obstructing the work of a methods man. His superintendent would now certainly hear of it and would be displeased to learn that a foreman had failed to tell him of such an important technical improvement. Furthermore, he knew that the aircraft industry was expanding at this time and that the demand for impellers had increased to such an extent that management was planning to set up an entire new plant unit devoted to this product.

7. Far-West Water District: Policy, Strategy, and Functional Problems*

Introduction

In August of 1980, James Rawlins, an experienced engineer and near graduate of a local university MBA program was looking for a potential career in management connected with irrigated agriculture. He was secure in his present staff position with a consulting engineer for the past ten years but there was no hope to lever into a line position and the workload was gravitating to another state.

One such management opportunity manifested with a smaller irrigation district not more than thirty minutes' drive from Rawlin's house. After following

---

*This case was prepared by Marketing Professors Jim D. Barnes and Brenda J. Moscove, along with Tim W. Collins, M.B.A., California State College, Bakersfield, as a basis for class discussion rather than to illustrate the effective or ineffective handling of an administrative situation. Distributed by the Harvard Business Case Service, Soldiers Field, Boston, Mass. 92163. All rights reserved to the contributors.

up on an ad in a local newspaper, he met with the District Manager on three
occasions and toured the District twice. Both parties were in agreement as to the
position of Assistant to the Manger," and compensation and terms were approved
during a final interview with two District Board members. The Board members
were pleased with Rawlins' qualifications and indicated in two years he would be
running the District as the present manager was too involved in politics and was
due to retire in five to seven years.

Rawlins accepted the position and spent the next three months closing out
his project accounts with his former employer.

The District

Actual land area comprises approximately 50,000 acres and the distribution
system consists of approximately 300 miles of earth canals, ditches, and surface
drains which have been in operation since the turn of the century. The system is
antiquated and in need of renovation. Furthermore, maintenance has deteriorated
in past years. Rawlins felt he could stay busy for two years just planning and
designing an improved system.

During the first month, Rawlins spent most of his time out in the field
learning the system and inventorying structures and conditions. He found
effective operation to be greatly hindered due to the run-down condition of the
system and maintenance problems.

Management

Within a short time, Rawlins knew the District organization was in trouble. There
was an extreme dislike of the manager by the field personnel. They described the
manager as a "penny pincher," moody, hard-nosed, uncommunicative, short-
sighted, unyielding, authoritarian, and untrustworthy. Rawlins characterized him
as a moody, conservative, unemotional, insensitive, pessimistic, short-range
planner concerned only with the status quo. The manager had been with the
District for over twenty years and his management style was reminiscent of the
1960s; however, today's turbulent 1980s are another era. There was a need for
change but the manager was not yet ready. Even the hiring of Rawlins was at the
request of the Board of Directors.

As with many not-for-profit organizations, political influences and constraints
tend to "hamstring" managerial effectiveness and achievement. With the District,
these constraining influences were manifested in the Board of Directors. Each
member had an individual style with separate wants, needs, desires, and political
aspirations. Other constraints were internal (organization and employees) and
external (landowners and water community politics).

Policy/Strategy

The direction in which a water district goes depends on its management, Board of
Directors, service mission, external/internal threats and opportunities, politics,
and societal obligations. Rawlins found that District policy was in the heads of a

few people, not on a formalized blueprint. The last document, dated 1948, set forth rules and regulations governing the distribution and use of water under the system operated by the District.

What was done in the past generally held for today and tomorrow. Administrative policy was handled by the manager on a one-to-one or item-by-item basis. Landowners, desiring any canal or structure relocations, improvements, or other requests, met directly with the manager and no one else knew what went on. Operational policy was largely with the chief ditch tender, the oldest employee of the District. Water measurement had record policy, previously with the manager, had gradually been transferred to the chief hydrographer. Maintenance policy also had been with the manager but was being transferred to the superintendent. The manager, under Board pressure, was in the process of delegating more authority downward.

A major strategy over the past two decades was to simplify operations to a bare minimum and cut costs. Prior to the 1960s there were forty employees and numerous pieces of equipment for maintenance of canals and structures on a year-around basis. Now much of the equipment stays parked in the District yard and the District operates with twelve full-time employees.

The manager stated that the Board had supported this strategy to keep maintenance and operation costs to a bare minimum for many years. Now he thinks the Board has a new strategy of spending more money. Consequently, Rawlins was hired to investigate the system, learn landowner, as well as District, problems and formulate an overall plan for future modernization. However, no clear goals, objectives, or policies were set. This was complicated by the pluralistic nature of policy-making of the Board and manager. It was difficult to achieve any sort of consensus on goals except at high levels of abstraction. Although the manager set short-range goals such as the annual budget, long-range goals, objectives, policies, and strategies were often discussed with no resultant action. Various committees to handle personnel matters, finance, etc., have been recently established, but no committee interfaces with the manager for long-range planning.

What Rawlins observed as a "disjointed incremental approach"[1] to policy matters characterized by proceeding one step at a time to alter and compromise policy and muddle through problems. After attending a few Board meetings, it was evident that policy decisions on problems had low priority and critical questions were ignored.

Board of Directors

Far-West has a small Board representing five geographical divisions within the District. Although District law requires elections every two years, elections rarely occur unless landowners become irate and desire change. Exhibit 1 briefly profiles each of the members and enumerates years of service to the District.

Of two opposite categories, functional or inside directors and honorific or outside directors,[2] the Board is composed of the former type, that is, all are

1. George A. Steiner, and John B. Miner, *Management Policy and Strategy*, 1977, p. 762.
2. Stanley Vance, *Boards of Directors*, 1964, p. 17.

Exhibit 1. Board of Director's Profile

Position	Name/Background	Committees/Service
President	Walter Braun, approximate age: 59. President/owner of three related agriculture service businesses, does not actively farm. Lives outside town but has one business office in town. Family has farmed and owned businesses in area since 1900s. Family and relatives farm 14% of District.	Ten years County Water Board
Vice-President	Hugo Moreno, approximate age: 62. Family has farmed the area since the 1920s. Currently his sons farm and Hugo is semi-retired, lives out of town.	Nineteen years Personnel Finance Engineering
Secretary	Vito Mazzie, approximate age: 56. Family has also farmed since the 1920s. He currently farms outside the District but lives in town. His brothers farm within the District.	Fourteen years Groundwater Engineering Legal
Member	Jess Einstein, approximate age: 47. Family has farmed since the 1930s. Jess lives out of town but he and his sons actively farm within the District as well as outside.	Nine years Personnel Finance Groundwater
Member	Craig Johnson, approximate age: 37. Manager of division corporate farmm within the District, lives out of town but is active in representing the District at state and local levels.	Eight years Legal County Water Board
Treasurer, Asst./Sec.	Lupe Martinez, approximate age: 28. Acts as secretary-bookkeeper for the District. Takes Board Minutes and acts as Controller. Handles assessments in excess of $4 million per year.	One year No voting rights
District Manager	Harry Johns, approximate age: 59. Has engineering background, does not come from farm family, but has lived in the area until just recently. Has run the District alone until just recently.	Twenty-four years County Water Board City Water Board No voting rights
Ex-member Constant Visitor	Reuben Goldstein, approximate age: 63. Successful entrepreneur and businessman. Does not actively farm but has manager run large acreage within District (10% land area). Descendant of wealthy landowner (1900s).	County Water Board City Water Board (Represents business interests)

landowners within the District. As the profile suggests, there is diversity as well as similarity among Board members. Rawlins observed certain voting trends and consensus in decision-making at the Board meetings.

The two predominately business-oriented individuals are Braun and Johnson. These two interviewed Rawlins and indicated the potential for a management position. During the Board meetings, Braun has complete control. When he is not present, not much gets discussed. Often, he and Goldstein get locked into water politics with Goldstein trying to make deals and Braun not giving an inch. Braun is adept at politics and playing other individuals against one another. Johnson is more reserved in the meetings but is always thinking ahead and definitely looks out for his employer's position.

The other three members are progressive farmers, conservative and slow moving on crucial decisions, especially personnel matters. Some promised merit raises for employees were not acted upon for two months. In the process, two individuals went to work for other employers. Mazzie is outspoken, explosive, disagreeable, but when outnumbered, usually votes with the consensus. Mazzie was previously removed from the personnel committee for his prejudice against any kind of raise. Einstein is also not sympathetic to raises regardless of the type, such as merit or annual. Einstein goes with the consensus and contributes little during the meetings. Moreno is a portly, soft-spoken gentleman who always agrees with Braun's opinion.

Lupe Martinez keeps Board Minutes and asks frequent questions to maintain order during discussions. She often complains that the manager completely re-edits the Minutes and substantially modifies the context, prior to final typing, to include indications of Board approval. Rawlins noted in several instances the "truth was stretched" in the official Minutes. Johns is active in the meetings on external matters but tends to play down internal problems the District faces. He reads the agenda but does not attempt to keep the meeting on course.

Although the District is in definite distress, this never surfaces at regular meetings. Perhaps during executive sessions these problems are discussed. Rawlins observed: members proceeding according to self-interest; lack of defined flow of authority for making decisions according to any carefully devised plan; non-maximization of leadership potential of Board and management; lack of regular and effective communications; inability to adapt to rapidly changing internal and external conditions; and short-run, rather than long-run, planning emphasis. In spite of all of these limitations, by definition the Board of Directors is the top-level policy-making body of the District. However, landowners should not completely dominate and membership should not be a matter of historical accident, favoritism, or even nepotism, but a consequence of logic.[3]

Political Events

From the day Rawlins started working, he sensed a tense work environment, disgruntled employees, and a moody, and sometimes semi-hostile manager. In recent months, more field personnel were hired, including a new superintendent, who was consciously trying to get things done and boost worker morale. To Rawlins, it appeared the superintendent was empire-building, solidifying worker support, and not conferring enough with the manager. The manager became defensive at the swift manner things were done with apparent disregard for cost.

A series of secret meetings took place between the Board of Directors, the President, and superintendent; President and manager; and a combination thereof. Soon after, the superintendent told Rawlins that the Board had stripped the manager of all field duties and he, the superintendent, was in charge and would now be responsible for all field activities. He also told Rawlins that the Board was planning to lay off Rawlins. Subsequently, a group of thirty to forty landowners signed a petition requesting the impeachment of management and

---

3. Stanley Vance, *The Corporate Director*, 1968, p. 9.

the Board if the present manager didn't leave. As an apparent short-term measure, the Board put all their eggs with the superintendent to get the District in shape.

Organization

At the suggestion of Rawlins, the manager devised an organizational chart which is described in Exhibit 2. The number in each square denotes the number of original employees; furthermore, the number in parentheses indicates new employees hired within the last six months during which the work force nearly doubled.

Exhibit 3 shows the current scheme in which the manager has more of an administrative role and the superintendent reports directly to the Board. Because of the political situation, the Board gave the superintendent mini-manager responsibility and authority regarding hiring and firing of field personnel and purchasing equipment/supplies to expedite the maintenance program. Maintenance was interpreted as everything from simple chemical spray to new construction, canal/structure improvements, and dealing with landowners.

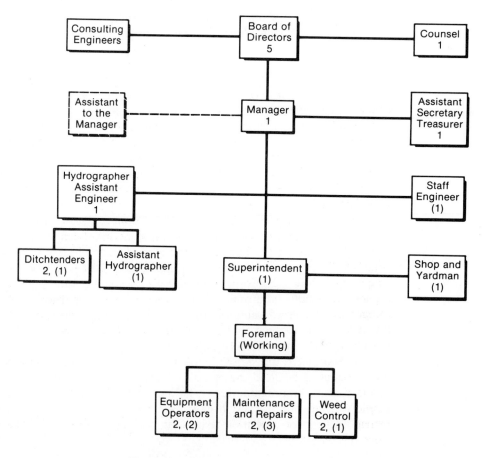

Exhibit 2. Organization Chart (Posted)

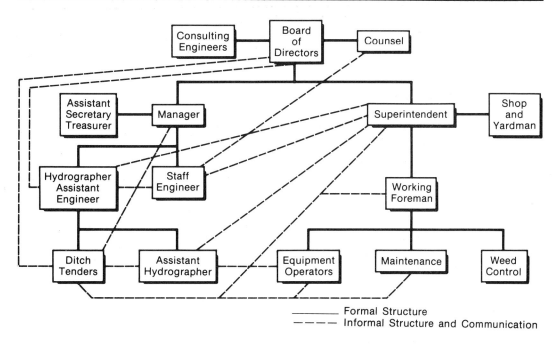

EXHIBIT 3. Organization Chart (Actual Working)

The separation of powers in Exhibit 3 presents unique problems without the further complications of personalities, value systems, formal and informal relationships, positions and work roles, individual and group behavior, and attitudes. The dashed lines of Exhibit 3 designate communication flow and informal structure. Previously, the manager and the Board kept tight control over wage increases following minimum cost strategies. However, a few direct contacts between the President of the Board and staff members concerning personnel issues and salary now occurred.

Under the new scheme, the superintendent hired more field people, upgraded positions, purchased new equipment and supplies, mobilized every piece of existing equipment, and started a crash maintenance and improvement program. This caused personnel problems. New workers were employed at high wages, especially heavy equipment operators. All maintenance people were cross-trained to operate equipment which theoretically put them in a higher pay category. Older employees, already disenchanted with management because of low pay and impossible workloads, rebelled and threatened to join a union for higher pay and personal recognition.

Consequently, the superintendent applied for eleven merit raises at the following monthly Board meeting. One was approved immediately and the others deferred to a committee for another month. In Exhibit 3, water operation employees, also disenchanted with pay and working conditions, spoke to the manager about these matters. Because they received little sympathy, they finally went to the Board President and superintendent.

On one occasion, the President approved a raise without notifying the manager. The wage situation snowballed to the point where even the secretary gave the manager an ultimatum. She requested proper compensation for the many jobs she performed (previously two people did the same thing) accompanied by a reasonable working relationship between the manager and superintendent. The manager didn't move quickly enough to resolve these problems and the secretary accepted another job.

Rawlins' Dilemma

Due to the disarray of the organization aggravated by the two mini-managers in a power struggle, Rawlins felt it best to take his case directly to the Board instead of getting involved in the struggle. A recent letter to the landowners by the Board President stating that the District was undergoing organizational changes and that any landowner requests or complaints should be directed to the superintendent or hydrographer confirmed Rawlins' suspicions that the Board intended to lay him off. After all, Rawlins originally was hired to deal with the landowners.

Rawlins wrote a memorandum to the Board (see Exhibit 4) defending his position against possible layoff and emphasizing the District's need for his services in organization, operation, and assistance in policy formulation/long-range strategic planning. He also addressed engineering and construction problems existing in the District. After completing the memo, Rawlins wondered if he had clearly identified the factors inhibiting strategic planning activities. He also speculated about the policies and strategies that might have resulted if the Board and present management had been impeached. Furthermore, he wondered if he had correctly assessed his situation and pursued the right course of action.

TO: BOARD OF DIRECTORS, FAR-WEST WATER DISTRICT
             Walter Braun
             Hugo Moreno
             Victor Mazzie
             Jess Einstein
             Craig Johnson

FROM: James Rawlins, Staff Engineer

SUBJECT: Position and Duties

DATE: March 6, 1981

As you know, the District has undergone recent organizational changes affecting the roles of the manager and superintendent. In the last Board Executive Session (February), apparently the differences were resolved and responsibilities, authority, and duties of each were clearly defined. Although there is a new organizational chart on the wall, it appears in actuality the Board is acting General Manager with a Manager of Water and Operations and a Manager of Maintenance and Construction under it.

What's alarming to me is that my position is in question. I know that during one of these personnel sessions, both the managing parties indicated to the Board that they saw no need for a Staff Engineer and couldn't utilize his help. If my understanding and perception of the situation are correct, the Board doesn't have any other recourse than to let me go. Before it goes to this extreme, I take this opportunity to present my case to the Board.

Upon the Board's review of this memorandum, I want to meet with them and discuss my current and future status with the District.

Organization

The District is still undergoing organizational adjustments due to the recent Board-initiated changes, as brought on by a landowner petition request to do so.

Under the new arrangement, the organization is still fragmented. I observe communication between office and field but it appears neither management entity has control over the overall organization unless both meet daily or weekly with the Board. I'm flexible but at the same time I like to know what's going on. If given the opportunity and time, I can assist both factions under the current organizational framework.

Already, I have brought the Hydrographer Section and superintendent together on the problem of coordinating turnout replacement invert elevations to ensure proper functioning of the stilling well. In the past, many have been installed too high on the canal banks, thus negating water measurement. Operation and maintenance of the turnouts will require coordination between Hydrographer, Ditchtender and Maintenance personnel. The majority of stilling wells I have observed do not function. This situation requires further study as the problem is not merely "normal maintenance."

A Staff Engineer is in an ideal position to define these and other District problems, provide alternatives, get all sides involved, and arrive at solutions that maximize benefit to the District as a whole. One reason for hiring the Staff Engineer was to get assistance with field problems, but the Board letter of February 17, 1981, to the landowners tends to negate these functions. This matter has to be clarified.

Beyond this current "maintenance crisis," other organizational and operational areas have to be addressed. As a minimum, plans have to be formulated and put in writing. Currently, there is no unifying force and the various factions appear to work in different directions. The Staff Engineer can lay out an organization plan, obtain input from all parties concerned, set broad goals and objectives, devise short- and long-range strategies to obtain goals, and propose an organizational structure to implement the strategies. Two months' observation in the field indicates the District may need up to two years just to catch up. Again, it's not just a maintenance problem.

Operation

The initial phase is one of learning the physical plant, canal and drainage systems, landowner boundaries. In addition, structures, turnouts, bridge and culvert crossings, and county road crossings must be checked. Based on these findings, present maps of ownerships, the above systems, and structures need updating. This update will serve two purposes: to acquaint the Staff Engineer with the District and to form a basis for use in planning, operation, and maintenance. At present, no one person in the District knows what's in the field and what condition it's in, other than in generalities. (Last structure update was 1960+.)

A second phase is to get involved with Hydrographers' and Ditchtenders' activities. This would require physically riding with each and becoming acquainted with water operation. It appears delivery into the District is monitored fairly well. At the farm level, deliveries are only estimated based on the Ditchtenders' or Hydrographers' experience. This area needs investigation, and perhaps more effective measurement methods can be designed within the same cost range.

A third phase is to prepare operational plans, policies, and procedures. The most "current" edition of the District's Rules and Regulations governing the distribution and use of water is dated May 7, 1948. Along with a standard operating procedure, the Rules and Regulations need to be updated. The Staff Engineer has the flexibility to work this in his schedule and can obtain input from all sources, to include the Board and District personnel. The operation plan needs input from the landowners as some utilize District facilities and go to the extreme of running water backwards. This will entail in-depth interviews as to what their current and future operational plans are and how they affect District canal and drainage operation.

The Board, in its February 17, 1981, letter to the landowners, made it clear that the Superintendent and Hydrographer will handle landowner problems. Although neither are engineers, both will encounter engineering problems. The Staff Engineer also has to become involved. Said letter further mentioned field investigations, landowner contacts, engineering and cost studies to be done by

District personnel, and outside contract help. Hiring a consultant is an alternative to an in-house Staff Engineer but there is the question of cost-benefit. Past work experience with a consultant shows engineer time is multiplied 2.25 to 2.5 times actual gross salary; that is, time to a client may be $25 per hour for a Staff Engineer, while actual gross take home is $10 per hour. Senior, Resident, and Principal Engineer costs are considerably more. Because of cost, a consultant and his staff would be limited in understanding District problems. It's questionable whether they could spend the time to learn the system, ride around with Ditchtenders, Hydrographers, and maintenance types, and landowner interviews would be limited. A subsequent report or plan may look good on paper but may not be practical from a District operational level.

Engineering and Construction

Along with an operational plan come feasibility, planning, design, construction, financing, operation and maintenance of existing or new structures, and distribution systems. If the objective is to maximize District benefit at least cost, then an overall plan with goals, objectives, strategies, District resources vs. outside help, formulation, and execution is necessary.

The current situation of "basic maintenance and repair work" actually leads into new construction with replacement items. Clearly some replacements require engineering design and inspection control, especially if we are dealing with road crossings, bridges or other canal crossings, and canal relocations. With increased activity comes increased liability. Furthermore, if a structure or facility built by District forces fails, who's responsible? The Staff Engineer can assist in design and inspection control.

Another area of short- and long-term implications is canal improvements. One example is the current Mirada relocation. The relocation calls for District plans, specifications, and procedures for construction control and for obtaining rights-of-way with legally binding agreements. If the District continues to function on verbal agreements, special interest groups will always prevail. Ultimately, the aggressive persons will do what they want, especially now with the District organization being splintered. The current situation is serious enough that immediate Board action is warranted. One alternative a landowner discussed is obtaining water delivery agreements with the other affected landowners, thus relieving the District of its obligations and responsibilities. If this becomes reality, the Board should settle for nothing less than a written, legally binding agreement between all parties concerned with review and approval by the District's legal counsel prior to any agreement execution.

Obviously, any future relocations will require involvement of the District Board, management, staff, or their representatives, and legal counsel at the planning stage with the landowner and should not be allowed to proceed to the construction stage without written legal agreements. The current Staff Engineer has both the engineering and legal experience required in this area.

Eventually, what is needed is a hydraulic study of the whole system from an operational standpoint to provide a plan and cost structure for future improvements. As in the Mirada case, other canals may be oversized, filled with sediment, and in deteriorated condition beyond the realm of normal maintenance. Landowner interviews by the same person that prepares the plan or under his direction are essential to planning. Upon modification, revisions, and final adoption by the Board, the plan can be finalized on paper as to design specifications, formally for outside contractors and/or landowners and informally for District forces.

Canal seepage in the northern and eastern portions of the District is a problem and has to be dealt with either prior to or at the same time as the hydraulic study. Discussions with four landowners indicate production has been and will continue to fall off near the District's canals. Whether seepage ditches and/or subterrain drains will solve the problem has to be investigated. Perhaps a pilot project should be engineered and initiated to serve as a basis for long-range planning. The Drainage District currently in the feasibility and planning stage should be seriously considered by the District. It is a difficult decision to make as it is similar to a cancer, in that ten to twenty years later you discover you have a problem (and it is too late).

Exhibit 4. Memorandum

Bibliography

Drucker, Peter F. *Managing in Turbulent Times.* New York, N.Y.: Harper and Row, 1980.

Steiner, George A., and John B. Miner. *Management Policy and Strategy.* New York, N.Y.: MacMillan, 1977.

Vance, Stanley C. *Boards of Directors.* Eugene, Ore.: University of Oregon Press, 1964.

————. *The Corporate Director.* Homewood, Ill.: Dow Jones-Irwin, 1968.

Webber, Ross A. *Management Pragmatics.* Homewood, Ill.: Richard D. Irwin, 1979.

Part II
Establishing Plans, Objectives, and Strategies

Cases Outline

- Whose Best Interests?
- Lyndon Johnson's Decision
- Not Enough to Go Around
- Sun Company/Gulf Oil/Mobil Corporation
- Peoples Trust Company
- "Perfectly Pure Peabody's"

8. Whose Best Interests?

James T. Delant is a regional manager for Elite Electonics, a light manufacturing concern that produces component parts for many computer and calculator companies. Jim has been with Elite Electronics for some sixteen years and has an excellent record. He joined the company right after getting his bachelor's degree in electronic engineering from a prestigious East Coast school. In addition, while working full time for Elite Electronics, he also completed his MBA. He has received one promotion after another and now makes approximately $70,000–$75,000 per year plus many benefits associated with upper management—stock options, expense accounts, use of company car, and so forth.

His present responsibility is the Eastern division of Elite Electronics. There are three other divisions all of which are involved in the development and manufacturing of calculator and computer components. Elite Electronics has a fine reputation in the industry as a quality producer of components. Jim Delant has been instrumental in the company gaining that reputation. Jim was responsible for many of the early electronic developments that put Elite "on the map." After early promotions, which removed Jim from the research and development areas of the company, he has been a tireless administrator. His reputation as an administrator is topflight. He is known to be hard, but scrupulously fair. Beyond that, he is known to be practically fanatical about quality control.

In the business, quality control is the key to success. Certainly, in any manufacturing business quality control is essential. In component electronics, however, the stakes are especially high. Even minor errors in computer components can and *do* lead to major problems with the finished product. Jim Delant's region has been the leader in quality control at Elite Electronics for years. Indeed, the quality control of his responsibility areas is practically a legend in the industry.

Expansion

The executive officers of Elite Electronics, with the blessing of the board of directors, have agreed to expand the operations of the company. A decision has been made to manufacture complete business-use computers under its own name rather than simply providing components to other manufacturers. This, of course, is a major move with a great deal of risk.

First, and foremost, there are many manufacturers in this area. Competition is brutal. It seems that every day some new manufacturer appears with one breakthrough or another. These breakthroughs take two primary forms. A computer will be made with more technical capability—it can do more things. Also, a computer can be made which, while it does not do more, is much more efficient. This may very well cause a large drop in price for the consumer. Both of these possibilities are real concerns to any manufacturer of these products. Obviously, if any other company can manufacture a product at the same price with greater capability or a similar product at a reduced price, then it can be expected to be a market leader.

Despite the tough competition and the speed of changes in the product line, Elite Electronics has decided to use its excellent reputation in the field as an edge for the production of a full line of business-use computers. Given the large risk attendant to this decision, the choice of the person to head this new operation is an important one. James Delant has been chosen to head this new division.

The Locations

The company is very pleased with the selection of James Delant to head the new division. His record is impeccable; they are particularly enthusiastic about his reputation for quality. A second issue, though, that has raised some controversy at Elite Electronics concerns the location of the new facilities. After much discussion with a variety of experts in the industry, three viable locations for the new plant to manufacture business-use computers have been identified. Naturally, there are several factors that are important in the choice of locations for such a facility. Among others, a location must be chosen in an area where there is an adequate supply of competent labor to work at the new facilities. Also, an important consideration is the nearness to reasonable transportation both to market the devices and to receive shipment of the parts and so forth necessary to assemble the final product.

Even with the number of possible locations reduced to three, there remains a good deal of controversy over which location should be chosen. Naturally, each location has its advantages and disadvantages. Each location has been studied carefully by a committee formed especially to address this problem. This committee has submitted a recommendation to the chief executive officer and the board of directors. This recommendation did not specifically exclude any of the locations. It did, however, prioritize them in the following order.

1. First selection (judged by the committee to be the best selection overall): Largetown, Midwest.
2. Second selection (judged by the committee to be the second best selection overall): Smalltown, Southeast.
3. Third selection (judged by the committee to be the worst location overall): Mediumtown, Northwest.

The chief executive officer, along with the board of directors, thanked the committee for its fine work on the selection process. Even so, there remains something of a controversy over the final selection. It has been decided, since James Delant will head the new facility, that he should have an input into the decision about the location of the facility. Accordingly, Mr. Delant has been provided with the written recommendation from the selection committee, reports from various experts and consultants hired for their expertise in these matters, and whatever other data could be assembled. Mr. Delant is to carefully study these materials and notify the chief executive officer and the board of directors of his decision about where to place the new plant facilities. Mr. Delant has been asked to respond within five days.

Tough Choice

James Delant's promotion to head the new division has, as you would expect, been a cause for celebration in the Delant household. He has two children, one currently in high school, the other in the seventh grade. Naturally, they have many friends in the community and are a little sad about moving. Even so, they are thrilled with their dad's promotion. There is, after all, a lot of money involved. The Delant family will probably be able to afford to do several things that they have done without in the past.

Rebecca Delant, Jim's wife, is also very pleased with the promotion. Mr. Delant has dedicated some sixteen years of his life to Elite Electronics. He has worked hard for this opportunity and she thinks he deserves it. Jim's wife knows what it is to work and be appreciated. Aside from raising a fine family, she is an accountant for a private firm in the community. She has been employed by this firm for just over ten years.

The choice of location for the new facility has been very difficult for Mr. Delant. He has studied the recommendation of the selection committee at length; he has also carefully reviewed all the reports from the various experts and the consulting firms. Based on the available information, he has decided that the recommendation of the committee is entirely accurate: Largetown, Midwest—first; Smalltown, Southeast—second; Mediumtown, Northwest—last. At least he thought that until last night.

Another Look

Last night, while Jim was reviewing the selection paperwork in his de   his wife came in with a cup of coffee. She asked what he was working on. He to   her that the choice for the location had essentially been left up to him. The company had a recommendation from a selection committee but since it was he who would head the new division, he would have a very strong way in the decision. In fact, Jim explained to his wife that he did not think that his recommendation would be rejected.

Naturally, his wife was very interested in the possible places to which the family might move. Jim briefly outlined the locations for her. At this point, she became very quiet and seemed a little upset. She, of course, had no idea that Mr.

Delant would have any say in the plant location. She assumed that those decisions would be made by others and the Delant family would go with little choice to the new area. She told her husband that she thought he should have discussed the selection with her before making his final choice.

In fact, she went on to explain that she did not like the idea of going to Largetown, Midwest (the company's first choice) one bit. She was very concerned about the large-city problems of the area and even more concerned about the education the children would receive in this location. Beyond that, she was very upset about the prospect of going to Smalltown, Southeast (the company's second choice) because she would probably not be able to find a reasonable accounting job in such a small community.

Mediumtown, Northwest (the company's last choice) would, on the other hand, be just fine. It was a nice area of the country. The schools were firstrate for the children and she would be able to find suitable employment very easily. Mrs. Delant made it *very* clear that she would be upset with a decision to go to either Largetown, Midwest or Smalltown, Southeast.

9. Lyndon Johnson's Decision*

When Lyndon Johnson was Senate Majority leader during the Eisenhower years, he was adamantly opposed to any American involvement in Indo-China. It was widely believed that it was his opposition which, in 1954 after the French defeat in Vietnam, made Eisenhower rule out any American military intervention against the strong pressure for it on the part of his Secretary of State, John Foster Dulles, his Vice-President, Richard Nixon, and his Chairman of the Joint Chiefs of Staff, Admiral Radford. Johnson continued his opposition to any American involvement in Indo-China when he became President Kennedy's Vice-President. He was outspoken about his desire to withdraw the American advisors whom Eisenhower had sent to bolster the South Vietnamese regime; and he strongly opposed the plunge into Vietnamese politics on the part of the Kennedy Administration when, in the fall of 1963—shortly before President Kennedy's assassination—it countenanced the coup against President Diem and thereby made the American government the guarantor of the successor regime, and the actual power in South Vietnam. Johnson continued this position after becoming President and resisted all through 1964 pressures for increased American involvement, especially from the Foreign and Defense Secretaries he had inherited from Mr. Kennedy. He strongly emphasized during his election campaign of 1964 his resistance to any

*"Lyndon Johnson's Decision," *Management Cases* by Peter F. Drucker, pp. 121–124. Copyright © 1977 by Peter F. Drucker. Reprinted by permission of Harper & Row.

attempt to expand the war in Vietnam or to make it an American war. Indeed, his opposition to our involvement in Vietnam was so great and so well known that it was widely feared in the Pentagon and the State Department—and even more in Saigon—that Johnson was encouraging the North Vietnamese to attack by, in effect, promising them that the U.S. would not resist.

Then, in the spring of 1965, Hanoi adopted a new and aggressive policy. Previously, Hanoi had confined itself to supporting insurgents in South Vietnam— with arms, advisors, and money. It had, in other words, matched the American policy of support for the South Vietnamese government and also the American decision not to become involved militarily on a large scale. Beginning in the spring of 1965—only a few weeks after Johnson was sworn in for his second term—North Vietnam began to send North Vietnamese Regulars, heavily armed with Russian armor and artillery, into South Vietnam, where they took over military operations from the South Vietnamese Viet Cong guerrillas. In late spring these North Vietnamese troops—by now the equivalent of about fifteen American divisions—launched a massive attack clearly aimed at cutting South Vietnam in two. North Vietnam's objective suddenly seemed to be a "military solution," that is, the defeat and destruction of the South Vietnamese military. In the face of this situation, Johnson changed his basic position. He decided that force had to be met with force. He sent a major American military force to Vietnam to take over the main burden of fighting the North Vietnamese. He argued—enough documents have been published to make this clear—that the South Vietnamese would not rise to join the North Vietnamese, as indeed they did not. In this situation a defeat of Hanoi's military thrust would rapidly induce Hanoi to re-establish the uneasy truce that had prevailed before, if not to replace it, as had happened in Korea ten years earlier, with a long-term armistice. Militarily the U.S. was at first fully successful. The North Vietnamese were beaten back with very heavy losses in manpower and almost complete loss of their equipment. By fall of 1965, the North Vietnamese were in full retreat, pulling their badly mauled divisions back into North Vietnam. There was every reason to believe that Johnson's basic premise, that such a defeat would lead to a valid armistice, would be proven right. We know that active negotiations via Moscow were going on and that around Christmas, 1965, an armistice was thought "to be in the bag" in Moscow, apparently as well as in Washington.

What happened then we do not know. One theory is that Brezhnev, until then only one of the three top men in the Soviet hierarchy, made his bid for supreme power in late 1965 and needed the support of the military (and it seems, especially of the Navy) which he only got by turning "hawk." To support this theory there is the fact that Russia began suddenly to step up military supplies to Hanoi—after telling Hanoi and the world in 1965 that supplies would be limited to replacement of lost equipment; that at the same time the Soviet Union, after long hesitation, decided on a crash program to build a three-ocean navy; and that it took over supplying India with arms on a massive scale. Another theory argues that the balance of power in Hanoi, between "doves" and "hawks," shifted decisively toward the "hawks," as Ho Chi Minh suffered a heart attack or stroke and could no longer control events (though he did not die until 1969). Another theory—the least likely one, by the way—maintains that growing American resistance to the Vietnamese war encouraged the Communists; but there was still very little resistance to the Vietnamese war in this country in early 1966, though it was beginning to grow and to be more vocal.

In any event, by January or February 1966, it had become clear that events were not following Lyndon Johnson's expectations. Hanoi had broken off truce negotiations. Instead it was pouring back supplies and men into South Vietnam. The Russians who, only a few months earlier, had acted as intermediaries between Washington and Hanoi were stepping up their support for Hanoi and refusing to use their influence to persuade Hanoi to moderate its demands for total surrender. And so President Johnson had to face the fact that his policy, despite its resounding military success, had been a political failure.

When he sat down with his advisors—mostly the crew he had inherited two years earlier from Presdient Kennedy—no one felt very good about the situation. But prevailing sentiment—and Johnson agreed reluctantly—was that there was really no choice but to hang on. It was now clear that the North Vietnamese could not win a military victory against American forces. It was equally clear that the South Vietnamese, while perhaps not enthusiastic about their regime, did not support the North Vietnamese government. So, the consensus ran, "sooner or later" Hanoi or their "real master," Moscow, would have to see the futility of the drive for a "military solution," and until then all the U.S. could do was to hang on.

No one liked this conclusion. But every one—Rusk, McNamara, McGeorge Bundy, the Joint Chiefs of Staff—went along, reluctantly. The only dissenter in the group, according to all reports, was George Ball, Undersecretary of State. He was primarily concerned with economic affairs, and until then, very far away from the Vietnam problem. Ball is reported to have said: "I don't know, Mr. President, what the right answer is. But I do know that continuing last year's policy is the wrong thing to do. It cannot work and must end in disaster. For it violates basic principles of decision-making."

10. Not Enough to Go Around

Divisional Companies

The Kennington Group is a divisionalized company. Simply, this means that the Kennington Group is involved in not one but several businesses. Normally, each business is handled by a general management group sometimes referred to as division management. The primary challenge for such a divisionalized company is to develop a reasonable—and, it is hoped, profitable—strategy for managing the diverse business interests of the entire company. In a simple sense, it is clear that what is good for the diesel truck division of a large corporation is not necessarily good for their tank division or their luxury car division, and so forth.

Kennington Group and Portfolio Management

The Kennington Group, like many other divisionalized companies, relies on a portfolio management strategy developed by the Boston Consulting Group (BCG) under its president, Bruce Henderson. It has been suggested that this approach to the management of divisionalized companies may represent the most significant contribution to strategic planning over the past two decades. As you would expect, the so-called BCG approach has its detractors. Still, the BCG model and its many extensions remain very popular in strategic planning today.

Basically, a divisionalized company like Kennington attempts to place its various businesses into one of four categories: stars, cash cows, dogs, and question marks. In order to responsibly classify operating companies in this way, both the business growth rate and relative market share must be identified. In other words, the divisionalized company should have some idea of the amount of growth in sales that it can reasonably expect in its businesses and the relative share of the market that its businesses do or will enjoy. With this information, a matrix is suggested.

Stars

A business with high growth rates and a high market share is usually labeled a "star" (see Exhibit 1). "Star" is an apt title inasmuch as such a company represents the best profit and growth opportunities for the divisionalized company. This is a business that a company like Kennington would carefully groom for the long run. Unfortunately, some stars do not actually make money in the shorter run. Very often, a business like this requires very heavy additions to investment to guarantee its growth potential. While such businesses have tremendous potential, they may not bring in enough money in sales to sustain their own growth and development. A divisionalized company may have to transfer funds from its other operating companies or obtain outside funding to fuel the rise of a star.

Cash Cow

A business with a high market share in a low growth market would be referred to as a "cash cow." This, in many ways, is a very envious position. Usually, a cash cow generates substantial cash surpluses far beyond the revenue needs for reinvestment and growth. Management hopes the "stars" of the past will become the "cash cows" of the present. While it is true that cash cows have very little growth potential, they are very valuable for the divisionalized company for a variety of reasons. There is an old expression about robbing Peter to pay Paul. This is a compelling analogy with the cash cow in portfolio management. Cash cows are regularly robbed to pay dividends to the divisionalized company's stockholders, to acquire other companies, and to provide funds for the "stars" of the future.

The objective in managing a cash cow is to maintain its market share (remember, there is little hope of increasing it) and preserve the flow of revenues for other purposes—particularly the reallocation of funds for business investments elsewhere.

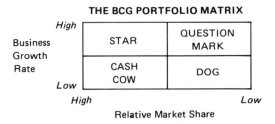

EXHIBIT 1.   The BCG Portfolio Matrix

Dogs

Businesses with a low growth rate (or none at all) and a low market share are rightfully labeled "dogs." Such companies are in an extremely weak competitive position with little or no profit potential. They do not, by and large, provide a sufficient cash flow to sustain their own operations. This, of course, makes it very difficult to maintain their current position (as bad as it is) in the market. Three primary strategies are generally suggested to deal with a dog-type business. First, it may simply be liquidated—assets and inventory sold off and the doors closed. Secondly, the dog business may be divested—sold at the best available price. Lastly, it may be what is referred to as "harvested." This essentially means that the company will be driven into the ground—no maintenance, no reinvestment, no support. In this case, the organization gets every last dime at absolutely minimum costs. When there is no longer a dime to be made, the doors are closed.

Question Mark

The designation "question mark" comes from the fact that rapid market growth makes the business potentially attractive but it is questionable whether profits will be realized because of the very low market share. The potential growth of the market really makes little difference unless a business can capture a reasonable share of the market. Such companies are often called "cash hogs" because they have a nearly insatiable demand for funds. In order to be competitive in the market, they need to invest large amounts of money. Unfortunately, they generate almost no revenue (because they have such a small share of the market). Businesses like this may develop into stars as they capture some of the market and then become cash cows. If, however, the enormous cost of developing these businesses does not warrant the risk, then they should be divested.

Back to Kennington

Kennington, as mentioned, is a divisionalized company that is in several businesses. Every year, the presidents of the businesses are required to submit their strategic plan for the following year and to submit a strategic plan for the next five-year period. Obviously, the object of such planning at the business level is to determine how the particular business can succeed—to improve the competitive position of the business, to concentrate on those segments of the business that seem most attractive, and so forth. Every business, as required, has submitted its one-year and five-year strategic plans to Kennington Group's chief executive officer for approval.

The Problem

The Kennington Group corporate officers have classified all its operating companies into the BCG categories. Unfortunately, based on the one-year and five-year plans to the operating companies, there is some disagreement about which business belongs in what category. In the "star" category, there is less disagreement. The Kennington Group and the operating businesses categorized as "stars" agree that the business growth potential is great, relative market share is good, and most importantly—a great deal of money will have to be invested to assure the promised profitability.

About here, the agreement stops. "Cash cows" agree that they make more money than they spend. However, in the one- and five-year plans, they have requested large increases in capital funds and personnel to expand their operations and develop new markets. They are, as you would expect, not anxious to turn over their large cash surpluses to develop markets and products other than their own.

The "dogs" do not see their plight as hopeless. They have no interest in being harvested, divested, or liquidated. They argue forcefully in their one- and five-year plans that with proper reinvestment, their market shares can be not only maintained but increased.

Lastly, Kennington has identified several businesses as "question marks." However, they have also decided that the enormous risk associated with developing a competitive stance for some of these businesses given the unknown market share is not warranted. The operating businesses, however, see things much differently. They have asked for enourmous injections of capital and personnel to aggressively develop and capture a market share in the areas where their business growth potential is great.

11. How Sun Co.'s Split Personality Works*

The specter of the oil industry's biggest problem looms somewhere in the next century: a permanent dry hole. But already the oil giants are beginning to prepare themselves for the day. Some integrated companies, such as Gulf Oil Corp. and Continental Oil Co., have carved themselves into functional companies, with each concentrating on a segment of the business: exploration and production or

*Reprinted from the November 8, 1976, issue of *Business Week* by special permission. Copyright © 1976 by McGraw-Hill, Inc., New York, New York. All rights reserved.

manufacturing and marketing. Others, such as Atlantic Richfield Co., which wants to acquire Anaconda Co., and Mobil Corp., which bought the giant retailer Marcor Inc., are diversifying against the day when oil and gas supplies simply are not there.

But no company has moved so far or so fast as the relatively small ($4.4 billion in revenues last year) Sun Co. to de-integrate its oil business in a carefully considered prelude to diversification. A year ago Sun Oil Co. was a totally integrated oil company with interests in a few non-related ventures. Today, with the word oil removed from the company name, Sun has fourteen new companies that are beginning to operate at arm's length from one another—learning, as Chairman H. Robert Sharbaugh puts it, "to view themselves as independent businesses."

The wrenching changes are responses not to any near-term crisis but to far-off eventualities, says Sharbaugh. "We still have a couple of decades of good healthy operation in the oil business," he says. "But it won't last forever. So we have moved to set up separate and distinct organizations, each capable of developing into free-standing companies."

Still with Oil

Most of the companies, of course, are still in a phase of the oil business. There are, for example, exploration, production, refining, and marketing companies. There are also gas, oilwell services, pipeline, and transportation companies, as well as a still fully integrated Canadian subsidiary. And Sun's computer and research operations have been folded into a catchall services company, called Suntech Inc. Outside the oil business are a shipbuilding and repair company, a company concentrating on the development of coal and geothermal energy, and a ventures company that runs such miscellaneous enterprises as a magnetic tape manufacturer, a trucking business, and a scattering of real estate developments.

While it is true that the new companies have basically the same operations that Sun had before, they already are showing their independence. "The new operating units have moved aggressively to build their organization, develop business plans, and establish their identities in their markets," says Sun President Theodore A. Burtis, who has overall operational responsibility for Sun.

The fact is that Sun, a company which until the 1970s was considered irreparably stodgy and rooted in the conservative mold espoused by the founding Pew family, is now becoming something of a swinger with its new split personality.

Sunmark Industries, the marketing company, is a far cry from the old marketing operation, for example. Its staff has been cut by 500, two layers of management were eliminated entirely, and a complex structure of five regions and thirty-three districts has become a more simplified twelve divisions. And Sunmark's business is changing with its structure. It sold 600 company-owned service stations this year and is willing to consider divesting all of its owned outlets.

Meanwhile, it purchased Stop-N-Go Foods Inc., a Trotwood (Ohio) self-service convenience food chain with 450 outlets, in order to build competence in nonpetroleum retailing and also to create more cut-price, self-service gasoline outlets. Sun plans to add pumps at some stores, and food sales at some stations.

Greater Control

The new exploration company is undergoing a similar upheaval. Sunmark Exploration Co. has cut its international drilling back substantially, operating in twelve countries this year, compared with twenty-one last year. Meanwhile, it has increased its efforts within the lower forty-eight states. A non-oil resource development company has also acquired 2.2 billion tons of coal reserves and will begin shipments next year from a mine in Wyoming with an annual capacity of twelve million tons.

Through the exploration company, Sun plunked $54 million, the industry's fifth biggest stake, into the Baltimore Canyon leaseholds. "We're free to call the shots onshore," says Sunmark Exploration's president, Marion D. Noble. "But I don't know any company that would give a person complete control over that size investment."

While the subsidiary presidents may not have complete control, they do have more control than many bargained for. Each company has spent the past year building its staff, learning about its direct competitors, and developing a long-term strategy for operations. "They are still heavily dependent on each other and our common services," says Sharbaugh. But he notes that a basic change is permeating the company. "When we were centrally controlled and tightly integrated, top management had a corporate development plan. We then asked the divisions to see what they could do that was consistent with our plan. Now they are given some guidelines, such as capital spending limits, but we ask them to develop their own business strategy." When the strategy is reviewed, the key question is: "Would doing that be inconsistent with where the company thinks it is going?"

Thus, the purchase of Stop-N-Go for about $5 million is consistent with the aims of a marketing company. "But if it reflected a corporate decision to move into the food business, we would be unlikely to invest in so small an acquisition," says Sharbaugh.

Responsibilities

Sunmark Industries' president, Harlan T. Snider, says, "The reorganization gives a much sharper focus on performance." Results for each segment of the business, says Snider, "were buried in information systems designed to show our combined performance. Now we're out there naked under the spotlight, and we have to take a harder-nosed attitude toward the economics of each of our businesses."

The production and gas companies have had to settle a number of disputes about who owns and operates wells in fields where both liquid and gas products are pumped. The exploration and production companies must negotiate who will drill and sell oil from "demarcation" wells drilled around an exploration well to mark the productive limits of a new field. "Those wells are producing while we determine the value of our asset," says Noble. "Who's responsible?"

The construction of a petrochemical expansion at the refinery in Toledo is now managed by a task force from Sun Petroleum Products Co. (SPPC), which runs the refinery and is responsible for its assets. It now contracts for engineering assistance from Suntech, whereas in the past the corporate engineers would have built the addition for the refinery operators to run.

The new relationships are not as clear-cut as they would be if the industry were deregulated, Sunmark must sell a stipulated amount of Sun Petroleum's refinery run to specified stations, and the refinery is locked into much of its supply. But there is no doubt among Sun Co. managers that the goal is for each to stand alone and, eventually, to buy and sell independently. Even now, Noble's exploration company can look for oil without considering whether Sun has economic refining and production gathering capacity. "We do give the production company first refusal rights," he says. The production company has been busy this year acquiring producing leases on its own account.

Testing Brands

At Sun Petroleum, President W. J. Magers says that except for controls, "we have no obligation to buy" from Sun Production, or to sell to the retailing company, Sunmark Industries. Indeed, Sun Petroleum wholesales its product to others, just as it does to Sunmark. And Sunmark is testing three different cut-price brand names and marketing approaches. A few months ago, SPPC lost a dispute over who should be responsible for selling the premium motor oil, Cam II, at wholesale to mass merchandisers such as Sears and K-Mart. Sunmark got the assignment because it was better qualified to handle consumer advertising of the product. Even so, Magers says, his company decides what products it will produce, where, and in what volume.

One president who frankly admits that he approached the 1977 budget planning period "with fear and trembling" is Fred M. Mayes of Suntech. "Our services," he explains, "had never been a direct cost before" to the other Sun companies that use them. While each company is free to contract its engineering or computer work elsewhere, the fact is that outsiders would have a hard time competing against established relationships, old friendships, and, in the case of computer services, customized programs. "In fact," says Mayes, "when we look into the pieces, we find more managers need more information." He expects his computer service sales to rise. On the other hand, the companies are concentrating on solving short-term problems, so Mayes expects at least a temporary decline in chargeable long-range research and engineering. But he notes, "These are big companies in their own right. In time they will each have research programs that match their strategies, and we will be looking at a half a dozen or more big programs rather than one."

Indeed, Sun's operations already have grown substantially in this first year of reorganization. The company announced just this week that net income rose nearly 69 percent to $270.8 million in the first nine months. Revenues were up 23 percent to $3.9 billion. The improved earnings, coupled with two dividend increases that doubled the $1 payout, which had been unchanged since 1925, have sent Sun's stock soaring 50 percent this year.

Progress has been rapid enough so that a year ahead of schedule, Sun President Burtis has appointed a top-level committee headed by Executive Vice-President J. Dwayne Taylor to assess progress, reevaluate the interrelations among the operating companies and between them and the parent company, and see if any changes are needed now.

"We've set these ships on their course," says Taylor. "We don't know just which ones will be sailing five years from now, or how their courses will change. But we do know there will be a number of them out there, each a free-standing company." As for today, he says, "they have all gone further than we had a right to expect."

Gulf Oil Goes Back to What It Knows Best[*]

Buffeted by political scandals and suffering from lack of direction, Gulf Oil Corp. has been a $16 billion a year laggard in the energy industry for a long time. Now Jerry McAfee, who took over as chairman and chief executive officer a year ago, after Bob R. Dorsey resigned under fire because of political contributions the company had made, is trying to get the company back in the race.

No longer will Gulf toy with making acquisitions outside the energy field, as it did recently with Rockwell International, CNA Financial, and Ringling Bros.– Barnum & Bailey—none of which was consummated. Instead, over the next five years, Gulf will put the three quarters of the $2 billion capital budget it plans to spend annually into petroleum exploration and development and coal and uranium operations. "We have decided to stick with the things we know best and to avoid acquisitions to which we can bring nothing but money," McAfee says. "We can see a sense of direction and purpose emerging. There is no longer any uncertainty about our strategy or our goals."

In the past, the conservative Mellon family, which owns about 20 percent of Gulf's stock, has been blamed for interfering with the management of the company, blocking commitments of capital and slowing down decision-making. But Nathan W. Pearson, financial adviser to the Mellons and a member of Gulf's board, says that he is pleased with the direction Gulf is taking under McAfee.

Oil Problems

Even concentrating on "things we know best" will be no easy task for lifelong oilman McAfee, who came to the chairmanship after heading the company's Canadian operations. Gulf is critically short of crude oil supplies. Some 80 percent of its average daily production of 1.7 million bbl. comes from overseas, and in the past three years its production facilities in Venezuela, Ecuador, and Kuwait have been expropriated. Since Kuwait took over Gulf's properties in 1975, for example, the company's daily supply from that sheikdom has dropped to 500,000 bbl. from 1.5 million bbl.

Without the Kuwait concession, says one London oil economist, Gulf no longer qualifies as one of the "Seven Sisters"—the major international oil companies that include Exxon, Mobil, and Texaco. He thinks Gulf now belongs in the second tier, among independents such as Continental Oil Co. and Standard Oil Co. (Indiana). Though Gulf's earnings increased 12.8 percent to $598 million in the first nine months of last year, the company still lagged behind the industry, whose profits averaged a 35.5 percent gain.

Still worse, McAfee must conduct the hunt for new oil sources while the company is still reeling from the after-shocks of a major corporate reorganization undertaken eighteen months ago by former Chairman Dorsey. Gulf, like Sun Co. and Mobil, has dropped its geographical organization and is now set up as seven independent strategy centers.

The centers—distinct companies with full profit and loss responsibility—are: Energy & Minerals, Refining & Marketing, Trading & Transportation, Science & Technology, Real Estate, Chemicals, and Canada. As part of the reorganization, Dorsey also recruited an elite group of sixty-five nonoil people to be Gulf's corporate planners. Their assigned job was to push the company into diversification and away from its heavy dependence on oil and gas profits.

The Tune-Up

McAfee is lukewarm to the new organization, but he has accepted it because he thinks it is impractical to revert to the old one. He is tampering extensively with it, however, and has sent many of the planners packing. He has also warned that "there is more fine-tuning to be done"—which sends shivers through middle management ranks.

Some Gulf people maintain that Dorsey went to the new setup to make any divestiture easier should Congress proceed with its threats to break up the major oil companies. Others say he made the move—at a time when he was under increasing fire in the political contribution scandal—to create enough pandemonium to make him indispensable as chairman.

The reorganization threatened to become a disaster. Right after it was accomplished—and as Dorsey's troubles mounted—authority temporarily passed to the hands of the chairman's council, composed of the chairman, president, and five senior staff vice-presidents. The head of planning, Juergen Landendorf, a former Harvard Business School professor, was virtually running the show. "Although the operating managers had authority to make decisions, many of them abdicated the responsibility because they knew that the guys on the council had the clout politically," says a source close to the executive suite.

With the staff vice-presidents in power, intense competition quickly developed among the strategic operating units, with the heads of the units trying to make their results look good at each other's expense. One widespread result: Inflated transfer payments among the Gulf units as each one vied to boost its own bottom line.

With Dorsey out, McAfee quickly turned the chairman's council into an advisory group, forcing responsibility back to the managers of the strategic units. President James E. Lee says that he and McAfee now "manage the managers," while the staff simply provides support services.

McAfee also cut back the internal competition. Lee emphasizes, "Gulf doesn't ring the cash register until we've made an outside sale." McAfee also changed one strategy center, Science & Technology—the research and development operation—from a profit center to a service organization. Two other profit centers, Trading & Transportation and Real Estate, hang in limbo while McAfee and Lee decide whether the same should be done with them.

"We overemphasized the profit-center concept in the beginning," McAfee admits. Now he is stressing total corporate profits, which makes some Gulf line managers unhappy.

Houston Calling

Another source of anxiety is the reshuffling going on within the strategy centers. The most sweeping changes have come in Gulf Refining & Marketing (GORAM), headquartered in Houston, which is responsible for $7 billion of Gulf's total sales. GORAM made a profit last year, but only because of some "ruthless" cost cutting "to stop bleeding from a thousand wounds," according to GORAM's president, Robert W. Balwin. He reduced the payroll by 1,200—including three regional vice-presidents—closed 400 service stations nationwide and a refinery in San Francisco, shrank the number of marketing districts from twenty-five to fifteen, and redesigned management reports to monitor everything affecting revenue. McAfee is still not satisfied, so more cuts are likely, particularly in the troubled European operation, which has 35 percent excess refining capacity.

At the Pittsburgh headquarters, there is fear that more jobs will be abolished. Already, scores of executives have been transferred from Pittsburgh to operations in Houston, Tulsa, and New Orleans. The ax fell heavily on Dorsey's planners— fifteen of whom have already departed—brought in two years ago and led by Landendorf. He masterminded Dorsey's reorganization and was roundly criticized by the old-time oilmen for being ignorant of the oil business. "The planning function has now been defined so that planning is merely a tool," McAfee says.

Now that McAfee intends to concentrate on energy for the next five years, there may not be much for the planners to do anyway. Some of the $1.5 billion that Gulf plans to spend annually over that half decade will go to develop oil sources in the North Sea. But most—$1 billion per year of it—will be spent in the U.S. About $140 million of it will go for coal and uranium development, the rest for oil and gas. The emphasis is on the U.S. because the profit margins on domestic oil are likely to be better than those on foreign crude, and the discoveries are not in danger of being expropriated.

McAfee's Difference

McAfee is proud that during his first year Gulf has arrested its six-year decline in domestic production of crude oil, and he is accelerating the company's bidding on offshore leases. Gulf has seven producing wells in the Gulf of Mexico and six more scheduled to start pumping this year. The company also holds leases in the Gulf of Alaska and off California.

But some oilmen remain unconvinced that Gulf is back in the game. In the Baltimore Canyon off the East Coast, Gulf mostly lost out to other bidders, coming away with only three tracts after the first auction in 1976.

"Frankly we were surprised at the high values that some bidders placed on this untested area," says Edward B. Walker III, the president of Gulf Energy & Minerals. But one Texas oilman says: "Gulf has not been aggressively bidding for twenty years, and there still is not any sign they are."

McAfee and Dorsey differ as much in personal style as they do in strategic thinking. McAfee is affable, Dorsey was aloof. Dorsey refused to ride in elevators with other employees, but McAfee rubs elbows with the rank and file in the lobby coffee shop of the Gulf building and often can be seen walking through the streets of Pittsburgh's Golden Triangle at lunch time. McAfee and Lee periodically appear on closed-circuit television to address employees, who refer to such telecasts as "The Jim and Jerry Show."

Still, middle managers at Gulf are jittery. They worry about more of McAfee's "fine tuning." McAfee, however, apparently has quieted the jitters of the board of directors and of Pearson, the Mellons' representative. This may be the key to McAfee's future, but not necessarily to Gulf's.

What Makes Mobil Run?*

"Why is Mobil Corp. investing substantial cash reserves in real estate development ventures . . . ?" asked the strange advertisement that appeared one day about a month ago in *The New York Times, The Washington Post,* the *Los Angeles Times,* and *The Wall Street Journal.* "Shouldn't Mobil be committing their efforts toward development of precious energy sources . . . ?" groused the copy.

The ad, it turned out, was paid for by interests associated with Taubman-Allen-Irvine Inc., Mobil's competition in the intense bidding for Irvine Co., the giant West Coast land developer. In the end, Mobil lost out, but the incident raised anew the nagging question that Mobil itself touched off in 1974, when it bought controlling interest in Marcor Inc., a holding company comprising Montgomery Ward & Co. and Container Corp. of America: Why are the oil companies buying nonenergy properties?

In 1975, Standard Oil of California (Socal) bought 20 percent of Amax Inc., primarily a metals mining company. Early this year, Atlantic Richfield Co. merged with Anaconda Co., a copper company. Two weeks ago, Union Oil Co. of California concluded an agreement to buy Molycorp Inc., which produces

*Reprinted from the June 13, 1977, issue of *Business Week* by special permission. Copyright © 1977 by McGraw-Hill, Inc., New York, New York. All rights reserved.

molybdenum and rare earths. Other oil companies have expressed interest in newspapers, insurance companies, aerospace manufacturers, even circuses.

But these examples pale in comparison to the bold moves by Mobil. While hardly a conglomerate, Mobil today gets about 20 percent of its income from businesses other than oil and gas (see Figure 1). Last year Montgomery Ward and Container Corp. together provided 17 percent of this $28 billion company's total revenues—even though Mobil owned only 54 percent of these companies for half the year. Like the rest of the oil industry, Mobil is moving rapidly into chemicals, too: In 1976 its chemicals business topped $1 billion in sales for the first time. And the company has been in real estate for some time, with development properties in the Far East and in northern California, and is apparently willing to buy a lot more land, as the Irvine bidding shows.

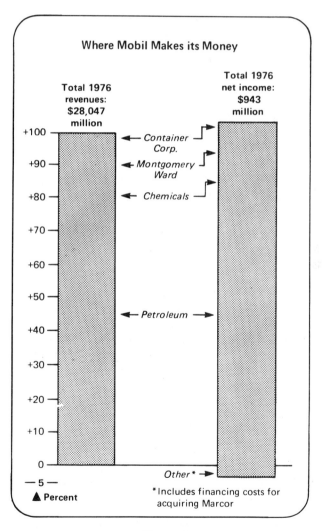

FIGURE 1

The Critical Question

To the oil industry's critics, such diversification is self-indicting. Why, they ask, should the industry and its supporters continually call for higher prices and higher profits—supposedly to support greater efforts at finding oil and gas—when the companies are clearly spending more and more money in areas that have nothing to do with energy?

It is a tough question—one that the companies cannot, in fact, answer satisfactorily. But there are some very good reasons why the oil industry is diversifying, few of them incriminating. And while these moves outside of oil may be inconsistent with the companies' public statements on price controls and government regulations, they make a lot of financial sense—as crude-poor but business-wise Mobil proves.

The main reason for diversification is the most obvious one: As the U.S., and eventually the world, runs out of oil, oil companies have no choice but to liquidate, add value to their products, or diversify. Though oil prices will no doubt continue to rise as supplies dwindle, there is no guarantee that prices will be high enough to provide sufficient profits with lower volume.

Alternative sources of hydrocarbons—shale, tar sands, and coal liquefaction and gasification—are logical options to invest in, and the oil companies do have substantial holdings and development programs in these fields. But the technology to tap these alternatives commercially is still primitive. In New York last week, John E. Swearingen, chairman of Standard Oil Co. (Indiana), made some of the highest estimates yet for the ever-escalating cost of these petroleum substitutes. Crude oil from tar sands, he said, would have to fetch $14 to $20 a bbl. to be profitable using existing technology. Shale oil would have to sell for about $25 a bbl. Coal liquefaction would cost $30 to $40 a bbl. Faced with such premium prices for substitute sources of domestic hydrocarbons, the U.S. would surely be better off buying oil for $13 a bbl. from the Middle East.

Alternatively, the companies might spend their money expanding coal production. They already account for one-fifth of U.S. coal output, though the bulk of that comes from just one company, Continental Oil Co., which owns Consolidation Coal Co. But coal production in the U.S. is already growing about as fast as labor, transportation, and environmental constraints permit.

Meanwhile, as the companies are fond of saying, the U.S. government keeps meddling in their traditional business. Last year Washington rolled back prices on new oil. Congress continually threatens to break up the companies. President Carter recently suggested that the government monitor the companies' highly guarded reserves and production data. Even more significant, both the executive and judicial branches of the government have blocked efforts by the companies to accelerate offshore exploration.

In short, whether from natural or political forces, the opportunities to invest in hydrocarbons production are shrinking, at least in the U.S. "The bigger companies already have huge reserves," notes Houston geophysical consultant Bill B. Crow. "Unless they find a major field, it hardly makes a dimple. Meanwhile, they have a hard time justifying the downside risk to their stockholders." And these days, new major fields are tough to come by, especially onshore in the so-called lower forty-eight states, where the companies operate under the fewest restraints.

But Mobil has even more reason to stray from oil than the other big international majors—it has less oil than they do (see Figure 2). Last year Mobil's domestic production of oil and natural gas liquids accounted for only 48 percent of the oil it processed in its U.S. refineries, vs. 73 percent for Exxon and 72 percent for Texaco. While Mobil's domestic production-to-refining ratio was better than Socal's (40 percent), Socal is awash with foreign oil. In contrast, Mobil's world supply of oil exceeds its own refining needs by only 5 percent. Indeed, further erosion in its global production-to-refining ratio would make it a net buyer of oil

Why Mobil is Straying from Oil

Of the major U.S. oil companies, Mobil ranks
second in gross revenues and net income. . .

| | Millions of dollars | |
	1976 revenues	1976 income
Exxon	$52,585	$2,641
Mobil	28,047	943
Texaco	26,047	870
Socal	20,600	880
Gulf	18,117	816

. . .but is weak in producing domestic oil
for its U.S. refineries. . .

| | 1976 production of petroleum liquids in the U.S. | 1976 refinery runs in the U.S. | Domestic production-to- refining ratio |
	Thousands of bbl. a day		
Exxon	927	1,277	0.73
Texaco	699	972	0.72
Gulf	401	815	0.49
Mobil	375	778	0.48
Socal	420	1,062	0.40

. . .and trails the pack in providing
oil for refinery operations worldwide

| | Total 1976 supply of petroleum liquids | Total 1976 refinery runs | Worldwide production-to- refining ratio |
	Thousands of bbl. a day		
Socal	3,542	2,258	1.57
Texaco	4,015	2,860	1.40
Exxon	5,576	4,359	1.28
Gulf	2,022	1,697	1.19
Mobil	2,156	2,049	1.05

FIGURE 2

instead of a seller. Yet, almost by definition, the "Seven Sisters" of international oil must be sellers, not buyers.

Mobil's crude-poor position dates back to its origins. It began in 1866 as Vacuum Oil Co., a sophisticated refiner of lubricants. (To this day the company remains strong in lubricants. Last year it introduced Mobil 1, a synthetic engine oil, and sales of this pioneering product have far exceeded expectations.) In 1879, John D. Rockefeller bought controlling interest in Vacuum and three years later he folded the company into his notorious Standard Oil Trust. At the same time he set up Standard Oil Co. of New York (Socony) as the trust's administrative arm, also making it responsible for refining and marketing in New York and New England.

When the Supreme Court broke up the trust in 1911, Socony and Vacuum were two of thirty-three companies that were spun off. Both quickly started growing on their own. Vacuum continued to expand in refining, and Socony integrated backward into production. In 1931, with the blessing of a federal court, the two companies merged. But although they complemented each other, forming a fully integrated oil company, the resulting Socony-Vacuum Corp. did not have the big crude oil reserves that its large integrated competitors had already accumulated. It never caught up.

In 1955 Socony-Vacuum changed its name to Socony Mobil to take advantage of what by then had become a familiar trade name, and it finally became Mobil Oil in 1966. Today the company is simply Mobil Corp., consisting of three major operating units: Mobil Oil, Montgomery Ward, and Container Corp.

Financial Emphasis

At the helm is Rawleigh Warner, Jr., who has been chairman and chief executive officer since 1969. Though a second-generation oil executive—his father was chairman of Pure Oil Co., now part of Union Oil—Warner is hardly typical of the Texas-bred oilman. Trim and dapper at fifty-six, he comes across more as a diplomat than a businessman. Unlike the more rough-hewn chemical engineers that run Exxon and Texaco, Warner has a liberal arts degree from Princeton. And instead of working his way up through the grimy refining end of the business, he climbed to the top on the financial ladder.

The financial ladder is well worn at Mobil. President William P. Tavoulareas, Mobil's tough operations man, joined the company in 1947 in the accounting department (and later got a law degree). Lawrence M. Woods, executive vice-president in charge of planning, also is an accountant.

Thus, it is not surprising that Mobil scores high marks from the experts for its financial performance. "Mobil is known as one of the best managed companies in the oil business," says one analyst whose firm buys a lot of oil securities. "It's much more financially oriented than the other oil companies." Says Bruce Lazier, an oil analyst with Faulkner, Dawkins & Sullivan who worked in planning and finance at Mobil for ten years, "Mobil is a lawyer-businessman company rather than an oilman-geologist company. Planning is the real essence of this company." For Mobil, the approach makes sense: It started life and remains today primarily a refining and marketing company, and this part of the oil business requires more financial skills than the other segments.

Mobil's financial bent comes across in its vocabulary. Mobil people talk of "portfolios" and "managing assets" like so many investment bankers. The Marcor acquisition was referred to as a "risk aversion investment" as opposed to a "profit maximization investment"—typical Wall Street lingo.

Whatever the terminology, Marcor was certainly a smart buy. Characteristic of Mobil, the decision to move into a nonoil business was made in 1968—six years before the controversial acquisition actually got under way. "I won't say that we could foresee greater involvement in our business by the *consuming* countries," says Warner of the original impetus to broaden the business. "But it is fair to say we could foresee the greater involvement of the *producing* countries. That meant a lesser role for us. So we got a policy decision from the board of directors to diversify."

A policy decision was one thing; actual approval on a specific property was quite another. "We looked at a hundred different companies," he recalls. "The moment we would bring up a candidate, we had to go over all the arguments for diversification once again."

The arguments were pretty persuasive, however. To begin with, Mobil was often criticized by the financial community for depending on foreign operations for too much of its earnings. Moreover, the real price of oil had been dropping for twenty years, and although the demand for gasoline and other products was strong, growth in dollar volume was uncertain. The best guess at the time was lower profit growth ahead.

The project to find a suitable company fell to Woods, who had taken over the planning and economics department in 1967. "We took a lot of time in screening," he says. To avoid antitrust complications, the company had ruled out anything that was not entirely outside energy. Woods reasoned that a natural mate would be a company in a capital-intensive industry, since it might be attracted by Mobil's fast-growing cash flow. His team—at peak, three people were working on the project—first considered the minerals industry but decided that this business did not offer the high growth rate Mobil was looking for. The company had also put a premium on a consumer-oriented business, and that led to retailing, which is also capital intensive.

"By 1973," recalls Woods, "we were looking at individual companies. Marcor had turned around—it seemed to have a management that knew what they were about yet it was not fully priced in the stock market." Mobil was not yet ready to make the big plunge. "But we had done our homework," says Woods. "We knew it was a good investment, so we went out and bought 4.5 percent of the stock. If nothing else, we figured we could get back in the market the money we had spent on the analysis."

Flush with Cash

Then came the Arab oil embargo. Oil prices skyrocketed, and the stock market went into a dive. What seemed like a good buy just months before suddenly began to look like a steal—and Mobil simultaneously found itself with a lot of extra cash on hand as the big profit spurt of 1974 got under way.

"We hadn't expected to get anything that soon," says Woods. "Nonetheless, we started talking to our management about whether to move."

Mobil brass approached Marcor executives and had a half-dozen meetings with them before deciding to make the tender offer. "Our average cost for stock bought in 1973 was $23," says Woods, adding that Marcor shares had not risen above $28 since 1968. "In 1974, by the time we tendered for control, it was still below $25. We were just dumb lucky," he admits.

The offer, coming at a time when the anomalous profit jump of 1974 was most visible and least understood, brought a storm of public protest. But Mobil was undeterred. "Frankly," confides Woods, "we thought the criticism was relatively mild. And we knew there was no legal basis for a challenge." Some industry critics in Congress tried to attack the Mobil-Marcor marriage on antitrust grounds, arguing that Montgomery Ward's auto service centers compete with Mobil for sales of tires and other accessories. But the Justice Department dismissed the notion that the deal would result in any restraint of trade.

Four Mobil executives went on the Marcor board to get familiar with the company from the inside. "We found no nasty surprises," says Woods, "and we discovered some strengths we hadn't identified." So on July 1, 1976, the merger went through.

Mobil has never revealed the total price for Marcor, but the deal must have cost the company in the neighborhood of $1.8 billion. Mobil spent some $800 million buying the first 54 percent in 1973 and 1974, including $200 million for a new series of Marcor voting preferred stock. "That was one of the major reasons Marcor was willing," says Warner. "Money was tight at the time, and some of their loans were costing them 16 percent. We gave them $200 million at 7 percent."

Thus, with the equivalent of one year's cash flow, Mobil got two companies that will add roughly $150 million to its domestic net income this year. Says analyst Lazier, "Without Marcor, Mobil would be earning substantially more overseas than domestically by the end of this decade. Marcor balances foreign and domestic income for Mobil."

Meanwhile, the company has been striving to improve financial performance in its traditional business. Over the past ten years, Mobil's earnings have grown at a compound rate of 10.2 percent, faster than those of any of its U.S. sisters. That boosted its aftertax return on common equity—a crucial oil industry parameter—to a respectable 13 percent last year, far better than the 10 percent to 11 percent that was typical in the late 1960s and early 1970s. Though Mobil's return on equity is still not as good as Exxon's (14.9 percent in 1976), it is equal to Socal's and better than Gulf's (12.2 percent) and Texaco's (9.8 percent).

Mobil does less well by other measures, however. Its aftertax return on invested capital during 1976 was an unimpressive 9.2 percent. Exxon (12.2 percent), Socal (11.2 percent), and Gulf (10.5 percent) all did better; only Texaco's 7.9 percent return was worse. Part of the explanation is that Mobil borrowed a lot of money to buy Marcor. Furthermore, the company has been spending a lot of money in recent years in the Gulf of Mexico, in the North Sea, and Indonesia, trying to catch up to its crude-richer competitors. That, too, has meant a lot of borrowing. But as these new fields start bringing in oil and gas, return on capital should rise.

Its return on assets, though, will probably remain low indefinitely. Last year Exxon led the field with an 8 percent aftertax return on average total assets. Gulf and Socal both had 7.2 percent returns. Then came Mobil with 6 percent and, finally, Texaco with 5.5 percent. Mobil's acquisition of Marcor did not help here, either, since retailers traditionally have a lower return on assets than oil companies do. But the main reason is that Mobil has more of its money tied up in refining and marketing facilities, which are more asset-intensive than production facilities. Nothing much can be done about this unless Mobil were to discover a mammoth new oil field. "It's tough to budge your return-on-assets ratio when you have $7 billion in assets," notes one insider in the financial section.

Priming the Pump

But Mobil is trying. After years of arriving in the oil patch too late with too little, the company is now hoping to beat its competitors at their own game. Mobil spent $147 million on lease bonuses in the U.S. last year and is stepping up spending outside the U.S. "We're making a point of getting into two or three new areas a year," says Executive Vice-President Alex H. Massad, who took over exploration and production at Mobil last month.

Such big outlays are the industry's best defense against critics who charge that it is diverting funds away from oil and gas to buy other businesses. In the past four years, Mobil has fattened its U.S. exploration and production budget by more than 50 percent. Last year alone it poured nearly $495 million into domestic exploration and production. And the company spent an additional $279 million overseas. According to *Oil & Gas Journal*, the domestic petroleum industry as a whole has budgeted a record $19.6 billion for 1977, up 14.6 percent from its 1976 budget—which in turn was up 31.9 percent from 1975.

If anything, all this activity may be a bit too much. Drilling rigs and other equipment are currently in tight supply. "Right now the system is overheated," Federal Energy Administrator John O'Leary told a recent Washington meeting. "Every measure you want to use—the price of steel, the demand for steel, the demand for skilled labor, all the rest of it—shows a classically overheated microeconomy."

If the oil companies did pour any more into domestic exploration, they would probably only wind up bidding up the cost of oil already being found, instead of actually finding more oil. As a result of their somewhat enforced restraint, however, most of the companies are fast accumulating cash. According to the White House's Office of Energy Policy & Planning, the top eighteen U.S. oil companies had $4.9 billion on hand at the end of 1975, vs. $1.9 billion at the end of 1973. That is what has prompted many of them to look for outside investments during the past two years. Those that have not—such as Exxon and Gulf—have wound up holding excess cash.

Mobil's compromise approach of both increasing exploration and making a large acquisition was probably best for this crude-poor company. But spending a lot of money does not guarantee finding a lot of oil—especially at Mobil. Although industry people rank the company along with Exxon, Shell, and Standard of Indiana as the most technically sophisticated of the big oil companies, Mobil has never had the success that should go along with such expertise. "Mobil has never been particularly good at finding petroleum," says one industry observer. He suggests that other oil companies are not diversifying as fast "because maybe they are more optimistic about their chances of finding oil."

A prime example of the more optimistic, less adventurous oil company is Texaco Inc. A perennial laggard in financial ratios, Texaco is no slouch at providing oil, which, after all, is what the oil business is all about. Worldwide the company has access to a staggering 20.3 billion bbl. of reserves. In the U.S., it has more than 3.1 billion bbl. of oil reserves, nearly 9 percent of the nation's total. Mobil, whose oil and related revenues are only slightly smaller, has just 1.1 billion bbl. in the U.S. "We consider our investment opportunities in conventional petroleum very promising," says a confident John K. McKinley, Texaco's president.

Unlike Mobil's Warner, McKinley is an oilman's oilman. He has a BS in chemical engineering and an MS in chemistry, both from the University of Alabama. McKinley started at Texaco's giant Port Arthur (Texas) refinery. He worked his way to upper management through research and petrochemicals and holds a number of patents in chemicals and petroleum processing.

He believes the conventional oil business has a long future before it. "We don't see any justification for some kind of crash program for diversification's sake," he says in his oil-land drawl. "We do have programs for evaluating investments outside hydrocarbon fields. But we don't see, as others do, an absolute urgency in which the main thing we would have to contribute is money." Texaco is already big in petrochemicals, and when further diversification comes, says McKinley, the moves will be similarly "synergistic."

As a result of its comfortable position in reserves, Texaco last year was the drilling operator for fewer exploratory wells than it was in 1975, 647 in all, according to Denver-based Petroleum Information Corp. Still, that was considerably more than Mobil's total of 377, lowest among the big oil companies. Gulf drilled 629. Exxon drilled 613. And some of the smaller majors, which do not have access to Middle East crude, have been even more active than the Sisters. Standard of Indiana drilled 781 wells. Shell Oil Co., the domestic affiliate of giant Royal Dutch/Shell, drilled 715.

Mobil's No Gambler

Mobil's exploratory drilling in the U.S. was not only less than the others' but also less venturesome. Though the company's total exploration and production expenditures were up 9.2 percent last year, most of the money was spent on production—exploration was actually down 17 percent. On average, reports *Oil & Gas Journal,* industry exploration budgets were up 19.1 percent. Mobil did not even rank in the top ten when it came to wildcat wells, the biggest gambles of them all. Petroleum Information Corp. recorded only 25 wildcats for Mobil last year, compared with 124 for Shell and 97 for Standard of Indiana.

But this fits Mobil's pattern of being short in oil and long on financial savvy. "No one drills a wildcat well as an investment," says one independent oilman. He believes that if a company is looking for secure growth in assets, as Mobil is, wildcats are too much of a risk in the U.S. today. Even if a big company is strong on exploration, he adds, it tends to gamble only on the biggest stakes. One big bet that Mobil made in late 1973 was on the disappointing Destin Anticline in the eastern Gulf of Mexico. The company spent $227 million in lease bonuses—and found not one drop of oil.

On the other hand, with merely the stroke of a pen (plus some big dollars, no doubt), Mobil "found" more oil in 1974 than most oil explorers come across in a lifetime. In the midst of the chaos caused by the Arabs oil embargo, when most experts were predicting an end to the majors' control of Mideast oil, Mobil negotiated with its partners in Arabian American Oil Co. (Aramco) to increase its share from 10 percent to 15 percent over five years, thereby gaining access to untold billions of barrels of oil that it might never have otherwise obtained. "I think it was a brilliant move on their part," says John H. Lichtblau, executive director of the Petroleum Industry Research Foundation.

Mobil's unique approach to the oil business has led it to adopt a public posture that many oilmen consider heretical. Rawleigh Warner has publicly endorsed oil price controls, for instance, though he does want them to be phased out gradually. The company has also supported the "entitlements" program, a complex scheme that requires refiners with access to a lot of cheap domestic crude to subsidize refiners shy of price-controlled oil. True, crude-short Mobil's competitive position is enhanced by these regulatory measures. But in oil land, any government regulation that does not provide an across-the-board subsidy for all always becomes the focus of contempt, and anyone who thinks otherwise is promptly branded a traitor. Warner clearly had to buck peer pressure in breaking from the fold.

To make matters worse, Mobil goes out of its way to publicize its liberal views; it also does not hesitate to defend itself and the industry from its critics. But traditionally, the big oil companies have preferred to keep their profiles as low as possible, and even today most make their executives as inaccessible to the press as they can. When officials do speak up, they almost invariably act out tribal rituals.

"But Mobil has an open policy," says one expert who deals with all the oil companies. "You can see it. At Texaco things are different. People are afraid. It goes back to Gus Long," he says, referring to Texaco's aloof and near-dictatorial former chairman. Interestingly, another company with a notably progressive viewpoint is ARCO , whose president, Thornton F. Bradshaw, did not even come from the oil business but was formerly a professor at Harvard Business School.

Mobil has its share of difficult personalities, however. "There are going to be problems with Tavoulareas," predicts one source who asks not to be named. "He's shown sheer genius with about 99 percent of the things he's touched. But it becomes more and more difficult to challenge him. If you were to take in a bad idea to Warner, he would tell you very diplomatically that your idea was bad. Tav would tell you the same thing in five seconds—and probably in four-letter language."

As this source sees it, Tavoulareas' headstrong personality was behind the intense bidding for Irvine. "The Irvine thing got way out of hand," he says. "Mobil is probably lucky it didn't get the property." When the bidding started in May, 1976, Mobil offered $24 a share, or a total of $202 million. Before bowing out last month, Mobil had bid more than $336 million for Irvine.

Curiously, the company does not consider the attempt to acquire Irvine a diversification move. Whenever the subject comes up, executives point out that Mobil picked up is first development land in Hong Kong twenty years ago. Mobil started building a new town of condominiums, called Mei Foo New Village, on the property in 1966; the town will house nearly 65,000 people when the last units are finished in 1979. The company also owns Redwood Shores, a residential development on San Francisco Bay.

Is Mobil now going to look elsewhere? For the moment, at least, apparently not. "We don't want to become a conglomerate," insists Warner. "We can only afford one major diversification." He adds that the planning department has disbanded the group that did the spadework for the Marcor acquisition.

Mobil, though, will no doubt look to expand its existing secondary businesses, including real estate and chemicals. Petrochemicals are especially attractive to the oil companies because they are currently highly profitable. Last year Mobil Chemical Co. provided 8.3 percent of the corporation's net income while accounting for only 3.7 percent of its total revenues. Mobil is the nation's largest manufacturer of plastic packaging, producing such common items as foam meat trays and polypropylene films.

The oil companies made a big foray into chemicals in the 1960s—and promptly got burned. For example, they overproduced fertilizer from natural gas and soon glutted the market. Most eventually sold out. Now, the industry again sees new opportunities to add value to its dwindling petroleum reserves by converting them to more expensive products. This time, however, the companies are likely to avoid integrating too far downstream. Instead, they will probably concentrate on basic petrochemicals and commodity plastics.

Washington's Attitude

As they do move into other fields, they will no doubt draw more fire from their critics. But there is currently little concern in Congress about diversification into either related oil businesses, such as petrochemicals, or unrelated businesses, such as metals mining. In fact, despite all the recent hoopla, there is little chance this year that Congress will even seriously debate the issue of horizontal divestiture (forbidding oil companies to own stakes in other energy sources). Senator Philip A. Hart (D-Mich.), the driving force for divestiture in the Senate Judiciary Committee, died last year. Senator Edward M. Kennedy (D-Mass.), who assumed Hart's place as chairman of the antitrust and monopolies subcommittee, is not expected to pick up the baton. Moreover, the makeup of both the committee and the subcommittee has changed; it is more conservative this year. And there never was much of a push for divestiture in the House.

As for the Administration, it is at most lukewarm on the issue. Before the President's recent energy message, Attorney General Griffin Bell privately informed Carter's energy chief, James R. Schlesinger, Jr., that the Justice Department sees no grounds for either horizontal divestiture or vertical divestiture (breaking up the oil companies along functional lines, such as production, marketing, and refining). "I don't think the outlook is very good," concedes Representative Morris K. Udall (D-Ariz.), who has introduced legislation to break up the industry. "The President is very cool on the subject," he explains, "and the companies have written their stockholders. I get a steady stream of mail from stockholders."

So it seems that oil industry diversification—which so far has been quite minor except at Mobil—can continue unimpeded. The companies poorer in oil will no doubt follow in Mobil's path eventually. But the steps will come cautiously. As James E. Lee, president of Gulf Oil Corp., puts it: "Gulf has in the past looked at various non-energy-related businesses for potential diversification opportunities. We recognize, however, that our principal line of business is energy resource development—which is the thing we know best. . . ."

12. Peoples Trust Company*

The Peoples Trust Company first opened its doors to the public on June 1, 1875, with a total salaried staff of eight members: a treasurer; a secretary; and six assistants (three of whom held the positions of day watchman, night watchman, and messenger). Located in a large, midwestern city, the original company had occupied the basement floor of a new five-story office building with an electric-bell system, steam heat, and steam-driven elevator.

During its early years, the Trust Company had concentrated its activities on providing vault services to its customers for the safekeeping of tangible items and securities. Management had been able to develop the reputation of being a highly conservative trust company that concentrated on a relatively small and select market of wealthy individuals from the local area. In the years following, the vault service had been retained as an accommodation to its customers, but the company's emphasis had slowly shifted from vault service to a wider range of banking and trust services.

Until the early 1900s, banking services had overshadowed trust services in terms of asset volume. Following the turn of the century, trust assets had begun to grow at an increasing rate. Over the years, the company had been able to achieve an impressive record of sound and steady growth. According to a story often told in banking circles: "Peoples Trust was so conservative that they prospered even during the Depression!"

In 1963, with the appointment of a new president, a new era began for Peoples Trust Company. Between 1963 and 1978, trust assets under supervision rose by $145 million, while deposits increased by more than $20 million. The company entered 1983 with about $2 billion in trust assets and $90 million in savings deposits.

Accompanying this recent growth has been the company's desire to fashion a new image for itself. In 1979, Mr. Robert Toller assumed the presidency of Peoples Trust. In 1982, he remarked: ". . . it should be said that the old concept of a trust involving merely the regular payment of income and preservation of capital is largely obsolete." Accordingly, the Investment Division of the company had been

*This case was prepared by Hrach Bedrosian and is used here with his permission.

expanded and strengthened. Similar changes had been effected in the Trust and Estate Administrative Group and other customer services. Among these were the improvement of accounting methods and procedures, the installation of electronic data processing systems, and complete renovation of the company's eight-floor building and facilities. Most recently, the company has extended its services into the field of management consulting. This had been acknowledged as a "pioneer" step for a banking institution. The president recently characterized the company as "an organization in the fiduciary business."

At the time these data were gathered, the company had a total of 602 employees. Of this number, 109 were in what is considered the "officer-group"[1] positions of the company. The company's relations with its employees over the years have been satisfactory. The Peoples Trust is generally recognized by city residents and those in suburban areas as a good place to work. The company hires most of its employees from the local area.

In the period before 1980 Peoples Trust had provided satisfactory advancement opportunities for its employees, and it had been possible for a young, high-school graduate who showed promise on the job to work his way up gradually to officer status. Graduates of banking institutions were also sought for employment with the company. Ordinarily individuals were considered eligible for promotion to the jobs above them after they had thoroughly mastered the details of their present positions.

Prior to 1980 the total staff of the company was small enough so that there was no need to prepare official organization charts or job descriptions. Virtually all of the employees knew each other on a first-name basis, and they were generally familiar with each other's area of job responsibility. New employees were rapidly able to learn "whom you had to go to for what."

In 1980 the company management called in an outside consultant to appraise its organizational structure and operations and to confer on the rapid expansion and diversification of banking services that the company had planned. The presence of the consultants and the subsequent preparation of organization charts and job descriptions reportedly "shook up a lot of people"—many feared loss of their jobs or, at least, substantial changes in the nature of work and assignments. However, there was little overt reaction among the officer-level employees in terms of turnover and/or other indices of unrest.

Over the years it had been the policy of the company to pay wages that were at least average or a little above the average paid by comparable banking organizations in the area. This, combined with favorable employee relations and the stable and prestigious nature of the work, resulted in a low turnover of personnel. The bulk of employee turnover occurred among the younger employees who filled clerical positions throughout the company's various departments.

Since 1980, the personnel picture at Peoples Trust has been shifting. Several changes have taken place in the top management of the company. By adding several new customer services, the company has altered the very nature of its business. This has resulted in a trend toward "professionalization" of many of the officer-level positions in that these positions now require individuals with higher

---

1. Membership in the officer group is determined by an employee's being legally empowered to represent the company in a transaction.

levels of education and broader abilities. The impact of these changes on current employees has been a matter of concern to several executives in the company, particularly to Mr. John Moore, Manager of the Organization Planning and Personnel Department. Mr. Moore described his picture of the situation to the researcher as follows.[2]

Interview with John Moore, V.P., Organization Planning and Personnel

Our problem here is one of a changing image and along with it the changing of people. As a trust company, we had no other ties with an individual's financial needs . . . we could only talk in terms of death. We wanted to be able to talk in terms of life, we we got active in the investment-advisory business.

The old wealth around here is pretty well locked up, so we wanted to provide services to new and growing organizations and to individuals who are accumulating wealth. Our problem is one of reorientation. We used to provide one service for one customer. We now want to enter new ventures, offer new services, attract new customers. The problem has become one of how to make the change . . . do we have the talent and the people to make the change?

We have a "band" of people (see Exhibits 1 and 2) in our organization . . . in the thirty-five to fifty age group who came in under the old hiring practices and ground rules. Given the new directions in which our company is moving and the changing job requirements, it's clear that, considering their current qualifications and capabilities, these individuals have nowhere to go. Some have been able to accept this; and this acceptance includes watching others move past them. Others have difficulty accepting it . . . a few have left . . . and we haven't discouraged anyone from leaving. For those who can't accept it, there is the problem of integrating their career strategy with ours. We've articulated our objectives clearly; now individuals need clarification of their own strategies.

As I see it, change caught up with these individuals. They had on-the-job training in their own areas, but that doesn't help them much to cope with the new demands. New functional areas are being melded on top of old ones. For example, marketing is new; so is electronic data processing. They both require qualities that our existing employee staff didn't have.

To date, we have not approached any of these people in an individual way to discuss their problems with them. Our objectives are to further develop these people, but we'll first have to get the support of the department managers who supervise them.

We want to find ways to further develop personnel of the kind represented by this group through a variety of approaches. I am thinking here not only of formal job training in management development, but also of management techniques that would help individuals identify new kinds of qualifications or possible new standards of performance they must take into consideration in planning their own personal growth.

---

2. Mr. Moore drew from his files a list of ten individuals who he felt were representative of the group whose lack of appropriate experience or qualifications created a road block to their future development and advancement with the company. These individuals are described in Exhibit 1.

Exhibit 1. Peoples Trust Company

Name	Age	Education	Date of Hire	Positions Held
Linda Horn	37	2-year technical institute of business administration	1975	Messenger Clearance clerk Accounting clerk Unit head (working supervisor) Section head (supervisor)
Richard Gaul*	30	2-year junior college program in business administration	1977	Business machines operator Section head (supervisor) Operations officer
Fred James	35	B.A. degree, local university American Institute of Banking	1976	Loan clerk Teller Accounting unit head (working supervisor) Section head (supervisor)
Fran Wilson*	35	1 year at a local university	1981	Methods analyst Operations unit head (working supervisor) Systems programmer Property accounting dept. head
Martin Pfieffer*	32	Prep school	1977	Messenger Accounting clerk Section head (supervisor) Department head
James Klinger	38	B.A. degree from local university	1972	Messenger Accounting clerk Records clerk Unit head (working supervisor) Administrative specialist
Karen Kissler*	35	B.A. degree from local university co-op program	1974	Messenger Real property specialist Assistant estate officer
Charles Ferris	42	2-year jr. college program in business administration American Institute of Banking	1962	Messenger Deposit accounting section head (supervisor) Unit head (working supervisor)
William Jagger	54	High school	1949	Messenger Trust liaison clerk Accounting clerk Bookkeeping section head
Thomas Geoghigan*	42	2-year jr. college program in business administration	1969	Messenger Securities accountant Property custodian Office manager Assistant operations officer

*Officer

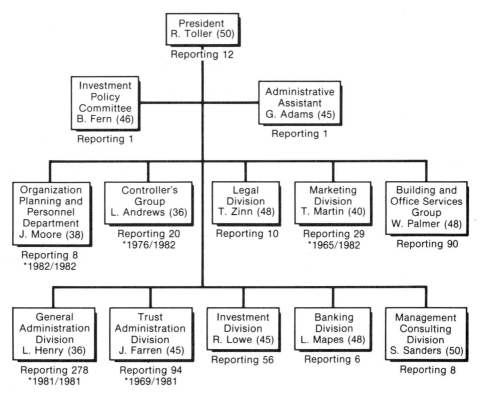

Note: Numbers in parentheses indicate manager's age. These are included for planning purposes only. Numbers below each position indicate number of subordinates.

*Indicates year in which manager joined the Company and year in which he assumed current position. For example, Mr. Larry Andrews joined Peoples Trust Company in 1976, and became Controller in 1982.

Exhibit 2. Peoples Trust Company Organization Chart (June 1983)

We also have to find ways to provide more opportunities for minorities and women in the organization, particularly at the officer level. Although Peoples Trust is not a federal contractor, we would like to be seen as and be an affirmative action employer and an organization where everyone has an equal chance for employment and promotion.

We have to change the conditioning of old times throughout the company. A recently hired MBA is now an officer. Years ago that couldn't have happened so rapidly. And not everyone here is in agreement that the appointment I just mentioned *should* have happened the way it did. We have to develop support in our company for the new recruiting image.

There are two things which really concern me most about this whole problem:

1. We have a problem in under-utilization of resources.
2. There is a problem which is presented to the growth and development of the company in having some of the individuals I have been discussing settled into key spots.

The company really bears the responsibility for the current situation as I described it. In addition, what this all means to me is that our personnel function may change considerably over the coming year.

After this interview with Mr. Moore, the researcher talked with other company executives to learn their views of the problems outlined by Mr. Moore. The findings from these interviews are presented below.

Interview with Fred Bellows—Human Resource Planning

Historically we have been conservatively managed . . . you might say "ultra-conservatively." But now we want to change that image. Several years ago there was a revolution in top management. In 1979, Mr. Toller took over and brought in young people, many not from the banking field but from other types of business and consulting organizations. Our employment philosophy may be stated as follows: "We want above-average people . . . for above-average pay . . . and we want to give them a chance to learn and grow and move with the organization." This applies mainly to those in whom we see management-level potential.

They are told in their employment interview that if they don't see opportunity with us, then they should leave. This is in contrast to the old philosophy that this is a secure place to work, that you can stay here by keeping your nose clean, and that you can sit and wait for pot luck to become a trust officer.

Many people are caught in this changing philosophy. A case in the Trust Administration Division is a good example. There we have an employee in a Grade 10 job who has been with the bank eight years. We just hired a new person out of college who we put in that same Grade 10. Now they're both at the same level, but they're entirely different people in terms of education, social background, etc.

Now the Head of our Trust Division bucks this sort of thing. She argues that we don't need all "stars" in the company. Yet, the president wants young, dynamic individuals who can develop and be developed. So I'm trying to get the Trust Division to define: what does the job really require?

We have a number of people with two years of accounting training who have been with the company anywhere from six to nine years. Under our old system they'd be okay, but under the new system they're not. They're not realistic about their future. Our problem is that we're being honest, but few are getting the message.

We bring in a new individual . . . ask others to train that person . . . and then promote that person over their heads. We have people whose jobs we could get done for a lot less money. When, if ever, do we tell them to go elsewhere?

Interview with Larry Andrews—Controller

There is no question but that there has been a complete revolution around here. In the past, we were in business to serve the community; to handle small accounts; to help the small investor who needed investment service. Our motto was "help anyone who needs help." Our employees were geared to this kind of work orientation and felt at home with it. They could easily identify themselves with this sort of approach to doing business. Most people were quite comfortable; their personal goals coincided with the company goal.

But we found that we couldn't make any money conducting this kind of business. So, we've had to extend our services to attract people who have money and can afford our service. Now the company goal has changed. For example, the Trust Department is now concerned with the management of property in general. The "dead man's bank" has become the "live people's service organization." So we've had to create a kind of snob appeal that too many of our people can't idenfity with or don't believe in.

Many problems have emerged from these changes. Before, individuals' knowledge of the details of their jobs was their greatest asset. They worked to develop that knowledge and protected it. Now—and I'm speaking of supervisory jobs—the important factor is to have some familiarity with the work but to be able to work with people; to get others to do the detail. Too many of our people still don't understand this. . . .

The route to the top is no longer clear. Over a five-year period this organization has changed. There have been reorganizations, new functions created, and some realignment of existing functions. Many who felt they had a clear line to something higher in the organization now find that that "something" isn't there anymore.

We've had lots of hiring-in at higher levels. Many old-timers have been bypassed. In some cases, the new, outside hirees came into jobs that never existed before, or were hired into a job that had previously existed, but which is now a "cut" above what it was before. What used to be a top job is now a second or third spot.

What we need now are people who are "professional managers"—by that I mean a supervisor versus a technical specialist. Years ago supervision could be concentrated in a few key individuals . . . but in the past five years we've grown 20 percent to 30 percent and have a management hierarchy. A person used to be able to grow up as a technical specialist and develop managerial skills secondarily.

To a small extent it's a matter of personality too. We have a new president, and what is acceptable to him differs from what was acceptable to his predecessor. There's a new mix of personal favoritism that goes along with the new vogue. Technical specialists are "low need" as far as the company is concerned. I estimate we now have about thirty people in this category in officer-level jobs.

Interview with Tom Martin—Marketing Division Head

There have been many changes over the past six years. Mr. Toller took a look at the entire organization . . . and then hired a consultant to do an organizational study. It was sort of an outside stamp of approval.

His hope was to move some of the dead wood . . . the senior people who were past their peak and didn't represent what the company wanted anymore in its managerial and officer staff. Few of these individuals have the capacity to change, and for others it may already be too late to change. Many had leveled off in their development long before these changes came about, and the changes just made it more apparent. Early retirement has been given to some of those over sixty. Others remained as titular head of their departments, but in essence report to a younger person who is really running the department.

Banking used to be a soft industry . . . you were hired and never fired. If you were a poor performer, you were given a lousy job that you could stay at. No one was ever called in and told to shape up. The pay was so poor it attracted people who wanted to work in a sheltered area, and they were satisfied to try and build a career in that area. So it was a job with low pay, high prestige, and some opportunity.

Our biggest problem is to convince people that they are not technicians anymore, that they are to *supervise* their subordinates and work to develop them. Apparently, for many older individuals, and younger ones too, this is an impossible assignment. They can do the jobs themselves, but having anyone else do it in any other way runs against their grain.

If our rate of personnel growth over the next ten years is as fast as the previous ten years, I'm afraid we can only absorb about 50 percent of our most promising people.

Interview with Jane Farren, Trust Administration Division Head

We have several people for whom there is very little opportunity anymore. We just don't see any potential in these people. There are about fifteen of them who are in their forties and are really not capable of making any independent decisions. We're trying to get them to see other opportunities . . . both inside and outside the company. For example, our Real Estate group was big in the 1960s and 1970s. We're trying to make it important again, and there may be some opportunities in that area.

To give you an idea of the problem we're faced with: One individual is really a personality problem. He's an attorney but he can't get along with others. He wants people to come to him; he focuses on detail too much; and he has great difficulty in telling others what to do and how to do it. He has to do the job all by himself.

Another individual: We gave him a section to supervise but he really hasn't measured up. But, he was the president's pet. I suppose we'll let him continue on . . . he's fifty-seven . . . and then retire him early.

Interview with Mr. L. Henry, General Administration Division

The company has been undergoing basic change. In the past, if people demonstrated technical competence they were promoted, and that was fine while the company was a small, stable group, and everyone knew what the other was thinking. But then, many in the senior group began to retire. With this "changing of the guard" and the growth of the company, many of us have lost communication with our counterparts. Many of us are new in this field, new to this company, and, of course, new to each other. But we recognize this, so half the communication problem is solved. In a sense, we're not constrained by "how it was done before."

My people have reacted to all this change by sitting back and waiting, seeing which way things are going to go, then I guess deciding whether they are going to join you or not. Most of my people are relatively recent employees—as a matter of fact, of the 278 people in my division, only 11 have been with the company more than ten years. Conversion to EDP will really create a lot of changes in my area.

13. "Perfectly Pure Peabody's"*

A Case of Affirmative Action for Women

The Peabody Soap Company was founded by Joshua Peabody, a smalltown pharmacist who patented his formula for "Perfectly Pure Peabody's" soap in 1909. by 1973, Peabody Soap had grown from a one-product mail order house to a $100 million publicly-held beauty business with 2,500 employees. The founder's grandson, George Hinton, now chairman and chief executive officer, had masterminded the recent growth, divisionalization, and international expansion of the company.

During the last ten years, Peabody Soap had received national recognition for its achievements in pollution control, community relations, and minority employment. George Hinton was personally responsible for spearheading activities in these areas and he was proud of the company's fine record.

Hinton was known throughout the industry as a business leader with outstanding instincts for developing both quality products and a sound management team. He began his career at Peabody Soap in 1945, having spent a year at a well-known consulting firm after graduation from Stanford Business School. He assumed the presidency in 1956, and became chairman in 1965.

However, in January 1974, the resignation of Chemical Research Manager Sarah Barrington (the company's top-ranking woman) made Hinton aware that he had not adequately addressed himself to a key corporate problem: women in management.

Peabody's Marketing: 1965–1973

Prior to 1965, the company had limited production to a highly successful and profitable line of soap, shampoo, and related skin care products. "Perfectly Pure Peabody's" consistently maintained better than a 20 percent share of the face soap

---

*Reprinted from *Stanford Business Cases 1974* with permission of the publishers, Stanford University Graduate School of Business. © 1974 by the Board of Trustees of the Leland Stanford Junior University.

market. In the mid-60s George Hinton decided to expand product lines domestically and open up new foreign markets.

To meet the domestic objective, he promoted Herbert Richardson, a 46-year-old production manager, to vice-president of marketing. Richardson, who had come up through the ranks, was considered a rugged individualist. His energy, directness, and work record made him a prime candidate to succeed George Hinton, who had already announced that the next chief executive officer wouldn't be a "member of the family."

Richardson's first move was to create a market research department. After a year of thorough market analysis by the new department, Richardson recommended that Peabody expand into the hypo-allergenic skin care products field. Because the company had experienced little need for research before the decision to broaden the line, its chemical laboratory was inadequately staffed for experimentation. As a result of his industry review, Richardson knew that several companies were experimenting with hypo-allergenics. He was convinced that the growth objective of the company depended on the caliber of the chemical research section and the speed with which it could develop new products. A "blind" ad for a product research manager, placed in several trade publications, *The Wall Street Journal,* and *The New York Times* brought in nearly eighty applications.

Richardson, who prided himself on his young and eager management team, was particularly impressed with one applicant—32-year-old Sarah Barrington, an unmarried research chemist. Barrington had spent the last three years as assistant laboratory director for Peabody's nearest competitor. Born and educated in England, she held a graduate degree in Business Economics and a doctorate in Organic Chemistry. Her total work experience was only four years but she had an outstanding record with both of her previous employers. Furthermore, her salary requirements were low ($15,000 per year) compared with other applicants.

After her initial interview with Richardson, Barrington was sent to the company's industrial psychologist who summarized his findings: "Sarah has good management potential, she is highly results-oriented with the proper balance of deference to authority. If, however, she cannot see the logic of a superior's request, she will seek an honest explanation. She is respectful, but also inquisitive and direct. She is ambitious as well, and will benefit from working toward long-term career goals." (See Exhibit 1.)

On the basis of her work record, the psychologist's assessment, and the knowledge that Hinton would be pleased to finally have a woman on his management team, Richardson selected Barrington for the job. In January 1967, she was named manager of chemical research and given full responsibility for setting up and staffing the lab.

Since fire laws prohibited the establishment of a laboratory in Peabody's headquarters, the research facility was located in a "loft" at a warehouse several blocks away. By March 1967, the laboratory was operational and Barrington hired a senior researcher, five assistant researchers, and a secretary. A year later, after a crash program involving close collaboration among the researchers, Peabody Soap was able to patent a process for the manufacture of "Peabody's Super Sensitives," a line of hypoallergenic products matched product by product to the regular Peabody Line.

INDUSTRIAL PSYCHOLOGIST'S REPORT ON SARAH BARRINGTON: 1/5/67

Miss Barrington is a conscientious, industrious, dependable woman
who takes herself and her responsibilities seriously. She enjoys
her work, is ambitious for career progress, and is willing to work
as hard as necessary to achieve her goals.

She is alert, intelligent, perceptive of what goes on around her,
and is eager to learn all she can about the processes with which she
works. Her strong points are trouble-shooting and problem-solving;
she is analytical, critical, and objective in her approach to situations of a technical nature. She works at a brisk pace, with strong
focus on tasks and takes pressure well. She plans effectively, is
well-organized and methodical, and can be counted on to meet
requirements. She sets high standards for herself and others and
faces up to issues squarely.

She likes activities that are challenging, stimulating, and rewarding
on which her capabilities will be utilized fully and which will
provide opportunities for further growth. Initiative is readily
available; she welcomes responsibilities and is eager to show what
she can do on her own. She likes to explore wherever clues lead,
will innovate and improvise as warranted, and is not reluctant to
take calculated risks to test the validity of her ideas.

Verbal and social skills are very good. She is articulate, precise,
fluent or terse as necessary, and typically puts people at ease.
While initially reserved with others, there is a warmth and dignity
about her to which people respond favorably. She enjoys working
with and through people and usually gets along with them.
Occasionally, nevertheless, some people may be disconcerted by her
somewhat unfeminine tendency to be forthright and outspoken when
provoked.

On the job she prefers to set her own pace and be in control over her
domain. Direction and criticism are used constructively, but she
dislikes close supervision after assignments are outlined for her.
She is most effective when allowed to participate in planning and
decision-making affecting her activities, given adequate authority
for implementing them, and support when needed. Generally, she
makes every effort to figure things out for herself before presenting suggestions or plans for discussion and approval.

Attitudes toward authority are favorable. She is appropriately
deferent, cooperates fully, and complies and conforms as required to
promote the organization's objectives. However, when directives or
procedures don't make sense to her she will raise questions and offer
her views--tactfully but unequivocally. She needs superiors who are
competent, strong, worthy of her esteem, and who keep communication
lines open. Above all, she needs to be dealt with honestly and fairly,
and be given adequate recognition for whatever she contributes to the
overall effort.

Her outstanding trait, perhaps, is her impelling drive for personal
achievement and career progress. And her strongest asset is indicated
potential for further growth. Thus, while she is young and her
experience is not extensive, and the fact that she's a woman will
make her sometimes less effective, she should be capable of getting
the new unit started.

EXHIBIT 1

The sales increase of 50 percent over the next two years was due, in great measure, to the introduction of the new products. In January 1970, the Company went public to raise much-needed capital for future growth—with funds earmarked for expansion in international markets. No new domestic product research of any magnitude would be required to meet these objectives.

Soon after the development and patenting of the "Super Sensitives" process the research staff was cut in half with the remaining members moving into quality control and analysis of new raw materials. Barrington received a citation from the Board of Directors and won an industry award for her work—but the company was no longer interested in expanding product lines. Realizing that she was at a dead end in her present position, Barrington hired a management trainee in 1970 so that she could prepare someone to assume her position. A year later the trainee was offered a promotion to assistant manager of market research. (Since he would receive more pay in the new position, company policy prohibited Barrington from refusing to let him make the move.) The following year, a similar promotion was accepted by his replacement.

In June 1972, separate product divisions were established. The work of the marketing function was to be phased out to the divisions over the next two years. At the same time, Richardson was promoted to president. John Carlisle, a distribution manager who was nearing retirement, was named marketing director. While most phases of the marketing divisionalization were easily achieved, the lab posed a real problem. Divisions were not interested in the additional overhead of separate labs. Yet, they all insisted that a company lab was necessary. Carlisle had little knowledge of the lab function and did not care to supervise the section. To deal with the situation, he held a meeting of all division managers to determine to whom the lab should report. They decided on quality control and sent Barrington a memo informing her of the new reporting relationship.

Equal Employment Opportunity at Peabody Soap

A family tradition of community involvement was a vital part of Peabody Soap's corporate policy. Joshua Peabody had a personal policy of donating one-quarter of his annual earnings to community organizations. His son-in-law, William Hinton, received nationwide recognition for his successful racial integration of the Peabody factory in the 1950s—long before such actions were required by law. It came as no surprise when, in 1967, George Hinton was appointed one of six Presidential advisors on the blue ribbon committee, "Minority Employment and the American Future."

Although laws requiring affirmative action for minorities were not promulgated until 1969, Hinton had set goals for the promotion and hiring of minority group members as early as 1966. By 1973, every Peabody plant had a workforce which reflected the racial composition of its community.

Finding an effective Equal Employment Opportunity (EEO) manager, however, had been a difficult task. After several men failed at the position, Richard Adams proved to have the necessary qualities for the job. Adams, thirty-five years old, had been a white activist in the Civil Rights Movement in the early sixties. His understanding of the problem of minority employment combined with his ability to establish good rapport with managers led to his success in Peabody's personnel department.

Peabody's workforce had always been about 50 percent female. While production jobs in some industries weren't considered "women's work," cosmetic soap manufacture was an acceptable industry for female workers. Peabody actually assessed potential plant sites based on labor surveys of the rate of female unemployment in the area. If the figure were high and other factors were favorable, the location was selected.

The precision involved in the work, clean working conditions, and low wages had also been cited as reasons why women were employed in the industry. Peabody Soap, like its competitors, had been slow in moving women into management. In 1973, Sarah Barrington was the highest ranking woman in the company—and one of only four women in middle or upper management.

In 1971, federal legislation requiring affirmative action for women was in the wind. George Hinton's own daughter was pressuring him to take a closer look at the underutilization of women and the related issues of day care and job restructuring. Hinton had an "open door" policy—any employee could come directly to him with a problem—and several women within the Company had used it to point out areas for improvement.

As a result, Hinton asked Personnel to add a woman to Adam's staff to handle female affirmative action. In fact, Hinton suggested his own secretary, 27-year-old Brenda Goldman, for the job. "She's been with us for five years now—she's bright, capable, and knows our management," Hinton explained to Adams, "and she's not one of those Women's Libbers. I hate to give her up, but I'd feel more comfortable with her in the job." Goldman became EEO assistant two weeks later. Announcement of her promotion included Hinton's policy statement regarding Equal Employment (Exhibit 2).

From the outset, rapport between Adams and Goldman was difficult.

Goldman: Where do I get started with the women's program, Dick? Guess I should begin by getting an idea of how we're going to be working together. . . .

Adams: I'm looking forward to getting this women's thing started, Brenda. But frankly, we're going to have to hold back on anything big for a while. Right now minorities—blacks in particular—are our biggest problem. That doesn't mean we're going to forget about women. You know, we've already made real headway. Sarah Barrington's doing a great job . . . she's one of the top twenty managers in the company. Besides, we're letting Carla O'Day and Helen Coates go on half-time jobs because they want to spend time at home with their young children. We've sent ten women to that "Women in Management Course" at company expense . . . we've liberalized our maternity leave policy. . . .

Goldman: You're right, we have taken some excellent steps and most of the innovation came from you, Dick . . . you must admit though, that we still have monstrous problems. Look at the statistics. Women have a worse problem at Peabody's than do minorities.

Adams: I disagree. Black men have always had a tougher time finding work than have women.

Goldman: Dick, we could go around in circles about this. I don't agree with you. Black men and women both have had a tough time . . . and, I hasten to add, so do the other minorities—you forget about Chicanos, Asians, and

---

TO: All Employees   December 5, 1971
FROM: George Hinton

    At Peabody's Soap, we have always been concerned with developing
our resources--both in terms of people and products. It has also
been our philosophy that discrimination, in any form, will not be
tolerated here. We now recognize that women, as well as minorities,
have suffered the effects of employment prejudice in the past.

    We are, therefore, establishing a program of Affirmative Action
for Women. Brenda Goldman, who joined the company as a secretary in
1968, will move up to become EEO Assistant for women reporting to
our EEO Manager. Her responsibilities, aside from the implementation
of the women's program, will include counseling, developing recruitment resources, and providing other supportive services.

    In the year ahead we will intensify our efforts in the identi-
fication of promotable women.

    At Peabody's Soap EEO is a corporate-wide policy. Every division,
department and facility is charged with the responsibility of setting
goals and every manager is evaluated on the action he or she takes to
insure that our commitment is met. Monitoring the program, providing
support services, and insuring that all personnel practices are
equitable is the duty of our Equal Employment Section.

    It is my sincerest hope that we will continue to direct our
energies toward EEO for women with the same vigor and enthusiasm
with which we approach all other pressing business problems.

EXHIBIT 2

American Indians. All of these groups are considered "Affected Classes" by
    the law.
Adams: Look, we've made progress and we'll keep making it . . . but we have
    to see this thing in perspective.

The conflicts were, of course, private; the reports which reached Hinton
showed progress. To his knowledge, the EEO function was being handled well
and the company's reputation continued to be virtually untarnished.

Another aspect of the EEO operation of which Hinton was unaware was
Goldman's "image" in the company. She had been accepted neither by her
"constituency" nor by management.

Barrington's Resignation

On January 15, 1974, George Hinton received this letter:

Dear Mr. Hinton:

    It is with deep personal and professional regret that I must submit my
resignation, effective February 1, 1974. While Peabody Soap has provided me with
the opportunity to make an outstanding contribution in chemical research, I find
no room for developing beyond this department.

The recent shift in reporting relationships in my section and the manner in which that shift was accomplished make it clear that my services to the organization are no longer of value. Furthermore, my ability to effect a promotion to other departments has been deliberately inhibited.

I suggest you personally audit your EEO Program for Women. Many problems with potential legal implications exist in the organization.

Thank you for your personal encouragement over the last five years.

Sincerely,

Sarah Barrington

Hinton, alarmed by the letter, called the personnel department and asked them to send up a copy of Barrington's latest review (Exhibit 3) immediately. After a quick reading of Barrington's review, Hinton confirmed his belief that Barrington was an above-average manager in all respects. Next, Hinton asked Richardson to come to his office.

The Hinton/Richardson conversation went as follows:

Hinton: Herb, did you know that Sarah Barrington resigned?

Richardson: No, George, but I did know she was unhappy here . . . it doesn't surprise me. For the last two years she's wanted to get out of the lab . . . but there's nowhere for her to go. She doesn't know any other function . . . and the fact that she's located in that other building just hasn't given her any exposure.

Hinton: Do you think it's because she's a woman?

Richardson: Oh, George, I just don't think that's a problem with Sarah. She's had an excellent job and makes good money for a woman.

Hinton: How have her raises been?

Richardson: Well, since she's been in the same job all this time . . . and this wage freeze has been in effect . . . oh, she makes a little less than twenty grand.

Hinton: Well, where could she go?

Richardson: George, I don't know.

Hinton: Well, what about her reviews?

Richardson: They're great. She's good at what she does . . . we've been very pleased, as you know, with the contributions she's made in research.

Hinton: We've never really talked about her for a promotion, have we?

Richardson: George, I don't think anyone's ready for her to take over a major function as yet. We considered her for that International job . . . but they just didn't think a woman could do the job.

Hinton: Herb, off the record, what do the guys think of her?

Richardson: That's a tough question . . . nobody really talks about her very much. She's effective for a woman. They respect her judgment . . . but we don't know much more about her. Her trouble is that she doesn't sell herself enough. She doesn't socialize. Frankly, George, I don't know what more we can do to keep her here.

Hinton: Thanks Herb, I appreciate your candor. Oh, one more question . . . how do you think Brenda is doing in her new job? You're closer to the action around here than I am. . . .

EMPLOYEE PERFORMANCE APPRAISAL		REVIEW PERIOD	
		From (Mo-Yr) DECEMBER 1971	To (Mo-Yr) DECEMBER 1973

Employee Name SARAH BARRINGTON	Position Title MGR. PRODUCT RESEARCH	No. Months in Present Position 10	No. Months Supervised by Rater 6	Seniority Date FEB 5, 1967	Field Location ADJACENT LAB

Responsibilities Performed (to be written by Employee)	Performance Appraisal (to be written by Rater)
List agreed upon objectives under each responsibility:	Evaluate employee's performance on each responsibility and related objectives
1. COMPLETE LISTS FOR ALL POSSIBLE NEW MATERIALS AND PROCESSES '72-'73.	1. EXCELLENT
2. ASSIST MARKETING GROUP BY NOTIFYING THEM OF TESTS OF ALL COMPETITORS' PRODUCTS.	2. EXCELLENT
3. SUPERVISE STAFF OF 4.	3. SARAH IS A GOOD SUPERVISOR.
4. DEVELOP BETTER EXPOSURE FOR LAB TO OTHER FUNCTIONS.	4. SARAH IS PROGRESSING IN THIS AREA.
5. MAINTAIN PROGRESS ON X-22 PROJECT.	5. X-22 COMPLETED SATISFACTORILY.

OVERALL JOB PERFORMANCE

☐ Unsatisfactory ☐ Fair ☐ Competent ☐ Highly Competent ☒ Exceptional

COMMENTS

Rater's Signature John Carmle	Date 12/3/73
Employee Signature Sarah Barrington	Date 12/5/73
Manager's Signature John Carlile	Date

ADVANCEMENT POTENTIAL

☐ Can Develop Further in Present Position ☐ Adequately Placed ☒ Ready for Advancement Now

COMMENTS

Describe Two or More of Employee's Strongest Points:

1. SUCCESSFULLY DELEGATES AUTHORITY.
2. DOES AN EXCELLENT JOB OF TRAINING SUBORDINATES.
3. RUNS AN EFFICIENT LAB, NEEDS LITTLE SUPERVISION.
4. VERY PROFESSIONAL IN HER APPROACH.

List Two or More Areas that Could Profit from Improvement:

1. SARAH IS SOMETIMES AGGRESSIVE... SOME OF THE MANAGERS SHE WORKS WITH FIND THIS "PUTS THEM OFF" IT MAY INHIBIT HER JOB PERFORMANCE.

2. SHE COULD BENEFIT FROM MORE INVOLVEMENT IN MANAGEMENT ACTIVITIES.

What Are this Employee's Career Goals?

FOR SOMETIME, SARAH HAS INDICATED AN INTEREST IN PROGRESSING TO ANOTHER MANAGEMENT POSITION. NOTHING IS AVAILABLE AT PRESENT.

Suggested and Agreed Upon Actions to be Taken for Self Improvement and Achievement of Career Goals:

SARAH IS OUR TOP FEMALE MANAGER AND THEREFORE IS A GOOD CANDIDATE FOR PROMOTION. TO DO SO, SHE MUST HAVE CLOSER COMMUNICATIONS WITH OTHER MANAGERS. SHE WOULD BENEFIT FROM A LITTLE "SOFTENING" TOO.... BEING A BIT MORE GENTLE IN HER APPROACH.

CURRENT SALARY:	Weekly 340		SALARY GRADE 30		
RECOMMENDED SALARY:	Weekly 397	Eff. Date JAN 1, 1974	CURRENT SALARY		
			Min	Mid	Max

EXHIBIT 3

Richardson: To tell you the truth, George, I've been meaning to speak to you about Brenda. Although the figures are up slightly, I haven't heard anything about an affirmative action program for women, and from what I have seen and heard I think Brenda may be having problems. Just what the cause of the difficulty is, I'm not sure; it may be the set up in that office, or it may be Brenda herself. Let me do some more probing and I'll get back to you.

Hinton: You really think Brenda may be at fault?

Richardson: Well, it's possible. We just may have to move her out.

Hinton: Thanks, Herb. Let me know what you find out.

Hinton then called Barrington and asked her to come to his office. Traditionally brief at his meetings, Hinton decided to break the rule with Barrington to delve more deeply into her side of the story. The relationship between Barrington and Hinton had always been cordial and open.

Hinton: Sarah, I really don't want to accept your resignation. I'd like you to stay on. Tell me exactly why you've made this decision . . . and don't be afraid of chewing my ear.

Barrington: I joined the Peabody Soap Company in 1967 because, as I stated on my application, I wanted the opportunity to grow with a growth company. In fact, I chose to go into industry because I hoped to move from strict chemical research into other related areas of the organization. The reasonableness of that goal is evident when one looks at the experience of the two trainees I've had. Both men hold degrees similar to mine. I hired them at Herb's urging . . . "You can't get promoted until you have a replacement," he kept stressing. But both Simon and Roger were offered promotions to other parts of the company. They make almost as much as I do now, and their work experiences and the exposure they're getting will make them more valuable to the company.

So much for what might sound like jealousy . . . and if it does, I'm sorry. I'm proud of Simon and Roger because I hired and trained them in the beginning. I mention them only as examples. In fact, my secretary was promoted to a training position in the Soap Division last month—so your Affirmative Action Program does work.

But, back to my problems. Although I've indicated to both Herb and my new supervisor that I want to progress beyond my present job, nothing has happened. Other managers have been promoted from technical to nontechnical jobs. Take Frank Everett, he was quality control manager and now he runs the "Super Sensitive" Division.

My reviews have been good and have indicated that I'm ready but when top jobs open up, no one even thinks of me. There was a job open for a research director in the International Division—it would have meant a big promotion in grade, pay, and status. I wasn't even considered, as I found out later, because they "didn't think a woman could do the job." It involved travel and dealing with raw materials suppliers—I do those things in my job now. And I had all the requirements, too. No one thinks I'm "strong" enough to negotiate or wheel and deal.

When Herb left—I had thought that he was my real mentor—things got worse. Carlisle doesn't know me or what we do in the lab, and frankly, he doesn't care. I discussed my desire to be promoted and he simply said he'd get back to me on it; he hasn't.

You wonder why I haven't pursued it further? George, have you seen my last review? *[He indicated that he'd just read it.]* Well, look at the strengths and weaknesses section. Carlisle listed aggressiveness as a weakness. If I come on too strong, I'm considered "brassy" or "pushy" . . . and unfeminine. If I'm the least bit reticent, they think I don't have the stuff managers are made of. No one seems to be able to cope with the idea of a woman manager.

Frankly, George, I've been discriminated against for the last few years. I've never been promoted; I've never had much of a raise; I've never received a stock option; I've never been invited to the Annual Management Meeting . . . probably because it's held at the Downtown Club, where women aren't even allowed.

It's harder for people to level with me, too. Herb never gave me many pointers about improvement. I hardly got any feedback, negative or positive. The other men here won't treat me as an equal either and there aren't any other women even near my level in the organization . . . so I have no one to emulate or consult.

George, there really isn't anything you can do about these things, I know. I don't mean to sound melodramatic, but I'm honestly fed up with having to perform like I'm "Superwoman" . . . and being treated like someone's little sister.

Hinton: I'm glad you've been so frank with me, Sarah. Have you talked to anybody in Personnel about this?

Barrington: Yes, I did give Brenda a call and we had lunch. We've known each other for a long time and I'd hoped she could give me some advice. She suggested talking it over with Herb. I did, but he didn't seem very concerned . . . I think he's lost interest in me since his promotion.

George, Brenda's in an impossible situation. Adams hasn't given her any guidance in counseling, he's jsut made a statistician out of her. She cited two cases where she's afraid we're going to have sex discrimination suits—but she can't get anywhere with Adams . . . he simply sees the women's program as a threat. Most of the women in the company don't even know who Brenda is. In fact, there's an indepedent Women's Group already holding meetings outside the company. It's common knowledge that Brenda is all but totally ineffectual.

At the close of their conversation, Hinton asked Barrington if she'd wait a few days before her final resignation. Barrington agreed and offered a handshake. Hinton then began to consider his course of action.

Part III

Staffing and Organizing

Cases Outline

14. Northeast Data Resources, Inc.*

George Wellington closed the door behind him and slumped into his desk chair with an air of resignation. He had just returned from a meeting of the Executive Committee of Northeast Data Resources where personnel layoffs had been decided upon. As director of personnel at NDR, he realized that he would be responsible for both developing the process by which the layoffs would take place and assisting the managers responsible for the actual implementation. It wasn't a pleasant task, particularly in light of the human resources program that he had begun to implement over the past four years.

Wellington pulled out a pad of paper from the top desk drawer and began to scribble notes. He had found that in times of pressure it was best to get some perspective on the situation before taking action. The drastic character of this situation required a review of the growth of Northeast Data Resources from its inception in 1969 to the present. It was the first crisis the young company had been forced to face.

Background of the Company

In 1969, four young engineers formed a partnership to form the basis of NDR. Three of them had worked for a large, national data-processing company. They had recognized the high potential in the computer industry particularly for a product which filled a vital need in this growing field. Another engineer working in a research program with a large university was asked to join them because of his expertise in the computer field.

Jack Logan was the prime mover of the new company. He had been working for nearly five years on a project within the large company to develop ways to protect its computer systems from being copied by competitors. The primary objective in this project was to ensure that a customer would have to purchase the entire system rather than being able to make use of a number of different systems.

---

*D. Jeffrey Lenn, School of Government and Business Administration, The George Washington University. This case is not meant to be an example of effective or ineffective personnel and human resource management but an example for teaching and discussion purposes. Reprinted by permission.

Jack saw the opportunity to sell a service to customers that would do just the opposite—provide a mechanism that would link various competing systems into an integrated unit.

He and a colleague, Charlie Bonner, developed a "black box" which had the capacity to connect at least two types of computer systems already on the market. They had worked in Jack's basement over a two-year period to perfect this instrument. Another six months of testing found that it was very effective. The two other engineers had begun to work with them in order to expand the box to tie together three other systems with which they had experience.

The four men decided to strike out on their own and found that their innovation and daring paid off. The first two years were both exhilarating and demanding. NDR subcontracted the production of the black box to a small manufacturing company while the partners divided responsibilities between marketing and continuing research. Jack and Charlie carried the marketing and organizational functions while George Miller and Al Grant worked to streamline the instrument itself.

Early success in securing contracts with some key customers and fears about loss of the exclusive information about the unpatented invention led to a decision to go into full production. An old plant was leased and renovated and workers were hired to begin the process of building the black box for distribution. Within two years the company had grown from four partners to nearly 100 people. By 1976 NDR had expanded to about 700 people and had become the focus of attention for a number of investors. The invention, now dubbed Omega I, had become a product competitors emulated but with little success.

Logan assumed the responsibilities of chairman and president with Bonner as executive vice-president in charge of operations. Miller and Grant stayed in the lab with more interest in research and development, being willing to act more in advisory capacity on managerial decisions.

Logan saw the need to consolidate and expand the overall operations of the company. Production and distribution now overflowed into three buildings separated by nearly ten miles. He negotiated a contract with the economic development committee of Newbury, a New England town about forty miles away, to help construct a new building to house headquarters and plant. The town agreed to help NDR through reduced taxes, water, and sewage hookups at a minimal charge, arrangements with local banks to secure a loan for construction of the plant, and development of a federal grant to train new workers at the plant. In exchange NDR agreed to move its entire operation to Newbury within the next two years. It helped Newbury in its search for new industry while assuring NDR of a secure base of operations for the future.

The Newbury headquarters was only forty miles from the old facilities so NDR lost few of its present staff because of the change. But the growth in business demanded an increase in personnel. Engineers with sophisticated skills in computer science were hired to expand the system capability. Often, international engineers were the only ones available and the importation of English and Australians with a spattering of Europeans gave an international flair to the small company. New factory workers from Newbury and surrounding towns were hired so that the production shifts could be expanded from one to two. The training grants secured by the town helped to equip new workers and the integration with more experienced workers moved smoothly. Empty managerial slots required hiring from the outside mostly. A new vice-president of manufacturing came from a large industrial company in the Midwest. The new vice-president of finance had a solid resume which included most recently financial experience with a large conglomerate but before that two stints with growing companies much like NDR. The staffing of the growing company proceeded professionally.

Future of the Company

The phenomenal growth of NDR in old industrial New England rivaled the computer companies developing in California's Silicon Valley. The workforce had evolved from 4 in 1969 to 100 in 1971, 700 in 1976, and 1,350 by 1982. Sales increased from two small initial contracts in 1969 of $75,000 to nearly $59 million by 1982. In 1975, NDR went public and was listed on the New York Stock Exchange in 1980. The opening price of 7 moved to between 8 and 9 and hovered there in 1981. But a feature article in a national stock advisory report about NDR led to an upward move in the summer in 1982 to 15. Even without paying a dividend in its thirteen years of existence, it had become an attractive investment.

Logan had taken time during the summer of 1982 to begin the process of strategic planning. Convinced that he and his executive committee could and should do this alone, he decided not to engage outside consultants to develop a costly set of plans. His projection was that the computer industry would grow nearly ten times in size over the next decade. Conservatively the company could expect to hold its share of the market which meant a doubling of sales in five years to $120 million and up to $210 million by 1992. Expansion was the key to maintaining market share and holding its own against the handful of competitors which had begun to appear by 1982.

In shaping the strategy, Logan began to map out a new marketing plan which would guarantee NDR's position in the national market instead of the eastern market alone. He saw new customer possibilities in the fields of insurance, financial institutions, and state and local governments. He negotiated an option to buy the factory of a watch company moving South. Its building was about thirty-five miles away in the heart of another old industrial New England town with a pool of skilled workers available to be retrained. He began to develop some ideas about how many new staff would be needed and the kind of capital necessary to finance this expansion.

George Wellington's Career at NDR

George stopped his writing and reviewed the rapid growth of NDR up to this point. He remembered vividly his first few months at the company in 1977. He had moved to a nearby town to retire in the serenity of New England. His career had begun immediately after completing his MBA from a leading eastern university where he had concentrated on management and personnel. He had begun work in the personnel area with a major corporation located in New York. Six years in the field had led him next into marketing and then strategic planning with another company. The last seven years had been with a prestigious consulting firm in New York where he had focused on a variety of problems for a host of clients. His decision to retire had been prompted by a dislike for traveling and a desire to settle down in the area where his children had located.

While retirement continued to bring part-time consulting work, George still found the travel excessive. But his ideas of relaxation in retirement quickly exposed his own need to be fully active in business to be happy. His search for a part-time job was successful as Jack Logan met him at a Chamber of Commerce luncheon in Newbury and hired him as a consultant to help with the transition from the old to the new facilities. He remembered the challenges associated with coordinating not only the efforts of NDR personnel but outside contractors and town officials as well.

The flawless nature of the transition into the new plant made the president recognize that he needed George full-time. Wellington agreed to stay only another six months as a special assistant to Logan. He carried out a variety of projects for Logan and quickly became an integral part of the management team at NDR.

The president called in George one day and showed him an organization chart which he was reworking. "George, I know that your six months are nearly up but I need you around here on a permanent basis. I just don't know where to put you on this chart. How about becoming director of personnel for NDR? That is the only important position which we haven't filled here in the past few months and it would allow me to have you close at hand for help on those big decisions."

George asked for some time to think through his decision and within a week agreed to a full-time position. While Logan still saw personnel as a somewhat unnecessary staff function, there would be a chance for George to help him understand the importance of human resources to this company.

Wellington began immediately to develop a plan for human resources at NDR. Logan encouraged him but wasn't excited about the use of the term "human resources." "I don't understand why you have to complicate this whole business of personnel with a new name. Why not still use the old 'personnel' for the department?" Logan asked. George saw a futile battle in this naming process so he clearly defined his function as that of director of personnel.

His plan for that function at NDR had three major elements:

The Program

Gathering Employee Information. He had his staff develop a file on each employee with a record of hiring date, previous experience and employers, salary, job title, etc. This was stored in a computer so that he could have rapid recall for evaluation.

Performance Appraisal System. He developed a new appraisal system which incorporated a three-page form to be completed twice a year by immediate supervisors. The annual review was tied to salary and bonus decisions. He experimented with it in two engineering sections over a two-year period and then was able to get Logan to mandate it for all of NDR beginning in 1981. The results from the 1981–82 year were compiled and filed for future use.

Personnel Policy Manual. In 1981, a new personnel policy manual was developed that detailed the policies and procedures as well as benefits for all personnel at NDR. There was some initial negative reaction by those who had enjoyed a variety of benefits from the early days of the company. But the imprint of Logan on the manual quelled the complaints and ensured uniformity in the policies.

EEO and Affirmative Action (AA) Program. The highly technical character of the NDR business and its presence in a small New England town made both EEO and AA difficult to pursue. A visit to Wellington by an EEO field investigator regarded the case of a former worker led him to move quickly to formulate this program. The data was gathered on minority hiring and promotion and then a plan designed for increasing the percentage of minorities in all categories and the number of women in management in particular. Logan resisted the immediate implementation of the program with the argument that the Reagan administration would soft-pedal civil rights in employment so that business people did not need to worry. George accepted this decision with reluctance but got an agreement to update the plan periodically as well as pursue informally a goal of more integration of the workforce.

Management Development Program. The rapid growth of NDR created many new managerial positions. Hiring from the outside became one method by which to increase the number of managers, but George believed that the key to the company's future lay in developing them from within. He negotiated a contract with a professor of management at a local university to design and teach a course in management for selected employees. George and the professor team-taught a six-week course for twenty middle level managers in 1980. Its success led to an offering three times a year to both managers and potential managers.

The Staff

George became director of personnel in the spring of 1979. He selected four professionals and two secretaries to work with him. Two professionals came from outside of NDR and two from within. All four had human resources management experience but needed more training. One was encouraged to enter an MBA program on a part-time basis with a concentration on human resource management. The other three were sent to local and national seminars to upgrade skills and understanding in the various areas of HRM. But at the heart of their training was George Wellington, drawing on his vast experience and encouraging his younger colleagues to learn through experimentation and discussion.

The Office Location

The final design of the NDR headquarters had not been decided when George became a consultant to the project so he had taken primary responsibility for the design of the corporate office area. Later, as director of personnel, he negotiated some changes in the office assignments so that personnel was located at one of the major entrances and exits of the building. It was a primary thoroughfare for engineers and managerial personnel arriving in the morning and leaving at night. It was also a stop along the way to the new cafeteria that had just opened.

George had chosen this location for a reason. He felt that human resources departments must have high visibility and availability. Being in the middle of a key thoroughfare allowed people to recognize the central function of personnel in the operation of NDR. It encouraged questions about policies and procedures. It also gave the HRM staff the chance to get to know all of the managers and professionals within a short period of time. This provided instant recognition and a capacity to deal with problems on a much more personal basis. George himself was always at his desk working before most of the staff arrived and usually left after 6:00 P.M. This gave him considerable visibility with managerial personnel who often worked late.

The images of the first few years were succeeded by thoughts about the past two months with his staff. He had begun to engage them in the planning process by asking them to think about NDR for the next five years. He had sketched out the growth projections of Logan and then provided some parameters within which to think about staffing. Each of his professional staff was to develop a short presentation on four consequences for HRM:

1. Impact on the size of our workforce
2. Impact on the mix of skills needed in the workforce
3. Impact on the recruitment efforts from outside NDR and development efforts from within
4. Impact on the working conditions within the company itself, both physically and organizationally.

The first meeting four weeks ago had produced some very good reports. With one exception, the four had done a lot of homework and some imaginative thinking about the future with regard to how HRM plans would fit into the NDR overall strategic plan. George had collated and refined the projections and redistributed them to the professional staff asking for further thought and more specific targets for the next five years. He asked for input for his own report to the president, which he had hoped would be ready by December 1982.

The Present Dilemma

That work had now come to an abrupt halt although he had not alerted the staff to the discussion taking place within the executive committee until the day before. Logan's projections about the future had been overly optimistic.

Two weeks ago, Logan had asked George to meet him at 8:00 P.M. He laid out a report on the results from the first quarter of this fiscal year and then a chart which traced the sales of the last nine quarters. The last two quarters showed a significant decline. Logan indicated to George that, "The decline is now a trend and not simply a blip on the screen as I had thought." The loss of five key contracts totaling nearly $5 million dollars over the past six months plus the entry of a new competitor in the southeastern market had been responsible for the dramatic sales drop. At the same time, profits had suffered as well because of the increased expenses from a decision to increase the size of the engineering and financial service departments. The president admitted that his projections had been too optimistic and that something had to be done immediately. The cash flow problem had emerged as the most important pressure in this situation. The budget had to be pared while efforts to increase revenue were intensified.

George studied the figures carefully and agreed reluctantly to both the conclusions and recommendations reached by Logan. The two men took some time to sort through the various options available but it always came back to drastic cuts in personnel. He urged Logan to call a meeting of the executive committee in the morning and provide the data to them with encouragement to diagnose the problem and solutions to it. He argued that any solution must be a product of consensus of the committee.

The meeting caught everybody by surprise as they had accepted the president's projections of growth despite a temporary decline in sales. Two weeks of intensive debate among the executives led to the meeting this morning which defined the exact personnel cuts to be made. It was agreed that twenty-five engineers, fifty production personnel (workers and supervisors), and twenty-five others from various departments would be laid off within the next two weeks. In addition, fifteen new marketing and sales personnel would be added as soon as possible to carry out a new marketing thrust aimed at a different market segment.

There had been heated discussion about the exact number to be laid off and hired, with considerable friction between the vice-presidents of production, engineering, and marketing. The blame for the crisis was shouldered by Logan who asked that the executives recognize that they had to work together to resolve this problem if the future of NDR was to be assured. Wellington as the director of personnel was given the task of coordinating the identification of the people to be laid off although the actual decision would rest in the hands of the three vice-presidents. There were no criteria for the decisions although all agreed that loyal and trusted employees who had been with NDR for a number of years should be released only as a last resort.

The Director's Responsibility

The acrimonious debate of the morning still echoed in George's ears that afternoon. He tore the pages on which he had been writing off the pad and began a new one as he started to determine how the layoffs should be handled. It was a far cry from the exuberance with which he had begun the process of developing a five-year human resource plan just two months ago. Cutbacks in personnel demanded the same precision and careful thought in planning and action as hiring and promotion. There was less excitement about retrenching than growing because it affected the livelihood of so many people.

George jotted down the important questions in three different areas as he mapped out his thinking on this problem.

1. *The Layoffs*
    - Criteria to be used?
    - Data available on employees?
    - Impact of EEO and AA on decisions?
    - Severance pay and benefits?
    - Procedure for layoffs?

2. *The New Hires*
   - Skills needed in marketing and sales?
   - Available resources for positions?
   - Salary and benefit package?
   - Procedure for hiring?
3. *The HRM Plan*
   - Immediate impact on HRM five-year plan?
   - What if only temporary reversal of growth trend? (Commitments to rehire or not?)
   - Impact on employee morale now and in future?

George recognized that he had a lot of work to do. He struggled to regain his sense of professionalism as he began to detail the options available to each of the questions. His days as a consultant and manager had given him little experience in the arena of layoffs. But Logan had given him the responsibility and he knew that the future of NDR would depend heavily on how it handled this crisis.

15. Bellefonte Rubber Works*

Works manager Bill Dalton looked pensively at the heavy raindrops as they beat against the glass sections of the window in his corner office at the Bellefonte Rubber plant. It suddenly occurred to Bill that in his four years as manager at the plant, he had never before allowed himself the luxury of watching the raindrops splash against the plant windows. He had been too busy with internal plant problems.

He thought to himself: "When it rains, it really pours at Bellefonte." Then he turned his back on the July cloudburst and looked at the letter of resignation on his desk. It was signed by Jack Fletcher, one of the day foremen. Jack had worked at the plant seven years—the last four years as a foreman of the Belt Department. Because of his apparent progress, Jack was promoted to a day foreman about a year ago on Bill's recommendation. Jack seemed to appreciate the prestige of his new position and the straight day shift, even though he was on call at the plant twenty-four hours a day if trouble developed in the Belt Department. However, Jack's attitude had changed considerably the last few months. Jack's problems on the floor had become more serious as well as more frequent.

The first sign of serious trouble in the Belt Department after Jack became day foreman developed in the weeks preceding December 31, 1962. The inventory at the end of the year showed a terrific shortage in the Belt Department where Jack assumed a consistent profit was being made. Jack became very antagonistic toward the Accounting Department head whose records showed that the materials

---
*This case was prepared by Ed L. Christensen and is used here with his permission.

and labor input in the Belt Department, when balanced against the value of the Belt Department's output, left a shortage of over $45,000 for 1962.

Jack refused to believe that the Accounting Department's monthly book inventory of work in process gave a true picture of his operation. (See Figure 1.) Even though he was no statistician, Jack could see where the materials drawn and the labor cost had deviated from the desired norm. He had tightened down on his crew's use of rubber and fabric drawn for belt making after July; and, as a result, the department approached the norm or a full accounting of the raw materials requisitioned in August and September. The chart did indicate this all right. He also had checked carefully the direct and indirect labor time card reports of his men during the same period. The chart reflected a favorable trend toward the desired norm during August and September. Then, after September, the amount of materials actually accounted for in belts produced dropped off, and the labor time going into the belts increased even though the actual belt footage produced did not increase.

It was the first week in January 1963 that Bill Dalton had a long talk with Jack about the need for operating the Belt Department as if it were a separate business in downtown Bellefonte. Bill pointed out the difficulty of staying in business very

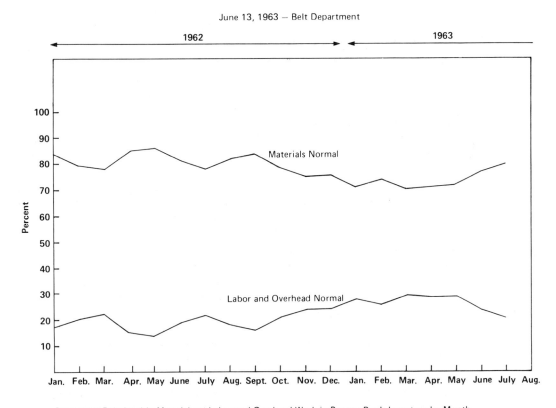

Percentage Relationship Materials to Labor and Overhead Work in Process Book Inventory by Month

Figure 1. Average Monthly Materials, Labor, and Overhead Outlays
at Bellefonte Rubber Works

long with raw materials being drawn for work in process only to have large amounts ending up as waste in the city dump. Didn't Jack think a foreman ought to hold his crew responsible for unusual and increasing material wastage?

Perhaps a bigger drain on the profit anticipated in the Belt Department was because of the way Jack was failing to control the time reported by his crew. Bill had insisted there was no point in arguing with the Accounting Department about the reliability of its reports on the belt operation. Jack was told that if he approved unreliable, inaccurate information on the time cards, he was likely to get back an unreliable, inaccurate summary of the month's operation. It was clear enough to Jack what Bill was trying to tell him.

Jack's men were paid a base rate plus an incentive for so many items produced above minimum set by a time-and-motion study. Time spent on directly producing belts was charged and paid as "direct labor." In case of a breakdown or other direct work stoppage, the men would go to work cleaning up, getting supplies, or doing other maintenance chores. Time spent in such "nonproductive" work was charged and paid as "indirect labor."

The record of so much direct or indirect labor time was submitted to the foreman at the end of the shift by each man. The foreman, who supposedly was aware of any direct labor interruptions which occurred during the shift, would verify the time card claim by initialing it. The reporting of time appeared to operate on the honor system, especially if the foreman gave the impression of blinking at or being oblivious to a "doctored" time card.

It was simple enough for a man to claim two hours of indirect labor, and claim—if questioned by the foreman—that he had trouble for that long. Yet during that two hours he could have been turning out belt footage for which he would receive incentive pay, also. It didn't take long for a workman to accumulate an hour of indirect labor through an ordinary day by reporting material shortages or work stoppages for a few short intervals.

Jack understood clearly what Bill meant, because Jack had passed out some pretty fat paychecks to members of his crew on payday. He had seen some of the men on a base pay of $40 a week come out with a $45 bonus! If a belt department had sixty employees doing this, the labor cost charged against the belt footage produced mounted up fast.

Actually, Jack had not given too much thought to the fudging of time cards which he signed daily. He didn't think of this practice as really cheating anybody, and he was sure most of the men didn't look at it as a dishonest practice. It was "just one of those things."

At the conclusion of their talk, Jack told Bill that the Belt Department would push both the materials and labor charges back into normal operating position. During the month of January, Jack made good on his promise of improvement, although the department still had a long pull ahead. Then suddenly, at the end of February, the Belt Department made its poorest production record in fourteen months.

Bill, who had been anxiously watching this plant trouble spot, maneuvered Jack into his office for a chat. The foreman half anticipated what was coming. In fact, he didn't wait for Bill to ask him about his family or about Jack's plans for a trip to Pittsburgh to see his son who was a freshman at Carnegie Tech. Jack came right to the point of issue by saying: "I know what's on your mind, Bill, but before you start boring into me about competition and profits, I want to tell you something."

"Good enough, Jack," Bill agreed. "Why don't you tell me what's on your mind?"

A deep sigh escaped Jack as he settled down in his chair and wondered momentarily where he should begin. "Have you ever seriously considered the pressures that I face every day out on that floor?" Jack began. Bill nodded understandingly and Jack, feeling encouraged, continued. "You know, I'm the fall guy for everything that goes wrong in the Belt Department. Not one man in my crew is faced with taking initiative to improve our operation. Not one of them will make the most trivial decision. I guess the union won't let them. Brother, when I was working on the line years ago—before the union came along—we felt responsible. Where is the pressure today? On the worker? Oh no! Right on the back of a foreman whose hands are tied more often than they are free to clean house out there.

"At our foremen's training sessions on Wednesdays, Bill, you have stressed the importance of the service departments [see Figure 2] to production. Without doubt you are right or you wouldn't keep them on the payroll. But they never have produced a single foot of belt that ever went out of this plant. Am I right?"

Bill nodded in partial agreement. "Yes, in a way. But I think you will agree that if, for example, the Planning Department failed to provide you with specifications; if the Laboratory didn't test and control the quality of your product; if Purchasing didn't supply you with needed materials; and if Selling didn't find an outlet for your belts—you just wouldn't be able to go it alone, Jack. Isn't that right?"

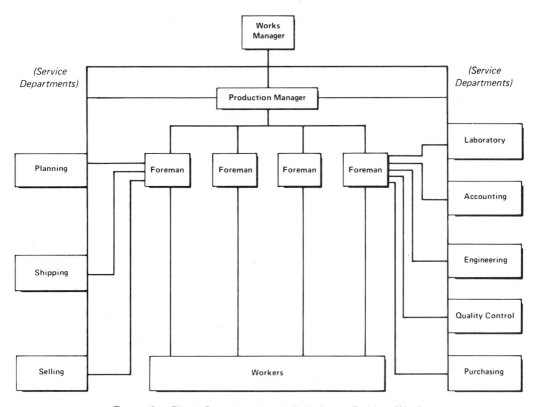

FIGURE 2. Plant Organization at Bellefonte Rubber Works

"Well, yes, in a way, but that isn't what I meant," Jack replied. "These services, like Accounting which is always making reports on our costs and output, are never under pressure. Their work—I guess they work—is specialized. Every contact I have with them turns out to be pressure on me, not on them. For example, the engineer is much better paid than I am, yet he has fewer problems. He works mostly with things, not people. If he has any headaches, I fail to see them. Most of these service people have quiet, clean, unhurried jobs. Don't they?"

Bill shook his head. "Sometimes we don't see all the pressures that are focused on the other fellow. They do wear different clothes than the men on the production line. However, I'm sure you wouldn't want them to try to do their work in a noisy place or on a greasy table. What are you suggesting that I do about this, Jack?"

"Well, I'm not suggesting anything. I'm only saying that a foreman has the toughest job in this plant. From the time I get a production order until I meet the time schedule that comes with it I'm on the spot. I must keep a variety of belts moving along those lines. I'm responsible for costs, waste, supplies, quality control, stoppages, breakdowns, maintenance. You name it; I seem to have it. Then I can't step on anyone's toes. I'm supposed to maintain discipline, and yet I have to be a good guy. My time schedules stay the same even though some joker doesn't show up for work. All the time I have quality control, the inspector, the shop steward, and the accounting guy with the sharp pencil on my back. How about my morale? Who gives a damn about Jack Fletcher or how he feels?"

"You're right in general, Jack," Bill responded, "but you are an important person in this whole operation. If this were not so, you wouldn't be the focal point of these pressures. You are the catalyst in this process. Although you are in the middle of it all, you have to keep everything under control. In fact, Jack, if we didn't feel these pressures in this competitive industry, we wouldn't be around long. These pressures aren't mean, or vindictive, or intended by anyone. They are a sign we are sensitive to potential trouble, and we ought to recognize them for what they are worth in our productive efforts."

Jack looked thoughtfully out of the window for a moment. Then he ventured, "You make this sound better than I feel about it. I don't know what a catalyst is, unless he is a guy with a thick skin and a thick head. Now you take last week. My paycheck was $437.50 for the month. I put in about ten hours a day five days a week, not to mention three Saturdays, for that check. When I handed out the checks to the crew that works for me, I noticed that about a dozen of the men made something over $500. A foreman must have a thick skull all right to stay here after every shift for an hour or two signing time cards, checking other things, and helping the next foreman get under way. I can't leave the minute the whistle blows like the hourly men do. In fact, if they have serious trouble in the Belt Department on the next shift, I might be called out here in the middle of the night, just because I'm day foreman. Do you think this setup is fair to a foreman, Bill?"

Bill shifted uneasily in his chair. He knew this was a tough one to explain. "I can honestly say I think you are worth more to this operation than one of those men who got a bigger paycheck than you did last month. But I also believe that your envelope didn't contain something you get in addition—something which goes only to a man in your position. If you should become sick, Jack, as you were two years ago, we carry you on the payroll, and we are glad to do it. We are not able to do that for your crew. If you need an afternoon off to take your family to Lewistown or your wife to a doctor, you need only suggest this to me. Moreover, you have been recognized by your men as a leader. I know they have confidence in you. People in Bellefonte respect you because of your position here at the plant. This prestige means something to your family, believe me. I might ask you, Jack, how many of those twelve who had a larger paycheck than you fully earned it? We can't account for their excess time in the inventory. I'm not so sure many of them were entitled to a larger check than you received."

Jack sat studying his safety helmet for a brief time. Then he stood up. "Thanks anyway, Bill," he said. "If it's all right with you, I'll give this thing another try. I better get back on the floor."

"Thanks for the chat, Jack. I know you can put the Belt Department back in the black, if anyone can," Bill said as he opened the door and gave Jack a parting pat on the back.

Bill had been pleased to observe that, during June and July, the Belt Department made obvious improvement in its operation. (See Figure 1.) Jack was apparently getting on top of all those pressures that had laid him low a couple of months ago. Then, out of the clear blue sky comes Jack's letter of resignation. The letter was brief:

Dear Bill:

This thing isn't getting any better. It may be even worse. I guess I want out. Can you use me in the Maintenance Department where they were short-handed this week?

Jack

Here was a chance to move someone else into the position of day foreman in the Belt Department. Bill wasn't certain whom he could confidently move into that position. He wasn't at all sure he wanted to let Jack step down, although he knew Jack was having a struggle. But this could be said about nearly every one of the other ten foremen at Bellefonte Rubber Works.

Bill felt he understood the situation faced by his foremen—especially the day foreman on the lead-off shift. He had followed a policy of placing the night-shift foremen on the day shift. This gave them some experience with the larger crews, the ringing telephones, and the full impact of contacts with the service departments as well as customers. After two weeks of this, the foremen were usually happy to get back on the night shift. There was good reason for Bill's paying the day foreman a little more money each month, which he did.

No one knew better than Bill that good foremen were scarce. A good foreman had to be many things. He had to be a diplomat, a disciplinarian, a counselor, an instructor, an example to his men, an engineer, a repairman, a lawyer, an inspector, a judge, a manager, a psychologist. While wearing all these hats, he had better arrange to be making a profit in his department. Bill just didn't keep this kind of man on reserve. In fact, if a foreman possessed a fair capability in these desirable areas, he was usually promoted to a higher position in management.

As Bill mentally scanned his roster of eleven foremen and those he considered potential foremen, he was not inspired. Yet, he would argue with anyone that his eleven foremen compared favorably with those in any other plant in his company. Still, each of his foremen had specific weaknesses and certain strengths. At the moment he could think of three men who had indicated an interest in becoming day foremen at the Bellefonte plant. They were Sam Craven Chuck Weatherby, and George Maitland.

Sam Craven had been a foreman twenty years ago for Sharon Rubber Products in Sharon, Pennsylvania. Although he had been fairly young at the time, Sam had established himself at the Sharon plant as a foreman who made things move. His crews turned out the items on schedule or else. He didn't spare himself, and he developed a reputation for not sparing his men. One of Bill's older friends told him that he had worked for Sam at Sharon. This friend confirmed the fact that Sam had an enviable record for output, but he had no friends among his crew. Bill was reminded, too, that Sam worked in a place where the plant was not unionized.

When Sam came to see Bill about possible openings at the Bellefonte plant, the former had expressed an interest in working as a foreman. This meeting had taken place last December. Sam had recently been retired from the U.S. Army as a master sergeant. According to his discharge, Sam had entered the Army soon after leaving his job as foreman at Sharon Rubber Products. The earlier part of his Army career had been spent in the infantry. The last twelve years Sam had been attached to a number of different finance-disbursing units.

Chuck Weatherby had been working for the past eleven years at the Bellefonte Rubber Works. During the last six years he had been a foreman on the night shift. Bill felt that Chuck leaned rather heavily on the day foreman whenever a problem of any consequence came along in his department. Moreover, he had only thirty-five men on his shift whereas the Belt Department typically had over seventy-five men on a day crew.

The men on Chuck's shift seemed to like him all right. At times Bill felt he had to practically force Chuck to use the tools and techniques available to a foreman. During the years, Chuck had attended all the training sessions that had been sponsored for the plant foremen on Wednesday afternoons. It was debatable how effective these sessions had been in upgrading his performance.

Bill recalled that it was on Chuck's shift that a costly mistake had been made on a large ore conveyor belt. The specifications had called for a belt 48" wide, ¾" thick, 1,000' long, six plys of cotton-nylon fabric, and a heavy rubber compound all around. The belt, which had to be out in three weeks, was contracted for $14,000. By mistake, Chuck had started the belt through with five, instead of six, plys of fabric. By the time the error was picked up, valuable time had been lost and an enormous waste had occurred. Chuck had blamed the error on "scheduling in" the custom order when his shift had a four-week backlog of other belts.

About two months ago, Chuck had mentioned that he was interested in the day shift and asked Bill to keep him in mind. Chuck said he could use the money that went with handling the larger crew on the day shift.

The third person who had expressed an interest in becoming a day foreman was a college graduate by the name of George Maitland. George, who was married and about twenty-five years of age, had majored in psychology at Pennsylvania State University. He had worked at the Bellefonte plant for the past three years. In fact, it was the only job he had ever held other than part-time summer work in a grocery chain store.

The foremen under whom George had worked were unanimous in classifying him as a very reliable and effective employee. However, this opinion was qualified in each instance by some reference to the fact that George was good in spite of his college education.

George had taken an interest in problems of the foreman. Occasionally, he had asked them questions about their work. Some of the foremen answered his questions; others let him feel he was getting a bit too "nosy." George did appear to show a great deal of insight into the forces that constantly impinged upon the individual foreman. They didn't know, however, that George was taking courses in foreman training in an extension program at Penn State.

Bill knew that George was taking classes in production control, labor laws, and human relations. One of the professors at Penn State had mentioned the fact to Bill during a Rotary luncheon some time ago. Later Bill had asked George about his evening courses and his plans for the future. It was during the ensuing conversation that George expressed a desire to get into management—the sooner the better. George had some ready answers, too, for plant problems that had bothered Bill and his foremen for a long time. It was clear this young man didn't lack confidence.

Could it be that Jack Fletcher, whose resignation Bill held in his hand, would want to reconsider? Bill looked again at the promising record of the last two months. Then his eyes settled upon the dismal record of the preceding months. Whatever he did, Bill would have to act promptly. He needed a day foreman to manage the Belt Department, the basic producing unit at Bellefonte Rubber Works.

16. Promotion to Police Sergeant*

Until recently selection of candidates for promotion to police sergeants at State University was done unsystematically. Job analysis was not the foundation for selection decisions but rather intuition and subjective judgments. The presence of a legal imperative and a desire to make better and more objective selection decisions resulted in a program to develop new promotion procedures.

State University is a large university with eight campuses spread throughout the state. Each campus has its own police department. Although the eight campuses are fairly autonomous and independent, there is a central administration group which coordinates certain functions, including personnel. Legally the police departments are responsible for their selection and promotion decisions; they are not governed by the personnel group in central administration

*This case was prepared by Susan E. Jackson, The University of Michigan. The example used is for teaching purposes only and is not meant to be an example of effective or ineffective management practice.

nor by the campus-based personnel departments. But the chiefs recognize that their expertise is limited and so they regularly seek advice and guidance from the campus and central administration personnel departments.

The eight campuses differ from each other in many ways, including size (from 4,000 students at the smallest campus to 30,000 students at the largest campus), location (both urban and rural), and age or time in existence (from as young as ten years to as old as more than 100 years). Corresponding to these differences among the campuses are differences in the composition, philosophies, and histories of the police department, each run by its own police chief. Of particular importance in 1983 was an ongoing rivalry between two large departments, one in the northern part of the state and the other in the southern part of the state; each was vying for recognition as the "best."

Despite competition among the departments, all eight police chiefs recognized the value of pooling their resources to maintain a single promotion procedure (or test) for selecting sergeants. By having a single procedure, a rank-ordered list of all university police officers qualified for promotion could be developed and made available to all campuses. Each list had a two-year life. During these two years, whenever a vacancy for sergeant came up on any of the eight campuses, the people at the top of the list had first priority for promotion. Approximately twenty vacancies occurred during a list's two-year life, and usually about 150 of the 250 police officers met the *minimum* requirements for promotion (i.e., two years of college credits, two years' police experience, and completion of a state-sponsored management training course).

Because of the attractive small selection ratio, the police chiefs wanted to improve their selection procedures so that the twenty vacancies were filled with the very best of the 150 eligible police officers. Accordingly, the university agreed to pay for a consultant to work with the police and personnel groups to design a high-quality promotion procedure for sergeants. They hired Gerri Smith from a prestigious consulting firm specializing in selection.

Getting Started

As with previous consulting assignments of this type, Ms. Smith knew that the development of a new promotion procedure would take time and involve several components. These components, beginning with job analysis, are outlined in the sequence through which Ms. Smith proceeded. This outline is shown in Exhibit 1.

Job Analysis

In 1979, six of the eight police departments had hired a firm to conduct job analyses of all jobs within their departments. The method the firm had used appeared to be the critical incident technique (CIT), but it was difficult to tell for sure because the documentation of the job analysis procedures had been retained by the consulting firm. The police chiefs contacted the firm after Ms. Smith pointed out to them that this documentation would be critical should they ever need to defend in court decisions they made using the results of the job analysis. Unfortunately, the particular consultant they had worked with four years ago was no longer with the firm and the documentation was nowhere to be found.

Exhibit 1. Components of the Promotion Test Developed by Ms. Smith

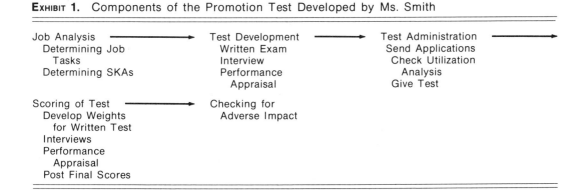

Job Analysis ——————→   Test Development ——————→   Test Administration ——————→
    Determining Job   Written Exam   Send Applications
        Tasks   Interview   Check Utilization
    Determining SKAs   Performance   Analysis
                                 Appraisal   Give Test

Scoring of Test ——————→   Checking for
    Develop Weights   Adverse Impact
        for Written Test
    Interviews
    Performance
        Appraisal
    Post Final Scores

Neither Ms. Smith nor the police chiefs had anticipated this problem. They had hoped to have their promotion list ready in four months. If they did a job analysis, they knew they might have to wait six or seven months before seeing that list. After discussing the matter at length, the chiefs decided that in the long run it was in their best interest to collect systematic, up-to-date job analysis information, so they asked Ms. Smith to get started.

Phase 1: Determining Job Tasks.   Usually, Ms. Smith likes to use an extended CIT method of job analysis but in this case it was not practical. To do so, she would have had to travel to eight locations that were hundreds of miles apart from each other. Both time and budget constraints ruled this out. Therefore, Ms. Smith decided to combine features of the CIT and GOJA methods. This creative solution was possible because the *Uniform Guidelines* recognize that there is no one best method of job analysis. As long as the method used provided information about the importance, frequency, difficulty, and trainability of one's job tasks, it would probably hold up to the scrutiny of the courts.

Ms. Smith conducted the job analysis for sergeants as follows: First, she asked each police department to send copies of the job descriptions for all of their sergeants. These gave her a general working knowledge of what the job of sergeant involved. Next, she developed a form that she would send to each sergeant to fill out. This form asked the sergeant to list all of his or her job duties and then, for each duty or task, to rate how frequently it was performed relative to other duties, how important it was to the job overall, how difficult it was to perform, and the amount of training that would be needed to teach someone to perform the duty. This form was sent to each sergeant, who filled it out and then reviewed it with his or her commanding lieutenant. If the lieutenant felt any qualifications or changes were needed, these were noted in a designated space. Both the sergeant and lieutenant then signed the form to indicate they had reviewed it together. Finally, the chief reviewed the form, added any comments he felt were appropriate, and signed it. The original copy of the form was kept by the campus police department and a photocopy was sent to Ms. Smith.

Using the information from the completed forms, Ms. Smith generated a list of eight job domains, which she believed, based on the data she had collected, represented the tasks relevant to the job of a sergeant. Then, for each domain, she listed all of the specific tasks that she felt belonged to the domain. For each task, she recorded the corresponding ratings of frequency, difficulty, importance, and trainability *(FDIT ratings)*. This list of domains and tasks was then sent back to twelve randomly chosen sergeants and three lieutenants who reviewed it. Ms. Smith asked these reviewers to study the list she had generated and evaluate whether the domains made logical sense to them and whether the tasks within each domain belonged there. They returned their suggestions for revision to Ms. Smith in writing. She then finalized the list, which is shown in Exhibit 2.

The last step in Phase 2 of the job analysis involved calculating frequency, difficulty, importance, and trainability values for each of the eight job domains. These values were calculated by averaging the FDIT ratings of the tasks within each domain and are shown in Exhibit 2.

Exhibit 2.   Job Domains for the Position of Police Sergeant

		Average Ratings			
		F	D	I	T[a]
Domain:	Law enforcement activities including patrolling, investigating, apprehending.	6.2	5.8	6.3	5.1[b]
Sample tasks:					
	1. responding to call for crime in progress				
	2. cultivating sources of street information				
Domain:	Adaptability to the job, including completing work in a timely manner, attention to detail, willingness to assume accountability for one's work.	6.4	3.3	5.7	4.0
Sample tasks:					
	1. accepting orders or assignments				
	2. keeping up-to-date files				
Domain:	Dealing with the public.	6.7	4.9	5.2	4.1
Sample tasks:					
	1. making death notifications				
	2. talking to news media				
Domain:	Communication, including communicating to others as well as understanding others.	5.5	3.2	6.1	4.2
Sample tasks:					
	1. referring citizens to other agencies				
	2. interviewing witnesses				
Domain:	Personal appearance and demeanor.	6.7	2.7	5.3	2.9
Sample tasks:					
	1. physical fitness activities				
	2. maintenance of uniform and equipment				
Domain:	Supervision and leadership.	4.7	6.4	4.8	6.7
Sample tasks:					
	1. working with a rookie or new transfer				
	2. supervising an investigation				
Domain:	Report writing.	5.9	4.6	5.5	5.1
Sample tasks:					
	1. writing up findings for an ongoing investigation				
	2. writing descriptions of events that occurred during on-site call				
Domain:	Teamwork, including working with other professionals both inside and outside of the department.	5.4	5.1	5.7	4.3
Sample tasks:					
	1. requesting assistance from other officers				
	2. teaching knowledge and skills to other officers				

[a]F = Frequency of task performance; D = Difficulty; I = Importance; T = Trainability.
[b]Ratings were made using a scale of 1 to 7. Values shown are means obtained by averaging across all items in the domain.

Phase 2: Determining Skills, Knowledge and Abilities (SKAs). Now that the major job tasks had been identified, Ms. Smith needed to determine the SKAs required to perform those tasks. Then methods of assessing applicants' relevant SKAs could be designed for use as a selection test.

To find out which SKAs were important for performing a sergeant's job, Ms. Smith went back to the experts—the sergeants and lieutenants. In order to record their judgments in a systematic way, Ms. Smith designed a simple matrix for the job experts to complete. The headings on the eight columns of the matrix were the names of the domains generated in Phase 1 of the job analysis. The labels for the seventeen rows of the matrix were names of abilities, knowledges, and skills that she believed someone might need to perform well as a sergeant.

This domains × abilities matrix was sent to all sergeants and lieutenants along with a list of the tasks that belonged in each domain and definitions of each ability. The job experts completed the matrix by indicating the importance of each ability for performing the tasks in each domain. Using these ratings, Ms. Smith determined the nine SKAs that were most important to assess in order to predict performance as a sergeant (see Exhibit 3).

Test Development

The police refer to the process through which sergeants are selected as the *Sergeants' Promotional Exam (SPE).* Traditionally, SPE has three components: a written exam, an interview, and an evaluation of past performance. These three components have always been used by the university police departments and they are typically used by city and state police departments as well. The police chiefs wanted Ms. Smith to maintain the three components of SPE, but they were eager to have the content of each component revised and updated. So, the major questions were: (1) Which SKAs should be assessed by each component? and (2) How exactly should each SKA be measured?

In deciding how to design the SPE, Ms. Smith kept several things in mind: First, she knew that written tests were more likely than interviews and

Exhibit 3.   SKAs Assessed by the Sergeant's Promotional Exam

			Exam Component in Which SKA Was Assessed[a]		
	Skills, Knowledges, & Abilities	I[b]	Written	Interview	Performance
1.	Knowledge of State and Federal Law	6.7	X		X
2.	Knowledge of Local Procedures and Regulations	6.6	X		X
3.	Writing Ability	5.2	X		X
4.	Communication Skills	5.8		X	X
5.	Reasoning Ability	5.0		X	X
6.	Skill in Interpersonal Relations	6.1		X	X
7.	Knowledge of General Management Principles	5.4	X		
8.	Reading Ability	4.9	X		
9.	Leadership Skills	4.8		X	X

[a]An "X" indicates the ability was assessed by that component of the exam.
[b]I = Importance rating of the ability. The value shown is a mean obtained by averaging the importance ratings of the ability for all job domains.

performance ratings to have adverse impact against minorities, especially blacks and Hispanics. Second, she was wary of interviews because she knew they are difficult to standardize and make reliable. Third, she preferred to assess as many SKAs as possible using the most job-related method possible, which in this case was the performance appraisal. Finally, she knew that each of the three methods at her disposal (written test, interview, performance ratings) had both strengths and weaknesses, so the best strategy would be to measure all SKAs using more than one method, if possible.

The three components of the SPE Ms. Smith designed are described in detail below. Throughout these next sections, reference is made to a Task Force. This Task Force was organized to assist Ms. Smith with her task of developing the tests. It consisted of three chiefs and two lieutenants.

The Written Exam.   During Phase II of the job analysis, seventeen SKAs had been rated for their importance to a sergeant's job performance. Of these, nine were judged to be relatively high in importance. Five of the nine were judged to be appropriately assessed in a written exam: *reading skills, writing skills, knowledge of basic management principles, knowledge of state and federal laws,* and *knowledge of university regulations and procedures* as described by the local General Orders manual. The two skill areas had been rated as relatively less important than the three knowledge areas, so the proportion of test items devoted to each skill or knowledge area was adjusted to reflect the importance ratings.

Usually, the most difficult part of developing a written test is writing the test items. Fortunately, the Task Force had the advantage of being able to obtain potential items from a state agency that maintained a bank of thousands of test items for law enforcement exams. Upon request, this agency randomly selected a total of 400 items relevant to the SKAs to be assessed on the exam. Each member of the Task Force then reviewed all 400 questions and noted any objections they had. At a group meeting, the Task Force discussed their evaluations of the 400 items. Their goal was to select a total of 100 of the best items. The decision rule they used to eliminate items from the pool of 400 was to eliminate any item to which any member of the Task Force had objections. This reduced the pool to fewer than 200. Finally, redundant items were eliminated and the final 100 items were chosen to fit the goal of distributing items across the five knowledge and skill areas according to the relative importance of the areas.

As already noted, one disadvantage of written tests was that minorities tend to score lower than whites, resulting in adverse impact for selection decisions based on written tests. Test experts now realize that a major source of unfairness in written tests is that often the reading skill needed to take the test is higher than the skill needed to do the job in question. To decrease the potential for unfair discimination, any written test used for selection should be checked to ensure that the readability level of the test is equal to or below the readability level of written materials typically encountered in the job. Therefore, as the last step in developing the written test for the SPE, Ms. Smith conducted readability analyses of the test and of samples of department memos, regulation manuals, legal documents, and correspondence taken directly out of the record files of current sergeants. This analysis showed the reading skill needed to take the test was somewhat less than the skill needed to read materials from the sergeant's actual files.

The Interview.   In the past, the police department interviewed only candidates who passed the written test. This practice meant that the chiefs had to decide on a cut-off point to define what a passing score would be for the written exam. They had always found this to be an extremely difficult judgment to make and wanted to avoid making that judgment this year. Their solution to the problem was to allow everyone to go through the interview process and not use the written test as a hurdle. This solution fit the chiefs' philosophy that someone who does well in the interview should be able to have that compensate for a low score on the written test, but it creates a practical problem: How could they interview approximately 100 candidates spread throughout a large state in a manner that everyone perceived to be standardized and fair, without incurring prohibitive expenses?

Ideally, it seemed that fairness and standardization could be best attained by having only one interview board (or panel), rather than having one panel at each of the eight campuses. But this would mean unbearably high travel costs—either the board members would have to travel around the state, or applicants would have to travel to the board. The Task Force decided the only practical solution was to set up two interview boards, one in the northern half of the state, and one in the southern half. This solution presented a real challenge to Ms. Smith who had to develop an interviewing procedure so sound it could not be attacked as possibly giving an unfair advantage to candidates in either half of the state. Ms. Smith realized that this challenge could be met only with a structured interview conducted by trained interviewers.

The first order of business was to solicit volunteers to serve as interviewers. The chiefs believed the interviewers should represent the following: the Affirmative Action officers from central administration, the general university community, the local communities by which the campuses were surrounded, the state law enforcement agencies, and their own departments. The group included the people to whom the chiefs felt most directly accountable, the people to whom the chiefs wished to demonstrate the credibility of their departments, and the people for whom the chiefs felt their departments should serve as role models. The Task Force was given the responsibility of creating two interview boards. Each board was to have one member to represent each of the five groups listed above.

After the interview boards were set up, Ms. Smith arranged a one-day training session for the interviewers. Her objectives for this training session were as follows:

- Develop a set of four or five questions that would be used for all interviews.
- Develop standards to use in evaluating candidates' responses to each question.
- Generate consensus among the interviewers about what they were to accomplish with the interview process.
- Give the interviewers an opportunity to role play an interview session.
- Develop an appreciation among the interviewers of the seriousness of their task and the problems inherent in accomplishing it (e.g., rater errors and biases, primacy and recency effects, and possible boredom and fatigue).

In order to accomplish these objectives, Ms. Smith did several things. First, prior to the training session she identified five SKAs (based on her job analysis) that could *potentially* be assessed in an interview. For each of these SKAs, she asked a few lieutenants to suggest interview questions that would tap the SKAs. Using these suggestions, she generated a list of about twenty potential interview questions. She sent this list, along with a short manual on interviewing and a job description for sergeants, to all members of the interview boards. The interviewers were asked to review this material prior to the training session.

At the training session, Ms. Smith reviewed several principles of interviewing and explained her objectives to the board members. She explained her belief that the only way to accomplish the objectives was for the interviewers to spend the day communicating and problem solving together. She turned over to them the task of selecting four or five questions that they all agreed were appropriate, and for which they were able to specify standards to be used in evaluating the candidates' responses. The interviewers struggled for several hours with this task, which they were surprised to find so difficult. By the end of the day, they had developed four questions they could all live with and a conviction that the interview process would be standardized and fair. At the end of the day, one of the interviewers—a twenty-year veteran of a large city's police department—admitted to Ms. Smith that he came to the training session believing the day would be a waste of time because there was nothing he didn't already know about interviewing. To his surprise he came away feeling that every interview board should go through a similar process before they began evaluating candidates, especially since their evaluations can strongly influence the careers of young officers.

Performance Appraisals.   The third component of the SPE was a performance appraisal of each candidate. Ms. Smith was happy to learn that the department already had a good performance appraisal procedure that was used for promotion decisions. The system worked as follows: For each candidate, all of the department officers who knew the candidate (this was typically three or four people) filled out a detailed appraisal form. The appraisal form assessed seven domains of job performance. For each performance domain, eight to twelve specific tasks were listed. The officers evaluated the candidate's performance of each task using a ten-point rating scale. These ratings were averaged and multiplied by ten to yield one overall performance score.

Administering the SPE

At the same time the three test components were being developed, Ms. Smith and the Task Force were planning for the administration of the tests. Only internal applicants were allowed to take the SPE, so the recruiting process was simple. All university police officers were sent a letter that described the testing procedures in detail. An application form was sent with this letter instructing all interested persons to apply by a particular date.

Although it was routine practice for the department to use only internal recruiting for the SPE, the chiefs always felt obliged to justify this practice. The major argument against the practice of internal recruiting was that it would perpetuate any existing underrepresentation of minority groups. To counter this argument, the chiefs sent a utilization analysis to the university's AAP officer, who compared this information to their routinely collected availability data. Because the police department had an aggressive recruiting program for entry-level positions, this comparison usually revealed that minority groups were not underrepresented in the pool of potential internal applicants.

The written exam was scheduled for a Saturday morning, and the police chiefs were all instructed to take this into account when assigning duties during that period. All interviewing was conducted the week after the written test. The officers completed their performance appraisals during that week also. Candidates were told the final list of total scores would be posted three weeks after the date of the written test.

Scoring the SPE

Final SPE scores were created by adding together the weighted scores from each component. The written test was weighted 50 percent, and the interview and performance appraisal were each weighted 25 percent. The final list of promotion candidates consisted of a rank ordering of everyone who had completed all three phases of the SPE based on the overall scores. This list was posted in each of the eight campus police departments along with a notice encouraging all applicants to speak with their chief to obtain detailed feedback.

The chiefs chose to weight the written test more heavily than the interview and performance appraisal primarily because they and their patrol officers all believed the written test was the most objective component of the SPE, and thus was the least subject to the criticism that favoritism determined the scores. Initially, the chiefs had suggested to Ms. Smith that the performance appraisal be weighted only 10 percent because it was the component believed to be most subjective. However, Ms. Smith countered that the performance appraisal was the most job-related component and therefore was probably the most valid predictor. The 50-25-25 weighting system was eventually agreed upon to take into account these and other similar types of concerns.

Checking for Adverse Impact

As noted previously, this university's police departments viewed themselves as leaders in the field of law enforcement practice. Consequently, they were particularly concerned about maintaining a force that was balanced with respect to the races and sexes. Recall that it was primarily this concern that led the departments to use a compensatory selection model rather than use the written test as a hurdle and therefore have to impose an arbitrary cut-off score for that component.

Ms. Smith believed that when management is sincerely concerned about the potential discriminatory effects of their selection procedures, the best quarantee for preventing unfair discrimination is information. Therefore, her last task for the police department was to conduct numerous analyses that illustrated the effects certain types of policies could have on their selection process. For example, one analysis involved computing adverse impact figures (using the 80 percent rule and a computer) under the assumption that the top ten, twenty, or thirty

Exhibit 4.   Analysis to Check for Potential Adverse Impact

Test Component	Asian (n = 23)[a]	Black (n = 37)	Hispanic (n = 11)	Am. Indian (n = 3)	White (n = 71)	Males (n = 118)	Females (n = 27)
	% of Subgroup Who Are Among the Top 20 Candidates						
Written	(5)[b]22%	(2)5%[c]	(1)9%[c]	(1)33%	(11)15%	(14)12%	(6)22%
Interview	(6)26%	(3)8%[c]	(1)9%[c]	(0) 0%[c]	(10)14%	(16)14%	(4)15%
Performance Appraisal	(5)22%	(5)14%	(0)0%[c]	(1)33%	(9) 13%	(15)13%	(5)19%
	% of Subgroup Who Are Among the Top 30 Candidates						
Written	(7)30%	(7)19%	(2)18%	(1)33%	(13)18%	(22)19%	(8)30%
Interview	(7)30%	(6)16%	(2)18%	(1)33%	(14)20%	(24)20%	(6)22%
Performance Appraisal	(5)22%	(6)16%	(2)18%	(2)67%	(15)21%	(25)21%	(5)19%

[a]n = indicates the total number of job applicants in the subgroup.
[b]Values in parentheses represent numbers of applicants.
[c]Indicates that adverse impact defined by the 80% rule exists for the subgroup in comparison to the majority group (whites or males).

candidates, respectively, would eventually be promoted from their list. This analysis revealed that strong adverse impact against blacks would occur if only the top ten candidates were promoted, that using the top twenty candidates would cause less adverse impact, and that no adverse impact would occur if the top thirty candidates were promoted (see Exhibit 4). Similarly, Ms. Smith demonstrated the adverse impact of each of the three components of the SPE and the effects that changing the weighting system would have with respect to adverse impact. Because adverse impact was associated only with the written test, the adverse impact of the total SPE was directly affected by the weight given the written test— the higher the weight of the written test, the more adverse impact of the SPE overall. To reduce the potential adverse impact of the SPE, the weight of the written test should be reduced.

Ms. Smith concluded her consulting assignment with the police chiefs. It is now up to them to fairly utilize, evaluate, and update the promotion procedures Ms. Smith helped them design. What problems, challenges, and issues face the police chiefs in carrying out the procedures developed by Ms. Smith?

17. International Metals Corporation*

In May 1961, Phillip Reisenger was wondering what action he should recommend to the president of International Metals Corporation in light of the internal problems the firm was facing. As part of his responsibilities as the company's personnel officer, Reisenger was in charge of organizational planning. He thought that most of the difficulties with which he was concerned could be traced to an organization change made in 1958 on the recommendation of his predecessor, Paul Wilson. Wilson had been the company's personnel officer until 1959 when he was promoted to the position of vice-president of its ore refining operations which were carried on by several foreign subsidiaries.

International Metals Corporation was engaged in an extensive international trade in nonferrous metals, and in the ore concentrates and by-products related to the refining of these metals. Anthony Cola started in the trading business in 1923 on a partnership agreement. In 1925, when his partner sold his interest in the business, Cola incorporated the firm and became its first president. He ran the company almost single-handedly during its early years.

It wasn't until the end of World War II that Cola felt able to relinquish some of his influence to a newly developing management team. In 1957 his nephew, Joseph Amante, was named to the presidency. As the chairman of the board, however, Cola, who was sixty-eight in 1961, remained active in the firm's day-to-day operations. Both he and his nephew, who was twenty-three years younger, maintained direct supervision over the company's trading division and also functioned as traders for copper and zinc, an activity which accounted for about 30 percent of the company's sales in 1960.

Anthony Cola referred to copper and zinc as the most speculative items which the company traded. "Prices on these commodities and profitability," he said, "may vary widely from year to year. Last year, for example, we operated at a net loss on these two items, although in some years they have contributed the bulk of our profits."

A business associate who had known Anthony Cola for many years described him as follows:

> All the success of International Metals can be attributed to one man, Anthony Cola. He has certainly built himself an empire. Of course, now both he and his nephew share in running the company. But it was only after a long period of training as a trader that his nephew was given this responsibility.

Characteristic of companies engaged in international trade, the history of International Metals Corporation was one of wide variations and shifting emphasis. For example, during World War II, when imports of all offshore commodities were taken over by the government, the company cultivated new sources of supply for ore concentrates in Mexico and Canada.

It was the firm's stated policy to shift quickly when a given source of supply was cut off. The firm was constantly seeking new opportunities; when market conditions changed, the scope of its activities likewise changed. It was mainly by seeking out new, profitable commodities in which to trade that the company had shown a rising trend in earnings as well as in sales in its recent years. As Anthony Cola put it,

> As soon as a lot of companies start trading in the same commodity, there is no profit in it for anyone. It seems that competition is quicker than it used to be in moving in on you these days with our modern high speed methods of communication. The commodity that has contributed the bulk of our products over the past three years is a product we call "Crystallium." It is a rare earth whose market we were the first to pioneer. Already a number of competitors have started to move in.
>
> To make a profit in this business, a trader first of all has to have vision. He has to be able to find and recognize new opportunities. Then he also must have a quick mind and must be willing to take risks and speculate.

Cola also pointed out that the firm characteristically operated on narrow margins. "Despite our small margins," he said, "we are able to show substantial earnings relative to our net worth since, in comparison to a manufacturing concern, we are able to operate on a small amount of equity capital." Over its thirty-five years International Metals grew to where, including its subsidiaries, it employed 400 people and achieved more than $80 million in sales in 1960. Income statements for the years since 1955 are shown in Exhibit 1.

Operations

By 1961, the company was represented by a branch office in San Francisco and by offices of subsidiary or affiliated trading companies located in Syndey, La Paz, London, Tokyo, and Osaka. The Sydney and La Paz offices were designated as buying offices. The San Francisco branch and the subsidiaries in England and Japan were manned by traders whose function it was to buy and sell for the parent company in the commodity market in their respective regions. Trading between each of these outlying offices was coordinated by the traders in the company's central headquarters in New York.

The two essential components of the company's business were its trading and traffic functions. Trading functions consisted of buying, selling, hedging, and negotiating contract terms. Traffic functions consisted of scheduling, booking space, chartering, and negotiating freight rates. Profits were realized by differentials existing between costs (purchasing, handling, storing, freighting, and financing) and market prices in the country to which a commodity was exported. These profits could be augmented by taking advantage of both fluctuating prices in the commodity markets and fluctuating prices in the shipping market. Therefore, the company occasionally speculated in the shipping market just as it did in the markets for the commodities it traded. Like his trading counterpart, a traffic man, for example, could "book" steamship space ahead of the firm's shipping requirements if he could thereby obtain a favorable rate. Often all the

	1960	1959	1958	1957	1956	1955
Sales	$82,048	$89,282	$62,759	$71,676	$79,981	$71,622
Expenses:						
Cost of sales	$76,310	$83,561	$58,343	$68,951	$77,102	$69,098
Storage & handling expenses	1,653	1,499	1,514	210	226	215
Selling & administrative expenses	2,218	2,194	1,679	1,447	1,450	1,379
Interest expense	689	532	438	434	508	473
	$80,870	$87,786	$61,974	$71,042	$79,286	$71,165
Net income before provision for income taxes	$ 1,178	$ 1,496	$ 785	$ 634	$ 695	$ 457
Provision for U.S. & foreign income taxes	558	741	396	223	345	173
Net income before deduction of minority interest	$ 620	$ 755	$ 389	$ 411	$ 350	$ 284
Minority interest in income of subsidiaries	24	93	80	8	7	6
Net income for year	$ 596	$ 662	$ 309	$ 403	$ 343	$ 278
Equity in income of affiliated companies	58	47				
Net income & increase in equity	$ 654	$ 709				

EXHIBIT 1. Income Statements for Years Ending December 31—in Thousands
(Source: Company Financial Statements.)

profits in a transaction were realized through the company's ability to obtain a favorable freight rate.

Each trade was composed of a purchase and a sale on the part of the trader. However, he did not necessarily have to make his purchase before his sale. If market conditions warranted it, he might sell first and then make his purchase. To buy, the trader kept in touch with the market conditions near his sources of supply, attempting to take advantage of cyclical variations so as to make his purchases at a favorable price. In selling his commodity, the trader would wire one or more of the firm's overseas sales offices stating the quantity he wanted to sell, the time at which he wanted to sell it and the sales price, including profit. Usually, the overseas office was given some price leeway with which to negotiate with potential buyers. However, a price was stipulated below which he could not go. This minimum was based on the price which the trader had to pay for the commodity; the transportation charges; direct selling expenses, such as labor, documenting, and insurance; financing charges; and other general overhead expenses which would be applied to the sale.

Upon receipt of an offer to sell, the office receiving the offer had to return a reply reaching New York before the opening of business the following day. Otherwise the offer was automatically rescinded. Sometimes it took several exchanges of cablegrams before a sale was negotiated. In cultivating a market for a new (to the firm) commodity, it took about one month to send samples, make a price offering, receive a counter offer, and negotiate final terms on a sale. On establishing commodities, however, negotiations were normally completed in two hours or less.

When the sale had been negotiated, the company's traffic personnel took over. Generally, one month ahead of the shipping dates, purchases were consolidated against sales since, in a given period, many individual purchases and sales were made. When shipping was tight, consolidation had to be accomplished as much as two months ahead of time. The consolidation completed, freight space was arranged for, or confirmed through a ship broker at the port. Ship brokers or steamship agents had a similar relationship to the steamship companies as manufacturers' representatives had to manufacturing concerns. They acted as independent sales agents for the steamship lines and were usually paid a commission of 1¼ percent of the freight by the steamship company to which they directed a given shipment. Finally, shipping instructions were sent to the suppliers instructing them on the quantities to ship and the date the commodity had to arrive at the port. A copy of the shipping instructions was also sent to a freight forwarder at the port of embarkation.

Generally, the company took physical possession of the commodity when the seller had loaded it on transportation destined for the port, the seller having paid the freight and insurance required for transit to the port. Upon arrival at the port, International Metals paid for all expenses incurred in storing and handling the commodity. The company's usual terms with a buyer were CIF, meaning that cost, insurance, and freight to the port of destination were included in the selling price. The buyer took physical possession of the commodity when it had been loaded on a vessel at the port of embarkation.

Representing the company's interests at the port of embarkation was a freight forwarder who was paid a commission by the company for each loading. His function was to prepare the bills of lading and the weight and quality certificates covering the shipment, and to see that the proper quantity of material was loaded on the vessel. The commission he was paid varied in accordance with the amount of work involved in a given loading. A freight forwarder depended on many shippers for his income. It was unusual for a firm the size of International Metals to have forwarders in its own employ since it shipped intermittently from many different ports.

The bills of lading, weight, and quality certificates were collected as soon as possible by International Metals' traffic personnel and were attached to sales invoices and drafts drawn on the buyer or his bank. These documents were then turned over to the treasury department for deposit or discount at the company's bank.

When the commodity reached its port of destination, the buyer or his agent checked the shipment. International Metals also paid a commission to a surveyor at this port to represent its interests when the shipment was checked. If the buyer had any claims against the company, they were first processed by traffic personnel to check for errors before being sent to the trader of the commodity involved for his approval or denial of the claim. If approved, the claim was sent to the comptroller's department for payment. If the trader denied the claim he would try to negotiate a settlement, failing which, the matter was taken to a court of arbitration as provided in the sales contract. In this case, the trader was responsible for drafting the arbitration briefs with the assistance of legal counsel. According to one of the company's traders, these claims arose quite frequently, but were usually settled out of court. Less than one in one hundred claims would go to arbitration.

Initial Organization

Prior to the 1958 realignment in the company structure, the trading and traffic functions were organized under separate departments. Both of these departments were structured along roughly parallel lines according to commodity groupings. For example, the trader for titanium and magnesium had his counterpart in the traffic department who specialized in transporting these commodities. The two departments differed in one respect. There was an intermediary between the traffic personnel and the president, while each trader reported directly to the president and the chairman of the board. In addition to these two departments which were considered line elements, personnel, treasury, and control staff departments filled out the organization. Exhibit 2 shows the firm's organization chart immediately prior to the change.

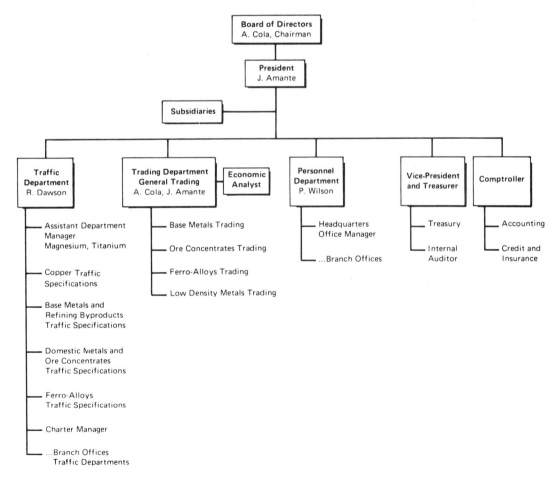

Exhibit 2. Organization Chart, April 1958

The trading department had not always been organized by commodity groupings. This change had been made in 1954 at the suggestion of Paul Wilson, the personnel officer, in anticipation of the change he was to propose in 1958. Previously the traffic department had been organized, as Wilson put it, "loosely," into two sections. The department manager headed a foreign traffic section while his assistant was in charge of a domestic traffic section. There was also a "loose" assignment of commodities to each traffic specialist. According to Wilson, the disadvantage he saw in this was that to complete a trading transaction, it was sometimes necessary for work and information to flow through each of the two traffic sections, thereby causing delays. In 1954 a more rigid assignment of commodities to each traffic specialist was made. In addition, most specialists were assigned the handling of both the foreign and the domestic aspects of transporting their respective commodities. Wilson said, however, that because of the different workloads involved for various commodities, it was impossible for the traffic department to parallel exactly the organization of the trading department.

Considerations Leading to a Further Change

In April 1958, Wilson made the proposal that the company further realign its organization by breaking down the trading department into separate trading sections, each centered around commodity groupings, and each staffed by a trader, a traffic specialist, and the secretarial personnel required to handle the necessary paper work. Wilson cited four reasons for his proposal.

First, it was designed to give each trader direct control over the freighting of his goods. Both Wilson and the president recognized this control as being very important since many trading opportunities were dependent upon freight considerations. It was also designed to provide direct communications between the trader and the traffic man who specialized in arranging transportation of his commodities and to give the trader a better chance to ensure that his transactions were executed as contemplated. Under the existing arrangement, when a trader needed information on shipping, he had to call or walk over to the traffic department. Because of the interruption and demand on the trader's time which this caused, he often relied upon his own familiarity with the transportation market rather than contacting the traffic specialist. In many cases, this resulted in errors in judgment on the trader's part in deciding the feasibility of a given trade. By improving communications, the change would also promote a better understanding and cooperation between trading and traffic personnel.

The second purpose behind the proposal was to shift administrative responsibility for trading and traffic detail to the trading section managers. This would provide a direct line of authority in the handling of all products, since it placed responsibility for all the operations necessary to complete a trade under each trader. With the trading and traffic operations divided into separate functional departments, it was difficult to pinpoint responsibility when problems arose. Moreover, there was a tendency for delays to creep into the system because only a few people in the traffic department were entrusted with making decisions of any importance. With many traffic personnel passing information upward for decision in their department, it was easy for bottlenecks to develop. Fast action in settling on the terms of a trade was of primary importance since, at the most, a trader had eight hours in which to reply to an offer or counteroffer. With a traffic specialist assigned to him, a trader could readily obtain the necessary traffic information. In addition, with his own department, each trader could organize and distribute his work in accordance with the requirement of the market in which he traded.

A third reason, correlative to the second, was to enable the company's traffic manager to devote more of his time to negotiating more favorable freight rates, setting traffic policy, investigating new ideas aimed at improvement of services or cutting of costs, analyzing and solving major traffic problems as they occur, and training all departments in better traffic methods. As a line manager, the pressure of day-to-day operations had left the traffic manager with little time for policy formulation and planning functions.

The fourth objective of the change was to give the company the opportunity to train its own traders. Typically it took five to ten years to train a trader. The chairman of the board and the president believed that this period of apprenticeship was necessary in order to cultivate the "intuitive feel" for trading which they felt was an essential attribute of a successful trader. Since the company did not have productive positions which would also serve as training positions in its existing organization, it left an inordinate portion of the trading burden on the president and on the chairman of the board. With a traffic specialist or an assistant traffic specialist assigned to a trader, it would be possible to train a prospective trader by having him work in the traffic positions throughout the company. He would therefore obtain valuable contact with the various trading elements while he performed productive work in the traffic function. The traffic job typically was more clerical than a trading position, and hence it took a shorter period to train a man as a traffic specialist. In recruiting men to handle traffic jobs, the company looked for those having bachelor's degrees in transportation. Prospective traders, on the other hand, were recruited from men with bachelor's or master's degrees in either economics or international trade. However, background alone would not guarantee success in trading. In the experience of the company's two chief executives, it took a unique set of personal characteristics and a long period of training to develop the necessary "feel" for trading. Even after a trader had been with the company for more than ten years, Joseph Amante and Anthony Cola kept close contact with his day-to-day trading decisions. They read all cablegrams sent from the company. Most of the traders also checked with them before making decisions which committed large amounts of funds or to which they felt the two chief executives might object for any reason. Each trader operated within credit lines and terms granted to his commodities by the president. To step outside of these limits required special permission from Joseph Amante.

Effects of the Change

After considering Wilson's proposal, Amante, with Cola's consent, decided to put the plan into effect in September 1958. Besides reassigning traffic specialists to the various traders, this involved a reapportionment of the main office building so that each trader had a section of the office which would accommodate the trader and the traffic specialists and clerks assigned to him. The change was first announced through a series of meetings with the traders and the traffic manager. After the physical move was made, a memorandum was circulated to all employees in which Wilson explained his reasons for the realignment and described the new reporting relationships and responsibilities of all employees who were affected by the change. Departmental responsibilities and job descriptions of the key people affected by the change as they appeared in this memorandum are shown in the Appendix. The firm's 1961 organization structure as it evolved after the change is shown in Exhibit 3.

In the series of personnel reassignments and promotions which followed the structural change in organization, Wilson was promoted to the new position of the company's director of manufacturing subsidiaries. He was subsequently given the title of vice-president in this position. As director of manufacturing, he acted as the contact man in the parent company to whom the general manager of each of the company's foreign ore refining subsidiaries reported. Previously, they had reported directly to the president. This post was designed to relieve the already great burden on the president's time. Wilson also initiated studies concerning the possibility of adding new manufacturing concerns to the company.

Several of the company's traders said that Wilson's promotion had come as quite a surprise to them. "Until he was promoted," one said, "the only path of advancement to top level management was through trading. Then we found that there was more importance attached to our overseas manufacturing and to a man with an engineering degree." Wilson had received a degree in metallurgy from a well-known midwestern college. He went on to receive a master's degree in business at the same school before joining International Metals.

Succeeding Wilson as personnel manager was Phillip Reisenger. Reisenger had an educational background similar to Wilson's. While studying for his business degree, Reisenger also did some part-time teaching in the areas of statistics and basic business organization. Toward the end of this program, Reisenger met Wilson, who interested him in International Metals and was instrumental in getting him a job with the company. Reisenger was hired in June 1957, as a management trainee, and thereupon was assigned several research projects under Wilson. Later he served for three months as a traffic trainee in one of the trading departments. In mid-1959 he was named as Wilson's assistant, and a year later took over the full responsibilities associated with the position of personnel officer.

When Reisenger took over his new job as personnel officer in 1959 there was still some confusion evident concerning the change. At the same time that the change had been put into effect, responsibility for billing domestic traffic was given to the traffic specialists. This, in effect, heaped more detail work on the traffic specialist and, according to Wilson, "may have caused some grievances on the part of the traffic specialists which were attributed to the change in organization rather than to the new assignment of duties."

It was not until a year later that Reisenger began to suspect that some of the problems with which he was concerned might be chronic, long-term situations resulting from the change, rather than the transitory type which would be eliminated once people had become accustomed to the new arrangements.

The first problem arose when Ralph Dawson, the traffic manager, began to complain to Reisenger that his control over traffic operations had been considerably reduced as a result of the change. He maintained that it had become increasingly difficult for him to obtain up-to-date information on the traffic

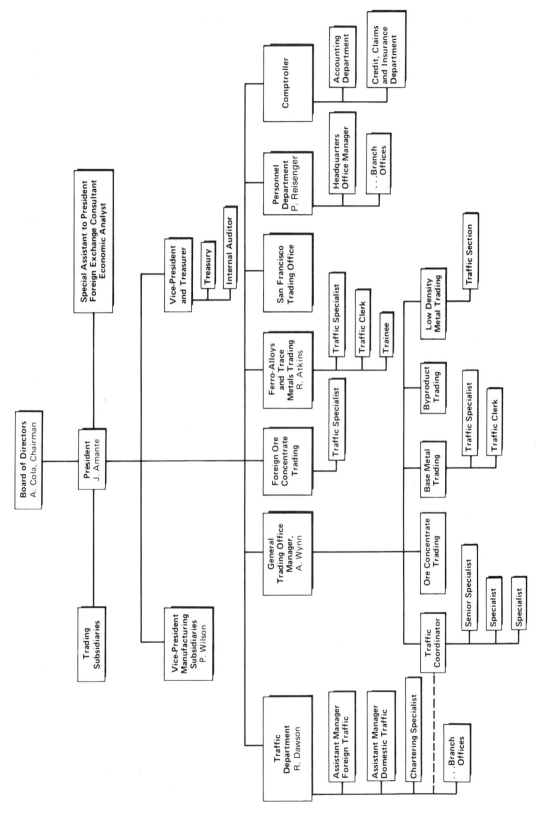

Exhibit 3. Organization Chart, May 1961

operations of the various trading departments. Even though he continued to review each shipping order made, he felt that he had lost contact with day-to-day traffic operations. Another weakness he pointed to was that he was no longer able to consolidate shipments of different commodities effectively. Under the old organizational arrangement, he said, he had been able to obtain significant freight savings by grouping shipments of various commodities so as to take up a more significant portion of a given ship's capacity.

After hearing Dawson voice his dissatisfaction with his new role in the company on several occasions, Reisenger decided to bring the matter to the attention of the president. When he did so, Amante asked, "Why doesn't Dawson come directly to me if he has a complaint? What has he done to try to correct the situation?" Reisenger concluded that Dawson had probably accepted the change as being irrefutable and something he had to live with in spite of his protests. During the conversation, Amante expressed the opinion that Dawson had lost nothing as a result of the change. As traffic manager he still had full responsibility for the company's traffic operations. The only thing that had changed was that each traffic specialist had been put in charge of all of the details necessary to complete the transportation phase of any trade in his assigned area. Since he reported to a man less familiar with the transportation function than he, this meant that each traffic specialist had to assume more responsibility than had been required under the previous organization structure. On the other hand, this meant that Dawson did not have to get involved in operating details but could devote more time toward planning and traffic policy formulation. It was Reisenger's opinion, however, that Dawson had continued to concern himself with following all the detailed phases of the traffic operation.

At one meeting in the president's office, the subject of Dawson's discontent with his role under the new arrangement came up when Wilson was present. Wilson made the suggestion that Dawson be moved over as head of all trading departments, thereby relieving the president from day-to-day trading responsibilities and allowing him to devote all of his time to "planning and controlling" the company's operations. Amante's reply to this suggestion was, "I don't think it will work. I don't think he is temperamentally suited to being a trader. He is far better qualified to supervise traffic work than trading. His weakness is in organizing his department, and he should be encouraged to spend less time on detail and more time on the broader aspect of his work, including organization."

Dawson, who was fifty-three in 1961, had joined the company in 1947 as traffic manager, with a background of long experience in the transportation field. His previous working experience had been in various jobs leading to his promotion to department manager for an east coast steamship company.

Another difficulty which Mr. Reisenger observed was that, in his opinion, even though the traders tended to be very independent people, most of them did not adequately fulfill their new role as department managers. This problem directly affected Reisenger's responsibilities as personnel manager, especially in the areas of personnel evaluation, development, and promotion. Some of the firm's traders, he observed, did not concern themselves with training their people or with how well they were doing. Under the previous organization, the traders were located in one room supported only by a secretarial pool. Therefore, they had no personnel responsibilities. Now with separate trading departments, each trader was required to make recommendations for promotion of their people and to pass out pay raises and promotions. Even though they were required to fill out a rating sheet on their people at least once a year, Reisenger felt that most traders did only a superficial job in supplying information which was called for on these forms.

Roger Atkins was in Reisenger's opinion the only trader, aside from the president, who adequately carried out his managerial responsibilities. But even he had indicated to Reisenger that personnel problems had now become a major concern, whereas previously he had only to concern himself with searching for trading opportunities. Atkins, who was forty, was considered by Reisenger to be the company's most enterprising trader. Vitally interested in his work, he often carried on trading in the evenings, initiating cablegrams from his home. He was constantly investigating new ideas on ways to operate his department, new methods of predicting trends in his markets, and new products in which to trade.

Some of Atkins' ideas took hold throughout the company. For example, on reading a *Fortune* article describing Consolidated Food Company's success with the profit center concept,[1] he proposed that International Metals try this out with its foreign subsidiaries. The company adopted this idea in late 1960 with its London subsidiary. He said that the change had a tremendous effect in boosting the morale of the traders in this subsidiary and improved is own working relationship with these traders. If the central office did not equal the best available terms, the subsidiary was authorized to trade outside the company. This also put the trader in the home office on his mettle in always trying to be able to offer the best terms.

Atkins' department had achieved the largest growth in sales volume of any department over the years since 1958. He said the president commented on this by saying, "OK, you've shown us that you can obtain sales volume, now see what you can do about profits." Atkins said that for 1961 he set for himself a goal of a profit of $200,000. This objective made him look critically at each of the commodities he was trading in terms of its contribution toward achieving it. He did this by comparing the gross margin of each potential trade with the direct expenses involved in making the trade, plus the general overhead which was allocated to his department. As a long-standing company policy, general overhead was allocated on the basis of the dollar sales generated by each trader. Atkins had broken down all of his costs to a per-pound basis so he could quickly determine the break-even point and profitability of any transaction. He was constantly searching for new profitable commodities in which to trade to replace those whose profit margins had eroded. Despite his concern with keeping his costs down, he had asked Reisenger several times in the past month to hire him an additional man. He already had the main office's only trader trainee in his department. A trainee from the London office was scheduled for training in his department starting in August 1961. Atkins said he had no difficulty in finding work for the people assigned to him.

At lunch one day, Reisenger questioned Atkins about his feelings about the change in organization. The following conversation ensued:

Reisenger: Roger, I'm trying to get an idea of how various people react to the new way we've organized. What do you think of our new setup?

---

1. C. Reiser, "Consolidated Foods: All over the Lot," *Fortune,* June 1960, p. 139.

Atkins: You mean our profit center idea?

Reisenger: No, I meant the change to separate trading departments.

Atkins: Didn't that happen about three years ago? I thought that was a dead issue. Don't tell me you're trying to instigate another shake up.

Reisenger: I'm trying to assess how well we're doing and see where we can make improvements.

Atkins: Well, frankly, Phil, I liked it better under the old setup. For one thing, there was closer association among the traders. We were located in one room, so when any of us got hold of any information which might be pertinent to someone else we could put him onto it right away. There is a strong interrelationship between all the commodities we trade. What happens in the market for one affects the markets for the others. So we could really help each other out under the old setup. Very little of this assistance takes place now. It's just too much trouble to get on the phone and get hold of another trader. For one thing, either he or his phone might be tied up. All of us are more tied up now looking after the administrative details in running our own departments. I think also that a sense of competition has crept in between trading departments. Even though we were judged on the basis of our sales before, just as we are now, there didn't seem to be much competition between traders. Now, about the only time the traders get together is to compare notes at the weekly trading meetings when we are given a rundown on the economic outlook for all our commodities. . . . Of course, under the old arrangement, it was easier for full sessions to develop among the traders since we had so much in common. I don't feel that I have so much in common with any of the people in my own department. . . . I guess the present arrangement is more business-like . . . it's probably better for the company.

Reisenger: Do you feel you are getting better help in your traffic operations?

Atkins: Yes, I can get the transportation end of a trade arranged much faster now. And I know that I can quickly get the answer to any traffic question without having to walk or call over to the traffic department.

Reisenger: How's Estes working out as a trainee?

Atkins: O.K. But I wish you wouldn't tell our trainees what position they've been hired for. It would give us a lot more flexibility if the man wasn't told that he was being trained to be a trader. Why couldn't you tell trainees that the job they end up with depends on the aptitude they display during training?

Reisenger: It might be hard to hire people on this basis. But let me think about that one for a while.

Reisenger asked William Morrow, whom he looked upon as a highly capable traffic man, for an opinion of the effects of the organization change. Morrow, the assistant traffic manager for foreign traffic, felt that the change served to give the traffic specialists more responsibilities and broader horizons to look forward to. Before the change, he said, they had been delegated pretty routine work.

In the course of the conversation, Morrow described how a Japanese trading company had been very successful with an organization composed of both traffic and trading line departments. Each of these departments was considered a profit center and evaluated on the profits it contributed to the company. Morrow indicated that he thought a similar arrangement at International Metals would work better than the existing organization. When the International Metals Corporation had been composed of both traffic and trading line departments, the profit center concept had not been practiced. The accounting system was the same then as it was in 1961. That is, direct costs were applied to each commodity traded and overhead was based on dollar volume of sales and also applied to each commodity. Hence, under the previous organization, the only indications that corrective action was necessary in the traffic department were when incorrect paper work was spotted or when a trader complained that he was given erroneous information on freight rates and shipping schedules by the traffic department.

Reisenger next approached George Bell, the traffic specialist in Atkins' department, to get his reaction to the change. Bell said:

> At first I couldn't see what the company was driving at with the change. But now that I've seen how it works, I definitely think it is a change for the better. I think it gives each person in our trading department even the secretaries, a feeling that they are part of a complete working unit. You get the feeling that you are a company within a company. By listening to the trader and the traffic specialist, everyone can see how a trade is put together and how the work they do fits in. Also, we can now wrap up a trade in minutes instead of hours. I think I am able to do my job better too. By getting to know the markets for the commodities we trade, I can plan my negotiations for freight space. I can also stand in for Atkins, and trade for him when he is away.
>
> As far as my relationship with the traffic department goes, I refer to them only on policy matters, like when we want to appeal to the Interstate Commerce Commission to have freight rates lowered in a new domestic marketing area we've opened up. I think it is pretty clear between what is a policy matter and what is an operating matter that I can handle myself. Of course, Bill Morrow, the assistant traffic manager, handles some of the traffic work on commodities we trade only occasionally. One of these items, though, really caught on, and we started trading it regularly. Morrow has continued to handle the traffic for this product. I'm so busy with my other work that I couldn't relieve him of this job even if I wanted to.

Later Reisenger told Atkins of Bell's enthusiasm for the present arrangment. Atkins countered with:

> Maybe he has a point there. But I still think there is the disadvantage that I am called upon to make decisions which should be made by other people in my department. Making these decisions myself, or trying to get the people in my department to take the responsibility for making them on their own, cuts in on the time I have to analyze my markets or to look for new trading opportunities.

The only other issue that Reisenger perceived had been raised as a result of the change in organization was brought to his attention by Carl Mitchell, the traffic coordinator in the general trading office. This office was located in quarters separate from company headquarters in another part of New York City. It had its own trading and traffic elements, but relied on support from the staff elements in the headquarters office. The general trading office had been a subsidiary trading company which was consolidated within the parent organization in 1960. The two New York offices had not been consolidated into one location because of lack of space. By 1963, however, the company planned to move to new quarters which would make it possible to combine both offices.

Mitchell's complaint was that the general trading office was employing a needless amount of traffic personnel. He argued that if all the traffic people at this location were organized as a central traffic section reporting to him, the company could eliminate two traffic specialists from the general trading office. This, he said, would result in an annual savings to the company of the combined salaries of these two men, roughly $15,000, plus another 30 percent of this amount, $4,500, for fringe benefits. Based on the 1.5 percent before tax return on sales which the company earned in 1960, it would take well over a million dollars in sales to cover the total cost of retaining these two surplus positions.

In the general trading office were located two trading departments which had traffic personnel directly assigned to them. Two other departments, however, relied completely on a central traffic department organized under Mitchell to handle their traffic work (see Exhibit 3). One of the reasons for this exception to the general organization plan was that the general trading office had only recently been consolidated within the parent company. It had previously been operated with a centralized trading department. Following the consolidation, two trading departments with traffic personnel assigned to them were moved from the headquarters office to the general trading office. Reisenger cited another reason why he felt there had been no action taken to assign all traffic personnel in the general trading office to individual trading departments there. He said that this office was generally looked upon in the company as an advanced training area for traders. Therefore, a certain amount of flexibility was required in that office as responsibilities for trading more commodities were shifted to a new trader as he progressed in his training. Alfred Wynn, manager of the general trading office, had long experience as a trader. Aged sixty-two, he was still active in trading certain commodities. As an adjunct to this trading duties he was valued as an excellent influence in helping develop traders who had advanced to the stage where they had been assigned a particular commodity to trade.

Reisenger was also familiar with still another alternative method of organizing a trading company. This was a method of dividing responsibility which was used by most European trading firms. There, the trader was responsible for buying, selling, and freighting his goods. A contract administration section in these firms was responsible for handling all documents, billings, claims, contract audits, and accounting. When a transaction had been initiated by a trader, contract administrators followed the transaction through to its completion and were familiar with every detail and cost involved.

Late in May 1961, Reisenger was expressing some of his misgivings about the way the firm was organized in a meeting with the president. At one point in their conversation, after Reisenger had enumerated a number of the difficulties in the situation which led to uncertainty as to what to recommend be done, Amante slammed his hand to the table with a loud report. "Damn it, Paul, we've dragged our feet long enough on this thing. At one time or another you've given me all the pros and cons involved in the way we're organized. Now it's your baby. Based on these pros and cons, what are your recommendations? How about giving me a report on this in three days?"

APPENDIX

Realignment of Duties of Traffic and Trading Personnel

The recent changes in the physical location of trading and traffic personnel in our New York office also signify some changes in responsibility, authority, and activity. More than even before, it will be the responsibility of each trading department manager to keep the general traffic manager and his assistant managers fully informed of all facts concerning the movement of their commodities and to consult with them when any question concerning traffic policy or procedure is not clear. Accordingly, the following line-up of functions and responsibilities will take place as soon as practicable within each department.

Organization of the Traffic Department

The traffic department is responsible for the establishment of policies concerning the storage and movements of all products bought and sold by the International Metals Corporation and its subsidiaries, in both foreign and domestic transactions. This work includes:

1. Chartering ships and booking large parcel space for the various trading departments.
2. Negotiating rates and rate adjustments with transportation companies.
3. Obtaining transit differentials and maintaining transit records.
4. Establishing policies relating to proper shipping and documentation in conformance with shipping instructions and contract provisions.
5. Overseeing marine and war risk insurance placement.
6. Investigating and developing any traffic techniques.
7. Inspecting traffic operations in other locations.
8. Training and guidance of all personnel in proper traffic procedure.
9. Maintaining adequate records of contracts of sales and purchases.
10. Invoicing domestic transactions and dittoing contracts and shipping instructions.

Organizing of Trading Divisions

The trading policy of the company is developed jointly by the chairman of the board and the president, assisted by the various traders and the economic analysis section. The chairman and the president trade in several commodities in their own right—assignment of these commodities to traders in the operating units will be secondary assignments.

Description of Jobs

General Traffic Manager—Ralph Dawson. The general traffic manager is responsible for the general supervision of all traffic and will coordinate all traffic work at New York, San Francisco, London, La Paz, Sydney, Tokyo, and Osaka.

Questions pertaining to general traffic policy and any problems in the coordination of traffic matters between the trading departments or other branch offices of the company are to be referred to him. He is responsible directly to the president, Joseph Amante. His major functions will be to establish and review general traffic policies, train and guide all personnel in proper traffic policy and procedure, anticipate trouble areas and help the departments concerned surmount them, and visit and inspect traffic operations in other locations.

Trading Department Manager. Within this framework, our trading department is divided into several commodity departments or operating units, each headed by a trading manager. Each manager is responsible to the president for general trading and administrative policy within his department, and shall keep him well-advised of the market situation and of his own position in the market within the credit, price, and trading limits authorized by the president. Each manager will be directly responsible for the purchase, sale, and movement (under the traffic policies laid down by the traffic department) of the particular commodities assigned to him, and for the supervision of the traffic people charged with their movement. Traffic policy will be subordinate to trading policy and will be modified when outweighed by trading considerations. If disagreement arises between the trading and traffic departments, the matter shall be referred to the president.

In addition to the above, each trading manager shall be directly responsible for the following in regard to his purchases and sales:

1. Operating profitability within credit lines and terms granted his commodities and keeping the treasurer well-advised of any sizable, actual, or anticipated changes approved by the president.
2. Checking with the credit department prior to sale to or purchase from new accounts and keeping well-posted on his accounts.
3. Preparation, signing, and following up of his contracts. It shall be his responsibility to see that contracts are issued the day the trade is executed, amendments are issued promptly, contracts and confirmations are carefully checked, and that signed copies are returned to us promptly and forwarded to our central contract file.
4. Checking on traffic work, billings, commissions, insurance, expenses, and accounting work relating to his contracts and following up any late deliveries or shipments.
5. Checking actual costs against estimates; furnishing yearly budget information.
6. Working closely with the credit and claims department to effect prompt settlements of all disputes.
7. Following up monthly on all past due accounts.
8. Working with our advertising agency (when required) in preparation of copying.
9. Handling traffic matters in the absence of his traffic specialist.
10. Checking position reports in collaboration with assistant traffic manager, foreign or domestic, whichever applicable.

Traffic Specialist. Operating under the general traffic policy of the company, the traffic specialist under each trading department manager shall be responsible for all traffic functions relating to the commodities assigned to his commodity section. He shall be accountable directly to the trader and will be responsible for:

1. Obtaining of options and booking of freight space. This is done either through the assistant traffic managers in connection with large movements or directly in cases of small shipments as defined by the general traffic manager; in all cases, the traffic department must be kept fully informed of his actions.
2. Issuing ship orders and shipping instructions to suppliers except where jurisdiction of London office applies.
3. Requesting and executing shipping instructions from our buyers.
4. Assisting in the negotiations of rate adjustments.
5. Maintaining records of open purchases and sales, and regularly preparing position-reports, open purchase and sales contracts.
6. Checking all shipping and insurance documents for conformance with shipping instructions and contract provisions.
7. Placing adequate marine and war risk insurance, filing of claims.
8. Arranging for pumping, storage, sampling, analysis, and discharge of shipments.
9. Preparation (except final extension and distribution) and checking of domestic invoices and preparation of billing instructions on foreign sales.
10. Passing claims information to the credit and claims department.
11. Handling trading matters in the absence of his trading department manager.
12. Notifying trading manager of possible late deliveries or shipments so trading manager can follow up with broker.

18. Chandler's Restaurant*

In discussing the kitchen as a status system, we have only incidentally taken account of the fact that the kitchen is part of a communication and supply system, which operates to get the food from the range onto the customer's table. Looking at it this way will bring to light other problems.

Where the restaurant is small and the kitchen is on the same floor as the dining room, waitresses are in direct contact with cooks. This does not eliminate friction, but at least everybody is in a position to know what everybody else is doing, and the problems of communication and coordination are relatively simple.

When the restaurant is large, there are more people whose activities must be coordinated, and when the restaurant operates on several floors, the coordination

---

*This case was prepared by William Foote Whyte and is reprinted here by permission of the author.

must be accomplished through people who are not generally in face-to-face contact with each other. These factions add tremendously to the difficulty of achieving smooth coordination.

The cooks feel that they work under pressure—and under a pressure whose origins they cannot see or anticipate.

As one of them said,

> It's mostly the uncertainty of the job that gets me down, I think. I mean, you never know how much work you're going to have to do. You never know in advance if you're going to have to make more. I think that's what a lot of 'em don't like around here. That uncertainty is hard on your nerves.

For a cook, the ideal situation is one in which she always has a sufficient supply of food prepared ahead so that she is never asked for something she does not have on hand. As one of them said, "You have to keep ahead or you get all excited and upset."

Life would be simpler for the cook if she were free to prepare just as much food as she wanted to, but the large and efficiently operated restaurant plans production on the basis of very careful estimates of the volume of business to be expected. Low food costs depend in part upon minimizing waste or leftover food. This means that production must be scheduled so as to run only a little ahead of customer demand. The cook therefore works within a narrow margin of error. She can't get far ahead, and that means that on extra-busy days she is certain sometimes to lose her lead or even to drop behind.

When the cook drops behind, all the pressures from customer to waitress to service pantry to runner descend upon her, for no one between her and the customer can do this job unless she produces the goods. From this point of view, timing and coordination are key problems of the organization. Proper timing and good coordination must be achieved in human relations or else efficiency is dissipated in personal frictions.

While these statements apply to every step in the process of production and service, let us look here at the first steps—the relations of cooks to kitchen runners to the service pantry.

When the restaurant operates on different floors, the relations must be carried on in part through mechanical means of communication. There are three common channels of this nature, and all have their drawbacks. Use of a public address system adds considerably to the noise of the kitchen and service pantries. The teleautograph (in which orders written on the machine on one floor are automatically recorded on the kitchen machine) is quiet but sometimes unintelligible. Orders written in a hurry and in abbreviated form are sometimes misinterpreted so that sliced ham arrives when sliced toms (tomatoes) were ordered. Besides, neither of those channels operates easily for two-way communication. It is difficult to carry on a conversation over the public address system, and, while kitchen runners can write their replies to orders on the teleautograph, this hardly makes for full and free expression. The telephone provides two-way communication, but most kitchens are so noisy that it is difficult to hear phone conversations. And then in some restaurants there is only one telephone circuit for the whole house, so that when kitchen and pantry runners are using it, no one else can put in a call.

The problems that come up with such communication systems can best be illustrated by looking at a particular restaurant, Chandler's where teleautograph and phone were used.

A kitchen supervisor was in charge of Chandler's kitchen, and pantry supervisors were in charge of each pantry, under her general supervision. There was also an assistant supervisor working in the kitchen.

The supplying function was carried on in the kitchen by two or three runners (depending upon the employment situation) and by a runner on each of the service-pantry floors. Food was sent up by automatic elevator.

The kitchen runners were supposed to pick up their orders from storage bins, iceboxes, or direct from the cooks. When the order was in preparation, the cook or salad girl was supposed to say how long it would be before it was ready, and the runner would relay this information by teleautograph to the service pantries. When the cooking or salad making had not been begun, the runner had no authority to tell the cook to hurry the order. Before each meal, the cook was given an open order (a minimum and maximum amount) on each item by the kitchen supervisor. She worked steadily until she had produced the minimum, and, from then on, she gauged her production according to the demands that came to her from the runner. That is, if the item was going out fast, she would keep producing as fast as she could until she had produced the maximum. Beyond this point she could not go without authorization from her supervisor. Ideally, the supervisor and cook would confer before the maximum had been reached in order to see whether it was necessary to set a new figure, but this did not always happen.

While the runner could not order the cook to go beyond her maximum, his demands did directly influence her behavior up to that point. He originated action for her.

That was at the base of his troubles. Among kitchen employees, as we have seen, the cooks have the highest status. In Chandler's, runners had a low status, just above potwashers and sweepers. The jobs were filled by inexperienced employees, women or men who, if they performed well, were advanced to something of higher status. Their wages were considerably lower than the cooks', and the cooks also had a great advantage in seniority. In this particular case, the age difference was important too. The runners were a young man, a teen-aged boy, and a young girl, while the cooks were middle-aged women.

The runners would have been in a more secure position if they had been in close touch with a supervisor, but here the communication was sporadic and ineffective. The supervisor was inclined to let the runners fend for themselves.

When the runners put pressure on them, the cooks were inclined to react so as to put the runners in their place. For example, we observed incidents like this one. One runner (Ruth) asked another to get some salmon salad from the salad girl. The second runner found that the salad girl had no more on hand.

"They want me to get some of that salmon salad," he said. "Couldn't you make it, please?"

"Who told you that?" she asked.

"Ruth did."

"You can tell Ruth that I don't take no orders from her. I have a boss, and I don't take orders from nobody else. You can just tell her that."

Now it may have been that the salad girl had made her maximum and could not go on without authorization from her supervisor, but the runner had no way of knowing that this was the case. He put his request to her politely, and she could have responded in kind by saying she was sorry that she could not make more without consulting the supervisor. Instead she responded aggressively, as if she felt a need to make it clear that no mere runner was going to originate action for her.

Even when they complied with the runner's requests, the cooks sometimes behaved so as to make it appear as if it were really they who originated the action. They always liked to make it clear that they had authority over the foods after they had been prepared, and that they could determine what should be done with them. While this was a general reaction, the salad girl was most explicit in such cases.

A runner went to look for some boiled eggs. The salad girl was not present at the moment, so he could not ask her, but after he had got the eggs from the icebox, he saw that she was back at her station. He showed her the pan of eggs, asking, "What about that?"

"I don't like that," she said belligerently. "You have no business taking them eggs out of the icebox without asking."

"Well, I'm asking you now."

"I have to know how much there is. That's why I want you to tell me. . . . Go on, you might as well take them now that you have them."

On other occasions when he asked her for salad, she would say, "Why don't you people look in the icebox once in a while?"

In such a case, whatever the runner did was wrong. The salad girl's behavior was irrational, of course, but it did serve a function for her. Behaving in this way, she was able to originate action for the runner instead of being in the inferior position of responding to his actions.

The runners also had difficulty in getting information out of the cooks. When there was a demand from the service pantries, and the food could not be sent up immediately, the runners were always supposed to give an estimate as to when they could furnish the item. This information they were expected to get from the cooks. The cooks sometimes flatly refused to give a time and were generally reluctant to make an estimate. When they did give a time, they nearly always ran considerably beyond it.

Incidentally, time seems to be used as a weapon in the restaurant. It is well known that customers feel and complain that they wait for a table or for service far longer than they actually do. Waitresses, as we observed them, estimated their waiting time on orders as much as 50 to 100 percent more than the actual time. While they were not conscious of what they were doing, they could express impatience with the service-pantry girls more eloquently by saying, "I've been waiting twenty minutes for that order," than by giving the time as ten minutes. In the front the house, time is used to put pressure on people. In the back of the house, the cooks try to use time to take pressure off themselves. They say that an item will be done "right away," which does not tell when it will be done but announces that they have the situation well in hand and that nobody should bother them about it. Giving a short time tends to have the same effect. It reassures the runner, who reassures the service pantries. When the time runs out, the pantry runners begin again to demand action, but it may take a few minutes before the pressure gets back to the cooks, and by that time the item may really be ready for delivery. Furthermore, the cooks' refusal to give a time turns the pressure back on runners and other parts of the house—a result that they are not able to accomplish in any other way.

In the case of some of the inexperienced cooks, it may be that they simply did not know how to estimate cooking time, but that would hardly explain the persistent failure of all the cooks to cooperate with the runners in this matter.

The management was quite aware of this problem but had no real solution to offer. One of the pantry supervisors instructed a kitchen runner in this way:

> "You have to give us a time on everything that is going to be delayed. That is the only way we can keep things going upstairs. On our blackboards we list all our foods and how long it will take to get them, and most of the time we have to list them 'indefinite.' That shouldn't be. We should always have a definite time, so the waitress can tell the guest how long he will have to wait for his order. We can't tell the guest we're out of a certain food item on the menu and that we don't know how long it will take to replace it. They'll ask what kind of a restaurant we're running."
>
> The runner thought that over and then went on to question the supervisor. "But sometimes we can't get that information from the cooks. . . . They won't tell us, or maybe they don't know."
>
> "Then you should always ask the food-production manager. She'll tell you, or she'll get the cook to tell you."
>
> "But the cooks would think we had squealed."
>
> "No, they wouldn't. And if they did, all right, it's the only way they'll ever learn. They've got to learn that, because we must always have a time on all delayed foods."
>
> "Yes, surely we couldn't tell on them if they refused to give the information."
>
> "Yes, you could. You have to. They'll have to learn it somehow."

The efficiency of this system depended upon building up a cooperative relationship between cooks and runners. For runners to try to get action by appealing to the boss to put pressure on the cooks is hardly the way to build up such a relationship. It is clear that, considering their low status in relation to the cooks, runners are not in a position to take the lead in smoothing out human-relations difficulties.

Some of the runner's problems arise out of failure to achieve efficient coordination and communication between floors. For example, on one occasion one of the upstairs floors put in a rush order for a pan of rice. With some difficulty, the kitchen runner was able to fill the order. Then, fifteen minutes later, the pan came back to the kitchen again, still almost full, but apparently no more was needed for the meal. The cooks gathered around the elevator to give vent to their feelings. This proved, they said, that the rice had not been needed after all. Those people upstairs just didn't know what they were doing. After the meal was over, the kitchen runner went up to check with the pantry runner. The pantry man explained, "I ran out of creole, and there wasn't going to be any more, so I had no use for any more rice."

This was a perfectly reasonable explanation, but it did not reach the cooks. As a rule, the cooks had little idea of what was going on upstairs. Sometimes there would be an urgent call for some food item along toward the end of the mealtime, and it would be supplied only after a considerable delay. By the time it reached the service pantries, there would no longer be a demand for it, and the supply would shortly be back. This would always upset the cooks. They would then stand around and vow that next time they would not take it seriously when the upstairs people were clamoring for action.

"In the service pantries," one of the cooks said, "they just don't care how much they ask for. That guy, Joe [pantry runner], just hoards the stuff up there. He can't always be out of it like he claims. He just hoards it."

A kitchen runner made this comment:

Joe will order something and right away he'll order it again. He just keeps calling for more. Once or twice I went upstairs, and I saw he had plenty of stuff up there. He just hoards it up there, and he has to send a lot of stuff downstairs. He wastes a lot of stuff. After I caught on to the way he works, I just made it a rule when he called for stuff and the first floor was calling for stuff at the same time, I divided it between them.

On the other hand, when Joe was rushed and found that he was not getting quick action on his orders, his tendency was to make his orders larger, repeat the orders before any supply had come up, and mark all his orders *rush*. When this did not bring results he would call the kitchen on the phone. If all else failed, he would sometimes run down into the kitchen himself to see if he could snatch what he needed.

This kind of behavior built up confusion and resentment in the kitchen. When orders were repeated, the kitchen runners could not tell whether additional supply was needed or whether the pantry runners were just getting impatient. When everything was marked rush, there was no way of telling how badly anybody needed anything. But most serious of all was the reaction when the pantry runner invaded the kitchen.

One of them told us of such an incident:

One of the cooks got mad at me the other day. I went down there to get this item, and boy, did she get mad at me for coming down there. But I got to do *something!* The waitresses and the pantry girls keep on yelling at me to get it for them. Well, I finally got it, or somehow it got sent upstairs. Boy, she was sure mad at me, though.

Apparently the cooks resented the presence of any upstairs supply man in the kitchen, but they were particularly incensed against Joe, the runner they all suspected of hoarding food.

One of them made this comment:

That guy would try to come down in the kitchen and tell us what to do. But not me. No sir. He came down here one day and tried to tell me what to do. He said to me, "We're going to be very busy today." I just looked at him. "Yeah?" I said, "Who are you? Go on upstairs. Go on. Mind your own business." Can you beat that! "We're going to be very busy today!" He never came down and told *me* anything again. "Who are you?" I asked him. That's all I had to say to him.

Here the runner's remark did not have any effect upon the work of the cook, but the implication was that he was in a superior position, and she reacted strongly against him for that reason. None of the cooks enjoy having the kitchen runners originate action for them, but, since it occurs regularly, they make some adjustment to it. They are not accustomed to any sort of relationship with the pantry runners, so when they come down to add to the pressure and confusion of the kitchen, the cooks feel free to slap them down.

It was not only the pantry runners who invaded the kitchen. The pantry supervisors spent a good deal of time and energy running up and down. When an upstairs supervisor comes after supplies, the kitchen reaction is the same as that to the pantry runners—except that the supervisor cannot be slapped down. Instead, the employees gripe to each other.

As one kitchen runner said,

> I wish she would quit that. I wonder what she thinks she's doing, running down here and picking up things we're waiting for. Now like just a minute ago, did you see that? She went off with peaches and plums, and we'd never have known about it if I hadn't seen her. Now couldn't she have just stepped over here and told us? . . . She sure gets mad a lot, doesn't she? She's always griping. I mean, she's probably a nice person, but she's hard to get along with at work—she sure is!

There were other pantry supervisors whose presence in the kitchen did not cause such an disturbance. The workers would say that so-and-so was really all right. Nevertheless, whenever a pantry supervisor dashed into the kitchen for supplies, it was a sign to everybody that something was wrong—that somebody was worried—and thus it added to the tension in the atmosphere and disturbed the human relations of the regular supply system—such as they were.

In this situation, the kitchen runner was the man in the middle. One of the service-pantry girls we interviewed put it this way:

> Oh, we certainly are busy up here. We don't stop even for a moment. I think this is the busiest place around here. It's bad when we can't get those foods, though. We get delayed by those supply people downstairs all the time. I could shoot those runners. We can be just as busy up here—but down there it's always slow motion. It seems like they just don't care at all. They always take all the time in the world.

On the other hand, the cooks blamed the inefficiency of the runners for many of their troubles. They felt that the runners were constantly sending up duplicate orders just through failure to consult each other on the progress of their work. Actually, according to our observation, this happened very rarely, but whenever a runner was caught in the act, this was taken as proof that duplication was common practice. The failure of the runners to coordinate their work efficiently did annoy the cooks in another way, as they were sometimes asked for the same order within a few seconds by two different runners. However, while this added to the nervous tension, it did not directly affect the flow of supplies.

Such were the problems of supply in one restaurant where we were able to give them close attention. However, as it stands, this account is likely to give a false impression. The reader may picture the restaurant as a series of armed camps, each one in constant battle with its neighbor. He may also get the impression that food reaches customers only intermittently and after long delays.

To us it seemed that the restaurant was doing a remarkable job of production and service, and yet, in view of the frictions we observed, it is only natural to ask whether it would not be possible to organize the human relations so as to make for better teamwork and greater efficiency.

According to one point of view, no basic improvement is possible because "you can't change human nature."

But is it all just personalities and personal inefficiency? What has been the situation in other restaurants of this type (operating on several floors) and in other periods of time?

Unfortunately we have no studies for other time periods, but we do have the testimony of several supervisors who have had previous experience in restaurants facing similar problems, and who have shown themselves, in the course of our study, to be shrewd observers of behavior in their own organizations. Their story is that the friction and incoordination we observed were not simply a war-time phenomenon. While increased business and inexperienced help made the problem much more acute, the friction came at the same places in the organization—between the categories of people—that it used to. The job of the kitchen runner, apparently, has always been a "hot spot" in such an organization.

This, then, is not primarily a personality problem. It is a problem in human relations. When the organization operates so as to stimulate conflict between people holding certain positions within it, then we can expect trouble.

19. Rider Tire Acquisition*

In 1972 Rider Tire Company purchased the physical assets of the Collington Tire plant of Trenton, New Jersey. Collington Tire was founded in 1925 by John F. Collington and remained a family-held corporation until the sale. Under pressure from major tire firm pricing policies, Rider president Wilton Collington (John's son) in 1963 had decided to stop producing Collington's diversified tire line and concentrate on military tires. The firm continued to market a line of passenger and light truck tires that were produced by another small firm, under the Collington name.

The company realized unexpectedly substantial profits as the Vietnam War escalated. This, however, created two problems. First, in order to meet their government contract obligations, Collington found it necessary to give in to greater and greater union demands in order to avert a costly strike. Second, the company needed to expand its facilities. Although land was available in the countryside near Trenton, Wilton chose to build three extensions onto the existing plant. The extensions were inefficient, based on present-day

---

*This case was prepared by Theodore T. Herbert, Concordia College. Reprinted with permission of Macmillan Publishing Co., Inc., from *Organizational Behavior Readings and Cases* by Theodore T. Herbert. Copyright © 1976 by Theodore T. Herbert.

manufacturing standards, but Wilton was opposed to borrowing money for a complete plant relocation. He had already borrowed heavily to pay off the inheritance tax on his father's holdings. He also realized the war would not last forever, and the company would soon need to reduce production while making the conversion to new products. As the war began to wind down and contracts diminished, Collington attempted to fill excess capacity by building light truck and passenger tires for the private brands market. Unlike the government market, this was an extremely competitive area. Collington underestimated the cost of new curing and building equipment needed for these tires and the impact of recently imposed government testing requirements. Within a short time, the company was losing money on its passenger tires business, which was no longer offset by cost-plus military contracts.

The company made several attempts at merger and finally outright sale. One look at the worn-out facilities convinced most of the major companies to stay away. Rider's offer to buy the physical assets was Collington's last resort.

The Rider Tire Company

The Rider Tire Company was also a privately held company, about the same size as Collington. It was a primary producer of specialty tires used on everything from lawn mowers to dune buggies. Located in Cadillac, a small town in northwest Michigan, Rider obtained its employees from the local population. The company was respected in the industry for its ability to compete successfully with the corporate giants of the rubber industry. Rider had been planning an expansion of its facilities for over two years, because a full 40 percent of company sales was being produced at other firms' factories, subcontracted for marketing under the Rider name. These sales produced only 3 percent return on investment, whereas the company could realize a 12 percent return if they had the facilities to produce the tires themselves. Suitable expansion sites were being investigated in North Carolina, where labor and land rates were attractive. Expansion plans and the firm's success were largely attributed to the abilities of one man, Garland Pierce.

Garland Pierce

Garland Pierce, age forty-seven, was married and had a son and daughter. He was taller than average, and quite thin. His blue-gray eyes tended to look through rather than at people and were in contrast to his boyish features. He had been brought up in Cincinnati and had earned a business degree while residing at home. He was an average student, being generally not interested in courses he did not consider relevant. He was active in campus politics but declined the nomination for class president. His reasoning was that he wanted to devote his efforts to becoming first-string center on the basketball team, a goal he never attained.

After college, Pierce began working as an industrial engineer in the Thomlinson Corporation furniture factory in southern Michigan where he was recognized as a "comer." Within two years he was production manager of the firm; within eight years he had been made vice-president of manufacturing. Pierce developed a reputation as an unrelenting taskmaster at Thomlinson. His outspoken manner and abrupt rejection of poorly conceived ideas made him both respected and feared. Managers who reported to him learned quickly that they were expected to share Pierce's management philosophy as well as his unrelenting drive for success in all undertakings.

Pierce was with Thomlinson for ten years when he met Dave Sumner, the president of Rider. Sumner recognized Pierce's abilities and in 1965 persuaded him to join Rider as vice-president of manufacturing at a considerably higher salary than he had been earning at Thomlinson.

Larry Rider

During the five-year period prior to Pierce's starting with Rider, profits had declined steadily to the point that the company was just breaking even. Its principal stockholder and chairman of the board, Larry Rider (the founder's son), began taking an active interest in the company late in 1966. After lengthy discussion with top management, he was moved to action. A complete reorganization was begun in which several top management people were fired, including Dave Sumner. Larry Rider took over the company presidency in addition to his duties as chairman of the board. Garland Pierce was made senior vice-president of manufacturing. In 1968 Pierce was elected as a member of the board.

The Acquisition

Over the next three years, Pierce distinguished himself as one of the leading union negotiators in the tire industry. Within the Rider Company, Pierce was considered an adept planner; his authority at Rider was rarely questioned by anyone, including Larry Rider. Rider was content to handle corporate public relations with dealers and the media, and let Pierce run manufacturing.

One morning in January 1972, Pierce received a call from Wilton Collington. Collington had contacted Pierce six months earlier with a merger offer, but Pierce had turned him down. Now with the last of Collington's other merger possibilities gone, Collington suggested a sale of the company. Pierce declined, but offered instead to buy only Collington's physical assets. Collington had anticipated Pierce's offer and had decided to accept the proposal as a last resort. That afternoon, Pierce sent his plant engineer and production manager to Trenton to look over the facilities and equipment.

Within two months Pierce had received the board's approval, and the sale was completed. Rider bought the land, buildings, and equipment for less than the equipment alone would cost on the used equipment market.

On the first Monday in April 1972, Collington workers arrived to find the gates closed and locked. Workers were told by Collington top management stationed at the gate that their personal effects, severance pay, and pensions would be sent to them at their homes.

At the next board meeting, Pierce made a presentation outlining a contingency plan for the Trenton plant. He believed the plant could be reopened on a profitable basis if a new union contract could be negotiated that would substantially cut the salaries and benefits formerly paid by Collington. Pierce reasoned that negotiations for land in North Carolina would not be completed for another month and a new building could not be erected before the beginning of 1973. The new plant would cost five times the amount paid for the Collington acquisition. Pierce concluded by saying:

> I don't intend for this to be a permanent solution. The plant is inefficient and operated at high cost. Its only advantage is that we can go into production within two months and be that much further ahead. In three years, when the next contract comes up, we can be ready to move out if the union shows signs of making outrageous demands.

As expected, the board (which was comprised of a majority of Rider executives) gave its approval, contingent on the negotiation of a new union contract.

Reorganization

The union was less than happy with Rider's proposal, but Collington had been the largest rubber company in the Trenton area, and its closing severely reduced the union's membership. The union was impressed by Pierce's open style and obvious abilities. It even agreed to allow Rider to rehire only the Collington employees Rider was certain had not been troublemakers. The union, however, issued a final warning:

> These wages may be acceptable in upper Michigan, but are below standard in Trenton. You may find it difficult to get any of the old-timers to return, or hire new workers for that matter.

Pierce had hired John MacDonald as his special assistant three months before the acquisition. MacDonald had been the plant manager in a small tire firm in central Michigan. Pierce approached MacDonald with the idea of making him plant manager when the North Carolina deal was completed. MacDonald had readily agreed. He had been brought up in Georgia, and jumped at the opportunity of returning to the South.

John, age thirty-five, had an engineering degree from Georgia Tech, and had been a standout on its football team. He had begun work at a major tire company in Akron and had advanced to production manager at the company's Iowa plant before accepting the position in central Michigan. In previous management positions, John was well liked by his subordinates for his easygoing manner and openness with all people. MacDonald encouraged worker participation in making decisions that affected them. To familiarize himself with the concerns of his workers, he often joined them for informal discussions during coffee breaks. John attended church regularly, and was devoted to his wife and two boys. He took the boys to sports events and played with them at every opportunity.

He was less happy about moving to Trenton, but reasoned the situation might be temporary. In any event he was determined to try his best.

The remainder of the Trenton staff was not as easily hired. Without adequate additional production, supervisory, and technical staff at Cadillac to staff the

Trenton plant, the decision was made to hire back all the Collington technical staff still available, and some of their production supervisors. Pierce wanted to make sure the plant was started properly with Rider's philosophy and proven record of success. Most of the individuals at Cadillac who had the necessary experience rejected the offer when approached for transfer. As a trade-off, Pierce decided to transfer younger staff members who were considered competent in their fields, but had no previous management responsibilities. Pierce reasoned that their aggressiveness would compensate for their lack of experience. Those who were transferred from Cadillac received a 20 percent salary increase. Pierce also believed that these new managers could get all the help they would need from the experienced people remaining in Cadillac. (A list of the important Trenton personnel in major management positions is given in Table 1. The new plant organizational structure is shown in Figure 1.)

Rider had maintained a policy of testing both white- and blue-collar workers before hiring. The blue-collar workers were required to take standardized tests that gave an indication of mechanical aptitude and personality profile. In addition to personality profile, secretaries and clerical employees were given spelling and basic mathematical ability tests. These were generally conducted in the office, and acceptance was based upon a minimum test requirement that the company had correlated with job performance. White-collar workers above the technician level were sent to East Lansing, where they were tested for one or two days by a private testing institute. The results of the test and the psychologists' recommendations went into the employee's personnel file for future reference.

Plant Operation

Trouble began the second week after start-up when several of the rehired Collington workers walked off the job to protest work conditions. MacDonald notified Pierce, who in turn instructed MacDonald to fire the violators and not let them in the plant. He then notified the union of his actions. The union complied with Pierce's decision.

TABLE **1**

	Age	Position	Background
Jim Hunter	31	Technical Manager	Had been with Rider for three years as a tire engineer. Prior to that had five years' experience with an Akron tire firm.
Bill Wagner	32	Plant Engineer	Had been with Rider six years as a maintenance foreman. Two years of college.
Mike Smiley	37	Personnel Manager	Hired directly to the Trenton plant from a carbon black firm where he had been assistant to the personnel manager.
Dick Shiner	29	Production Manager	Had been with Collington for eleven years, most recently as building room foreman. No college.
Gene Wiley	55	Automotive Sales Manager	Had been with Collington for twenty-six years, most recently as vice-president of sales.
Brian Yamokoski	28	Industrial Engineer	Had been with Rider three years as an industrial engineer.

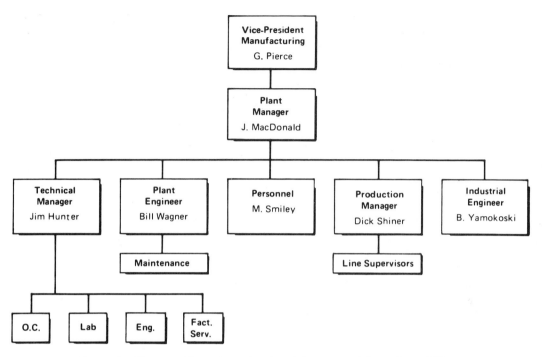

FIGURE 1. Trenton Plant Organizational Structure (Note: Gene Wiley, Sales Manager, Moved to Cadillac.)

Finding new workers to fill these vacancies and the remaining available positions was difficult. The low wages generally attracted only minority groups from the central city; 90 percent were unable to pass the written or medical tests given. Of the applicants remaining, only one-half showed up for work. One in five hirees continued to return to work after his first six weeks on the job. When contacted by Mike Smiley, former employees generally stated they quit because the pay was too low. All new employees were put on trial for their first ninety days on the job. Workers who failed to meet production quotas by this time could be fired or moved to a new position at the company's discretion. In the latter case, the transferred employee would begin a new ninety-day trial period.

The plant was not designed to enable a marginally adequate workforce to maintain three shifts for five months after plant start-up; production workers were therefore asked to work double shifts to make up for lost time. By that time many of the old Collington employees had found higher-paying jobs and had left. In many cases inexperienced workers were left to train the newly hired employees. The production defect rate ran as high as 10 percent of production totals.

The Maintenance Department was the most difficult group to staff. Qualified mechanics and electricians were being paid 20 percent more in other industries within Trenton. But Pierce believed the company could not meet this demand without causing production workers to demand higher wages too. In addition, it would create too large a differential between the two Rider plants.

Breakdowns became a daily fact of life. After repeated calls to the beleaguered plant engineer, frustrated supervisors told production workers to go back to work if the machine would still run or shift to another task. The breakdowns and constant shifts to new jobs extended the learning period for the workers and reduced their individual productivities, monitored daily by Brian Yamokoski.

MacDonald and Pierce talked daily by telephone. MacDonald kept Pierce informed of equipment breakdowns, production achievements, and productivity of new workers. It was generally agreed that the start-up was taking much longer than planned, but that there were extenuating circumstances that hadn't been considered.

In early November 1972, after the close of the fiscal year, the profit-loss statement showed that the Trenton plant had dragged profit down further than management's worst expectations. Pierce disliked giving excuses as much as he disliked accepting them. He was determined that the plant would begin producing near its break-even point within the next two quarters. Up to this time, Pierce had rejected a sales request to start up a line of passenger tires at Trenton. Sales had received several calls within the past two months from a large discount house eager for tires. These tires could be produced on the old Collington equipment and cured in molds owned by the discount house. Pierce considered this and reasoned that if the specialty tire production remained constant and the passenger line started, the plant would break even. He gave in to pressure from the Sales Department.

As task force of Cadillac personnel was organized. It was charged with getting the new product line into production while holding present production constant. The task force was composed of the Cadillac plant engineer, technical manager, production manager, a production scheduler six maintenance men, and one foreman from each department to aid in training. The group stayed one month at the plant. Time spent at Trenton was considered "banishment," so each member of the task force was flown home on weekends to alleviate this feeling. The task force succeeded in starting up the passenger tire line and actually increased production of the four specialty lines by 10 percent. Although everyone at Trenton recognized the task force's contributions, few were sorry to see the group return to Michigan. One production foreman summarized the general feeling:

> They descended on us like a conquering army and treated us like a bunch of incompetents.

By February production had declined 15 percent from the previous high, and the first shipment had yet to be made to the discount house. Workers and supervisors were asked to work on Saturdays and then on Sundays. Unfortunately this increased absenteeism on straight-time days by as much as 10 percent.

John MacDonald's daily conversation with Pierce became more argumentative. MacDonald had presented a program to Pierce that would expand the production workforce above the minimum level needed. The program would expand the production and maintenance staff to compensate for the number of people in training. In addition he proposed hiring qualified supervisors from other rubber companies. Rider would need to pay them accordingly. He also believed the workers should participate in more decisions, and their opinions should be solicited. Pierce disagreed. First, there was no money available to hire excess workers or experienced supervisors; personnel would have to come out of either the Cadillac or Trenton organizations. Pierce lectured MacDonald:

> John, there are only three things to managing people: tell them what they have to do, be certain they know how to do it, and follow up to see that it's done. Participative management is sharing your responsibility with the worker. Once introduced, you'll never be able to make a decision without its being questioned.

By early April results of the second quarter showed the company had lost more ground. There were several environmental factors which made the loss appear worse than could be attributed solely to production. The prime rate, fuel costs, and raw materials costs had all increased, while the company's tire prices were held in the price freeze. Nevertheless, it was apparent no real improvements had been made in Trenton.

The attitude toward Pierce by both the board and the banks began to be strained. Pierce took decisive action. On April 8 Pierce arrived in Trenton and called the department heads together.

> I am sorry to announce that I have terminated John MacDonald. John has tried hard here, but we keep losing money. I think John was misplaced. He'd make a good plant manager at a settled plant. But this plant calls for innovation and a firm hand, and John doesn't have either.
> I'm not going to name a successor immediately. I'll be staying at the plant for three or four days a week, however, so you'll be answering directly to me.

The more time Pierce spent in the Trenton plant, the more he realized that a great deal of time was being wasted as a result of poor scheduling of priorities on the part of the department heads. He believed their youth and lack of experience was to blame. This, he believed, could be overcome if the managers were provided with proper training in the use of planning devices such as Gantt Charts. He therefore worked with each manager for a full week during which time he outlined the use of managerial devices and helped the manager set up his priorities. These "blitzes," as they came to be known among the department heads, were unpopular. Pierce's presence was difficult to deal with and his visits to their offices for hours on end disrupted their work. Each manager had become accustomed to spending at least twelve hours per day at the plant, and usually worked all of Saturday and part of Sunday. They felt that the meetings with Pierce undermined their status with their subordinates; the presence of Pierce in a manager's office became a sign to others that the manager was "in training."

Within two months, Dick Shiner was promoted from production manager to plant manager. The promotion came as a surprise to the production workers and office staff alike. One production foreman remarked:

> He never made a good foreman under Collington and he's been a pretty poor production manager here. I wonder why Pierce thinks he'll be a good plant manager? I gave Pierce more credit than that.

Nonetheless, Pierce had been impressed with Shiner's aggressiveness, neatness, and efficiency. Although Shiner spent more time at the plant than anyone else, the staff saw him as largely uneducated, unintelligent, and incompetent. He was generally distrusted by the production foremen because, as production manager, he had skillfully passed blame for low production onto them. Production workers generally disliked his inconsistent behavior toward people and his failure to admit that he did not understand the production process. Shiner soon developed a reputation for emulating Pierce. As Jim Hunter told Brian Yamokoski:

> You can tell when Pierce has been talking to Shiner. Afterwards, Shiner will call you in, and he'll look, act, and sound just like Pierce. Unfortunately, no brains; it's a recording!

Weekly staff meetings were instituted by Pierce through a memo issued by Shiner. The staff considered this more efficient than MacDonald's method of meeting with each department head separately. But the meetings as conducted by Shiner consisted of making weekly assignments and warning the staff:

> You people have to get this plant moving. We can't afford any more losses.

In early June the discount house canceled the remainder of its order. They had not been satisfied with Rider's shipments. In looking for another supplier the discounter had been offered a complete line of new concept radial tires which would be made in the supplier's molds.

The Trenton plant by this time was producing six lines of specialty tires in a full range of sizes. Pierce decided to replace the discounter's passenger line with two more lines of specialty tires and to introduce a new line of farm service tires. Jim Hunter was less than pleased, and approached Dick Shiner:

Jim: In a little over one year, we have had to develop forty-two different tires for production here. These new specialty tires will add twelve more. The farm tires are something else. There isn't a person in this company who has ever seen a farm tire produced. We've got our hands full just trying to take care of problems caused by poor equipment and poorly trained workers. The farm tires are altogether different; who's going to train the people needed for this new line? I just can't see the reasoning behind this.

Dick: The farm tires are high profit. We can't afford not to produce them. If you need help, call Cadillac.

Jim: I've tried that and I've been put off. Cadillac doesn't know our equipment!

Dick: We'll manage. Just see that *you* do.

Under Pierce's guidance, the specialty lines were in production by September. Development problems delayed the farm service line until mid-October.

The fiscal 1973 figures published in November indicated an overall loss for the company of $500,000. In an emergency session of the Board of Directors, Larry Rider outlined his plans:

> The banks have called for a review of our Trenton plant. In accordance with their wishes, I have hired a consultant to review the operation to see if it can be made profitable. I believe it would be beneficial if I personally spent a good deal of time viewing the problems firsthand.

For the next three weeks, Rider talked with Trenton production personnel getting opinions and viewing the operation. At the end of the visit, he had a number of ideas which he talked over with Pierce. Pierce agreed to all but one, to which he objected strongly. Rider thought the farm tire program should be abolished and emphasis placed on producing passenger tires. Pierce objected. He had been relieved when the discounter had canceled his order. Pierce felt the passenger tires had caused a high loss in scrap and were to difficult to produce. He stated:

> We don't have the caliber of people or equipment at Trenton to produce those tires. I can't see us getting back into them.

20. Dowling Flexible Metals*

Background

In 1960, Bill Dowling, a "machine-tool set-up-man" for a large auto firm, became so frustrated with his job that he quit to form his own business. The manufacturing operation consisted of a few general purpose metal working machines that were set up in Dowling's garage. Space was such a constraint that it controlled the work process. For example, if the cutting press was to be used with long stock, the milling machines would have to be pushed back against the wall and remain idle. Production always increased on rain-free, summer days since the garage doors could be opened and a couple of machines moved out onto the drive. Besides Dowling, who acted as salesman, accountant, engineer, president, manufacturing representative, and working foreman, members of the original organization were Eve Sullivan, who began as a part-time secretary and payroll clerk; and Wally Denton, who left the auto firm with Bill. The workforce was composed of part-time "moonlighters," full-time machinists for other firms, who were attracted by the job autonomy which provided experience in setting up jobs and job processes, where a high degree of ingenuity was required.

The first years were touch and go with profits being erratic. Gradually the firm began to gain a reputation for being ingenious at solving unique problems and for producing a quality product on, or before, deadlines. The "product" consisted of fabricating dies for making minor component metal parts for automobiles and a specified quantity of the parts. Having realized that the firm was too dependent on the auto industry and that sudden fluctuations in auto sales could have a drastic effect on the firm's survival, Dowling began marketing their services toward manufacturing firms not connected with the auto industry. Bids were submitted

*This case was prepared by Floyd G. Willoughby, Oakland University, Rochester, Mi. © 1980 by Floyd G. Willoughby. Reprinted by permission.

for work that involved legs for vending machines, metal trim for large appliances, clamps and latches for metal windows, and display racks for small power hand tools.

As Dowling Flexible Metals became more diversified, the need for expansion forced the company to borrow building funds from the local bank, which enabled construction of a small factory on the edge of town. As new markets and products created a need for increasingly more versatile equipment and a larger workforce, the plant has since expanded twice until it is now three times its original size.

In 1980, Dowling Flexible Metals hardly resembles the garage operation of the formative years. The firm now employs approximately thirty full-time journeymen and apprentice machinists, a staff of four engineers that were hired about three years ago, and a full-time office secretary subordinate to Eve Sullivan, the Office Manager. Their rapid growth has created problems that in 1980 have not been resolved. Bill Dowling, realizing his firm is suffering from growing pains, has asked you to "take a look at the operation and make recommendations as to how things could be run better." You begin the consulting project by interviewing Dowling, other key people in the firm, and workers out in the shop who seem willing to express their opinion about the firm.

Bill Dowling, Owner-President

"We sure have come a long way from that first set-up in my garage. On a nice day we would get everything all spread out in the drive and then it would start pouring cats and dogs—so we would have to move back inside. It was just like a one-ring circus. Now it seems like a three-ring circus. You would think that with all that talent we have here and all the experience, things would run smoother. Instead, it seems I am putting in more time than ever and accomplishing a whole lot less in a day's time.

"It's not like the old days. Everything has gotten so complicated and precise in design. When you go to a customer to discuss a job you have to talk to six kids right out of engineering school. Every one of them has a calculator—they don't even carry slide rules anymore—and all they can talk is fancy formulas and how we should do our job. It just seems I spend more time with customers and less time around the shop than I used to. That's why I hired the engineering staff—to interpret specifications, solve engineering problems, and draw blueprints. It still seems all the problems are solved out on the shop floor by guys like Walt and Tom, just like always. Gene and the other engineers are necessary, but they don't seem to be working as smoothly with the guys on the floor as they should.

"One of the things I would like to see us do in the future is to diversify even more. Now that we have the capability, I am starting to bid jobs that require the computerized milling machine process tape. This involves devising a work process for milling a part on a machine and then making a computer process tape of it. We can then sell copies of the tape just like we do dies and parts. These tapes allow less skilled operators to operate complicated milling machines without the long apprenticeship of a tradesman. All they have to do is press buttons and follow the machine's instructions for changing the milling tools. Demand is increasing for the computerized process tapes.

"I would like to see the firm get into things like working with combinations of bonded materials such as plastics, fiberglass, and metals. I am also starting to bid jobs involving the machining of plastics and other materials beside metals."

Wally Denton, Shop Foreman, First Shift

"Life just doesn't seem to be as simple as when we first started in Bill's garage. In those days he would bring a job back and we would all gather 'round and decide how we were going to set it up and who would do it. If one of the 'moonlighters' was to get the job either Bill or I would lay the job out for him when he came in that afternoon. Now, the customers' ideas get processed through the engineers and we, out here in the shop, have to guess just exactly what the customer had in mind.

"What some people around here don't understand is that I am a partner in this business. I've stayed out here in the shop because this is where I like it and it's where I feel most useful. When Bill isn't here, I'm always around to put out fires. Between Eve, Gene, and myself we usually make the right decision.

"With all this diversification and Bill spending a lot of time with customers, I think we need to get somebody else out there to share the load."

Thomas McNull, Shop Foreman, Second Shift

"In general, I agree with Wally that things aren't as simple as they used to be, but I think, given the amount of jobs we are handling at any one time, we run the shop pretty smoothly. When the guys bring problems to me that require major job changes, I get Wally's approval before making the changes. We haven't any difficulty in that area.

"Where we run into problems is with the engineers. They get the job when Bill brings it back. They decide how the part should be made and by what process, which in turn pretty much restricts what type of dies we have to make. Therein lies the bind. Oftentimes we run into a snag following the engineers' instructions. If it's after five o'clock, the engineers have left for the day. We, on the second shift, either have to let the job sit until the next morning or solve the problem ourselves. This not only creates bad feelings between the shop personnel and the engineers, but it makes extra work for the engineers because they have to draw up new plans.

"I often think we have the whole process backwards around here. What we should be doing is giving the job to the journeymen—after all, these guys have a lot of experience and know-how—then give the finished product to the engineers to draw up. I'll give you an example. Last year we got a job from a vending machine manufacturer. The job consisted of fabricating five sets of dies for making those stubby little legs for vending machines, plus five hundred of the finished legs. Well, the engineers figured the job all out, drew up the plans, and sent it out to us. We made the first die to specs, but when we tried to punch out the leg on the press, the metal tore. We took the problem back to the engineers, and after the preliminary accusations of who was responsible for the screw up, they changed the raw material specifications. We waited two weeks for delivery of the new steel, then tried again. The metal still tore. Finally, after two months of hassle, Charlie Oakes and I worked on the die for two days and finally came up with a solution. The problem was that the shoulders of the die were too steep for forming the leg in just one punch. We had to use two punches (see Exhibit 1). The problem was the production process, not the raw materials. We spent four months on that job and ran over our deadline. Things like that shouldn't happen."

Charlie Oakes, Journeyman Apprentice

"Really, I hate to say anything against this place because it is a pretty good place to work. The pay and benefits are pretty good and because it is a small shop our hours can be somewhat flexible. If you have a doctor's appointment you can either come in late or stay until you get you time in or punch out and come back. You can work as much overtime as you want to.

"The thing I'm kind of disappointed about is that I thought the work would be more challenging. I'm just an apprentice, but I've only got a year to go in my program before I can get my journeyman's card, and I think I should be handling more jobs on my own. That's why I came to work here. My Dad was one of the original 'moonlighters' here. He told me about how interesting it was when he was here. I guess I just expected the same thing."

Gene Jenkins, Chief Engineer

"I imagine the guys out in the shop already have told you about 'The Great Vending Machine Fiasco.' They'll never let us forget that. However, it does point out the need for better coordination around here. The engineers were hired as engineers, not as draftsmen, which is just about all we do. I'm not saying we should have the final say on how the job is designed, because there is a lot of practical experience out in that shop; but just as we haven't their expertise neither do they have ours. There is a need for both, the technical skill of the engineers and the practical experience of the shop.

"One thing that would really help is more information from Bill. I realize Bill is spread pretty thin but there are a lot of times he comes back with a job, briefs us, and we still have to call the customer about details because Bill hasn't been specific enough or asked the right questions of the customer. Engineers communicate best with other engineers. Having an engineering function gives us a competitive advantage over our competition. In may opinion, operating as we do now, we are not maximizing that advantage.

"When the plans leave here we have no idea what happens to those plans once they are out in the shop. The next thing we know, we get a die or set of dies back that doesn't even resemble the plans we sent out in the shop. We then have to draw up new plans to fit the dies. Believe me, it is not only discouraging, but it really makes you wonder what your job is around here. It's embarrassing when a customer calls to check on the status of a job and I have to run out in the shop, look up the guy handling the job, and get his best estimate of how the job is going."

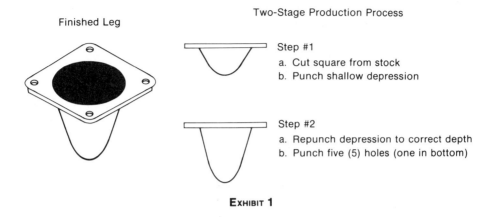

EXHIBIT 1

Eve Sullivan, Office Manager

"One thing is for sure, life is far from dull around here. It seems Bill is either dragging in a bunch of plans or racing off with the truck to deliver a job to a customer.

"Really, Wally and I make all the day-to-day decisions around here. Of course, I don't get involved in technical matters; Wally and Gene take care of those, but if we are short-handed or need a new machine, Wally and I start the ball rolling by getting together the necessary information and talking to Bill the first chance we get. I guess you could say that we run things around here by consensus most of the time. If I get a call from a customer asking about the status of a job, I refer the call to Gene because Wally is usually out in the shop.

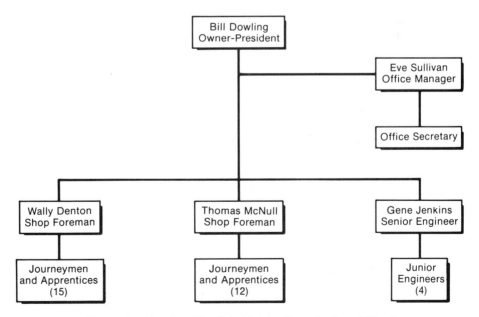

EXHIBIT 2. Dowling Flexible Metals Organizational Chart

"I started with Bill and Wally twenty years ago, on a part-time basis, and somehow the excitement has turned into work. Joan, the office secretary, and I handle all correspondence, bookkeeping, payroll, insurance forms, and everything else besides run the office. It's just getting to be too hectic—I just wish the job was more fun, the way it used to be."

Having listened to all concerned, you returned to Bill's office only to find him gone. You tell Eve and Wally that you will return within one week with your recommendations.

21. Sunday At Al Tech *

Saturday, August 14, 1982, 9 P.M.

George Hayes, Assistant to the President at Star Manufacturing, Inc., was sitting in his motel room in a small city near Chicago with his feet propped up on the bed recalling the events which had prompted his being there. On Thursday, only two days earlier, he had attended a meeting of the top managers at the Star corporate headquarters on the east coast. The day's agenda centered on his analysis of the recent performance of the company's various divisions. One in particular, Al Tech, was receiving an unusual amount of attention that day.

George had the numbers on the table next to him. Sales, net income, and return on investment (ROI) for Al Tech were down from the previous year and below budgeted performance levels. The results were somewhat understandable given the unexpected severity of the current economic downturn and Al Tech's sensitivities to such conditions. Just when George had felt the meeting was about to adjourn, the president asked him for more details concerning Al Tech's new expansion and equipment acquisition plans. George knew those numbers all too well. He had reviewed them prior to Star's approval of the project. He had even been sent to the equipment manufacturer for a first-hand look at the technology and accompanying manpower and facilities requirements. George recalled that this had been the trip which had caused him to miss the tenth birthday of his twin daughters.

The meeting had continued with George reporting that the building addition at Al Tech was nearing completion and the equipment was scheduled for installation during the month of October. The management group then had

*Lynda L. Goulet and Peter G. Goulet, Instructor and Associate Professor, respectively, University of Northern Iowa. Reprinted by permission. Copyright © 1983, 1984. All rights reserved. This case describes a hypothetical company based on a composite of several actual experiences in a similar industrial setting.

briefly discussed Al Tech's forecast for the year beginning in January 1983, the first full year the new equipment would be operational. Several forecasts had been prepared, each based on different assumptions concerning the utilization of the new technology. The most pessimistic forecast—utilizing less than 50 percent of the new capacity and having no new product lines—still resulted in overall profit performance for the division which was better than that from 1981 or from the current year's adjusted projections.

George had also reported that if the most optimistic forecast were attained, Al Tech would become one of the corporation's most profitable divisions. Though marketing new product lines would require development time and the acquisition of experience with the new technology, it was still plausible to expect some sales of new products by the end of the upcoming year.

George's mind wandered. Al Tech had been his pet project for the last four years. He had first heard of the company while attending his ten year college reunion in Illinois over four years ago. George's former fiancee, Julie, who had broken their engagement to marry Ben Brown, introduced him to her husband at the reunion. Ben had just been promoted to Personnel Manager at Al Tech. George recalled, however, that Ben wasn't certain how long he would be able to retain that position as the Carter family, who owned the firm, wished to sell it to settle an estate. Only the Vice-President of Sales, Stuart Carter, was a family member. The President, Russell Wainscott, had been hired several years earlier when the founder of the company retired. Following the founder's death, everyone in the family except Stuart wanted the firm to be sold, for cash rather than for stock in another firm. George remembered the many hours of work and travel time he had invested analyzing this potential acquisition for Star Manufacturing. The work had all come to fruition in late 1978 when Star purchased Al Tech from the Carter family estate.

A door to a nearby room slammed shut. George was jarred back to thoughts of the last few minutes of last Thursday's meeting at Star. At long last Star's President made it clear why Al Tech had been the focus of attention. Russell Wainscott, who had been retained as the General Manager at Al Tech after the acquisition, had been severely injured in a car accident and would be hospitalized for an unknown, though substantial, period of time. George was to assume responsibility for the division as its Acting General Manager until Wainscott was able to assume his duties again.

George slipped into bed early, knowing Sunday would be a very long day. He had made arrangements to spend the day at Al Tech, alone, preparing for his first week as GM. Before going to sleep he felt both apprehension and excitement. Finally he would have the opportunity to get the line management experience he needed to advance his career. However, with line responsibility, especially under these circumstances, comes high visibility. George nervously drifted off to sleep.

Sunday, August 15, 8 A.M.

The keys to the Al Tech office building and the GM's office were in the box at the motel desk when George went to breakfast. A note from Wainscott's secretary, Barbara Curtis, was in a manila envelope with the keys. It read:

Mr. Hayes:

As you requested in your Friday telephone call, all the managers prepared memos relating any problems under their responsibility which must be resolved in the near future. Five of the memos are in envelopes on Rusty's [Wainscott] desk. Richard Simcox told me he would slip his memo under the office door as he wasn't able to complete it before I left Friday. In addition, I prepared a summary of Rusty's agenda for next week with some explanations of any meetings to the best of my knowledge. Finally there is a stack of mail on the desk. Some of it is left over from before the accident and some arrived since then. I hope this is satisfactory. I'm looking forward to working for you in Rusty's absence and will arrive early Monday morning to help you begin your first week.

(Signed) Barb Curtis

Sunday, August 15, 9 A.M.

When George arrived at the office he found the following items awaiting his attention:

Memos from managers (Exhibits 1–6)
Agenda for the week of the sixteenth (Exhibit 7)
Correspondence (Exhibits 8–17)

Before he began working George scribbled on a piece of paper and added that to the pile on top of his desk (see Exhibit 18).

Place yourself in George Hayes' position. Plan your activities for the week of August 16. What meetings must be held? When? With whom? What decisions must be made? When? Which decisions can be delegated? To whom? A note on Al Tech appears below to provide you with additional background. An organizational chart is also provided as Figure 1.

A Note on Al Tech

Al Tech is a vertically integrated firm which converts aluminum billets (cylindrical ingots of aluminum) into aluminum extrusions which are then converted into finished products. Aluminum extrusions are produced by hydraulic presses which force billets heated to just below the melting point through profile dies of hardened steel. The hot extrusions run out onto long tables for cooling. These extrusions are cut to length, heat treated, and machined through various operations, typically in punch or brake presses, to produce the constituent parts for numerous products. Al Tech makes extrusions for its own lines of windows, storm sash, patio doors, screens, and extension ladders.

The major suppliers for Al Tech are companies which provide the aluminum billets, flat glass, and screen cloth. Al Tech's customers include nearly 500 firms, though their major source of revenue derives from about twenty manufacturers of recreational vehicles (RVs) and manufactured housing (MH) and two chains of discount retailers who purchase the ladders for sale under private labels.

The major investment to which Al Tech recently committed itself is a series of machines which electrostatically paint extrusions. The equipment requires a facility with a forty-foot ceiling as the extrusions are painted while suspended vertically. Al Tech's new installation will allow it to paint extrusion lengths among the longest that can be painted in any U.S. facility. Aluminum is very difficult to paint successfully because the paint doesn't adhere to the surface easily. Though painted aluminum also scratches easily, it must still be painted before machining to achieve necessary economies.

There is a great deal of demand for painted aluminum products because painting both colors the surface and prevents the unsightly oxidation of the bare metal characteristic of aluminum. Anodizing also accomplishes these purposes and produces a harder, more durable finish than that achieved with painting. However, the cost of anodizing is so high as to be prohibitive for almost all uses but curtain walls for high-rise office buildings and high-valued decorative products. Painting also offers a greater variety of colors and finish textures than anodizing.

Al Tech built its paint facility for internal use. However, with this facility and its extrusion operation, it felt it could develop demand for high-margin custom-extruded, custom-painted parts for current as well as new markets.

From: Ben Brown
To: George Hayes
Date: August 13, 1982

George:

Looking forward to working with you for a while—too bad it had to be under these circumstances. Barb passed your message along and I guess there are several issues we need to discuss pretty soon.

1. Sam Howarth, one of our designers, has been suspected of the "appropriation" of minor amounts of company materials for a long time. Two weeks ago, Dick Simcox inadvertently caught him piling some obsolete screens into his car. These screens probably would have been sold for scrap. Dick, Rusty, and I decided to let him take some vacation time until we decided what to do about it. We'd have fired him on the spot but the truth is he is a good designer and our designers are underpaid and turnover is terrible. Howarth has been with the firm for over fifteen years and is responsible for a couple of innovations that have been really profitable. His vacation time will run out at the end of the week so some decision must be reached by the 20th.

2. The new paint process equipment is scheduled for delivery and installation during October. I have placed an ad for a supervisor in that department and I have an application in hand for a good man. He used to supervise a line that painted cabinets for TV sets. The problem is that one of our assembly supervisors wants the job. Dick tried to convince her to stay in assembly but she's being a hard-nose about it. She is not qualified for this job from the standpoint of having run a paint room. She probably could be trained eventually but we don't know how good a job she would ever do. It will also delay us for a long time if we go this route. As I see it all she really wants is the money or the prestige associated with the new position. What she doesn't understand, or won't accept, is that the higher wages for the paint room job reflect the level of skill required. She says she'll cause some trouble if she doesn't get the job this week but none of us knows what she means by "trouble." The final kicker is that this is our only female manager at any level.

3. You probably aren't aware of this, but every year Al Tech has a company party for its employees and their spouses. I have been in charge of the arrangements for the last few years. It's next Saturday at the local Elks club. Some of the people around the office have wondered if it wouldn't be wise to postpone it because of Rusty's accident. My feeling is that it's a bit late to cancel. Besides, it'll be months before Rusty can get back on his feet again. The Carter family started the tradition fifteen years ago and Stuart hates to see it abandoned. Al White thinks it's an awful waste of money but Dick says it's a real morale booster for his workers. I need to know about this no later than Monday afternoon.

4. One final thing, and this is a real winner. Somewhere in Rusty's pile of stuff there should be a copy of a letter from our receptionist. I'll just let you read it for the pure joy of the moment. When you have gotten off the floor let me know and we'll talk about it. By the way, she officially works for me.

EXHIBIT 1

From: Aaron McClosky
To: George Hayes
Date: August 13, 1982

Welcome aboard.

The fellows in engineering have been busy working up some new designs to expand our product lines. Stu Carter, Dick Simcox, and I have been going around for months trying to decide what to do with the extra capacity of the new paint line. We're all in agreement that the window and door lines will go on first. I guess you've got the figures on this, too. There is a lot of demand for white and brown frames on both the RV and MH window lines and the margins are a good deal better than for the unpainted units. However, I believe we'd better develop some new products quickly if we want to get above the low capacity utilization our current products will provide. Dick thinks there's no real problem here because he feels we can land a lot of contract painting jobs. As far as I know Stu hasn't even tried to check out that possibility.

I'm having one of the designers collect some of our more promising designs. She should have them ready for you by Monday. We've been working on the designs for a line of picture frames, some designer curtain rods, and a dynamite set of shower doors. For the last several years there has been talk around the sales office of redesigning our lines for the retail market but we never seem to get anywhere on this. Just when the designers get excited about a new product design, it seems like Stu comes up with a variation on our windows that the mobile home guys just "have to have." By the time that's taken care of the new products get lost in the shuffle. I sure hope that doesn't happen with the paint line ideas.

We really ought to move on this business so my department can develop prototypes by yearend. After that it'll take at least six months to work out the bugs, let the dies, and get into production.

EXHIBIT 2

From: Albert White
To: George Hayes
Date: 8/13/82

Mr. Hayes:

Having just recently corresponded with you at headquarters concerning the latest quarterly report, I am certain you are well aware of our current position. This week I have been reviewing the updated estimates for the fourth quarter. In doing so I have been reminded of a potential problem to which you should be alerted. The details are attached but I have summarized the situation below. [Attachment not shown.]

On July 28, Stuart Carter got an order for 10,000 window units with storms and screens, and 1000 patio doors. [Attachment shows this order to be worth just under $300,000.] The customer, a new one for us, is a large condominium developer with units in five states. The order was to be delivered by November 5. Normally an order of this size would be greatly appreciated. However, these units are all non-standard product for us. Though assembly will not be a problem, the glass will be. For some reason we cannot find any way to cut the glass without a great deal of waste. The upshot of this is that in figuring the costs on this order, given the price Stuart quoted, we would be selling the whole order at about breakeven.

Rusty and I talked about this situation and decided that one solution to this problem might be to try to resell the order using painted extrusions from the new line. We sent Stuart back to the customer and the developer said he would let us know this Wednesday if the order would be changed. By changing to painted windows we were able to quote a price that covered us for the painting and the excess waste and provide a profit. However, there is a catch. The customer is willing to wait a bit longer to give us a chance to operationalize the paint line, as he is in the design stage of the development. However, he wants a penalty clause in the order in case we are late in delivering under the revised order. If for any reason the equipment isn't ready to go on time we will either have to pay a penalty or have the extrusions painted outside. Either way, we would lose about $10,000 on the order if the revised quote is accepted and the paint room isn't ready by November.

EXHIBIT 3

From: Stu Carter
To: George Hayes
Date: August 13

Sorry I won't be in town when you arrive at Al Tech. I've had a big sales trip planned to meet with several of our major window customers in the South. Rusty wanted me to drum up some firm orders for the new painted metal lines since we're going to be going on line soon. He was apparently concerned our customers wouldn't order the more expensive, painted products, given the recession. I told him not to worry, though, as the expensive stuff usually sells OK anyway, especially in the South where the economy isn't as hard hit.

Barb was lucky to catch me before I left. I'll be swinging on back through Cincinnati for the Manufactured Housing Suppliers Show, then home for the big party!

Oh, before I forget, sooner or later you're bound to hear about it. In fact, the lawyer was going to meet with Rusty this week. While I was on the road recently the Groves kid broke into my office. I know he rifled my desk because the drawers were an awful mess. I don't care what he says he was after, he's had it in for me ever since I fired his dad from the sales force a year ago. How did I know his old man, Marv, would end up marrying my secretary! I have a good notion to fire her when I get back. Marv Groves went over my head to McClosky, insisting he could sell more to the chain stores if we had more retail lines. I told Marv to keep his nose out of the design department and when he didn't I finally fired him. Those guys in design would spend all their time on the new stuff instead of helping me out on the window lines. The MH guys are always hot for slick-looking new window designs. Now McClosky is convinced that the new paint line was put in just so his department could have some fun.

Gotta run.

EXHIBIT 4

From: Charles Weber
To: George Hayes
Date: 8/13/82

Mr. Hayes:

Ms. Curtis suggested I prepare a memo to advise you of any problems I may be encountering in Purchasing. I foresee two areas of concern.

First, it will be necessary for me to locate long-term, reliable sources of supply for the paint facility. We have temporary sources for the materials we need for the forecasted window and door production through December. Beyond that we need to be concerned about the demands of any new product lines and/or contract paint work. We also have not accounted for the condominium order, should it require painting.

Second, I have been hearing some rumors that two of our major aluminum suppliers may be cutting back production further. In the last major recession several of the "majors" shut off some potlines [smelting equipment] to artificially tighten supplies so they could raise prices even in a period of slack demand. This strategy worked well last time, so I suspect the rumors may be true. I may know more by the middle of next week. One of our suppliers will have their regional sales manager in the area on the pretext of training a new territory representative. You might wish to join us on the morning of the 18th, should you be available.

The last time billets were in short supply both of our contract suppliers instituted a very restrictive policy before supplying us with metal. For each pound of aluminum we wished to purchase we had to turn in a pound of scrap at the going price. Obviously, we could not keep up such a practice for very long without severe production cutbacks. Otherwise, we would be forced into the spot market to fill our remaining needs. To anticipate this possibility it might be wise to begin stockpiling our scrap. This will hurt our quarterly cash flow, but may help protect our supply of new metal. The next regular scrap pickup is scheduled for Friday the 20th.

Just a reminder, the engineers from the paint equipment company will be here Tuesday. It might be a good time for you to learn more about the new facility firsthand.

If I can be of any additional help, please don't hesitate to ask.

EXHIBIT 5

From: Dick Simcox
To: George Hayes
Date: August 14, 1982

Just before shutdown on Friday I got a phone call from one of our large customers. Apparently Stu had left on his sales trip already, and due to the urgency of the call, his secretary transferred the call to me. Here's the trouble. Our trucks just delivered a shipment of our new hexagonal windows to our biggest MH customer. These babies were right on spec, exceeded federal standards by a mile-- the designers did a bang-up job. These are the most expensive windows we make because of the unusual shape. The tooling is incredible and glass-cutting is a real chore. I was real proud of assembly when I inspected these before loading. My supervisor, Judy Mills, did a great job on this. I sure wish she'd get off her horse about this paint job; I need her here. Anyway, the bums wouldn't accept delivery of the order. They told the driver the latch was on the wrong side. What's more like it is that their business is really off and they stopped producing the model that uses the hex windows. The driver's bringing them back this weekend.

What's got me worried is that this was just the first batch. The order was for three times what we shipped. We got a big set of tools and hired and trained a guy just for this product, hoping to get some more customers for it next year. If we could get in touch with Stu we could get him to see the customer at the show this week. The next batch was already started but I cancelled them on Friday night until we find out what gives here. Not filling this order will do some damage to our sales targets for the quarter.

What worries me most is that this could be a trend. If all our customers are hurting now, how are we going to sell the painted stuff? We've been counting on the higher margins there to offset some volume declines in other products. Rusty's been worrying about this, too. He told me just last week. But Stu is convinced there's no problem. Seems to me we ought to be out looking for some contract painting. It'll be a bad Christmas for a lot of our people if we have to cut back in the last quarter.

I can free up an hour or two any time after 10 A.M. Monday if you need me.

EXHIBIT 6

From: Barbara Curtis
To: George Hayes
Date: August 13, 1982

Below is a summary of Rusty's agenda for the week of August 16.

1. Luncheon with Alan Holtman at noon on Monday.

    Mr. Holtman is the attorney retained by Al Tech. The subject of the meeting is the trespass, breaking and entering charge pending against Mitchell Groves, age 16, stepson of Stu Carter's secretary.

    On July 31, the boy was apprehended inside our office building after he set off the silent alarm. He claims to have been looking for proof that his step-mother was having an affair with Stu. They both deny this. When the police searched the boy, they found nothing in his possession belonging to Al Tech. The Groves think the situation can and should be worked out at home, though they want the boy to pay for damages. Stu seems to want to press for prosecution.

2. Tuesday, 11 A.M. to 3 P.M. meet with Janice Schulcraft and Dennis Sanchez.

    These are the engineers from the paint equipment manufacturer. The subject of their visit concerns the finalization of the delivery and installation plans. Rusty had planned a tour of the building addition, now almost completed, lunch, and then a briefing session to include Messers Weber, White, and Simcox.

3. Wednesday, 7:45 A.M.

   Rusty had reservations to leave O'Hare for Cincinnati for the MH Suppliers Show, returning Friday after dinner. He was to meet Stu upon his arrival.

4. Saturday, 6 P.M. to midnight, annual party, Elks club

   Rusty was to deliver a short speech after dinner.

EXHIBIT 7

Unopened letter dated August 12, 1982:

Dear Mr. Wainscott:

   Our office has on file your plans for the construction of an addition to your facility on Eleventh Street, including the remodeling of the south-side entrance. You may be aware of the fact that last Monday, August 9, the City Council approved proposed building code modifications which go into effect immediately.

   One section of the revised code may impact on your current construction. This notification is intended to provide you with some warning that, as filed, your new premises may not pass inspection. It is to your benefit to discuss this situation with your architect and your general contractor as soon as possible.

   Enclosed is a copy of the changes in the code as approved by the council. [Enclosure not shown.] If my office can help you in interpreting these changes or in answering any other questions, please let me know.

Sincerely,
(Signed) Stanley Lerner, City Engineer

EXHIBIT 8

Manila envelope containing petition:

August 2, 1982

We the undersigned request that the management of Al Tech repair the employees' parking lot. Many of us damaged our tires and suffered wheel alignment problems after last winter from the deep ruts, potholes, and frost heaving problems. We also request that in fall the apples from the trees by the lot be swept up regularly so the lot is not an obstacle course to walk through.

[253 signatures followed]

EXHIBIT 9

Unopened letter dated August 10, postmarked New York:

Dear Mr. Wainscott:

   For the past two years you have supplied our chain of stores with your aluminum extension ladders. Let me express to you again how pleased we all are here with the high quality and timely delivery of this product. It continues to be a strong item for us.

   In light of recent and expected changes in both demographics and the economic climate, we have redefined our corporate merchandising strategy. It is our intention to provide more variety in home improvement products and hardware. To implement this strategy we are seeking reliable suppliers in such product lines to provide our chain with private label merchandise. We would be interested in talking with you about the possibility of contracting for an exclusive line of windows, doors, and porch enclosures.

Since this may require some rethinking of your firm's priorities, I have decided to approach you directly rather than contacting your sales department. We are very anxious to proceed and I am hopeful we can expand our already cordial business relations further. I am planning to be in Chicago for a regional meeting on the 19th of this month. If you will be available it would be no trouble for me to drive out to your office on the 20th to discuss this in more detail. If you wish to get together at that time please call my office by the 18th.

Sincerely,
(Signed) John Colby
Vice President,
Merchandising

Exhibit 10

Letter postmarked August 9, addressed to "Al Teck." Letter was handwritten and is reproduced verbatim below:

To the man who runs things at Al Teck,

I was at your factry a few weeks back to get a job that was in the Want Ads. The boss woodn't hire me. Over the week end I seen my sister inlaw She says I can sue your place cause I am a pertecked class. To be nice I give you one more chance befor I get a loyer.

Marie Grace

Exhibit 11

Letter dated July 23, 1982, opened by Wainscott:

Dear Mr. Wainscott:

County General Hospital is vitally concerned with the increasing number of job-related accidents occurring in our community. In an attempt to ameliorate this trend we have added a Safety Consultant to our hospital staff. His job is to suggest specific improvements which can be implemented with minimal expense in offices and factories in our community.

The services of our Safety Consultant will be made available to local businesses under one of two programs: a per-diem consultation or our charitable contribution plan. The per-diem rate is $500. The charitable contribution plan is based on the actual savings accruing to each firm through the reduction in expenses from reduced insurance costs and direct company-borne medical costs. If your company institutes any of the improvements suggested by our Safety Consultant, rather than pay the per-diem expense you may elect to contribute 10 percent of the first year's actual dollar savings to our hospital.

We at County General sincerely believe this program will benefit both the community and the businesses that are so critical to its welfare. Please feel free to make an appointment with me at your earliest convenience so we can confer on this matter.

Respectfully,
(Signed) Michael Franz, Administrator
County General Hospital

Exhibit 12

Unsigned, handwritten note, no date, found on the floor near the office door on Sunday morning:

To the new Acting General Manager

Sir, the foremen here at Al Tech got together after quitting time on Friday and talked about the situation since Rusty's accident. We're sure you're a good guy and all or the company wouldn't have sent you. We just want you to know that we think Dick [Simcox] should have gotten the job. It didn't need to go to an outsider.

EXHIBIT 13

Letter dated August 4, 1982, opened by Wainscott, postmarked St. Louis:

Dear Rusty,

It's about that time again. We need to make plans for this year's holiday break. Some of the others want to spend the week after Christmas lolling on the beaches in either southern California or Florida. I'm partial to the Gulf side of Florida because my in-laws are in the area and my kids could spend the week with them. Do you have any preference?

This sure was one heck of a good idea. I don't remember exactly whose it was though—it's been three years now. Doesn't really matter. Since all the divisions are shut down for the holidays anyway and the only thing going on is inventory, we general managers might as well enjoy ourselves. Besides, last year Frank said our gossip about HQ really helped him when it came time to put together the report on closing down his Kirksville plant. Knowing how the guys at HQ felt about things saved him a couple of months time.

Well, give me a call as soon as possible so we can finalize our plans and make reservations. Say hi to your good-looking wife for me.

(Signed) Jonas [Calder, General Manager, Metal Stampings]

EXHIBIT 14

Envelope, hand addressed to Mr. Hayes:

I have been a bookkeeper in the Accounting Department for eight years and heard about your temporary assignment to Al Tech on Friday morning. My parents are retired and vacation in Florida during the winter. Their two-bedroom home is located about a mile from our office at 2132 Elm St. It's near an elementary school. I called my folks over the lunch hour and they offered to rent the house to you for $250 a month. They are leaving after Labor Day and won't be back until Easter. It's really a good deal as two-bedroom apartments in town are scarce and rent for about $350 a month. Let me know early in the week if you are interested.

Dotty Simmons

EXHIBIT 15

Handwritten note from Ben Brown, clipped to the letter below, dated August 11:

Rusty,

This is a xerox of a letter I just got today from Joyce Riley, the new receptionist. I don't know what you want to do about this, but we should talk about it on Friday, the 13th (unless you want to meet at the Olympus Club Saturday).

Ben

Dear Mr. Brown

Since you are both my boss and the Personnel Director, I felt it was right to mention a problem I'm having to you. I feel I am being harassed on my job.

When I interviewed for work here I asked if it was all right to moonlight and you said I could use my own time as I wished. The truth was that I had a job then, and still do, working Friday and Saturday nights at the Olympus Club on Sycamore Street. Sooner or later you're bound to hear it so I'll tell you now that I work there as an exotic dancer.

It seems some of the workers who I know work in the factory told a couple of the office people about my moonlighting and several of them came to see me at work. The club was really busy the last couple of weekends. Now rumors are all over the place about me. I know it's true because I overheard some of the workers in the lunchroom talking about drawing straws to see who gets to bring paperwork over to the office from the factory. Some of our office people must even have told customers who call here, because visitors to our office have said a few things to me. I'm not really complaining about what they say to me or how they look at me. I'm used to that. But what happened recently really bothers me.

A woman called here two days ago, wouldn't say who she was, and accused me of all sorts of things with her husband. I finally got over that and then yesterday another woman called and said I was a loose woman who shouldn't be allowed to work in an office where nice husbands worked. She said if I didn't quit my job she'd tell the other wives and get me fired. I enjoy my work but I don't play around with married men and I don't want to give up either job. Can you help me?

(Signed) Joyce Riley

EXHIBIT 16

Letter dated August 4, 1982, opened by Wainscott:

Dear Mr. Wainscott:

In preparation for the coming year the Board of Education has voiced its continuing support for our Career Day program at Central High School. Your firm's participation last year was appreciated and we hope you will again donate your time and effort to help ensure the success of this year's program.

Career Day is scheduled for Friday, January 7, 1983, from 9 o'clock to 4 o'clock. This year the Board has decided to cancel all classes for the day so the participating firms will have more space for displays and meetings than we had last year.

We need your response by August 20 so we may make the necessary arrangements. Thank you for your cooperation in our efforts.

Sincerely,
(Signed) Robert Wood, Superintendent of Schools

EXHIBIT 17

Note written to himself by George Hayes when he arrived in the office:

Catch 8:30 P.M. United flight from O'Hare on Friday for our anniversary on Saturday—get present.

Exhibit 18

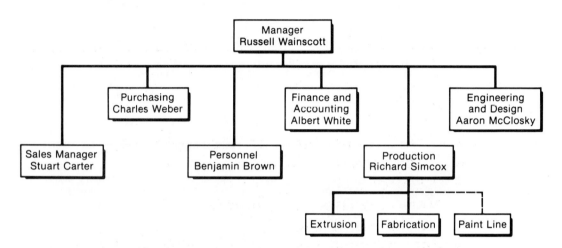

FIGURE 1.   Organization Chart—Al Tech Division

Part IV

Controlling and Monitoring Activities and People

Cases Outline

- The National Insurance Company
- The Luggers Versus the Butchers
- Control from Afar
- The Two Edges of Control
- Leases and Losses
- International Systems Corporation—Ajax Plant

22. The National Insurance Company*

Jerry Taylor has been involved with the administrative functions of the National Insurance Company for almost twenty years. About three months ago, Jerry was appointed group manager of the Policyholder Service and Accounting Departments at the home office. Before he actually assumed the job, Jerry was able to get away for a three-week management development program at the State University College of Business. One of the topics covered in the program was the concept of job enrichment, or job redesign. Jerry had read about job enrichment in several of his trade journals, but the program was his first opportunity to think about the concept in some detail. In addition, several of the program participants had had some experience (both positive and negative) with job redesign projects.

Jerry was intrigued with the idea. He knew how boring routine administrative tasks could become, and he knew from his previous supervisory work that turnover of clerical personnel was a real problem. In addition, his conversations with the administrative vice-president and Joe Bellows, the personnel manager, led him to believe that some trials and redesigning the work would be supported and favorably regarded.

Description of the Work

Group Policyholder Service Department

The principal activities undertaken in this department are the sorting and opening of incoming mail and then matching to accounting files; reviewing of group insurance bills from policyholders; and coding required changes to policies (e.g., new employees and terminations). These activities are carried out by approximately twenty-eight people; 53 percent of them are over age thirty-five, 82 percent female, 89 percent high school graduates, and 53 percent have less than two years' experience in their current job.

---

*This case and the analysis are adapted (with permission) from Antone F. Alber, *An Exploratory Study of the Benefits and Costs of Job Enrichment,* Ph.D. dissertation, The Pennsylvania State University, 1977. Several figures are reproduced directly, and major portions of the text are quoted directly. The case was written in conjunction with Henry P. Sims, Jr., and Andrew D. Szilagyi, Jr.

Organizationally, the department is headed by a manager. The employees are grouped into the four functional categories of clerical support, senior technician, change coder, and special clerk. The general work flow and a more specific list of the tasks carried out within each functional category are shown in Exhibit 1.

The Group Policyholder Service Department shares the same physical working area as the Accounting Department. The people within Policyholder Service who work in the different functional categories are in very close proximity to one another, frequently just one desk away. The files for the department are located at one corner of the work area and the supervisors have offices along one side (see Exhibit 2).

In the last few months, Jerry has observed that the functional breakdown and the accompanying physical arrangement of people and files lead to a number of problems. Since work is assigned or selected on a random basis, there is no personal accountability for it. Files are at one corner of the work area where they can be retrieved by the clerical group and distributed to a senior technician who randomly distributes them to be processed. After a file is coded, it is placed in a holding area for processing by the Accounting Department. Here, assignment of

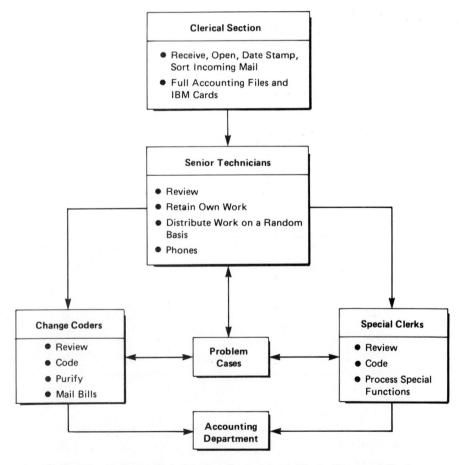

Exhibit 1. Policyholder Service Department Work Flow and Tasks

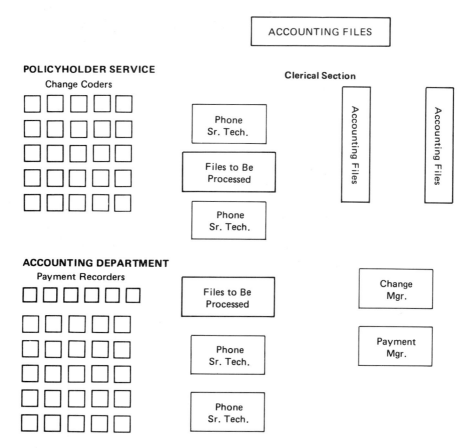

Indicates relative positions and not actual number of employees or floor space occupied.

Exhibit 2. Policyholder Service Department
and Accounting Department Physical Layout

work is also done on a random basis. It is difficult to respond to phone calls or written requests for information promptly, because it is frequently difficult to find a file. In fact, several people are kept busy doing nothing but looking for files.

The typical employee performs a job which consists of two tasks on approximately an eleven-minute cycle. All work is cross-checked. The training for the job is minimal and there are a number of individuals performing the same set of tasks on files randomly issued. A clerk occasionally corresponds with a policyholder, but all correspondence goes out with the manager's signature on it. The manager thus receives all phone calls and correspondence from policyholders.

Because of the random distribution of work, individual performance is difficult to measure. There are spot checks on some completed work by someone other than the doer, but it is difficult or impossible to determine the specific individual who was responsible. Consequently, it is not possible to provide specific information to individuals at regular intervals about their work performance.

Accounting Department

The Accounting Department processes the files, bills, and checks received from the Group Policyholder Service. Premiums are posted on IBM cards and worksheets. Necessary adjustments are made to accounts and the checks, cards, and worksheets are balanced. Approximately twenty-eight people are employed at any one time performing these tasks. Seventy-seven percent of the work force are under thirty-five years of age. Everyone has at least a high school degree and 54 percent have less than two years' experience in the job they were performing.

The department has both a manager and a supervisor. The employees are divided into senior technicians, premium posters, and special clerks. The general work flow and tasks carried out in each of these functional areas are shown in Exhibit 3. As shown in Exhibit 2, the Accounting Department shares its work and files with Policyholder Service.

Work is selected on a random basis. Clerks go to a bookcase file and choose the cases they wish to do. Occasionally, correspondence with a policyholder is necessary, and is signed by the manager.

The Problem of Change

Jerry believes that if the work in his department can be *properly* redesigned, then departmental effectiveness can be improved. In addition, he believes that substantial improvements can be made in terms of individual employee work satisfaction.

In thinking about redesigning the work, Jerry has separated the problem into two parts. First, he is concerned about the *process* of change. How can he best

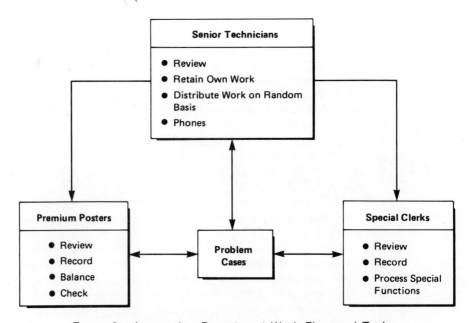

EXHIBIT 3. Accounting Department Work Flow and Tasks

accomplish a job redesign project? Second, Jerry has been concerned with the arrangement of the tasks themselves. Before he begins such a project, Jerry hopes to have at least some preliminary ideas about the feasibility of such a change.
Let's help Jerry out.

First, *as an individual,* how would you actually redesign the work in Jerry's department?

_____

_____

_____

_____

_____

_____

Second, *as a group,* how would you redesign the work in Jerry's department?

_____

_____

_____

_____

_____

_____

23.   The Luggers Versus the Butchers*

Food Merchandising Corporation had one of its warehouses in a small city in northern New Jersey. The main operation of the warehouse was to stock certain goods, and then ship them on order to various stores. The meat department handled packaged meats, and wholesale cuts of lamb, veal, and beef. Beef, by far the biggest and most expensive commodity, was generally bought from midwestern packers and shipped either by railroad or truck. On arrival at the warehouse, the beef was in the form of two hindquarters and two forequarters, each weighing close to two hundred pounds. The problem was to get these heavy pieces of meat off the trucks (or freight cars) and onto the intricate system of rails within the warehouse. Freight was paid by the shipper.

Company and union rules proscribed warehousemen from unloading trucks. It became the function of the general warehouseman (designated "lugger") to assist in the unloading of the trucks, but with no lifting. If, however, the beef was shipped by rail, it became his function to unload the freight cars. After the meat was placed on company rails, it was pushed through the doors into the 35° warehouse where it was placed in stock until it was butchered. The butchery process involved several men. First, the meat went to the sawman. While someone

_____

*Robert E. C. Wegner, Leonard Sayles, *Cases in Organizational and Administrative Behavior,* 1972, pp. 42–48. Reprinted by permission of Prentice-Hall, Inc., Englewood Cliffs, New Jersey.

steadied the meat on the rail, the rib, plate, brisket, and shoulder bones were severed. Then it was passed on to the cutters, who butchered it into several smaller wholesale cuts. After that the meat was again placed in stock to be shipped out by the night crews.

The "Luggers" Versus the "Butchers"

The operation of the warehouse involved two distinct functions: to unload and stock the beef, and then to butcher it. The unloading process was wholly different from the butchering. It required physical strength and coordination to lift 200 pounds of beef all day. Furthermore, when the workload slowed down, the luggers were given different tasks. There was a degree of variety in their work. But the butchering function was very different. The men were geographically confined to the cutting line and performed the same basic operations day after day.

When the warehouse was unionized eight years ago, the men who had most seniority were given first option as to the jobs they preferred. Since many of these men were on the older side, they gravitated away from the more laborious general warehouse work toward the higher-wage butcher jobs. Consequently, two different types of individuals became associated with the two different types of jobs.

The eight butchers were engaged in the skilled practice of butchering meat. Most of them had been with the company for many years. For the most part, they were family men with many off-the-job responsibilities, were by no means in union affairs, and probably had more loyalty to the company than to the union local. They had a high number of social activities off-the-job such as group picnics, bowling, golf, et cetera. The tedious boredom of their job was somewhat mitigated by these mutual activities, and an atmosphere of good humor usually prevailed in their corner of the warehouse.

There were nine luggers, but two of these had been butchers until very recently. More will be said later about these men. A third man usually worked in another section. Thus the term "lugger" referred to a specific group of six general warehousemen. These men were younger and generally had less company time than the butchers, but this is not to say that they were young or new. Most of them were married, but treated their home responsibilities differently. For instance, the typical butcher would spend his night at home, and most of the luggers would spend their night working a part-time job.

Hank, Josh, and Mr. Abrams

Hank was the foreman. When he became foreman about ten years ago, the men considered him a walking terror but a good foreman. Now he was considered neither. There were several reasons for this change. First, the coming of the union had made Hank more careful in the way he handled the men. Second, Hank had lost control of the luggers. After several fiery confrontations, he more or less left them alone. When it was necessary to give them an order, great explanations and apologies often accompanied it. His relationship with butchers, however, remained fairly intact. In effect, Hank was afraid of the luggers but not of the butchers. Third, when Mr. Abrams became manager two years ago it was his policy to use close personal supervision of the men to ensure efficiency. Mr. Abrams, therefore, usurped considerable portions of Hank's responsibility.

Josh was the union representative. He had built up a great friendship with Carl, the shop steward, and the other luggers. His relationship with the butchers, however, was strictly on a business basis. As a consequence, Josh tended to favor the luggers in any controversy. Usually this meant that the butchers complained about the luggers, but nothing really important was done about it.

Mr. Abrams' assistant was Lyle, nicknamed "the Puppy." Lyle used to follow Mr. Abrams everywhere he went, to the great enjoyment of the men. Thus came the nickname "Puppy."

The butchers took the brunt of Mr. Abrams' close supervision, mainly because they were confined to one spot and were easy to observe. Also, this was where the real pressure had to be applied, for if the meat was not butchered, it could not be sent out and stores would run short. Mr. Abrams had the responsibility to ensure that stores were not short. He evidently felt that standing over the men (with the Puppy at his side) would cut down on the little games the men developed to break up their boring routine (talking, bathroom breaks, et cetera). The net effect was that the men, being old timers, took their breaks anyway but grumbled about being watched over. The luggers were harder to watch, being more spread out, and they also managed to gain some control over Mr. Abrams. He knew that an ill-timed remark or too much supervision would only result in later slowdowns by these men.

A Slow Change in Status

Six years ago the butcher's job was considered much more desirable than that of the luggers. At that time most of the meat was shipped by railroad. This necessitated a great deal of heavy work. Most of the men would have preferred the cold monotony of cutting meat to lugging 200 pounds of beef from a railroad car to a loading dock. It was at this point that two luggers, Brent and Terry, began to think of developing a system of portable rails that would be adaptable to the large variety of freight cars which came to the warehouse. The rails were successfully designed and developed by the two men. With the passage of time, skill in their use was achieved and the job of unloading freight cars became quite simple.

The ingenuity of two luggers was widely heralded about the warehouse and in the company, and recognition was given in due proportion. More importantly, a job that was undesirable before became quite attractive because the chief reason for its undesirability had ceased to exist. The main attractions of the butcher's job were reduced to the companionship of the group, the waning prestige of being a skilled workman, and the higher-wage-more-overtime benefits. This was quite sufficient to keep them satisfied, if not as happy as before.

Hank's foremanship also suffered. At this date, his position had already been dealt a few blows by the union and the men. Now an innovation was introduced that had no place in his way of doing things. He preferred to completely ignore the rails and allow the luggers to use them as they saw fit. From the company's point of view, the use of rails in freight cars meant very little. Four men were still required in each car. Efficiency remained about the same because it took time to assemble and disassemble the rail system.

If the use of the rails had resulted solely in physical advantages, it is probable that the situation would have gone along unchanged. But the luggers were quick to discover an economic value in their use. The trucks coming in on the front docks had to be unloaded. Since freight was paid by the shipper, the company and union had worked out an agreement in which the trucker was responsible for delivering the meat to the dock. The warehouse workers were only to assist peripherally, and were not permitted inside the trucks unless it was absolutely necessary.

The drivers were not happy with their lot of unloading up to 35,000 pounds of beef. Consequently, they often hired warehouse vagrants—men who sat around the warehouse waiting for such opportunities. The going rate was one dollar per 1,000 pounds: between $30.00 and $35.00 a truck. It generally took two hours to unload one truck. The enterprising luggers redesigned the rails for use on the trucks, and made it known that a tip of two dollars was in order for anyone who cared to use them. Since the railroad was making more and more use of piggyback services, the number of trucks as well as the amount of the tips began to increase.

A Dispute Develops

Last year, two butchers were given the option of working as luggers. They exercised the option, partly hoping to recuperate some of their wage losses by sharing in the tip money. It was not long before serious arguments developed between the old and new luggers. Beforehand, the luggers had worked out a one-for-you and one-for-me system with the trucks. Such an informal understanding was possible because this tightly cohesive group knew that petty bickering would soon take the problem out of their own hands. The two ex-butchers, however, had no desire to work with the old group. They were in no way amenable to tacit understandings that cut them out. Consequently, when the big trailers turned into the driveway, there began a jockeying for position.

Arguments developed, and other work suffered. When, the two ex-butchers turned to the union, they found their upward paths of communication thoroughly blocked. Carl, the shop steward, was a lugger. It was to his disadvantage to press hard on behalf of the two ex-butchers. Josh, the union representative, was much too friendly with the luggers and no progress could be made here. Hank, the foreman, was worthless in this matter, and Mr. Abrams was too new at this stage to take action. For these reasons, and because of a normal reluctance to push grievances, little pressure was placed on the union.

Early last spring, following a series of flare-ups over equipment usage and truck tips, two "clubs" were formed: Club "Six" and Club "Three." Brent, one of the two rail designers, originated the idea of formalizing the two groups. Each club was given a separate locker for equipment. No exchanges were to take place. Members of Club Three (the two ex-butchers and a third who worked in a different part of the warehouse) were permitted to work a share of trucks proportional to club membership. Members of Club Six (the six original luggers) began a practice of pooling tips and dividing them equally.

At first the formalization of the two groups appeared to be a good solution. There were fewer arguments, and Club Three was reasonably satisfied. However, an unfortunate side effect developed. Previously, the distinctions between luggers and butchers were implicit and the warehouse as a whole was a friendly place. People knew who got along with whom, and friendships often crossed group lines. With the formalization, however, people began to class themselves as "in" or "out." Club Six members began to be more and more isolated among the twenty-five men who worked in this section of the warehouse. Butchers and luggers constantly complained about each other. Members of Club Six refused to work with members of Club Three, and much ill feeling was generated. But even so, had there been nothing else, these difficulties would probably not have caused any lasting problems. There was, however, something else—the piggyback development.

The railroads were making more and more use of piggyback trucking. This is a system whereby trailers are hauled part of the way by rail, and part of the way by road. As the number of freight cars decreased and the warehouse volume increased, more trucks began coming. These trucks had to be unloaded, and unloading was an expensive and time-consuming proposition. The use of rails on the trucks had cut down the time it took to unload. A good crew could "knock one off" in less than an hour, though the average time was about two hours. The luggers began to move into this very lucrative area. It became quite a steady thing for them to bring home an extra $30.00 or $40.00 per week. Occasionally, if things were slow enough, the luggers would work a truck on company time. Or they would begin setting it up about 3:30, so there would be no delay in getting it started at 4:00.

From the company viewpoint, there was no problem. Trucks were being emptied faster than ever before, even on the rare occasion when a truck came in purposely late. The more usual situation was either that there were too many trucks to unload in the normal day or that the truck was legitimately delayed. At any rate, the rails enabled the ordinary trucks to be unloaded much more rapidly and the experienced luggers often finished their after-hour trucks in half the normal time. Warehouse efficiency did not suffer.

The butchers, however, were not a happy group. They continued to work the same boring routine in the same 35°. Their income did not change. They watched the luggers develop into a very cohesive group and usurp their status position. They resented the different treatments meted out to the two groups. The luggers were given too much freedom, and the butchers were too closely supervised. The luggers quite often "couldn't" stay overtime, yet they could almost always work a truck. Nothing was ever said when luggers made excuses; but if the butchers did not want to stay, they were given a great deal of grief.

Pressure was applied, and it was not a rare thing to find butchers working three hours overtime for half the money the luggers made in an hour by working a truck. The obvious inequity was deeply resented. The luggers used company time to work trucks, or to set them up, and this violated the union contract. Yet nothing concrete was ever done to stop them. The butchers felt totally frustrated and disenchanted with what they had once considered as high-status jobs. Despite their innate conservatism and procompany attitude they seriously considered a massive walkout to get their grievances heard.

24.   Control from Afar

Background

Westways Utility Services is a company whose operations are limited to the northwest region of the United States. While they do have other minor interests, their main business is providing telephone service. As a public service, they are subject to rather close scrutiny by state utility commissions. Westways' companies actually come under the jurisdiction of three different western states.

Public telephone companies are watched very closely, especially with respect to quality of service. In most states, one of the primary methods of assessing the quality of telephone service is through the "customer service index." There is a relatively complicated formula for determining this number. It is really a combination of factors. Among other things it includes the number of customer complaints about service outages (telephones not working for one reason or another) per hundred lines in use.

The customer service index also includes the number of complaints which are made directly to the public utility commission by customers. This happens rarely but is considered a serious matter. Only a few complaints of this nature will cause the "customer service index" to be very low. A complaint of this nature usually indicates one of two things. First, a customer has received very poor service over a long length of time. For one reason or another, this telephone just never seems to work properly. Another reason for a direct complaint to the public utility commission is an inability of the telephone company to fix a problem to the satisfaction of a customer. Suppose, for example, that a customer has complained about "noise" on the line. The customer feels that almost every time that he is on the telephone there is static or background noise or something of that nature. The telephone company, however, tells the customer that they have tested the line and can find nothing wrong. Businesses are usually more likely to make complaints directly to the public utility commission.

There are a couple of reasons for this. First, as you would expect, continuing problems are ordinarily more serious for a business. For many individuals a telephone out of order is an inconvenience. For commercial concerns, some of which may rely on their telephone service for nearly all their business, bad telephone service is more than inconvenient. There is a second reason also. Frankly, most individuals do not realize that they can complain directly to the public utility commission about poor service.

There is another major factor which is included in the customer service index. Most utility commissions occasionally (usually once a month) test telephone equipment. They do this by installing automatic dialing equipment in a telephone office. This device dials a certain number of calls. Suppose, for example, that the device dials 100 numbers. Obviously, if all 100 numbers are completed, then the service would appear to be reasonable. On the other hand, if several of the calls are not completed, then there is evidence that something is wrong with the telephone company's equipment.

It should be noted that 100 telephone calls is very few. In the average telephone central office (the location where these calls take place) hundreds of thousands of calls would be made each day. The principle of the automatic dialer, however, is like checking for the quality of light bulbs in a manufacturing company. In order to assure the quality of light bulbs, you do not have to plug in every light bulb that is manufactured. You might, however, select a random sample of light bulbs to test. If all the light bulbs you check work as they should, there is some evidence that the entire batch of light bulbs is all right. On the other hand, if you select 100 light bulbs to check and seven of them do not work, that is strong evidence that something is seriously wrong.

These three measures—number of customer complaints, complaints to the public utility commission, errors on the automatic dialing devices—are combined to form the "customer service index." The combination of these factors is adjusted so that 100 is a perfect index. It indicates an extremely high level of customer service. Anything less than 94/95 is cause for concern. A customer service index less than 94 would be a very serious matter which would require immediate action. Telephone companies are very sensitive about this number. It is ordinarily calculated every month. It is an important number. It is likely to be brought up, for instance, when a telephone company asks for an increase in rates for its service or if the telephone company wants to expand its services. Opposing groups may argue that the current service is poor (based on the customer services indexes) and therefore question whether an increase in rates or a service expansion should be allowed.

The Meeting

"Thank you for your attendance on such short notice. I'll tell you why I called this meeting," remarked Adrienne Parkins, vice-president of operations for Westways Utility to a group of operations officers. "Quite frankly, I am not pleased with last quarter's reports from the northern divisions of this state. Our operations in the other states are reasonable, even good at times. I have been watching the customer service indexes from our northern divisions and they are abysmal. The customer complaints are way out of line with our guidelines; the overall customer service index is low by any standards," continued Ms. Parkins.

"Well, as you know, the majority of our facilities in that region are remote equipment locations. We typically have one supervisor per five or six locations. The day-to-day operations are handled by a few nonmanagerial employees without direct supervision," offered Dale Jorgensen, a company general manager. "The obvious solution is to put a first-level supervisor at each site. Presumably, the performance of the workers, especially the completion of our routine preventive maintenance will be improved by closer supervision," finished Mr. Jorgensen. "As you know, the key to maintaining service indexes at acceptable levels is our routine preventive maintenance. You have to catch problems before they happen."

"Well," countered Ms. Parkins, "I am not going to continue to pay those people to merely babysit that equipment, to put out fires as problems are reported. I want that routine preventive maintenance done and I want it done right. I know that there are no supervisors on those shifts. Frankly, I am hesitant to put a supervisor on shifts with so few people. In fact, I will not hear of adding first-line supervisors to those remote sites. We would probably be talking about a dozen or so supervisors. I cannot justify that expense," concluded Ms. Parkins.

Several people present at the meeting argued that short of putting new first-line supervisors at the currently unsupervised locations, there was no way to assure the quality necessary to improve the customer service indexes in the region.

To this Ms. Parkins replied, "In the near future, Westways Utility intends a major expansion in the northern division. In order to finance that, we will ask for rate increases. It should be clear that we will have an uphill battle all the way if our service indexes do not improve dramatically. I will not authorize new supervisors for those remote locations. Nonetheless, I want improvement in the quality of our services in those regions."

25.   The Two Edges of Control

"Tom, do you have a minute?" asked David Morrison.

"Sure, come in," responded Tom Davidson, plant manager of Mayberry Manufacturing. "What do you have on your mind?"

"I'll tell you, Tom. At times it is just frustrating as hell around here. Sometimes you can't get a straight answer from anyone. There are times when absolutely no one can seem to help you," answered Mr. Morrison with some irritation.

"What specifically is bothering you, Dave?"

One Story

"It's just one thing after another. For instance, two days ago one of my employees asked me for a six-week leave of absence for surgery and a recuperation period. Frankly, I was not familiar with the leave of absence policy around here. I must have asked a half a dozen people including the other shift supervisors what the policy is. I have been told that there is no specific policy and that I will have to use my best judgment on the matter. I am to examine the circumstances of the request and decide accordingly. I thought I had better check with you before I acted in one way or another on the request for the six-week leave," explained Mr. Morrison. "Ordinarily, I wouldn't bother you with something like this. I just can't seem to get a policy anywhere else."

"Well, I appreciate the fact that you checked with me. The advice that you have received, however, is essentially correct. We don't have a specific policy for leaves of absence. In the past, it has been a case-to-case basis. I will say this, though. I don't think that this request has come at a very opportune time. As you know, we have a large order due for delivery and we will need every employee we can get. In fact, I will be very surprised if we get through this without paying a lot of overtime. Obviously, I hate to see us give any employees that much time off when we will have to replace them with employees on overtime and time-and-a-half," countered the plant manager, Tom Davidson.

"You haven't heard the half of it," continued Mr. Morrison. "Yesterday, another employee requested a six-week leave of absence as well. It seems that this employee's daughter works for a major airline and can get tickets to Europe for very reasonable rates. I don't know exactly what is happening there, but apparently the airline is in the middle of some kind of promotion for their overseas flights and employees are entitled to some extraordinary discount. To hear my employee tell it, this is the dream of a lifetime—the opportunity to visit Europe for very little money. There is no telling when, if ever, the employee will have this opportunity again."

"Given our circumstances," said the plant manager, "I can hardly see how that leave of absence could be justified."

"Well, I really have a problem," replied Mr. Morrison. "Both of these are excellent employees. At first, I thought that I could justify the leave of absence on medical grounds for the surgery, but would have trouble with the vacation. However, I looked into the matter a little more carefully and it turns out that the surgery is elective—it is not life threatening. The surgery could be put off for a time. Interestingly, the vacation really can't be put off. Well, of course it can be put off but only at great expense. We can be sure of one thing. The vacation is at least as important to the one employee as the elective surgery is to the other. I really wish we had a policy on this. It would make things a lot easier for me," finished Dave Morrison with some irritation.

"I see your point, Dave, but let me share a problem that I recently had which involves policy," said the plant manager.

Another Story

"We were talking about overtime a few minutes ago. Our corporate headquarters recently sent down a memorandum to all department heads concerning the use of overtime. The memo essentially stated that, in the future, no overtime could be authorized without the personal permission of the plant manager. In this case, of course, such permission would have to come from me. Let me remind you that I did not send the memo to the department managers. That memo was sent by corporate headquarters. I was, as you would expect, notified of the memo," explained the plant manager.

He continued, "Now, in the past any department manager could authorize overtime for his or her department if the need should arise. Evidently, the corporate offices are concerned about the amount of overtime which has been authorized and sought to control it by having all overtime okayed by me before its use. The company is trying to reduce costs and the reduction of overtime is a high priority item.

"This worked fairly well for a while. Of course, the department heads did not especially like the new policy. The policy did, however, have the effect of reducing overtime somewhat. The department heads were a little more careful.

For the most part, I approved any overtime that was requested. I think that the department heads just thought it over a bit more carefully before they called me.

"This all came to an unfortunate conclusion last Friday. As it happens, I was out of town that Friday. At the same time, two unforeseen circumstances caused a problem in the shipping department. First, there was an unusually high incidence of employee absenteeism so shipping was very shorthanded. Second, there was a delay in sending the finished goods from production to the shipping department. In other words, they were short of people, and the goods they were to send out were coming in late. It became absolutely obvious to Ms. Bates, head of the shipping department, that there was no way that all the orders were going to be dispatched by Friday's deadline. The following Monday was a holiday. So, if these orders did not go out on Friday, they would not be processed until Tuesday. The sum of this is that the orders will go out four days late," continued the plant manager, Tom Davidson.

"What happened?" asked David Morrison.

"Nothing, and that is the problem," replied the plant manager with some exasperation. "The department head of shipping, Ms. Bates, tried to reach me. I was out of town. She knew that in the past orders which were not processed by deadline have been returned by customers and subsequent orders canceled. The memo clearly stated that my personal permission was required to authorize overtime. She badly needed that overtime so that the orders could be processed Friday and not wait until Tuesday. If she had authorized the overtime, she would have exceeded her authority. Of course, if she doesn't go ahead with the overtime, we run the risk of product returns and cancellation of future orders."

"What did she do?" asked Mr. Morrison.

"Oh, she took the safe course. She did not use the overtime," answered the plant manager disgustedly. "It would seem, Tom, based on your recent experiences and mine, that policy is a two-edged sword."

26. Leases and Losses

Prestige Properties

Prestige Properties is a company in a midwestern city which owns and operates several apartment complexes. They currently own and manage four complexes of approximately equal size. Each complex has just over 100 apartments for a total of 432 rentable units. The total revenue for these operations is approximately 1.25 million per year.

Although some of these apartments are two- and three-bedroom units, the vast majority are efficiency (no separate bedroom) and one bedroom. Moreover, three of the four complexes are within a mile or so from a major university. The location of these apartments plus the demand for efficiency and single-bedroom units make these apartment complexes very attractive to the students of the nearby university. Aside from the nearness and the smaller units, all three apartment complexes have large swimming pools, leisure areas, laundry facilities, and every unit has a carport. These features make the apartment complexes that much more attractive to students.

The fourth apartment complex is literally on the other side of town. Although it has the extras offered by the other apartment complexes, it is several miles from the university and very few students have ever rented units at that location. Because the near-university complexes attract a very different tenant from the across-town complex, the management problems at each location are quite different.

What a Difference Five Miles Makes

At the across-town complex, the situation is quite stable. Over 60 percent of the renters there have been in the same apartment for over three years. Basically, the tenants here are a little older and work in the community. As a result, the turnover of tenants is relatively uncommon. In a given year, for example, only 20 percent of the tenants will move. This, of course, leads to lower maintenance costs for Prestige Properties. Except for unusual circumstances, the apartment units are only painted, recarpeted, and so forth when tenants move out of the units. In other words, any time a tenant moves out, the apartment is gone over very carefully so that it is in reasonable condition for the next tenant. Since people in the across-town complex do not move out very often, these costs are necessarily minimal for Prestige Properties.

The situation at the near-university complexes is another story. Years in which tenant turnover has approached 100 percent are not unusual. This does not necessarily mean that every person has moved out during the year. Tenant turnover rates can actually be greater than 100 percent. For example, in a given year perhaps three different people have come and gone from apartment number 22. Therefore, tenant turnover percentages are related to the total number of departures, not the number of different apartments which are involved. Even so, rates near 100 percent are very high and very expensive. Obviously, every time someone moves out of an apartment, maintenance crews must restore the unit to reasonable condition. This surely means a thorough cleaning. Beyond that, it may well include repainting, major repairs—whatever is necessary so that the next tenant will be pleased with the apartment. On the average, the cost of restoring an apartment to rentable condition is just under $200 for the near-university apartments. This will vary, of course; sometimes the costs are less than this; sometimes, they are much higher.

The point is that students move out a great deal more often in the near-university complexes than do the tenants in the across-town facility. Sometimes they quit school; sometimes they transfer schools; they get married; they decide to move in with their friends to reduce expenses; couples decide to live together. Unfortunately for Prestige Properties most of these decisions are not made in a time frame which allows the moving tenants to give sufficient notice to the manager of the apartment complexes. There are two major problems here. First, there is the issue of the broken lease. Legally, Prestige Properties does have recourse. The tenants who have broken the lease can be sued for the lost rents. Given that the landlord has made a good faith attempt to rent the abandoned premises, Prestige Properties would have the right to all lost rents over the term of the lease. In other words, if a lease is broken in the eighth month and Prestige Properties has made a reasonable effort to rent the apartment, the old tenant would have to pay four months' rent if the apartment remained vacant. This is an especially difficult problem when it occurs in the summer. Many students leave town in the summer to return home or to work elsewhere. In a university town, it becomes something of a problem to rent apartments in the summer because of this.

While this is legally true, it is also very naive. The truth is that tenants who break such leases are not ordinarily staying around to be sued. Even if they did stay around, they would not ordinarily have the funds to pay the losses. Lastly, except in the summer, property owners should be able to rent the vacated apartment in a reasonably short time.

Not giving notice is really the greater problem. Very often, landlords do not even know that an apartment is vacant until the rent is not paid at the first of the month. They find out that the tenants have moved out when they try to collect the rent. By the time that the apartment is ready to be rented again (ignoring the lease issue), several weeks of rent are lost. When the tenant turnover is over 100 percent, as it is in the Prestige Property near-university complexes, this amounts to many thousands of dollars a year.

Different Dollars for Different Difficulties

The real problem that Prestige Properties is having involves setting the monthly rental amounts for its apartments. Obviously, the near-university complexes have much higher costs—more broken leases, more maintenance costs, less notice, and so forth. The obvious solution is to raise the rents in the near-university complexes to cover these additional costs.

Unfortunately, this has an undesirable side effect. There is no need to raise the rents in the across-town complex. Simply, this complex does not have the problems which the near-university facilities have. If, however, you raise the rents at the near-university facilities and leave the across-town prices at their current levels, you will encourage students to drive the extra distance (five miles or so) to take advantage of the lower prices at the across-town complex. Again, the obvious solution to this problem is to raise the prices in the across-town complex as well. Certainly, if these prices are raised the students will have no incentive to rent the across-town rather than the near-university complexes. This would take care of the student problem. It does, however, leave a very difficult question unanswered.

The tenants in the across-town complex are not students and they have very little interest in living in the student-type complexes. They are not, however, immobile. If the prices are raised at the across-town complex to keep them constant with the near-university apartments, then current tenants in the across-town complex may move to other, cheaper apartments. Only the near-university complexes have the additional costs because of rapid turnover, short notice, and high maintenance. If the across-town complex moves its prices up to be even with the near-university apartments, then the nonstudent apartments will be overpriced in relation to other nonstudent apartment housing in the area.

What Now?

The principal owner of Prestige Properties, as you would expect, is aware of these problems. He has asked for a detailed report outlining exactly what the breakeven points are for all four complexes. He is, of course, particularly interested in the breakeven analysis of the near-university versus the across-town complexes. The object of this report is to determine exactly how much higher rents will have to be in the near-university complexes than those across-town. The main issue is: exactly how much higher would the near-university complexes' rents have to be raised to break even?

27. International Systems Corporation— Ajax Plant*

You are Robert Bedford, the new plant manager of Ajax Plant, part of the International Systems Corporation. Prior to this, you had been manager for research and development for another of International's plants in a different part of the country. You spent a week at Ajax in Central City getting acquainted with the plant and the people. Then, you had to spend a week at your old plant to finish up some business there. You arrived back in Central City late Sunday night. You came to the plant an hour early Monday morning, March 10, to catch up on your work and to review what had happened since you left.

The Ajax plant had been growing steadily under the management of Kenneth Chandler, the previous manager, who left the company for a better job. The plant now has a capital investment in excess of $24,000,000 and produces a variety of electronic and electromechanical testing and analyzing equipment for both military and civilian markets. The plant staff, excluding top management now includes 55 engineers and 35 technicians; there are approximately 1,100 production employees who work in two shifts.

The department manager in charge of production is William Silva. He has been with the company about fifteen years, but has been in his current job for less than a year. The department manager in charge of marketing is Joseph Fleming, who has been in the job approximately two years. Before then, he had been a regional sales manager. His present functions include sales promotion,

---

*Reprinted from *Behavior in Organizations: A Systems Approach to Managing* (2nd ed.), E. F. Huse and J. L. Bowditch, Addison-Wesley Publishing Co., 1977. Reprinted by permission.

merchandising, market research and development, and sales. Eighty-five employees are under his supervision.

Al Mumford, the section manager in research and development, is an electronics engineer. Prior to his promotion less than a year ago, he headed up the electrical engineering subsection in the engineering department. His functions are shown on the organization chart. He had thirty-eight engineers and fifteen technicians and draftsmen working for him. Because of Chandler's strong interest in research and development, close to 7 percent of the plant's profits are allocated to this function.

The finance manager is James Cardinal, who has held this job for about three years. His functions include general and cost accounting, accounts receivable and payable, payroll, and the computer unit. He has a staff of about twenty-five people.

Charles Gray, the employee and community relations manager, has a staff of approximately eighteen people. He transferred from the corporate staff a little over six months ago.

On the following pages are some memos and other correspondence. On a separate sheet of paper, outline and briefly describe what action you would take on each item. *Everything you decide or do must be in writing.* You might write on the items themselves or make memos to yourself about things you want to do later. Draft letters, if appropriate, for your secretary to type. Outline plans or draw up the agenda of meetings you want to call. Sign papers, if necessary. Actually write out memos to your subordinates or to others or make notes of anything you plan to say to them at some future time. (Do not, however, assume what they may say to you in return.) Enter any planned interviews, confirming letters or memos, telephone calls, meeting agenda, notes to yourself or others, and whatever thoughts you may have in connection with each item on the calendar pad. *Each time you make a decision, record fully the reasons behind your actions.*

INTERNATIONAL SYSTEMS CORPORATION

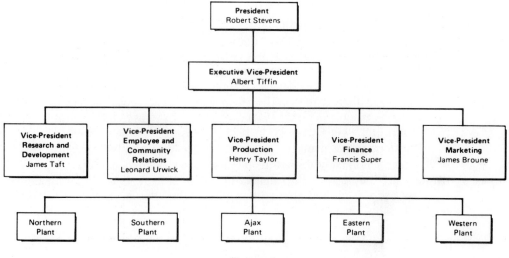

FIGURE 1

AJAX PLANT — CENTRAL CITY

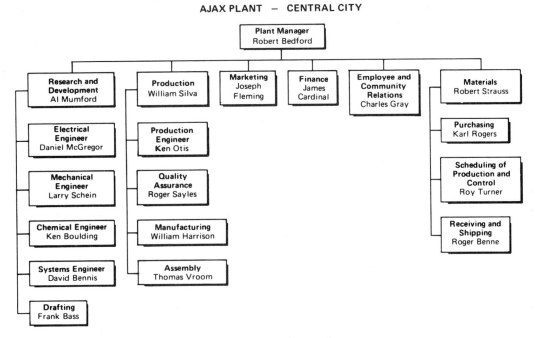

FIGURE 2

Calendar Pad—March 1969

Sunday	Monday	Tuesday	Wednesday	Thursday	Friday	Saturday
						1
2	3	4 *Out of plant all week*	5	6	7	8
9	10	11	12	13	14	15
16	17	18	19	20	21	22
23	24	25	26	27	28	29
30	31					

FIGURE 3

```
                    AJAX PLANT  —  CENTRAL CITY

OFFICE MEMORANDUM                                    March 6

TO:      Mr. Robert Bedford, Plant Manager
FROM:    Charles Gray, E. & C.R.
SUBJECT: Employment of the Disadvantaged

According to information I received at a personnel meeting last night,
both the State and Federal Equal Opportunity people will shortly be
giving a hard look at industrial plants in this area.  Currently, our
ratio of disadvantaged to white employees is extremely low, and we
may be in serious trouble.
     I would recommend that we put on a crash program to recruit and
employ at least 70-80 nonwhites, in all areas of the plant.  I
would further recommend that we not use our normal testing program
for these new employees, since the use of our regular intellectual
and aptitude tests can also open us to charges of discrimination.
We should continue to use the tests for our normal employment of
whites.
     I realize that a crash program may involve, for the short-run,
increased training and labor costs, but this is preferable to losing
our defense contracts or the bad publicity coming from an investiga-
tion.  Besides, I think that this is the right thing to do.
```

FIGURE 4

```
BR  XCL   292  RQ - WVX                    March 7

NY   NY                                     4:30 PM


MR.  ROBERT BEDFORD, PLANT MANAGER

MR.  JOSEPH FLEMING, MARKETING MANAGER


GOOD NEWS STOP HAVE JUST LEARNED THAT ED BAKER OF
BAKER & BAKER READY TO PURCHASE LARGE NUMBER OF
MODEL 80 SYSTEMS AND RELATED ACCESSORIES STOP
CONTRACT APPEARS LIKELY IF WE CAN PROMISE EARLY
DELIVERY ON GUARANTEED BASIS STOP ADVISE ME OF
ACTION STOP

                              JIM BROUNE
```

FIGURE 5

AJAX PLANT — CENTRAL CITY

OFFICE MEMORANDUM   March 5

TO: Bob Bedford
FROM: Robert Strauss
SUBJECT: Increased Materials Costs

As you know, I've been concerned for quite a while about parts
shortages, high inventory, and the steadily increasing materials
costs. This is particularly true since more than half of our direct
costs come from purchased materials, due to the nature of our
business.

My people are working hard to reduce costs and establish decent
manufacturing schedules, but we can't do it by ourselves. We are
continually having to revise our production schedules because of
manufacturing problems, particularly with the new models. As a
result, my purchasing people don't get the word early enough on what
we need to buy, and everything needs to be on rush order and
expedited. About the time we get it into the plant, there is another
design change, and sometimes the parts we have just rush-ordered are
then obsolete. As a result, our materials costs are skyrocketing.

We need to get designs locked in so that we can establish decent
manufacturing and purchasing schedules. For example, the Model 95
is supposed to go into manufacturing shortly, but as yet we have
been unable to get a parts listing that we can rely on.

FIGURE 6

AJAX PLANT — CENTRAL CITY

OFFICE MEMORANDUM   March 6

TO: Plant Manager
FROM: Jim Cardinal, Finance Operation
SUBJECT: Integrated Management Information System

Two months ago, we completed and debugged our computer-based
integrated management information system at a cost of $80,000.
This system is aimed at providing us with much more timely and
accurate information about sales figures, production and assembly
scheduling, vendor order status, and the like. I have been
particularly concerned with the fact that the new System would
provide me with considerably better cost-accounting data.

However, the new system is not working well. Its effectiveness has been considerably reduced by the fact that many managers
do not use it, but instead maintain duplicate records and do not
update the computer files regularly. Further, they appear reluctant to give me the cost-accounting figures that I need and do
not fully adhere to the new policies and procedures necessary to
make the new system work.

Any and all assistance in this matter would be greatly
appreciated.

FIGURE 7

INTERNATIONAL SYSTEMS CORPORATION
CHICAGO, ILLINOIS

INTRACOMPANY MEMORANDUM   March 4

TO: Mr. Robert Bedford
FROM: Henry Taylor, Vice-President
SUBJECT: Meeting   Production Division

I plan to come to Central City on March 25 to meet with you now that
you have had a chance to become acquainted with the plant. In
addition to the routine general review, I would like to take enough
time for us to discuss the problem of increasing our rate of new
product introduction. We need to increase our research and development emphasis in both personnel and facilities, especially since the
rate of product obsolescence is being considerably affected by our
competitors. I would like to have you prepare a special report on
this subject for me.

   In addition, the latest budget reports indicate that the plant
is running well above the projected operating expenses for both the
last quarter and the year to date. Furthermore, does the current
slight decrease in sales constitute a signal of a downward trend?
We will want to look at this for both near- and long-term
implications.

   You may ask any members of your staff to meet with us should you
feel it is appropriate.

                                                        Henry Taylor

HT:hs

FIGURE 8

AJAX PLANT — CENTRAL CITY

OFFICE MEMORANDUM   March 6

TO: Bob Bedford
FROM: William Silva
SUBJECT: Model 80 retrofit

Although we had a discussion about the Model 80 last week, I thought
it wise to drop you a note on the subject. It does not appear
possible to make the schedule for the Model 80 retrofit and at the
same time make the schedule for the new Model 80s coming out. My
production engineering people are going flat out trying to make the
necessary production design changes and at the same time help the
production people with the retrofit program. I would recommend
stopping production on both the retrofit and new production until
we get the design problems cleaned up once and for all.

   The mistake that I made was accepting the Model 80 for production
when I knew that there were a lot of design bugs in it. I won't make
that mistake again.

   By the way, can you get the finance people off my back for a
while? They are trying to put in the computer system. It still
hasn't been fully debugged, and I'll be glad to help them out in a
month or so when I've had a chance to get caught up with production
problems.

FIGURE 9

AJAX PLANT — CENTRAL CITY

OFFICE MEMORANDUM   March 7

TO: Robert Bedford, Plant Manager
FROM: Joseph Fleming, Marketing Manager
SUBJECT: Slippage of the Model 95

The latest word that I have is that the Model 95 will not go into
production for another month. As you know, we have had repeated
delays on introducing this system. Originally, it was supposed to
go into production last August. Our sales for this year were forecast
on the firm promise from R&D that the Model 95 would be ready for
production by January 1 of this year. Apparently, the earliest date
now is April 15.

    Our sales forecasts are based on the expectation that new products
will come into the plant and go into production on specific dates.
Any further delays in the introduction of the Model 95 will seriously
reduce sales for the year, particularly since delays on the 95 will
also affect other models in the series, especially the 96 and 97.

FIGURE 10

AJAX PLANT — CENTRAL CITY

OFFICE MEMORANDUM   March 4

TO: Mr. Robert Bedford
FROM: Al Mumford
SUBJECT: Project Status Report

This is a brief status report with some accompanying recommendations.

    1. Model 95. Although there have been some slippages, the Model
95 is close to coming into production. We have had one brief hangup
due to the failure of the system to pass the packaging tests, but we
anticipate no further difficulty, and the project should be ready to
hand over completely to production in the next few weeks.

    2. Models 96 and 97. As you know, the Model 96 is a simplified
and less complex version of the 95. The 97, as an ancillary system,
adds considerably to the capability of the 95. Both are progressing
and should be ready to be put into production within the next two
months.

    3. We would like to begin design on a completely new and original
system for hospital-laboratory analysis. What we have in mind is a
multichannel digital system which can conduct as many as ten different
blood analyses almost simultaneously. However, we are having difficulties, since Jim Cardinal tells us that funds cannot be made available within the current year.

    Recommendations:

    1. We recommend that you seriously consider hiring some really
capable people in production engineering. We don't want to repeat the
Model 80 problem again. We gave those people a good design, and they
were unable to follow it through.

    2. We recommend that you talk to Cardinal about considerably
increasing funding for the purpose of going into the digital blood
system.

FIGURE 11

Part V

Motivating and Leading Individuals and Groups, and Career Planning

Cases Outline

28. Managerial Systems Ltd.*

Introduction

It had been a rough week for Managerial Systems Ltd. By Thursday, MSL's president, Ken Long, had received upsetting phone calls from consultants Phil Mercer, Ray Terrell, and Fred Sargent concerning client difficulties. He had also talked at length with Karen Webster about conflicts between her personal and professional lives. Crises always seemed to come in avalanches. Tomorrow's staff meeting promised to last the entire spring day, ruining any plans Ken had for sailing.

Managerial Systems Ltd.

Managerial Systems Ltd. was a behaviorally based consulting organization focused on helping client companies improve the effectiveness of managerial systems through the application of sophisticated behavioral science technologies. (Exhibit 1 briefly explains the basics of behavioral consulting.) MSL consultants worked with client organizations to help define needs and then identify the proper methods for satisfying those needs. (Exhibit 2 lists the types of services provided in the past.) All MSL consultants had at least a master's degree in the behavioral sciences and most had obtained a doctorate in a related field. Many had worked in the behavioral area in either private practice or with institutions prior to joining MSL. (Exhibit 3 is a selected biography of representative consultants' backgrounds.)

MSL incorporated in 1977 when Ken Long, the president, resigned his professorship at a prominent southern business school in order to devote his full time to the company. In the past four years MSL had expanded to ten consultants, two research assistants, and five support staffers. MSL's primary clients had been in

*This case was written by Molly Batson and Nancy Sherman under the supervision of Associate Professor Jeffrey A. Barach, A.B. Freeman School of Business. This case has been prepared as a basis for class discussion rather than to illustrate effective or ineffective administrative practices. Copyright © 1982 by the School of Business, Tulane University. Reproduced with permission.

Organizational Development (OD) is a process by which behavioral science principles and practices are used in an ongoing organization in a planned and systematic way. It is utilized to attain such goals as developing greater organizational competence while improving the quality of work life and the organization's effectiveness. (Effectiveness refers to setting and attaining appropriate goals in a changing environment.) OD differs from other planned change efforts such as the purchase of new equipment or floating a bond issue to build a new plant, in that the focus includes the motivation, utilization, and integration of human resources within the organization and is focused on total system change.

OD is a vehicle for helping organizations adjust to accelerated technological and social change. OD is not a specific technique, such as sensitivity training, job enrichment, group team-building, or management by objectives. OD may use specific techniques, but only after the relevance and utility of a special technique has been clearly demonstrated by careful diagnosis.

Interventions or techniques can be grouped in ten basic classifications:
- Individual consultation (counseling-coaching) usually involving a change agent in a one-on-one helping interaction with a single client.
- Unstructured group training involving individuals in a group lacking specific task purpose except that of understanding individual or group dynamics.
- Structured group training including management and group development courses structured to change participant attitudes, convey knowledge, or develop skills.
- Process consultation involving small groups or work teams identifying and solving common problems.
- Survey-guided development, involving collection of data about client work-group or organizational functioning and feeding back data to work groups to use in problem solving.
- Job redesign involving altering the tasks, responsibilities, interactions patterns, or the technical and physical environment intrinsic to the work itself.
- Personnel systems involving implementation through traditional personnel functions.
- Management information and financial control systems involving tracking and evaluating employee or work-group performance.
- Organizational design involving a structural change in organizational authority and reporting relationships.
- Integrated approaches including more than one of the methods described above.

Exhibit 1. Description of Organizational Development (OD)

Source: Edgar F. Huse. *Organization Development and Change,* 1980.

the petrochemical industry. However, attempts to implement a strategy of diversification had begun this year.

The diversification into other industries presented something of a problem for MSL. MSL's consulting expertise had been developed and proven in the petrochemical field. But potential clients questioned how well that expertise would translate to their specific types of problems. To help overcome these questions, Ken had decided to concentrate in three areas related to the prior experience of MSL. These included flow process plants, e.g., petrochemical, energy services and equipment companies, and banking. Ken anticipated no major problems transferring techniques from one industry to the others. This was because MSL tailored each behavioral intervention to a client's particular set of needs.

Ken wanted each consultant to bring in at least one new client by the end of the year. Each consultant was asked to make contacts in new companies and

Organizational Development initiation, planning, and execution
Managerial effectiveness training
Supervisory skills training
Organizational team-building
Organizational diagnostic surveys
  - Organizational climate
  - Employee attitude assessment
  - Specific areas of concern
Managerial expectations clarification
  - Goal setting
  - Organizational dissemination
  - Individual superior-subordinate clarifications
Performance feedback enhancement
  - Establishing organizational systems
  - Expectations setting/feedback skills training
Development of organizational systems
  - Progressive discipline
  - Managerial communications
  - Work system redesign
  - Managerial succession system
Employee Assistance Programs
  - Individual managerial counseling
  - Employee psychological services
  - Alcoholic/drug abuse program
  - Assisting terminated and retiring employees
Effective planning and implementation of organizational changes
EEO Audit simulation
EEO Assimilation Programs
Research Studies
  - Attrition problems
  - Employee acceptance/rejection of anticipated change
  - EEO-related employee attitudes
  - Organization-wide training systems
Workshops on special topics
  - Management of stress situations
  - Assimilation of new managers
  - Problems faced by temporary supervisors
  - Successful specific conflict resolution
Facilitating development of overall top management goals

Exhibit 2.   Consulting Services Rendered to Clients—1980

arrange a presentation of MSL's array of services to management. Several of the consultants expressed their feelings of uneasiness in taking on a sales role. They felt they lacked sufficient experience to decide which companies and executives to approach as potential clients. Once they managed to make contact, the consultants were worried about how to make an effective presentation. To alleviate these concerns, Ken had begun training the consultants in sales techniques. The consultants were taught basic sales techniques tailored to MSL's particular marketing needs.

Long felt it was important for MSL's consultants to have divergent backgrounds both academically and professionally. However, he insisted that potential consultants have a fundamental belief in the benefits of a capitalistic society. When hiring consultants he discussed at length how the individual felt about working for major oil companies. If there was a wide gap in the beliefs of MSL and the consultant, Ken would refuse to hire them. He felt the strains of

Karen Webster,	30, MBA from Tulane University, B.A., psychology, had been with MSL for four years. Prior to joining MSL, Karen worked in a managerial capacity in private business. Her consulting expertise was primarily in management and supervisory development.
Fred Sargent,	55, had been with the firm for three years, joining MSL upon completion of a doctorate in Adult Education. He spent twenty-five years in the Army and rose to the rank of Colonel. During his military career, Fred held many managerial positions, planning and implementing numerous training programs. He also earned an MBA from Syracuse University while in the Army. His Army experience carried over easily in behavioral consulting where Fred focused on development and execution of organizational needs analysis and management training programs.
Ray Terrell,	32, received his Ph.D. in clinical psychology following a master's degree in counseling. He had joined MSL on a part-time basis one and a half years ago while continuing to teach at a local university. Small group facilitation had been Ray's specialty within MSL.
Phil Mercer,	36, had been with MSL on a part-time basis for a year. He continued to teach in the Social Work Department at a local university. His academic credentials included an MSW, an MPH, and a Ph.D. in Human Ecology, a discipline which works against exploitation of the environment. This degree strongly reflected Phil's personal values. He spent many years "throwing rocks at big business from the outside" but had never been a part of that world. He went into consulting to learn more about how big business works and to help improve conditions for people working in the system.

EXHIBIT 3.   Selected Biographies of MSL Consultants

working to improve a system one did not believe in would be detrimental to the consultant's working abilities and effectiveness. Ken encouraged the consultants to come to him to talk about any problems they were having on the job. He felt this minimized the chances of a consultant working him/herself into a corner over an issue.

Ken emphasized the importance of doing a thorough job with a client company. Many times a client company would bring in MSL to solve a specific problem that management had isolated. MSL wanted to gather their own data in order to determine the validity of management's point of view and to find out if there were any additional problems related to the ones indicated. MSL was prepared to walk away from a contract if management refused to allow them to do the necessary research or if management wanted their services for any reason other than to improve working conditions.

The Dilemmas

Phil Mercer

Phil had just completed a large project on the reasons for the engineer attrition rate for a major oil company. The report and final recommendations would be ready the following week. Phil was quite pleased with the results. He attributed the success of the project to the agreement of management to release the report and the final recommendations to the engineers. The engineers took this as a sign that management was making a serious effort to correct many of the problems they faced at work. Therefore, they cooperated fully and candidly with Phil in the interviewing process.

Phil called Mr. Spencer, the Vice-President of Personnel, Engineering, to inform him of the date the report would be ready. He also inquired about distributing the report to the engineers. Mr. Spencer said the report would not be released as planned. A two-page summary of it would be made available. The recommendations would be omitted.

This upset Phil. He had given his word to the engineers that they would receive copies of the report and the recommendations. He reminded Mr. Spencer of management's promise to release it. All the positive effects of the promised release would be negated and the engineers' attitudes would sour. Phil questioned the wisdom of such a move. Mr. Spencer blamed the change in plans on MSL's failure to stay within the contracted budget. He said there were insufficient funds available to copy the report. Phil was at a loss on what to reply, so he terminated the conversation, promising to call again in the next few days.

Phil reviewed his alternatives. He could try again to convince Mr. Spencer to release the results regardless of the costs involved. He thought this would be fruitless based on the previous conversation. Phil considered going directly to the engineers and giving them the report and the recommendations without management's approval. After all, they had been promised a copy of the report and he could provide it verbally anyway. He also thought about going to someone higher in the company who could countermand Spencer's decision.

Phil called Ken to talk about the situation. Ken suggested that Phil bring up the issue at tomorrow's staff meeting. Before hanging up Ken mentioned that the company had contacted him about another consulting job. He wanted Phil to think about whether or not MSL should accept the job in light of the situation with Mr. Spencer.

Fred Sargent

Hugh Cavanaugh was the Operations Manager of a medium-sized petrochemical refinery located on the Louisiana coast. The refinery was part of a large, well-known energy concern. Cavanaugh was from the traditional school of management ("seat of the pants" or "we've always done it this way"). At sixty-two, his physical condition was excellent, considering his recovery from open-heart surgery two years earlier. Although every other member of the Management Committee supported the Plant Manager's initiation of MSL's organizational development (OD) efforts within the refinery (which included supervisory training, teambuilding, and EEO development work) Cavanaugh thought OD was a waste of time. He reportedly said, "young turks come in and try to change the organization when they don't even understand its history . . . besides, the refinery was maximizing production capacity way before all this new OD rubbish came up." Cavanaugh constantly refuted the OD effort along with other organizational changes. He was against the massive computerization then underway, and blatantly expressed his feelings throughout the refinery. As Operations Manager with thirty-seven years of experience, Hugh was in a potentially powerful position on the Management Committee. As a result, his negative attitude hindered the effectiveness of the Management Committee in the change process.

Dennis Kline, the refinery's young, aggressive Plant Manager, was a strong supporter of OD and realized its potential for improving the refinery's productivity. He had been in his present position for one year and one of his first actions had been to initiate the OD effort with MSL's assistance. This was a good way to revitalize the workforce while improving the bottom line. The OD effort would help him gain the respect of the refinery employees by demonstrating his concern for their working environment. Hugh had been his only obstacle to implementing the OD effort. He had tried to energize Hugh by utilizing him as a leader to work decisions and assume responsibility for part of the OD effort. Kline figured that if Cavanaugh felt ownership of the ideas and participated in them from their inception, he would realize their value and be won over. However, Cavanaugh refused to get involved in any way and stonewalled all of Kline's efforts over the entire year. Kline had tried everything short of firing Hugh.

Fred Sargent, MSL's senior consultant working with the Management Committee, knew that the members of the committee recognized Hugh's biases against OD, but they really did not have the professional insight and objectivity to see that he had no capability for change. Some of the committee members had blinders on due to their longtime friendship and respect for Hugh. As a result, the whole Management Committee was having a difficult time accepting the realities of the situation. But it was quite obvious to Sargent, based on his past consulting experience, that as long as Cavanaugh was a forceful member of the Management Committee, MSL's OD efforts could never reach their full potential.

Should Fred work with the Management Committee to accept the fact that Hugh would never change, he would be the catalyst for Hugh's encouraged early retirement. This would then allow Sargent to facilitate the OD process. But, if Fred was linked to Hugh's encouraged retirement, he might be labeled as a "hit man," which could inhibit his ability to work with the Management Committee and other members of the refinery organization. They might see Fred's actions as part of a conspiracy to do some housecleaning and thus find working through behavioral dilemmas with him quite threatening. In addition, the loss of Cavanaugh could be detrimental to the refinery's operations. His position as Operations Manager was a subtle link in labor negotiations currently underway as a result of a recent wildcat strike. Cavanaugh was well-respected by his subordinates, and quite effective in the technical aspects of his job which gave him influence on the union negotiations. It was Fred's feeling that Cavanaugh's work was his life and crucial to his survival, both psychologically and financially.

Feeling extremely frustrated, Fred approached George Davenport, Process Division Manager, Management Committee member, and a longtime friend of Hugh Cavanaugh. George was in his early sixties, but, unlike Hugh, had been able to adjust to organizational changes quite well. He was able to see the potential benefits of OD and could look at the situation from a broad perspective.

Fred: George, I'm really concerned about the slow progress of the Management Committee in this recent OD effort concerning EEO and team building. What do you see as the barrier?

George: I seem to be having the same feelings that things are moving rather slowly. If only we could get Hugh on board . . . I think things would take

off. I've tried to talk to him about the value of the OD efforts, but I can understand his objections. After all, our past experience with consultants billing
themselves as OD experts has not been too good. They cost an arm and a leg
and talk in generalities, never touching on our specific problems. However,
your company has tailored its efforts to our specific needs. Also, Hugh's
knowledge and understanding of company history can't be matched—even
by the Plant Manager! He really feels outside consultants aren't qualified to
facilitate changes in the organization.

Fred: But, George, everyone else on the committee seems able and ready to
accept the OD efforts. Hugh is living in the past. He's dug in his heels and
won't budge.

George: Well, I do know he's too valuable not to have on the Management
Committee at this point.

Fred Sargent was in a bind and didn't know what to do. If he didn't take any
immediate action and chose to buy time, hoping to either change Hugh
Cavanaugh or wait for his scheduled retirement, the entire OD effort might be
doomed. Cavanaugh would do everything in his power to stop the effort, if not
through the Management Committee, then verbally throughout the refinery.
Another option for Sargent was to take on the biggest challenge of his career and
spend all his time trying to change Hugh Cavanaugh. If he could somehow work it
so Cavanaugh received full credit for part of the OD effort and was recognized by
corporate headquarters for this accomplishment, he'd have no choice but to go
along with the continuation of the effort.

Other options open to Fred included convincing Dennis Kline to "force"
Hugh's early retirement with all the usual fanfare; going to corporate headquarters
Human Resources Vice-President or the Vice-President of Refining (who were
both strong OD supporters) and explaining the situation; going to Hugh directly
and asking him to retire; slowly showing the Management Committee in a
calculated way that Hugh was damaging the refinery's effectiveness; or creating a
scandal in order to get Hugh fired if he refused to retire.

Fred decided that the next step would be to bring his dilemma to MSL's
monthly staff meeting for discussion.

Karen Webster

Karen had several problems at work to think about that night. She usually
discussed things with her husband, Jack, in order to put things into a better
perspective. The weekly staff meeting was coming up and she wanted to be
prepared to present her dilemmas as clearly and concisely as possible to the other
consultants to get their opinions.

Karen joined MSL at its inception and had been very active in helping the
company to reach its current size and in building its good reputation. She was the
only woman consultant for several years. MSL did most of its consulting in flow
processing plants and many of the plant managers were products of the "Good
Ole Boy" syndrome. They had grown up in the back country and had been taught
that women stayed at home. There were few, if any, women working in the plants
because of the rough nature of the work. Karen found that it was difficult to get the

managers to accept her as a professional, knowledgeable consultant. She had to prove herself time and again. She found that she couldn't allow her clients to think of her as a woman first and a consultant second. Her professional reputation had been built with these men through much hard work and continuing efforts to educate them.

After working for MSL for five years, Karen and Jack had decided to begin a family. A lot of thought had gone into this decision. Karen had no plans to stop working after the baby was born. This opened several areas of potential conflict between raising the baby and Karen's career. However, after carefully evaluating the situation, they decided to have a child. As soon as Karen found that she was pregnant, she began planning her projects so any traveling would be completed by the end of her seventh month of pregnancy. Back in December she had confirmed plans for an eight-day team-building session at a plant seventy-five miles away. She planned to commute every other day. This session would be the culmination of almost a year of hard work.

Several days ago the client company had contacted Karen and stated that the session would have to be pushed back. The new dates coincided with the end of the eighth month of her pregnancy. She was very concerned about this change. The thought of having to drive to and from the plant every other day was not pleasant. She also disliked the idea of staying at the plant for the entire week. She knew Jack would be upset if she were gone from home so late in her pregnancy. She would tire more easily and would not be as effective as usual. However, she had made a commitment to the client to complete the team-building process. Karen felt very strongly about fulfilling her obligations to MSL and to her career.

Karen considered her options. On some projects it would be possible to bring in another consultant to complete the training. However, this was not the case with team-building. Team-building's purpose was to improve the effectiveness and performance of people who work together closely on a regular basis. Because of the difficulty and time necessary to build a close, trusting relationship between the consultant and the group, it would be impossible for another consultant to take over. She could also go back to the client company and try to convince management to allow the original dates to stand. She could refuse to do the training now and try to complete it after she returned to work.

As Karen talked with Jack she voiced these possibilities and wondered how the other consultants would react to her situation. She was worried about the impact cancellation would have on her career and professional reputation. There was even a possibility that MSL would lose the client if she cancelled. How would her decision affect Ken's decisions to hire other women consultants? Karen wanted to get some feedback from the other consultants at the staff meeting before making her decision.

Ray Terrell

Back at MSL's New Orleans office on the morning of the monthly staff meeting, Ray Terrell's mind began to wander. Only twenty-four hours ago he had been in Dallas, Texas, in the midst of a tension-filled Management Committee meeting and a potentially explosive discussion with Bill Matthews, Vice-President of Refining—Southwest Region for a major energy concern. Ray had decided that this was an issue to be discussed by the entire MSL professional staff, as it had serious implications for MSL's future. He began to jot down notes in preparation for the meeting. . . .

During the first quarter of this year, Ray had become involved in an OD effort at one of the company's Southwest Region refineries located in Corpus Christi, Texas. Terrell, representing MSL, spent approximately three weeks in the data-gathering phase of the OD process, which included employee-consultant interviews in all refinery divisions. According to MSL's standard practice, prior to conducting the employee interviews, Ray had assured the employees that any information obtained during the interviews would be kept confidential. The Management Committee was aware of this practice but had no explicit confidentiality agreement with MSL. MSL had no formalized written statement on the subject of confidentiality in their signed contracts due to their philosophy of tailoring each OD effort to the particular client. It was strongly believed by all MSL consultants that their current practice was in the best interest of the client organization, the individual, and the consulting firm. This was based on the premise that a consulting organization's ability to collect accurate data about individuals and corporations was critical to successful performance. Effective data-gathering depended on trust that the information would not be used to the possible detriment of the individual unless clearly indicated up front.

Upon completion of the data-gathering phase, Ray compiled his results into a written document and presented it to the refinery's Management Committee which included Bill Matthews as an Ex Officio member. The report emphasized a heavy concern for race relations as expressed by black wage earners in particular. Ray had stated, in a broad general sense, that blacks felt mistreated given their seniority and the jobs they got in relation to other refinery workers with similar seniority. He supported this racial concern by stating that blacks felt they were not receiving as adequate career counseling and development as white workers were (both in technical areas and otherwise) so that blacks could compete for higher level positions. Ray's report concluded with recommended action steps which specified supervisory training in EEO awareness and counseling skills as the first steps. In addition, Ray would undertake an intensive study and revamping of the company's employee training program and practices.

Following Ray's presentation, Plant Manager Ron Gallagher called for a discussion. The EEO issue was of great concern to the entire committee, given an impending Department of Labor audit within a few months. Negative audit results could cause significant delay in the expected promotions of Ron (to a headquarters divisional V-P position) and Bill Matthews (to President of the corporation's small Chemical Division) at the end of the year. It was obvious to Ray that he had hit one of the company's most vulnerable spots. This meant that chances for successful implementation of his recommendations were even greater than he had expected. As a result, MSL could probably count on at least six months of steady billing. This would definitely please Ken.

The Management Committee discussion did not seem to be accomplishing anything. It was apparent the members were quite uncomfortable with the topic of EEO in addition to being defensive of their own subdivisions' non-discriminatory posture. Finally Bill Matthews spoke. He congratulated Ray on his effective presentation, reiterated his deep concern for the findings, and stated that he was all for immediate action. However, it would be essential for the

Management Committee to find out exactly who had expressed these concerns so that steps could be taken to rectify their situation right away. After all, Ray and MSL were working for management. Of course, his major concern was for the employees, but there was the upcoming audit to consider, since EEO charges or possible lawsuits could easily result in a prolonged audit and bad publicity. Once the situation was under control, the problem as a whole could be tackled.

When Matthews finished there was an awkward silence in the room. Ron Gallagher made an attempt to neutralize the situation by acknowledging the refinery's potential racial problem and admitting that blacks never came to any of the refinery's social gatherings.

Terrell could not believe that Matthews had the nerve to ask for identification of his information sources in front of the entire Management Committee! He was even more enraged that no one had objected to the request. Terrell did not know how to respond. As a management consultant he did have a responsibility to management, but had Matthews overstepped the professional boundary? This company was currently MSL's largest client, having produced the majority of projects and billing days throughout MSL's short history. If this situation got out of control, there was the possibility that the relationship would be severed. This could be devastating to MSL since their diversification strategy targets for this quarter had not been realized. At this point MSL was relying heavily on its current clients to produce further projects in other areas of their organizations. This vertical penetration marketing strategy had worked very well with almost no specific sales effort on the part of MSL consultants and now seemed crucial to the firm's immediate survivial.

Since all refinery divisions were represented on the Management Committee would Ray be putting MSL's immediate financial future on the line if he did not divulge his information sources? Additionally, if Gallagher and Matthews did get those promotions into the upper echelons of the company, would he be jeopardizing MSL's future with the entire corporation and MSL's reputation in the industry? Finally, one of his goals as an MSL consultant was to improve organizational effectiveness. If he gave the Management Committee the information Matthews wanted, he could be the catalyst needed for the refinery to address the racial concerns affecting the organization's effectiveness.

Ray's mind raced through his confused thoughts. Matthews would be expecting an answer. Ray decided to hold his tongue for the moment and told the Management Committee he'd be in touch with them at their meeting next week.

The Staff Meeting

Ken opened the staff meeting with a brief discussion of the various projects in progress. He then asked the consultants if they had any problems they wanted to discuss. Four hands shot up and Karen, Phil, Ray, and Fred then presented the problems confronting them. Once the initial recitals had been made, Ken recommended a fifteen-minute coffee break so everyone could digest the problems they had just heard about. He asked the group to think about possible courses of action for each situation, the pros and cons of each, and what their final recommendations would be.

29. Traveler Import Cars, Incorporated*

Background

Randy Traveler had been a partner in Capitol Imports, one of the most prosperous foreign car dealerships in greater Columbus, Ohio, selling expensive European automobiles. His wife, Beryl, a holder of an MBA degree from a respected private university, was a consultant specializing in automobile dealerships.

In 1979, Randy and Beryl decided to go into business for themselves. Since between the two of them they had four decades of automobile dealership experience, they elected to acquire their own dealership. With some luck, they obtained a dealership selling a brand of Japanese cars that had become known in the United States for its very high quality. Randy became president and Beryl executive vice-president.

Evolution of the Firm

Stage 1. After obtaining the Japanese dealership, Randy and Beryl decided to locate it approximately two miles from Capitol Imports. The decision was made on the basis of immediate availability of a suitable facility. This location, however, was several miles from a major shopping area of any kind, and the closest automobile dealership was Capitol Imports. Furthermore, the location was approximately three miles from the nearest interchange of a major interstate highway. Nonetheless, the dealership was located on a busy street within easy access to half a dozen upper-middleclass-to-affluent neighborhoods with residents predisposed to purchasing foreign automobiles with a high quality image.

A number of key employees were enticed by Randy and Beryl to leave Capitol Imports and join Traveler Import Cars. Stuart Graham, who was in charge of Finance and Insurance at Capitol Imports, became general manager at Traveler Import Cars. Although Graham is sixty years of age, he lacked any managerial experience prior to assuming the position of general manager at Traveler Import Cars. Before specializing in finance and insurance, Graham was a car salesman. Several mechanics and car salesmen also left Capitol Imports to join Traveler Import Cars. As a rule, the policies and procedures that pertained at Capitol Imports were relied on at Traveler Import Cars, Inc. for the first five years of operations.

No one at Traveler Import Cars was unionized, but the mechanics were given everything that unionized mechanics received at other dealerships in order to remove the incentive to unionize. By everything, it is meant direct compensation, indirect compensation (fringe benefits), and work rules.

Randy and Beryl viewed their dealership as a family. This was in some measure due to the fact that the dealership was part of a Japanese Corporation (which viewed its employees as family), and partly due to the beliefs that Randy and Beryl shared about organizations. Randy and Beryl made every effort to involve subordinates in day-to-day decision-making. As tangible evidence of her commitment to democratic leadership, Beryl decided to introduce a quality circle into Traveler Import Cars, Incorporated. This was done by selecting five non-supervisory employees (one from each part of the organization) to meet once a month with Beryl and Stuart Graham in order to discuss problems, possible solutions, and implementation strategies. No training whatsoever regarding quality circles was provided anyone involved with the so-called "quality circle," and this includes Beryl and Stuart.

Stuart Graham, on the other hand, was a benevolent autocrat, although he tried to create the facade of a democratic leader because he understood well Randy and Beryl's leadership preferences. Most employees agreed with Randy and Beryl that Traveler Import Cars was a family. Furthermore, most employees felt free to voice an opinion on anything to Randy, Beryl, and Graham, or to any other supervisor or manager, for that matter.

Stage 2. As long as the dealership was small everything went well, largely because Randy and Beryl made all key decisions, provided daily direction to supervisors and managers (including the general manager—Stuart Graham, who should have been running the dealership on a day-to-day basis), and resolved problems through face-to-face communications with the involved individuals. As the dealership grew and prospered, it generated enough money for growth. Expanding the dealership rapidly was impractical because of the limited allotment of cars due in large measure to the so-called "voluntary" import quotas by the Japanese car manufacturers. The demand for these cars was so great that cars were even sold from the showroom floor, leaving at times few models for new customers to view.

The first acquisition that Randy and Beryl made was a car leasing company, which they located next to the dealership. Randy elected to spend most of his time building up the car leasing company, leaving the operations of the dealership to Beryl. The second acquisition consisted of another car dealership located approximately ten miles from the original one. The new dealership sold another make of Japanese cars and an expensive European make. The newly acquired dealership was located in the midst of automobile dealerships on a main road, but was housed in inadequate facilities and beset by many problems. Beryl became the chief operating officer of the second dealership as well. Soon after acquiring the second dealership, Randy and Beryl decided to construct new facilities adjacent to the existing ones.

Stage 3. The newly acquired dealership created a great deal of additional work for Beryl, but she understood and accepted that reality because she and Randy knowingly acquired a business that had been plagued by problems prior to acquisition. What bewildered and frustrated Beryl was the fact that the operation of Traveler Import Cars, Inc. took so much of her time as well as physical and psychic energies. After all, it has been five years since she and Randy purchased that dealership. Many key supervisory and managerial personnel now have five years of experience with the dealership, yet the task of running Traveler Import Cars is just as consuming at this time as it was when the dealership was new. Frequently, Beryl would tell one of the managers to do something, but it wouldn't get done. Decisions were reached at management meetings, but they did not get implemented. Programs were initiated, but were frequently permitted to drift and disappear. Important deadlines were being missed with increasing frequency. Mechanics and salesmen were coming to work late and taking excessive lunch breaks with greater frequency. Beryl knew that these problems were not due to insubordination or lack of motivation. Yet, if she did not directly oversee implementation of an important decision, it did not get implemented.

In order to relieve herself of some of the work load, Beryl hired two experienced managers. In order to justify their salaries, however, they spent half of their time at Traveler Import Cars and the other half at the newly acquired dealership. The newly hired managers had good ideas, yet Beryl was working just as hard as ever, and the problems that motivated Beryl to hire two experienced managers remained practically unchanged. In spite of the problems, the dealership grew as rapidly as the increase in the quota of cars that was allotted to the dealership by the manufacturer permitted. In addition, Traveler Import Cars began wholesaling parts to service stations and car repair shops, and started to lease cars in direct competition with the leasing operation managed by Randy. Although an organizational chart did not exist, it would look like Figure 1, if Randy and Beryl bothered to construct one.

About this time, Randy and Beryl's marriage had come undone, and Randy remarried a lady considerably his junior. Even so, Beryl and Randy maintained their business relationship, and were able to work together professionally without visible acrimony. Beryl now had more money than she knew what to do with, and was about to make much more because the newly acquired dealership was being turned around rapidly, largely due to Beryl's considerable talents, the new facility, and the rapidly recovering economy. Yet Beryl no longer wanted to work as hard as she had in the past.

Beryl understood that Stuart Graham lacked the right stuff to be general manager of a car dealership in a metropolitan area, and she approached Randy on the matter. His response was: "Stuart Graham is too valuable of an asset because Traveler Import Cars, Inc. had generated a $500,000 after tax profit last year. He must be doing something right."

Even though Beryl had been a consultant to automobile dealerships for twenty years, she decided nonetheless to retain a consultant. Beryl was fortunate to contact a particularly astute consultant by the name of J. P. Muzak. Her request was that Muzak straighten out the quality circle, which she felt wasn't living up to her expectations. Muzak, however, was reluctant to get involved unless he was permitted to conduct a thorough needs analysis before selecting any kind of intervention strategy. Beryl, after thinking the matter through, assented to Muzak's proposal. The organizational needs analysis relied on confidential structured interviews with all the managers, supervisors, and select non-supervisory personnel. The summary of Muzak's organizational needs analysis follows.

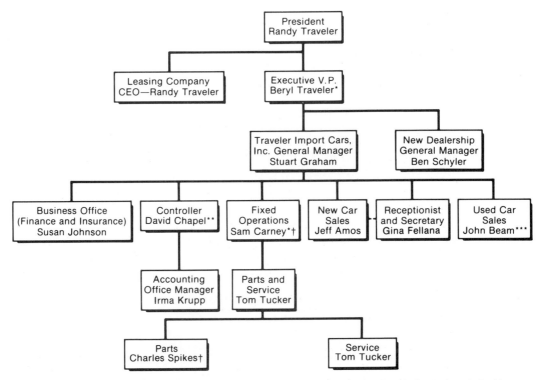

* These individuals spent approximately one-half of their time at Traveler Import Cars and one-half at the new dealership.

** David Chapel is the controller for Traveler Import Cars, the new dealership, and the leasing company. He spends about one-half of his time at Traveler Import Cars and one-half at the new dealership.

*** John Beam frequently is asked by Randy Traveler to assist with matters pertaining to the leasing company.

† Sam Carney owned and operated his own small business prior to joining Traveler Import Cars, Inc. Charles Spikes was a supervisor at a local office of a national automobile parts distributor before coming to work for Traveler Import Cars, Inc.

FIGURE 1. Organizational Chart of Traveler Import Cars, Inc.

Possible Problem Areas

Goals. Although general goals (such as providing the best customer service possible) exist at the organizational level, many individuals report that what is expected of them, in terms of specific and measurable objectives, isn't clearly defined. It is difficult to make a superior happy if the subordinate isn't sure just what it is that the boss wants.

Also, there does not appear to be a philosophy for setting goals. For example, should goals and objectives be imposed unilaterally by the superior on the subordinate, or should the goals and objectives be set jointly between the superior and subordinate?

Organizational Structure. The organizational structure in a number of instances appears to be confusing. Specifically, a number of individuals appear to be reporting to two or more superiors. Irma Krupp reports to David Chapel and Stuart

Graham. Tom Tucker reports to Sam Carney and Stuart Graham. Charles Spikes reports to Tom Tucker, Sam Carney, and Stuart Graham. Susan Johnson seems to work for John Beam and Stuart Graham. John Beam had Susan Johnson's job before he became manager of used cars. David Chapel believes that he reports to the two general managers, to Beryl, and to Randy. Gina Fellana appears to report to everyone.

There is the perception that few managers know what they can do on their own authority and what they must get approved and by whom.

Communications.   There appear to be too many meetings and they do not seem to be as productive as they could be. On this point there is a consensus.

A paper flow problem exists in several areas. The Accounting Office at times does not receive properly filled out forms from the Business Office. It appears that Susan Johnson does not have the time to fill out carefully and on a timely basis all the forms and attend to her other finance and insurance duties. The Accounting Office at times does not receive the necessary paper work from New Car Sales. The Parts Department at times doesn't receive on a timely basis the necessary information from New Car Sales.

Some individuals complain that their superiors do not keep them informed. Everything is a secret.

Training and Development.   A number of individuals have risen through the ranks into supervisory and managerial positions. Since these individuals have never received formal managerial training, the void must be filled by coaching. In a number of cases, the void has not been filled by coaching, and these persons are learning through trial and error—an expensive and time-consuming way of learning, indeed.

The consensus is that the computer equipment is adequate to the task, but the operators need additional training to realize the potential of the equipment. The mechanics receive the latest training from the manufacturer.

Performance Appraisal.   Many people reported that they do not receive a periodic formal appraisal. Thus, their need for performance feedback is frustrated.

Wage and Salary Administration.   Numerous individuals have reported that it is the subordinate who has to initiate a wage or salary increase. Most individuals report that they would like to see the superior initiate wage and salary action at least annually. Moreover, a number of individuals are not sure on what basis they are remunerated. The absence of a systematic periodic performance appraisal is responsible, in part, for this perception.

Discipline.   In a number of instances, individuals arrive late, take extended lunch breaks, and violate rules with impunity. This creates a demoralizing effect on others.

Control System.   The financial control system at the top of the organization appears to be satisfactory. The operational control systems in the rest of the organization are problematic.

Morale.   While there is still the feeling that the organization is a family and the best place the employees have ever worked, the feeling is starting to diminish.

Sundry Problems.

1.   Quality circle may need restructuring along traditional lines.
2.   The time it takes to make decisions should be shortened.
3.   The organization has difficulty implementing decisions that have been made.
4.   Lack of follow-up presents serious problems.
5.   Policies and programs are permitted to drift and disappear (motivator board is an example).
6.   Managers may not be delegating enough.
7.   New car salesmen do not always turn customers over to the Business Office, resulting in loss of revenue to the dealership.
8.   Service desk is crucial and it has been a revolving door.

At a meeting, Muzak presented the findings of his needs analysis to the management team of Traveler Import Cars, Inc., and a discussion ensued regarding each of the possible problem areas. Randy Traveler did not attend since he relegated the operation of the dealership to Beryl. At the end of the discussion, the management team agreed that all the problems uncovered by Muzak were real and, if anything, understated.

Muzak did not present at the meeting his assessment of the potential of the key managers. This he did in a private discussion with Beryl. In summary, Muzak concluded that Stuart Graham was too set in his ways to change. Moreover, he displayed too much emotion publicly, and lacked the respect of his subordinates. Jeff Amos was considered by his subordinates to be a nice guy, but was indecisive, lacked firmness, was manipulated by subordinates, and did not enjoy the respect of his subordinates. Tom Tucker was probably in over his head in his present position. He was only a high school graduate, he was not a mechanic, was unsure of himself, and lacked the confidence of his subordinates. Lastly, he was quite impulsive. His previous experience was as a service desk writer (the person to whom the customer explains the car problems and who writes the work order). All the other managers and supervisors were thought to possess the necessary potential which could be realized through training and experience.

30. Lordstown Plant of General Motors*

Introduction

In December 1971, the management of the Lordstown Plant was very much concerned with an unusually high rate of defective Vegas coming off the assembly line. For the previous several weeks, the lot with a capacity of 2,000 cars had been filled with Vegas which were waiting for rework before they could be shipped out to the dealers around the country.

The management was particularly disturbed by the fact that many of the defects were not the kinds of quality deficiency normally expected in an assembly production of automobiles.[1] There was a countless number of Vegas with their windshields broken, upholstery slashed, ignition keys broken, signal levers bent, rear-view mirrors broken, or carburetors clogged with washers. There were cases in which, as the Plant Manager put it, "the whole engine blocks passed by forty men without any work done on them."

Since then, the incident in the Lordstown Plant has been much publicized in news media, drawing public interest. It has also been frequently discussed in the classroom and in the academic circles. While some people viewed the event as "young worker revolt," others reacted to it as a simple "labor problem." Some viewed it as "worker sabotage," and others called it "industrial Woodstock."

This case describes some background and important incidents leading to this much publicized and discussed industrial event.

This case describes some background and important incidents leading to this much publicized and industrial event.

The General Motors Corporation is the nation's largest manufacturer. The company is a leading example among many industrial organizations which have achieved organizational growth and success through decentralization. The philosophy of decentralization has been one of the most valued traditions in General Motors from the days of Alfred Sloan in the 1930s through Charles Wilson and Harlow Curtice in the 1950s and up to recent years.

Under decentralized management, each of the company's car divisions, Cadillac, Buick, Oldsmobile, Pontiac, and Chevrolet, was given a maximum autonomy in the management of its manufacturing and marketing operations. The assembly operations were no exception, each division managing its own assembly work. The car bodies built by Fisher Body were assembled in various locations

*This case was prepared by Hak-Chong Lee, State University of New York at Albany, and is used here with his permission.

This case was developed for instructional purposes from published sources and interviews with the General Motors Assembly Division officials in Warren, Michigan, and Lordstown, Ohio. The case was read and minor corrections were made by the Public Relations Office of the GMAD. However, the author is solely responsible for the content of the case. The author appreciates the cooperation of General Motors. He also appreciates the suggestions of Professor Anthony Athos of Harvard and Mr. John Grix of General Motors which improved this case.

1. The normal defect rate requiring rework was fluctuating between 1–2 percent at the time.

under maximum control and coordination between the Fisher Body and each car division.

In the mid-1960s, however, the decentralization in divisional assembly operations was subject to a critical review. At the divisional level, the company was experiencing serious problems of worker absenteeism and increasing cost with declines in quality and productivity. They were reflected in the overall profit margins which were declining from 10 percent to 7 percent in the late 1960s. The autonomy in the divided management in body manufacturing and assembly operations, in separate locations in many cases, became questionable under the declining profit situation.

In light of these developments, General Motors began to consolidate in some instances the divided management of body and chassis assembly operations into a single management under the already existing General Motors Assembly Division (GMAD) in order to better coordinate the two operations. The GMAD was given an overall responsibility to integrate the two operations in these instances and see that the numerous parts and components going into car assembly get to the right places in the right amounts at the right times.[2]

The General Motors Assembly Division (GMAD)

The GMAD was originally established in the mid 1930s, when the company needed an additional assembly plant to meet the increasing demands for Buick, Oldsmobile, and Pontiac automobiles. The demands for these cars were growing so much beyond the available capacity at the time that the company began, for the first time, to build an assembly plant on the west coast which could turn out all three lines of cars rather than an individual line. As this novel approach became successful, similar plants turning out a multiple line of cars were built in seven other locations in the east, south, and midwest. In the 1960s the demand for Chevrolet production also increased, and some Buick-Oldsmobile-Pontiac plants began to assemble Chevrolet products. Accordingly, the name of the division was changed to GMAD in 1965.

In order to improve the quality and productivity, the GMAD increased its control over the operations of body manufacturing and assembly. It reorganized jobs, launched programs to improve efficiency, and reduced the causes of defects which required repairs and rework. With many positive results attained under the GMAD management, the company extended the single management concept to six more assembly locations in 1968 which had been run by the Fisher Body and Chevrolet Divisions. In 1971, the GM further extended the concept to four additional Chevrolet-Fisher Body assembly facilities, consolidating the separate management under which the body and chassis assembly had been operating. One of these plants was the Lordstown Plant.

The series of consolidation brought to eighteen the number of assembly plants operated by the GMAD. In terms of total production, they were producing

---

2. A typical assembly plant has five major assembly lines—hard trim, soft trim, body, paint, and final—supported by sub-assembly lines which feed to the main lines such components as engines, transmissions, wheels and tires, radiators, gas tanks, front and sheet metal, and scores of other items. The average vehicle on assembly lines has more than 5,500 items with quality checks numbering five million in a typical GMAD assembly plant in a sixteen-hour-a-day operation.

about 75 percent of all cars and 67 percent of trucks built by the GM. Also in 1971, one of the plants under the GMAD administration began building certain Cadillac models, thus involving GMAD in production of automobiles for each of the GM's five domestic car divisions as well as trucks for both Chevrolet and GMC Truck and Coach Division.

The Lordstown Complex

The Lordstown complex is located in Trumbull County in Ohio, about fifteen miles west of Youngstown and thirty miles east of Akron. It consists of the Vega assembly plant, the van-truck assembly plant, and Fisher Body metal fabricating plant, occupying about 1,000 acres of land. GMAD, which operates the Vega and van-truck assembly plants, is also located in the Lordstown complex. The three plants are in the heart of the heavy industrial triangle of Youngstown, Akron, and Cleveland. With Youngstown as a center of steel production, Akron the home of rubber industries, and Cleveland as a major center for heavy manufacturing, the Lordstown complex commands a good strategic and logistic location for automobile assembly.

The original assembly plant was built in 1964–1966 to assemble Impalas. But in 1970 it was converted into Vega assembly with extensive arrangements. The van-truck assembly plant was constructed in 1969, and the Fisher Body metal fabricating plant was further added in 1970 to carry out stamping operations to produce sheet metal components used in Vega and van assemblies. In October 1971, the Chevrolet Vega and van-assembly plants and Fisher Body Vega assembly plants which had been operating under separate management were merged into a single jurisdiction of the GMAD.

Workforce at the Lordstown Plant

There are over 11,400 employees working in the Lordstown Plant (as of 1973). Approximately 6,000 people, of whom 5,500 are on hourly payroll, work in the Vega assembly plant. About 2,600 workers, 2,100 of them paid hourly, work in van-truck assembly. As members of the United Auto Workers Union, Local 1112, the workers command good wages and benefits. They start out on the line at about $5.00 an hour, get a 10¢ an hour increase within thirty days, and another 10¢ after ninety days. Benefits come to $2.50 an hour.[3] The supplemental unemployment benefits virtually guarantee the worker's wages throughout the year. If the worker is laid off, he gets more than 90 percent of his wages for fifty-two weeks. He is also eligible for up to six days for holidays, excused absence, or bereavement, and up to four weeks' vacation.

The workforce at the plant is almost entirely made up of local people with 92 percent coming from the immediate area of a twenty-mile radius. Lordstown itself is a small rural town of about 500 residents. A sizable city closest to the plant is Warren, five miles away, which together with Youngstown supplies about two-

---

3. In GM, the average worker on the line earns $12,500 a year with fringe benefits of $3,000.

thirds of the workforce. The majority of the workers (57.5 percent) are married, 7.6 percent are homeowners, and 20.2 percent are buying their homes. Of those who do not own their own homes (72 percent), over one-half are still living with their parents. The rest live in rented houses or apartments.

The workers in the plant are generally young. Although various news media reported the average worker age as twenty-four years old, and in some parts of the plant as twenty-two years, the company records show that the overall average worker age was somewhat above twenty-nine years as of 1971–72. The national average is forty-two. The workforce at Lordstown is the second youngest among GM's twenty-five assembly plants around the country. The fact that the Lordstown plant is the GM's newest assembly plant may partly explain the relatively young work force.

The educational profile of the Lordstown workers indicates that only 22.2 percent have less than a high school education. Nearly two-thirds or 62 percent are high school graduates, and 16 percent are either college graduates or have attended college. Another 26 percent have attended trade school. The average education of 13.2 years makes the Lordstown workers among the best educated in GM's assembly plants.

The Vega Assembly Line

Conceived as a major competitive product against the increasing influx of foreign cars which were being produced at as low as one-fourth the labor rate in this country, the Vega was specifically designed with a maximum production efficiency and economy in mind. From the initial stages of planning, the Vega was designed by a special task team with the most sophisticated techniques, using computers in designing the outer skin of the car and making the tapes that form the dies. Computers were also used to match up parts, measure the stack tolerances, measure safety performance under head-on collision, and make all necessary corrections before the first 1971 model car was ever built. The 2300-cubic-centimeter all-aluminum, 4-cylinder engine, was designed to give gas economy comparable to the foreign imports.

The Vega was also designed with the plant and the people in mind. As the GM's newest plant, the Vega assembly plant was known as the "super plant" with the most modern and sophisticated designs to maximize efficiency. It featured the newest engineering techniques and a variety of new power tools and automatic devices to eliminate much of the heavy lifting and physical labor. The line gave the workers an easier access to the car body, reducing the amount of bending and crawling in and out, as in other plants around the country. The unitized body in large components like pre-fab housing made the assembly easier and lighter with greater body integrity. Most difficult and tedious tasks were eliminated or simplified, on-line variations of the job were minimized, and the most modern tooling and mechanization was used to the highest possible degree of reliability.

It was also the fastest moving assembly line in the industry. The average time per assembly job was thirty-six seconds with a maximum of 100 cars rolling off the assembly line per hour for a daily production of 1,600 cars from two shift operations. The time cycle per job in other assembly plants averaged about fifty-five seconds. Although the high speed of the line did not necessarily imply greater work load or job requirement, it was a part of the GM's attempt to maximize economy in Vega assembly. The fact that the Vega was designed to have 43 percent fewer parts than a full-size car also helped the high-speed line and economy.

Impact of GMAD and Reorganization in the Lordstown Plant

As stated previously, the assembly operations at Lordstown had originally been run by Fisher Body and Chevrolet as two plants. There were two organizations, two plant managers, two unions, and two service organizations. The consolidation of the two organizations into a single operating system under the GMAD in October 1971 required a difficult task of reorganization and dealing with the consequences of manpower reduction such as work slowdown, worker discipline, grievances, etc.

As duplicating units such as production, maintenance, inspection, and personnel were consolidated, there was a problem of selecting the personnel to manage the new organization. There were chief inspectors, personnel directors, and production superintendents as well as production and service workers to be displaced or reassigned. Unions which had been representing their respective plants also had to go through reorganization. Union elections were held to merge the separate union committees at Fisher Body and Chevrolet in a single union bargaining committee. This eliminated one full local union shop committee.

At the same time, GMAD launched an effort to improve production efficiency more in line with that in other assembly plants. It included increasing job efficiency through reorganization and better coordination between the body and chassis assembly, and improving controls over product quality and worker absenteeism. This effort coincided with the plant's early operational stage at the time which required adjustments in line balance and work methods. Like other assembly plants, the Vega assembly plant was going through an initial period of diseconomy caused by suboptimal operations, imbalance in the assembly line, and somewhat redundant workforce. According to management, line adjustment and work changes were a normal process in accelerating the assembly operation to the peak performance the plant had been designed for after the initial break-in and start-up period.

As for job efficiency, the GMAD initiated changes in those work sequences and work methods which were not well coordinated under the divided managements of body and chassis assembly. For example, previous to the GMAD, Fisher Body had been delivering the car body complete with interior trim to the final assembly lines, where oftentimes the workers soiled the front seats as they did further assembly operations. GMAD changed this practice so that the seats were installed as one of the last operations in building the car. Fisher Body also had been delivering the car body with complete panel instrument frame which made it extremely difficult for the assembly workers to reach behind the frame in installing the instrument panels. The GMAD improved the job method so that the box containing the entire instrument panels was installed on the assembly line. Such improvements in job sequences and job methods resulted in savings in time and the number of workers required. Consequently, there were some jobs where the assembly time was cut down and/or the number of workers was reduced.

GMAD also put more strict control over worker absenteeism and the causes for defect work; the reduction in absenteeism was expected to require less relief men, and the improvement in quality and less repair work were to require less repairmen. In implementing these changes, the GMAD instituted a strong policy of dealing with worker slowdowns via strict disciplinary measures including dismissal. It was rumored that the inspectors and foremen passing defective cars would be fired on the spot.

Many workers were laid off as a result of the reorganization and job changes. The union was claiming that as many as 700 workers were laid off. Management, on the other hand, put the layoff figure at 375 to which the union later conceded.[4] Although management claimed that the changes in job sequence and method in some assembly work did not bring a substantial change in the overall speed or pace of the assembly line, the workers perceived the job change as "tightening" the assembly line. The union charged that the GMAD brought a return of an old-fashioned line speedup and a "sweatshop style" of management reminiscent of the 1930s, making the men do more work at the same pay. The workers were blaming the "tightened" assembly line for the drastic increase in quality defects. As one worker commented, "That's the fastest line in the world. We have about forty seconds to do our job. The company adds one more thing and it can kill us. We can't get the stuff done on time and a car goes by. The company then blames us for sabotage and shoddy work."

The number of worker grievances also increased drastically. Before GMAD took over, there were about 100 grievances in the plant. Since then, grievances increased to 5,000, 1,000 of which were related to the charge that too much work had been added to the job. The worker resentment was particularly great in "towveyor" assembly and seat sub-assembly areas. The "towveyor" is the area where engines and transmissions are assembled. Like seat sub-assembly there is a great concentration of workers working together in close proximity. Also, these jobs are typically for beginning assemblers who tend to make the work crew in these areas younger and better educated.

The workers in the plant were particularly resentful of the company's strict policy in implementing the changes. They stated that the tougher the company became, the more they would stiffen their resistance even though other jobs were scarce in the market. One worker said, "In some of the other plants where the GMAD did the same thing, the workers were older and they took this. But I've got twenty-five years ahead of me in this plant." Another worker commented, "I saw a woman running to keep pace with the fast line. I'm not going to run for anybody. There ain't anyone in that plant that is going to tell me to run." One foreman said, "The problem with the workers here is not so much that they don't want to work, but that they just don't want to take orders. They don't believe in any kind of authority."

While the workers were resisting management orders, there were some indications that the first-line supervisors had not been adequately trained to perform satisfactory supervisory roles. The average supervisor at the time had less than three years of experience, and 20 percent of the supervisors had less than

4. All of the workers who had been laid off were later reinstated as the plant needed additional workers to perform assembly jobs for optional features to Vega, i.e., vinyl top, etc., which were later introduced. In addition, some workers were put to work at the van-assembly plant.

one year's experience. Typically, they were young, somewhat lacking in knowledge of the provisions of the union contract and other supervisory duties, and less than adequately trained to handle the workers in the threatening and hostile environment which was developing.

Another significant fact was that the strong reactions of the workers were not entirely from the organizational and job changes brought about by the GMAD alone. Management noted that there was a significant amount of worker reactions in the areas where the company hadn't changed anything at all. Management felt that the intense resentment was particularly due to the nature of the workforce in Lordstown. The plant was not only made up of young people, but also the workforce reflected the characteristics of "tough labor" in steel, coal, and rubber industries in the surrounding communities. Many of the workers in fact came from families who made their living working in these industries. Management also noted that the worker resistance had been much greater in the Lordstown Plant than in other plants where similar changes had been made.

A good part of the young workers' resentment also seemed to be related to the unskilled and repetitive nature of the assembly work. One management official admitted that the company was facing a difficult task in getting workers to "take pride" in the product they were assembling. Many of them were benefiting from the company's tuition assistance plan which was supporting their college education in the evening. With this educated background, obviously assembly work was not fulfilling their high work expectations. Also, the job market was tight at the time, and they could neither find any meaningful jobs elsewhere nor, even if found, could they afford to give up the good money and fringe benefits they were earning on their assembly-line jobs. This made them frustrated, according to company officials.

Many industrial engineers were questioning whether the direction of management toward assembly line work could continue. As the jobs became easier, simpler, and repetitive, requiring less physical effort, there were less and less traces of skill and increased monotony. The worker unrest indicated that they

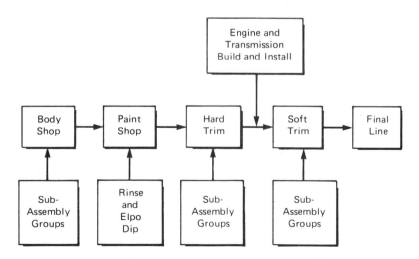

Exhibit 1. Flowchart of Major Assembly Operations

not only wanted to go back to the work pace prior to the "speedup" (pre-October pace), but also wanted the company to do something about the boring and meaningless assembly work. One worker commented, "The company has got to do something to change the job so that a guy can take an interest in the job. A guy can't do the same thing eight hours a day year after year. And it's got to be more than the company just saying to a guy, 'Okay, instead of six spots on the weld, you'll do five spots.'"

As the worker resentment mounted, the UAW Local 1112 decided in early January 1972 to consider possible authorization for a strike against the Lordstown Plant in a fight against the job changes. In the meantime, the union and management bargaining teams worked hard on worker grievances; they reduced the number of grievances from 5,000 to a few hundred; management even indicated that it would restore some of the eliminated jobs. However, the bargaining failed to produce accord on the issues of seniority rights and shift preference, which were related to wider issues of job changes and layoff.

A vote was held in early February 1972. Nearly 90 percent of the workers came out to vote, which was the heaviest turnout in the history of the Local. With 97 percent of the votes supporting, the workers went out on strike in early March.

In March 1972, with the strike in effect, the management of the Lordstown Plant was assessing the impact of the GMAD and the resultant strike in the Plant. It was estimated that the work disruption because of the worker resentment and slowdown had already cost the company 12,000 Vegas and 4,000 trucks amounting to $45 million. There had been repeated closedowns of assembly lines since December 1971, because of the worker slowdowns and the cars passing down the line without all necessary operations performed on them. The car lot was full with 2,000 cars waiting for repair work.

There had also been an amazing number of complaints from Chevrolet dealers, 6,000 complaints in November alone, about the quality of the Vegas shipped to them. This was more than the combined complaints from the other assembly plants.

The strike in the Lordstown Plant was expected to affect other plants. The plants at Tonawanda, New York, and Buffalo, New York, were supplying parts for Vega. Despite the costly impact of the worker resistance and the strike, the management felt that the job changes and cost reductions were essential if the Vega were to return a profit to the company. The plant had to be operating at about 90 percent capacity to break even. Not only had the plant with highly automated features cost twice as much as estimated, but also the Vega itself ended up weighing 10 percent more than had been planned.

While the company had to do something to increase the production efficiency in the Lordstown Plant, the management was wondering whether it couldn't have planned and implemented the organizational and job changes differently in view of the costly disruption of the operations and the organizational stress the plant had been experiencing.

31. The Hovey and Beard Company*

Part 1

The Hovey and Beard Company manufactured wooden toys of various kinds: wooden animals, pull toys, and the like. One part of the manufacturing process involved spraying paint on the partially assembled toys. The operation was staffed entirely by women.

The toys were cut, sanded, and partially assembled in the wood room. Then they were dipped into shellac, following which they were painted. The toys were predominantly two-colored predominantly two-colored; a few were made in more than two colors. Each color required an additional trip through the paint room.

For a number of years, production of these toys had been entirely hand-work. However, to meet tremendously increased demand, the painting operation had recently been re-engineered so that the eight women who did the painting sat in a line by an endless chain of hooks. These hooks were in continuous motion, past the line of women and into a long horizontal oven. Each woman sat at her own painting booth, so designed as to carry away fumes and to backstop excess paint. The woman would take a toy from the tray beside her, position it in a jig inside the painting cubicle, spray on the color according to a pattern, then release the toy and hang it on the hook passing by. The rate at which the hooks moved had been calculated by the engineers so that each woman, when fully trained, would be able to hang a painted toy on each hook before it passed beyond her reach.

The women working in the paint room were on a group bonus plan. Since the operation was new to them, they were receiving a learning bonus which decreased by regular amounts each month. The learning bonus was scheduled to vanish in six months, by which time it was expected that they would be on their own—that is, able to meet the standard and to earn a group bonus when they exceeded it.

Part 2

By the second month of the training period, trouble had developed. The women learned more slowly than had been anticipated, and it began to look as though their production would stabilize far below what was planned for. Many of the hooks were going by empty. The women complained that they were going by too fast, and that the time-study man had set the rates wrong. A few women quit and had to be replaced with new women, which further aggravated the learning problem. The team spirit that the management had expected to develop automatically through the group bonus was not in evidence except as an

*Abridgement from pp. 90–94 of "Group Dynamics and Intergroup Relations" by George Strauss and Alex Bavelas from *Money and Motivation* by William F. Whyte. Copyright © 1955 by Harper & Row, Publishers, Inc. Reprinted by permission.

expression of what the engineers called "resistance." One woman whom the group regarded as its leader (and the management regarded as the ringleader) was outspoken in making the various complaints of the group to the foreman: The job was a messy one, the hooks moved too fast, the incentive pay was not being correctly calculated, and it was too hot working so close to the drying oven.

Part 3

A consultant who was brought into this picture worked entirely with and through the foreman. After many conversations with him, the foreman felt that the first step should be to get the women together for a general discussion of the working conditions. He took this step with some hesitation, but he took it on his own volition.

The first meeting, held immediately after the shift was over at 4:00 in the afternoon, was attended by all eight women. They voiced the same complaints again: The hooks went by too fast, the job was too dirty, the room was hot and poorly ventilated. For some reason, it was this last item that they complained of most. The foreman promised to discuss the problem of ventilation and temperature with the engineers, and he scheduled a second meeting to report back to the women. In the next few days the foreman had several talks with the engineers. They and the superintendent felt that this was really a trumped-up complaint, and that the expense of any effective corrective measure would be prohibitively high.

The foreman came to the second meeting with some apprehension. The women, however, did not seem to be much put out, perhaps because they had a proposal of their own to make. They felt that if several large fans were set up so as to circulate the air around their feet, they would be much more comfortable. After some discussion, the foreman agreed that the idea might be tried out. The foreman and the consultant discussed the question of the fans with the superintendent, and three large propeller-type fans were purchased.

Part 4

The fans were brought in. The women were jubilant. For several days the fans were moved about in various positions until they were placed to the satisfaction of the group. The women seemed completely satisfied with the results, and relations between them and the foreman improved visibly.

The foreman, after this encouraging episode, decided that further meetings might also be profitable. He asked the women if they would like to meet and discuss other aspects of the work situation. The women were eager to do this. The meeting was held, and the discussion quickly centered on the speed of the hooks. The women maintained that the time-study man had set them at an unreasonably fast speed and that they would never be able to reach the goal of filling enough of them to make a bonus.

The turning point of the discussion came when the group's leader frankly explained that the point wasn't that they couldn't work fast enough to keep up with the hooks, but that they couldn't work at that pace all day long. The foreman explored the point. The women were unanimous in their opinion that they could keep up with the belt for short periods if they wanted to. But they didn't want to because if they showed they could do this for short periods, they would be expected to do it all day long. The meeting ended with an unprecedented request: "Let us adjust the speed of the belt faster or slower, depending on how we feel." The foreman agreed to discuss this with the superintendent and the engineers.

The reaction of the engineers to the suggestion was negative. However, after several meetings, it was granted that there was some latitude within which variations in the speed of the hooks would not affect the finished product. After considerable argument with the engineers, it was agreed to try out the women's idea.

With misgivings, the foreman had a control with a dial marked "low, medium, fast" installed at the booth of the group leader; she could now adjust the speed of the belt anywhere between the lower and upper limits that the engineers had set.

Part 5

The women were delighted, and spent many lunch hours deciding how the speed of the belt should be varied from hour to hour throughout the day. Within a week the pattern had settled down to one in which the first half hour of the shift was run on what the women called medium speed (a dial setting slightly above the point marked "medium"). The next two and one-half hours were run at high speed; the half hour before lunch and the half hour after lunch were run at low speed. The rest of the afternoon was run at high speed with the exception of the last forty-five minutes of the shift, which was run at medium.

In view of the women's reports of satisfaction and ease in their work, it is interesting to note that the constant speed at which the engineers had originally set the belt was slightly below medium on the dial of the control that had been given the women. The average speed at which the women were running the belt was on the high side of the dial. Few, if any, empty hooks entered the oven, and inspection showed no increase of rejects from the paint room.

Production increased, and within three weeks (some two months before the scheduled ending of the learning bonus) the women were operating at 30 to 50 percent above the level that had been expected under the original arrangement. They were collecting their base pay, a considerable piece-rate bonus, and the learning bonus which, it will be remembered, had been set to decrease with time and not as a function of current productivity. The women were earning more now than many skilled workers in other parts of the plant.

Part 6

Management was besieged by demands that this inequity be taken care of. With growing irritation between superintendent and foreman, engineers and foreman, superintendent and engineers, the situation came to a head when the superintendent revoked the learning bonus and returned the painting operation to its original status. The hooks moved again at their constant, time-studied designated speed; production dropped again; and within a month, all but two of the eight women had quit. The foreman himself stayed on for several months but, feeling aggrieved, then left for another job.

32.   National Lumber Company*

Frank Jensen was general manager of the Fabricated Components Division of the National Lumber Company. Located in Trenton, New Jersey, the Fabricated Components Division manufactured and sold a line of prefabricated components such as walls, floors, and roofing systems to building contractors on the eastern seaboard. By utilizing the products of the Fabricated Components Division contractors could, under certain circumstances, achieve great economy in construction of their projects.

The Fabricated Components Division was significantly different from the other operations of the National Lumber Company. National Lumber Company manufactured and sold a wide range of lumber products from a series of plants and wholesaling points throughout the United States. The National Lumber Company was a large, successful organization which had been in business for over seventy-five years. The Fabricated Components Division had been started on an experimental basis, as the management of the National Lumber Company felt that prefabricated components offered real promise in the construction industry, and it wished to be aware of the problems and opportunities in the field. By establishing this division, management felt that valuable experience and insights could be gained and that the National Lumber Company would be in a good position to capitalize on the expected boom in components.

A large modern plant, more than adequate for the expected level of immediate operations, was erected in Trenton. Mr. Jensen, who had a great deal of experience in the fabricated components business as manager of one of the small independent organizations which were engaged in this type of activity, was hired for the purpose of supervising the construction of the plant and for heading the operations of Fabricated Components Division after the plant was completed. He was considered to be a very capable administrator by executives of National Lumber Company.

During the first year of operation many diverse things had to be done: building an organization to both manufacture and sell the products, staffing the office force, working at production and control difficulties, and establishing a market for what was basically a new, relatively untested concept in the building industry. Many problems were encountered, but at the end of the first year the

*Copyright © 1976 by Harry R. Knudson, Graduate School of Business, University of Washington. Reprinted by permission from *Organizational Behavior: A Management Approach,* Harry R. Knudson and C. Patrick Fleenor, Winthrop Publishing Co., 1978.

Fabricated Components Division had shown a profit of $24,000 on sales of $800,000 and an investment of $500,000.

The second year was, according to Mr. Jensen, a continuation of the "shakedown period." Changes in both the product and the organization were made, additional capital was invested in the plant, and advertising and selling expenditures were increased. The product line seemed to be gaining the approval of many contractors, although competition with the more traditional methods of construction was severe. At the end of the second year the operating statements showed a net loss of $8,000 on sales of $700,000 and a net investment of $600,000.

The third and fourth years of the life of Fabricated Components Division were, in Mr. Jensen's words, "a madhouse." Several new products were introduced, the plant was again expanded, advertising expenditures were increased still more, and a great number of people were added to the organization to handle the increased volume of business. Sales for the third year totaled almost $2 million. However, a net loss of $126,000 was realized. Mr. Jensen stated:

> It was mass confusion and things just got away from us. We had too many things to do and too many people involved. When we lived through the third year without going under, we expected things to go very well from then on, but we had unexpected problems with some of our people quitting. We also lost a lot of money on a big government order, partly because we didn't have good enough control of our operations. During the fourth year of operations we lost $160,000 on the big job and overall $254,000. But I felt that we were learning through our mistakes and that we still had great potential in this part of the business. We had pretty well perfected our manufacturing operations in Trenton, had added some new equipment and had our organizational problems pretty well worked out.
>
> I was concerned about the increasing pressure I was subjected to from National Lumber, however. Naturally, I didn't expect top management to be overjoyed by our performance. When we started, both they and I knew that we would have some difficult times, but neither of us expected our financial picture to be quite so bleak. Although we were doing some very good work and were by far the most outstanding outfit in this part of the business, we did not seem to be able to make any money.

Pressures from above increased greatly during the fifth year. At one time or another Mr. Jensen was called on by literally every member of the top management of National Lumber, including the chairman of the board of directors. According to Mr. Jensen, these visits were relatively pleasant, but unproductive and prevented him from attending to what he considered at that time to be the most important part of his job—getting sufficient sales so that the large plant could be operated on a profitable basis. Mr. Jensen stated:

> We were like Grand Central Station! I couldn't get anything done, and the constant stream of top-level visitors was upsetting to our plant and office people. They knew that we hadn't yet proved ourselves financially, and all the top brass made them nervous.
>
> Some of our visitors were quite candid. One man told me he had no faith in the basic ideas of our organization and that he stopped by just "to see the rathole we're pouring all our money down." And when I found out many of our visitors were charging the expenses of their visits to our operations and we were getting billed for them through interdivisional charges, I really got pretty angry.

But the main thing was that we got little realistic advice or help from these people. Several suggested we "do better," but didn't tell us how we might.

There were several things that I felt they could have done—but I got nowhere. Everyone had a gloomy attitude except me. I knew what our capabilities were and had great hopes. I didn't feel that many people understood the differences between running an old established business such as National Lumber and a new, struggling business such as the Fabricated Components Division.

During the fifth year Mr. Jensen was under considerable pressure from his immediate superior, Avery Randell, Eastern Regional Manager for the parent company. Mr. Randell sent Mr. Jensen a "confidential memo" about every other week in which he commented upon events that had occurred or decisions that Mr. Jensen had made that did not meet with his approval. Mr. Jensen regularly ignored these memos. He kept them locked in his desk—to which only he had a key—as he did not want their contents known to his subordinates for fear of the effect upon their morale. Mr. Randell also frequently asked Mr. Jensen to have lunch in New York, where Mr. Randell's office was located, so that he could keep in closer touch with the activities at Fabricated Components Division. Often Mr. Jensen would decline these invitations, but he did have lunch with Mr. Randell in New York City about every two weeks. In an effort to satisfy Randell's demands for information, Mr. Jensen started to send him a weekly report on the activities of Fabricated Components Division. The information that went into this report was carefully screened by Mr. Jensen so that nothing that would upset Randell or increase his demands on Jensen's time was included. According to Jensen, "The sole purpose of these reports was to keep him off my back."

Mr. Jensen made the following comments about his relationship with Mr. Randell:

Avery's OK, but he's quite nervous about our operations. His division almost runs itself. His people are experienced and well trained, and he really doesn't have too much to do. He plays golf a lot and cruises on his boat for long weekends, while I'm at the plant seven days a week and most evenings. He doesn't know much about what we're trying to do and this makes him uncomfortable. We're a thorn in his side and the only "disreputable" part of his division financially. He inherited us because we're geographically close to him, but he doesn't have much sympathy for or understanding of what we're trying to do and the problems we face. I keep telling him that I'll take all the blame for our operations, but with all the attention we're getting from top management he's very much interested in taking part in many of our decisions—even though he doesn't know what is going on and is technically incompetent to assist in managing Fabricated Components Division. Personally, I like him and enjoy his company. Our meetings are very pleasant and we go to some very nice places for lunch. Avery does give us some kinds of help, too. For example, we've had some minor legal problems which he has gotten off our hands. But, in general, he is more of a hindrance than a help. He doesn't know enough about our operation to really help us, and the things he could do, he doesn't. I've wanted to hire another salesman for a long time, but I can't get Avery to approve it. It would cost us about $3,000 a month, but we need more sales and a good man would pay for himself in no time. But Avery's so upset about our losses that he won't let me hire anyone else without his approval, and he won't give it. I would guess that I spend 30 percent of my time either dealing with Avery or worrying about our relationship. I've told him that if I answered all of his memos, I wouldn't have time for anything else. He's been a real problem for me, and it keeps me from doing the really important things. I'd like to hire some kid to do all of that kind of thing so I would have time to run the business.

About two months before the end of the fifth year of operations, a meeting of top management of the National Lumber Company was held in New York to decide the future of Fabricated Components Division. Mr. Jensen was not asked to attend this meeting, which irritated him considerably. He was asked to submit his plans for the next year's operations, as well as several alternative plans and a capital and expense budget for the coming year. He spent a great deal of time preparing this information and submitted alternative plans ranging from considerable expansion of operations to shutting down of the plant completely and going out of business. In the letter submitting this information, he requested that he be permitted to attend the meeting. He received no reply to this request.

Two weeks after the meeting had been held Mr. Jensen had not been informed of what decision, if any, had been made. As he had had no information to the contrary, he assumed that operations for the next year would continue about as they had in the past. About three weeks after the meeting, Mr. Jensen began to hear rumors that the Fabricated Components Division would be shut down at the end of the year. These rumors came from sources both within and outside the company. On hearing these rumors, Mr. Jensen called Mr. Randell who told him that, "Things are still undecided, but don't spend any more money than you have to." Mr. Jensen then called the chairman of the board of directors who informed him that the company had decided to shut down the Fabricated Components Division and go out of that part of the business. Shortly thereafter, Mr. Jensen received a letter from the president of National Lumber Company confirming this information. Mr. Jensen then began making plans for closing down the Fabricated Components Division. He felt that a poor decision had been made, but that it would be useless to attempt to have the decision reversed.

During these last few weeks of operation Mr. Jensen was faced with several unique problems.

He was not sure what, if anything, to tell his employees—or what the timing should be. He was not greatly concerned about the fifty men in the plant, for they were skilled workers who could easily find other employment without suffering financial losses. He was especially concerned about the future of the production manager, the sales manager, and the office manager, all of whom had been with him since the start of Fabricated Components Division. Because none of these people had been with the National Lumber Company for very long, they would get little severance pay and, though capable people, could well be faced with a period of unemployment until they found other jobs. He wanted to give these people adequate time to find new positions, yet felt that if the news was out, efficiency would drop considerably and the Fabricated Components Division would have an even greater loss than anticipated for its fifth—and last—year of operation.

Mr. Jensen also faced another kind of problem. He still had great faith in the kind of thing that the Fabricated Components Division was doing and had often considered the advantages of operating his own company in this field. When he had learned that the Fabricated Components Division was to be shut down, he had quietly explored the possibilities of buying the business and had found that he could arrange adequate financing without too much difficulty. Much of the equipment was specialized and not readily saleable. He didn't know of anyone—other than himself—who might want to buy the Fabricated Components Division and felt that he could get everything that he needed to operate with at a reasonable price. Thus, if the Fabricated Components Division showed a great loss for the year, this might discourage any other prospective buyers, as well as increase National Lumber Company's desire to get out of an unprofitable venture for any kind of recovered investment, thus driving down the price he might have to pay.

Along these same lines, Mr. Jensen was undecided about what action, if any, should be taken regarding several large sales that were in the closing stages. It would be quite easy to defer action on these sales until after he had purchased the operations and thus start on his own with a considerable order file. If the sales were closed now, the customers would probably revert to the conventional construction techniques when they learned that Fabricated Components Division was not going to be in business. Or it was possible that these orders would be farmed out to small independents by National Lumber Company before Mr. Jensen could get operating on his own.

In reflecting upon the history of the Fabricated Components Division Mr. Jensen observed that this was an excellent example of a good idea that had been defeated because of lack of support and meddling on the part of top management. "They bought the idea of the Fabricated Components Division in theory but refused, or were literally unable, to recognize the kinds of problems that would arise. When these problems did arise—and almost any new operation faces the same kinds of problems—they wouldn't leave me alone long enough to solve them. Certainly, I must take a great share of the blame for our poor record, but I sincerely believe that if we hadn't had so many visitors and so much attention from top management, we would have had a respectable, if not spectacular, financial success."

Avery Randell made the following comments regarding the Fabricated Components Division:

> Frank Jensen is a very capable man, but we never really got him to operate as part of the company. He ran the Fabricated Components Division as if it were an independent organization and never really accepted or respected our advice. This past year in particular we had the very definite feeling that Frank wanted no part of us, even though several of our top management people went considerably out of their way to help him. Frank has not yet learned how to live in a relatively large organization and, because of his inability to accommodate the organization, creates a lot of problems for himself and detracts considerably from his excellent technical skills. He probably knows more about prefabricated components than anyone in the country, but, because of his inability to adjust to the organization, he has been an unsuccessful manager for us.

33. Bob Knowlton (A)*

Bob Knowlton was sitting alone in the conference room of the laboratory. The rest of the group had gone. One of the secretaries had stopped and talked for a while about her husband's coming induction into the Army, and had finally left. Bob, alone in the laboratory, slid a little further down in his chair looking with satisfaction at the results of the first test run of the new photon unit.

He liked to stay after the others had gone. His appointment as project head was still new enough to give him a deep sense of pleasure. His eyes were on the graphs before him but in his mind he could hear Dr. Jerrold, the laboratory head, saying again, "There's one thing about this place that you can bank on. The sky is the limit for a man who can produce!" Knowlton felt again the tingle of happiness and embarrassment. Well, dammit, he said to himself, he had produced. He wasn't kidding anybody. He had come to the Simmons Laboratories two years ago. During a routine testing of some rejected Clanson components he had stumbled on the idea of the photon correlator, and the rest just happened. Jerrold had been enthusiastic; a separate project had been set up for further research and development of the device, and he had gotten the job of running it. The whole sequence of events still seemed a little miraculous to Knowlton.

He shrugged out of the reverie and bent determinedly over the sheets when he heard someone come into the room behind him. He looked up expectantly. Jerrold often stayed late himself, and now and then dropped in for a chat. This always made the day's end especially pleasant for Bob. It wasn't Jerrold. The man who had come in was a stranger. He was tall, thin, and rather dark. He wore steel-rimmed glasses and had on a very wide leather belt with a large brass buckle. Lucy remarked later that it was the kind of belt the Pilgrims must have worn.

The stranger smiled and introduced himself. "I'm Simon Fester. Are you Bob Knowlton?" Bob said yes, and they shook hands. "Doctor Jerrold said I might find you in. We were talking about your work, and I'm very much interested in what you are doing." Bob waved to a chair.

Fester didn't seem to belong in any of the standard categories of visitors: customer, visiting fireman, stockholder. Bob pointed to the sheets on the table. "There are the preliminary results of a test we're running. We've got a new gadget by the tail and we're trying to understand it. It's not finished, but I can show you the section that we're testing."

He stood up, but Fester was deep in the graphs. After a moment, he looked up with an odd grin, "These look like plots of a Jennings surface. I've been playing around with some autocorrelation functions of surfaces—you know that stuff." Bob, who had no idea what he was referring to, grinned back and nodded, and immediately felt uncomfortable. "Let me show you the monster," he said, and led the way to the workroom.

*This case was prepared by Professors Alex Bavelas, A. H. Rubinstein, and H. A. Shepard for courses in Management of Research and Development conducted at the School of Industrial Management, Massachusetts Institute of Technology, Cambridge, Massachusetts, and is used with their permission.

After Fester left, Knowlton slowly put the graphs away, feeling vaguely annoyed. Then, as if he had made a decision, he quickly locked up and took the long way out so that he would pass Jerrold's office. But the office was locked. Knowlton wondered whether Jerrold and Fester had left together.

The next morning, Knowlton dropped into Jerrold's office, mentioned that he had talked with Fester, and asked who he was.

"Sit down for a minute," Jerrold said. "I want to talk to you about him. What do you think of him?" Knowlton replied truthfully that he thought Fester was very bright and probably very competent. Jerrold looked pleased.

"We're taking him on," he said. "He's had a very good background in a number of laboratories, and he seems to have ideas about the problems we're tackling here." Knowlton nodded in agreement, instantly wishing that Fester would not be placed with him.

"I don't know yet where he will finally land," Jerrold continued, "but he seems interested in what you are doing. I thought he might spend a little time with you by way of getting started." Knowlton nodded thoughtfully. "If his interest in your work continues, you can add him to your group."

"Well, he seemed to have some good ideas even without knowing exactly what we are doing," Knowlton answered. "I hope he stays; we'd be glad to have him.

Knowlton walked back to the lab with mixed feelings. He told himself that Fester would be good for the group. He was no dunce, he'd produce. Knowlton thought again of Jerrold's promise when he had promoted him—"the man who produces gets ahead in this outfit." The words seemed to carry the overtones of a threat now.

The next day, Fester didn't appear until mid-afternoon. He explained that he had had a long lunch with Jerrold, discussing his place in the lab. "Yes, said Knowlton, "I talked with Jerry this morning about it, and we both thought you might work with us for a while."

Fester smiled in the same knowing way that he had smiled when he mentioned the Jennings surfaces. "I'd like to," he said.

Knowlton introduced Fester to the other members of the lab. Fester and Link, the mathematician of the group, hit it off well together, and spent the rest of the afternoon discussing a method of analysis of patterns that Link had been worrying over for the last month.

It was 6:30 when Knowlton finally left the lab that night. He had waited almost eagerly for the end of the day to come—when they would all be gone and he could sit in the quiet rooms, relax, and think it over. "Think what over?" he asked himself. He didn't know. Shortly after 5:00 P.M. they had all gone except Fester, and what followed was almost a duel. Knowlton was annoyed that he was being cheated out of his quiet period, and finally resentfully determined that Fester should leave first.

Fester was sitting at the conference table reading, and Knowlton was sitting at his desk in the little glass-enclosed cubby that he used during the day when he needed to be undisturbed. Fester had gotten the last year's progress reports out and was studying them carefully. The time dragged. Knowlton doodled on a pad, the tension growing inside him. What the hell did Fester think he was going to find in the reports?

Knowlton finally gave up and they left the lab together. Fester took several of the reports with him to study in the evening. Knowlton asked him if he thought the reports gave a clear picture of the lab's activities.

"They're excellent," Fester answered with obvious sincerity. "They're not only good reports; what they report is damn good, too!" Knowlton was surprised at the relief he felt, and grew almost jovial as he said goodnight.

Driving home, Knowlton felt more optimistic about Fester's presence in the lab. He had never fully understood the analysis that Link was attempting. If there was anything wrong with Link's approach, Fester would probably spot it. "And if I'm any judge," he murmured, "he won't be especially diplomatic about it."

He described Fester to his wife, who was amused by the broad leather belt and the brass buckle.

"It's the kind of belt that Pilgrims must have worn," she laughed.

"I'm not worried about how he holds his pants up," he laughed with her. "I'm afraid that he's the kind that just has to make like a genius twice each day. And that can be pretty rough on the group."

Knowlton had been asleep for several hours when he was jerked awake by the telephone. He realized it had rung several times. He swung off the bed muttering about damn fools and telephones. It was Fester. Without any excuses, apparently oblivious of the time, he plunged into an excited recital of how Link's patterning problem could be solved.

Knowlton covered the mouthpiece to answer his wife's stage-whispered "Who is it?" "It's the genius," replied Knowlton.

Fester, completely ignoring the fact that it was 2:00 in the morning, proceeded in a very excited way to start in the middle of an explanation of a completely new approach to certain of the photon lab problems that he had stumbled on while analyzing past experiments. Knowlton managed to put some enthusiasm in his own voice and stood there, half-dazed and very uncomfortable, listening to Fester talk endlessly about what he had discovered. It was probably not only a new approach, but also an analysis which showed the inherent weakness of the previous experiment and how experimentation along that line would certainly have been inconclusive. The following day Knowlton spent the entire morning with Fester and Link, the mathematician, the morning meeting having been called off so that Fester's work of the previous night could be gone over intensively. Fester was very anxious that this be done and Knowlton was not too unhappy to call the meeting off for reasons of his own.

For the next several days Fester sat in the back office that had been turned over to him and did nothing but read the progress reports of the work that had been done in the last six months. Knowlton caught himself feeling apprehensive about the reaction that Fester might have to some of his work. He was a little surprised at his own feelings. He had always been proud—although he had put on a convincingly modest face—he had been proud of the way in which new ground in the study of photon measuring devices had been broken in his group. Now he wasn't sure, and it seemed to him that Fester might easily show that the line of research they had been following was unsound or even unimaginative.

The next morning, as was the custom in Bob's group, the members of the lab, including the girls, sat around a conference table. Bob always prided himself on the fact that the work of the lab was guided and evaluated by the group as a whole and he was fond of repeating that it was not a waste of time to include secretaries in such meetings. Often, what started out as a boring recital of fundamental assumptions to a naive listener uncovered new ways of regarding these assumptions that would not have occurred to the researcher who had long ago accepted them as a necessary basis for his work.

These group meetings also served Bob in another sense. He admitted to himself that he would have felt far less secure if he had had to direct the work out of his own mind, so to speak. With the group meeting as the principle of leadership, it was always possible to justify the exploration of blind alleys because of the general educative effect on the team. Fester was there; Lucy and Martha were there; Link was sitting next to Fester, their conversation conerning Link's mathematical study apparently continuing from yesterday. The other members, Bob Davenport, George Thurlow, and Arthur Oliver, were waiting quietly.

Knowlton, for reasons that he didn't quite understand, proposed for discussion this morning a problem that all of them had spent a greal deal of time on previously, with the conclusion that a solution was impossible, that there was no feasible way of treating it in an experimental fashion. When Knowlton proposed the problem, Davenport remarked that there was hardly any use of going over it again, that he was satisfied that there was no way of approaching the problem with the equipment and the physical capacities of the lab.

This statement had the effect of a shot of adrenalin on Fester. He said he would like to know what the problem was in detail, and walking to the blackboard, began setting down the "factors" as various members of the group began discussing the problem and simultaneously listing the reasons why it had been abandoned.

Very early in the description of the problem it was evident that Fester was going to disagree about the impossibility of attacking it. The group realized this and finally the descriptive materials and their recounting of the reasoning that had led to its abandonment dwindled away. Fester began his statement which, as it proceeded, might well have been prepared the previous night although Knowlton knew this was impossible. He couldn't help being impressed with the organized and logical way that Fester was presenting ideas that must have occurred to him only a few minutes before.

Fester had some things to say, however, which left Knowlton with a mixture of annoyance, irritation, and, at the same time, a rather smug feeling of superiority over Fester in at least one area. Fester was of the opinion that the way that the problem had been analyzed was really typical of group-thinking and, with an air of sophistication which made it difficult for a listener to dissent, he proceeded to comment on the American emphasis on team ideas, satirically describing the ways in which they led to a "high level of mediocrity."

During this time, Knowlton observed that Link stared studiously at the floor and he was very conscious of George Thurlow's and Bob Davenport's glances towards him at several points of Fester's little speech. Inwardly, Knowlton couldn't help feeling that this was one point at least in which Fester was off on the wrong foot. The whole lab, following Jerry's lead, talked if not practiced the theory of small research teams as the basic organization for effective research. Fester insisted that the problem could be approached and that he would like to study it for a while himself.

Knowlton ended the morning session by remarking that the meetings would continue and that the very fact that a supposedly insoluble experimental problem was now going to get another chance was another indication of the value of such meetings. Fester immediately remarked that he was not at all averse to meetings for the purpose of informing the group of the progress of its members—that the point he wanted to make was that creative advances were seldom accomplished in such meetings, that they were made by the individual "living with" the problem closely and continuously, a sort of personal relationship to it.

Knowlton went on to say to Fester that he was very glad that Fester had raised these points and that he was sure the group would profit by reexamining the basis on which they had been operating. Knowlton agreed that individual effort was probably the basis for making the major advances, but that he considered the group meetings useful primarily because of the effect they had on keeping the group together and on helping the weaker members of the group keep up with the ones who were able to advance more easily and quickly in the analysis of problems.

It was clear as days went by and meetings continued as they did that Fester came to enjoy them because of the pattern which the meetings assumed. It became typical for Fester to hold forth and it was unquestionably clear that he was more brilliant, better prepared on the various subjects which were germane to the problems being studied, and that he was more capable of going ahead than anyone there. Knowlton grew increasingly disturbed as he realized that his leadership of the group had been, in fact, taken over.

Whenever the subject of Fester was mentioned, in occasional meetings with Dr. Jerrold, Knowlton would comment only on the ability and obvious capacity for work that Fester had. Somehow he never felt that he could mention his own discomforts, not only because they revealed a weakness on his own part, but also because it was quite clear that Jerrold himself was considerably impressed with Fester's work and with the contacts he had with him outside the photon laboratory.

Knowlton now began to feel that perhaps the intellectual advantages that Fester had brought to the group did not quite compensate for what he felt were evidences of a breakdown in the cooperative spirit which he had seen in the group before Fester's coming. More and more of the morning meetings were skipped. Fester's opinion concerning the abilities of others of the group, with the exception of Link, was obviously low. At times, during morning meetings or in smaller discussions, he had been on the point of rudeness, refusing to pursue an argument when he claimed it was based on the other person's ignorance of the facts involved. His impatience with others led him to also make similar remarks to Dr. Jerrold. Knowlton inferred this from a conversation with Jerrold in which Jerrold asked whether Davenport and Oliver were going to be continued on; and his failure to mention Link, the mathematician, led Knowlton to feel that this was the result of private conversations between Fester and Jerrold.

It was not difficult for Knowlton to make a quite convincing case on whether the brilliance of Fester was sufficient recompense for the beginning of this breaking up of the group. He took the opportunity to speak privately with Davenport and with Oliver and it was quite clear that both of them were uncomfortable because of Fester. Knowlton didn't press the discussion beyond the point of hearing them in one way or another say that they did feel awkward and that it was sometimes difficult for them to understand the arguments he advanced, but often embarrassing to ask him to fill in the background on which his arguments are based. Knowlton did not interview Link in this manner.

About six months after Fester's coming into the photon lab, a meeting was scheduled in which the sponsors of the research were coming in to get some idea of the work and its progress. It was customary at these meetings for project heads to present the research being conducted in their groups. The members of each group were invited to other meetings which were held later in the day and open to all, but the special meetings were usually made up only of project heads, the head of the laboratory, and the sponsors.

As the time for the special meeting approached, it seemed to Knowlton that he must avoid the presentation at all cost. His reasons for this were that he could not trust himself to present the ideas and work that Fester had advanced because of his apprehension as to whether he could present them in sufficient detail and answer such questions about them as might be asked. On the other hand, he did not feel he could ignore these newer lines of work and present ony the material which he had done or had been started before Fester's arrival. He felt also that it would not be beyond Fester at all, in his blunt and undiplomatic way (if he were present at the meeting, that is) to make comments on his own presentation and reveal the inadequacy which Knowlton felt he had. It also seemed quite clear that it would not be easy to keep Fester from attending the meeting, even though he was not on the administrative level which was invited.

Knowlton found an opportunity to speak to Jerrold and raised the question. He remarked to Jerrold that, with the meetings coming up and with the interest in the work and the contributions that Fester had been making, he would probably like to come to these meetings, but there was a question of the feelings of the others in the group if Fester alone were invited. Jerrold passed this over very lightly by saying that he didn't think the group would fail to understand Fester's rather different position and that he thought that Fester by all means should be invited. Knowlton then immediately said he had thought so too and that he felt that Fester should present the work because much of it was work that he had done; and that, as Knowlton put it, this would be a nice way to recognize Fester's contributions and to reward him since he was eager to be recognized as a productive member of the lab. Jerrold agreed and so that matter was decided.

Fester's presentation was very successful and in some ways dominated the meeting. He attracted the interest and attention of many of those who had come, and a long discussion followed his presentation. Later in the evening, with the entire laboratory staff present, in the cocktail period before the dinner, a little circle of people formed about Fester. One of them was Jerrold himself, and a lively discussion took place concerning the application of Fester's theory. All of this disturbed Knowlton and his reaction and behavior were characteristic. He joined the circle, praised Fester to Jerrold and to others, and remarked on the brilliance of the work.

Knowlton, without consulting anyone, began at this time to take some interest in the possibility of a job elsewhere. After a few weeks he found that a new laboratory of considerable size was being organized in a nearby city, and that the kind of training he had would enable him to get a project head job equivalent to the one he had at the lab, with slightly more money.

34.   Southern Bank *

History and Organization

Southern Bank, established shortly after the Civil War, had developed over the years a distinguished record for prudent, conservative financial service. An independent, single-location bank located in a medium-sized city, it now (1965) employs some 550 persons and is one of the largest institutions of its kind in the area.

The bank is organized into eight divisions: General Administration; Banking; Investment; Trust Administration; Business Development; Management Consulting; Marketing; and Legal. (See Figure 1.) In addition, there are three service groups: Planning and Personnel; Building and Office Services; and the Controller's Group. There are six levels of management in the bank: President; Division; Group; Department; Section; and Unit.

About 100 of the bank's employees are officers, of whom six are women; another 100 employees are men in various stages of professional banking careers. The remaining 350 employees are women, about 50 of whom are highly trained career specialists. Approximately one-half of the female employees are young, unmarried high school graduates. These girls typically remain with the bank for two or three years before leaving to be married or for other reasons.

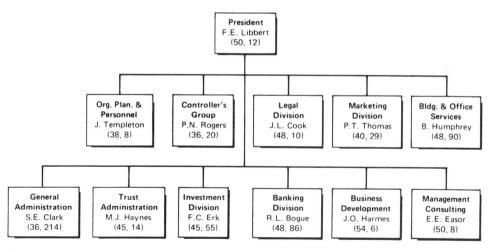

NOTE: Numbers in parentheses indicate manager's age and number of subordinates. For example, Mr. Cook, Head of the Legal Division, is 48 years old and has 10 people in his Division.

FIGURE 1.   Organizational Chart for Southern Bank

---

*This case was prepared by Professor Jack L. Rettig, Oregon State University, and is used here with his permission.

Since the inauguration of a new president in 1959 and the subsequent employment of a number of "bright young men," the bank has aggressively been exploring new ways of rendering financial services to its customers. This combination of aggressiveness and innovation has proved to be highly successful in promoting the growth and profitability of the bank. The Management Consulting Division, for example, was established to meet a perceived need and has not only become a profitable new service in its own right, but also has served, through its activities, to bring valued new accounts to the bank.

The top management people in Southern Bank believe that if the institution is to continue to grow through aggressiveness and innovation, the ideas and cooperation of all employees at all levels should be solicited and encouraged. In other words, excellent communication is considered by top management to be vital to the successful operation of this dynamic organization. To this end, Mr. Harold Walsh of the Personnel office was designated in 1963 as the coordinator of communications and training. Also to this end, a variety of communication techniques, channels, and devices, described on the following pages, have been adopted.

Officers' Meetings

The President meets formally with the Board of Directors once each month. A day or two after this meeting, the President holds his regular monthly meeting for the bank's officers. In this meeting, the President reports on selected topics from the Board meeting and reviews the monthly financial statements. At the end of this presentation, which usually lasts about fifteen minutes, the President asks for and responds to questions from the officers in attendance.[1]

As the conference room is not large enough to accommodate all of the bank's 100 officers at one time, the monthly officers' meetings are held in two sections on successive days, with approximately one-half of the officers attending each session.

Each officer is free to decide for himself which of the nonconfidential topics covered in the officers' meetings, if any, will be reported back to his subordinates. Officers typically do not hold group meetings for this purpose.

The officers' meetings are the only regularly scheduled meetings in the bank designed for the purpose of routinely disseminating information.

"COMCOM"

"COMCOM" (popular abbreviation for "Communications Committee") was the brainchild of Alice Davey, an officer in the bank, who suggested her idea to President Libbert at a cocktail party one evening in 1963. Mrs. Davey had been concerned about the discontinuation of the bank's house organ, *Southern Messenger,* earlier that year, and felt that something was needed to bolster communication to and from the lower levels of the organization. The stated

---

1. More will be said later about the sources of these questions.

objective of "COMCOM" was to "promote internal understanding of all matters of common concern at all levels throughout the organization."

President Libbert accepted Mrs. Davey's suggestion and announced the establishment of "COMCOM" in White Paper No. 81, dated October 2, 1963. (See Figure 2.) The functions of "COMCOM" were described by the President in White Paper No. 86, dated November 25, 1963. (See Figure 3.)

Each of the eleven members of "COMCOM" is an officer in the bank; all eight divisions are represented on the committee. George Storm and Alice Davey are the co-chairmen. Each "COMCOM" member is expected to solicit questions from employees at all levels in his division for submission to President Libbert for discussion at the monthly officers' meetings. Questions on any topic except grievances and personalities are welcomed.

"COMCOM" members report that they devote perhaps two hours each month to the task of gathering questions. These questions are reviewed at a regular monthly "COMCOM" meeting held one week prior to the officers' meeting. Suitable questions are agreed upon and then forwarded to the President well in advance of the officers' meeting. Typically, about five members attend "COMCOM" meetings.

"COMCOM" presents to the President an average of four questions per month. Most of these questions originate with the "COMCOM" members themselves or from persons in the top three levels of the organization. One of the "COMCOM" co-chairmen stated that perhaps twenty questions per month could be submitted to the President if the members had more time to devote to the task and if "people thought in terms of communications problems."

No. 81   October 2, 1963

                            COMMUNICATIONS COMMITTEE

    For an extended period of time, I have personally felt that a committee should be established to serve as an organized pipeline for the flow of information throughout the organization. We all like to know "what's going on when it's going on," and I believe that the Communications Committee can provide this type of information for all of us. I have appointed the following to serve on this committee:

        George Storm - Co-Chairman   Roy Munford
        Alice Davey   - Co-Chairman   Elmer Nagel
        Ronald Brooks   Jack Phillips
        John Cassidy   Ed Ralston
        Norman Euler   George Robinson
        Ruth Hobgood

    The committee is currently in the organizational stage, and when its program for effective internal communications has been established, it will be announced.

                                          Frederick E. Libbert
                                          Frederick E. Libbert

---

FIGURE 2.   Example of a Southern Bank White Paper

```
No. 86                                      November 25, 1963

                    COMMUNICATIONS COMMITTEE

    Our Communications Committee, which I appointed last month, has
recommended several steps to improve our communications program.

    The Committee feels strongly, and I agree, that all employees
should be informed promptly of what we're doing, why, and how it
affects them; and that they should be able to communicate their
ideas to top management and get timely answers to their questions
and requests.

    If you have any questions or ideas you want to pass along, see
your supervisor or a bank officer, or use our Suggestion System if
it is a formal suggestion you wish to make.  And during the formative
stages of the new program, members of the Committee will welcome your
suggestions, recommendations, and questions.

    Members of the Committee are:

        George Storm - Co-Chairman      Roy Munford
        Alice Davey  - Co-Chairman      Elmer Nagel
        Ronald Brooks                   Jack Phillips
        John Cassidy                    Ed Ralston
        Norman Euler                    George Robinson
        Ruth Hobgood

                                        Frederick E. Libbert
                                        Frederick E. Libbert
```

FIGURE 3. Example of a Southern Bank White Paper

The President feels that "COMCOM" is working well; the "COMCOM" co-chairmen feel that the committee is reasonably successful in reaching its objectives; the Personnel Manager feels that "COMCOM" is failing to attain its objectives and wonders how it might be made more effective.

Southern Messenger

The *Southern Messenger,* the bank's unusual house organ, originated in 1946 through spontaneous employee interest. A few employees volunteered to produce the publication on their own time if the bank would provide the necessary supplies and equipment. The paper was started on this basis.

Typewritten, then reproduced by the mimeograph process, the *Southern Messenger* was primarily a "gossip sheet" published approximately quarterly. Over the years the paper grew until, by early 1963, an issue might consist of as many as 100 single-spaced, typewritten pages.

By this time, however, employee interest in the paper apparently had declined, and when the volunteer editor left the bank for other employment in 1963, *Southern Messenger* collapsed from the lack of volunteer workers.

Largely through the efforts of Alice Davey and "COMCOM," *Southern Messenger* was reactivated in September 1964 as an official house organ.

Southern Messenger is now published bi-monthly, entirely on company time and entirely at company expense. The present editor spends about 40 percent of her time at the editor's job; the remainder of her time is spent at a clerical job in the bank. The paper now runs six 8½″ x 11″ pages in length; the bank allocates $500 per issue to cover printing, photographic, and other costs. Seven hundred fifty copies of each issue are printed.

The editor has twenty people (including three officers), scattered throughout the bank, who serve as informal reporters. These reporters serve on a voluntary basis and tend to obtain and report news items on an opportunistic, rather than a systematic, basis.

According to the editor, *Southern Messenger* space allocations run about as follows:

⅓	News about company plans and activities
⅙	Information regarding company policy
⅙	"Profiles of New Employees"
¹⁄₁₂	Gossip and personal items
rest	Crossword and scientific puzzles

The puzzles have proved to be highly popular with the employees, partly because of their intrinsic appeal and partly because of the prizes offered for the best solutions. The winner for each puzzle receives a pair of theater tickets. The crossword puzzles often contain words related to business and banking.

Although *Southern Messenger* is mailed to each employee at his home, the paper often finds its way back to the bank, where stimulating discussions regarding the puzzles sometimes occur.

Task Force

The Communications Task Force was established in February 1965 at the suggestion of John Templeton, Vice-President and Personnel Manager for the bank. Templeton felt that the Task Force might be more successful than "COMCOM" had been in improving communication to and from personnel in the lower echelons of the bank. The Task Force consists of five nonofficer employees nominated for the part-time assignment by their respective Division heads. Task Force members were notified of their appointments by interoffice memorandum from Mr. Templeton. (See Figure 4.)

The Task Force's basic assignment, as seen by the chairman, Stuart Seaton, is to circulate among and talk with lower level employees to discover questions, problems, and suggestions from the ranks. These items are then cleared by "COMCOM" which may modify but not block them, after which they are passed on to the Management Committee.[2] John Templeton's concept of the Task Force's assignment is presented in Figure 4.

The Task Force, which has now been in existence for five months, had a flurry of meetings immediately following its establishment but has had only one

---

2. The Management Committee consists of the President and four key Vice-Presidents.

To: Stuart Seaton

    cc: June Hugger   Louis Newton
         Benjamin Allen   Byron Edwards

The Management Committee of Southern Bank is interested in the
effectiveness of communications within the Company, especially as it
affects the ability of supervisors and officers to apply and to
interpret to others the policies and procedures of the Company, and
to supply information about new developments that should be of
interest to all employees.

The Committee requested nominations from Division Heads and selected
you to organize and direct the project. You will be assisted in this
task force study by the persons listed above as recipients of copies
of this memo.

For purposes of this project, "communications" refers to formal and
informal exchange and diffusion of information about such matters as:

    a. Responsibilities and authorities
    b. Policies governing personnel administration
    c. Applications of various procedures, such as performance
       review, purchase requisitions, expense approvals, etc.
    d. Information about significant new developments, new
       personnel, changes in benefit programs
    e. Problems in supervision and administration which require the
       attention of higher levels of management.

To carry out this project, the task force will be expected to:

    a. Determine the best way to assess communications; e.g., by
       interviews, questionnaires to supervisors, etc.
    b. Consult with the Chairmen of the Communications Committee,
       with personnel officers, and with the Supervisory
       Development Groups, to establish the kinds of possible
       communications problems that may exist.
    c. With the Chairmen of the Communications Committee, meet
       with the Management Committee to discuss findings.

I shall be available to assist in whatever way seems appropriate
to the task force.

John Templeton
John Templeton
February 1, 1965

Figure 4. Interoffice Memo of Southern Bank
Outlining Communications Committee Responsibilities

meeting during the past two months because of vacations and the demands of
other work. To date, the Task Force has made six suggestions to the Management
Committee via "COMCOM."

The Communications Task Force is only one of several task forces presently
operating in the bank. Others include the Training, New Services (Marketing),
and Trust Administration task forces. Conceptually, each task force is assembled to

accomplish a particular, well-defined job and upon completion of that job, or task, it is to be disbanded.

Chairman Seaton indicated that Communications Task Force members spend perhaps one hour per week on this assignment, and that most of the group's suggestions to date have originated from among its members.

When asked what caused him to believe there was a need for a Communications Task Force, the Personnel Manager replied, "There's no feedback around here, particularly from the lower levels. An order, report, or policy change is sent down the line and we wait for questions, or complaints, or some kind of response. What we get back is silence. Absolutely nothing. We find it very difficult to measure the impact of, say, a policy change. It's like shouting down a well and getting no echo. It's eerie."

Asked whether employees complain about poor communication in the bank, the Personnel Manager replied, "No. Oh, there is an occasional comment in the lunch room, but these are not specific and are mentioned in a very casual way. No one appears to be disturbed about it."

The chairman of the Communications Task Force, when asked about the condition of the bank's grapevine, replied, "Healthy."

Suggestion System

Southern Bank's suggestion system has been in continuous operation since its installation in 1952. Suggestion boxes are conveniently located on all floors, with a rack of blank suggestion forms attached to each box.

Suggestion forms are collected monthly. Over the years the input of employee suggestions has consistently averaged about ten per month. Most of the suggestions come from the Operations Group of the General Administration Division and deal with improving the heavy flow of paper processed by that group.

The suggestions are reviewed and evaluated by a six-man Suggestion Committee, presently comprised of both officers and nonofficers, representing the Trust Division (three members), the General Administration Division (two members), and the Investment Division (one member). An effort has been made to staff the committee with younger people from the lower echelons of the bank in the hope that this might stimulate employee interest in the suggestion system.

Committee members serve staggered two-year terms. When a replacement is needed, the committee meets to discuss individuals who may be interested in and suitable for a Suggestion Committee assignment. The most promising prospect is then contacted, and if he is willing to serve he is added to the committee after the approval of his supervisor is obtained.

When a suggestion is to be evaluated, it is given to the committee member most familiar with the operations of the department from which the suggestion came. This member then discusses the suggestion with the person who made it and with the head of the affected department(s). The member then reports back to the full committee, making a recommendation as to the disposition of the suggestion. The committee ordinarily accepts these recommendations.

If a suggestion is deemed to be practical and useful, the committee's next task is to determine the amount of money appropriate as the suggestion award.

The usual award range is from $10 to $50. The criteria used to determine the amount of the award are the estimated amounts of time and/or money saved by the suggestion. The committee often finds it difficult to arrive at the amount of this saving.

Every two months the committee issues a report listing all the suggestions made and the awards given during the preceding period. A copy of this report is placed on each bulletin board in the hope that it will stimulate further suggestion. When an award is given the report indicates the suggestor's name; suggestions receiving no award are listed by number.

The committee's decisions as to whether or not a suggestion is deserving of an award and the amount of the award are final. Approximately one-third of the suggestions submitted are considered worthy of awards.

Performance Review

Top management at Southern Bank believes that the bank's system of regular performance review provides an excellent opportunity to foster communication between each supervisor, at whatever level he might be, and his subordinates. The private performance review sessions, which deal primarily with the employee's job performance, also provide an opportunity for the employee to talk with his boss about his problems and for superior and subordinate to plan together the employee's future growth and progress.

Performance reviews are held after ninety days for new employees, then annually on the employee's anniversary date.[3] The reviews, which are keyed to the employee's job description, average perhaps thirty minutes in length. The same basic system is used for all employees—from clerks to vice-presidents.

A few days before his anniversary date, the employee receives from his supervisor a form notifying him when the review will occur, and inviting him to write on the form any questions that he would like his boss to answer during the review. This form is then returned to the supervisor. It is not uncommon for employees to write questions on these forms which the supervisor considers sensitive and/or difficult to answer. Nevertheless, the supervisor is expected to answer the questions. The form is destroyed after the review session.

Supervisors use a checklist form in rating their subordinates and use this form as a basis for the performance review discussion. Items on the checklist include such things as job knowledge, quality of work, effort, dependability, teamwork, communication, and profit-mindedness. The applicability of each item on the form with respect to the employee's particular job is recorded. The supervisor then checks whether the employee's performance "exceeds," "meets," or "falls short" of standard on each item. The resulting profile provides the core of the review discussion.

The supervisor retains the checklist rating form and notifies the personnel office regarding the result of the review in a separate summary report. Most employees receive a pay increase following their annual performance review. The amount of this increase, which usually ranges between 5 percent and 10 percent

---

3. Reviews may be held more frequently if the supervisor considers this desirable. The Personnel Officer encourages more frequent reviews to facilitate communications.

of present rate, depends upon the supervisor's evaluation of the employee's performance. The typical supervisor in the bank has from eight to ten subordinates to review during the course of a year.[4]

The Personnel Manager believes that many of the performance reviews are too superficial, but wonders how much time and effort a supervisor should spend in reviewing a young, female clerk who may marry and leave the bank next month. He also is concerned about what he believes to be inadequate training in interviewing techniques on the part of some supervisors in the bank. (Supervisors receive nine hours of in-bank training on the performance review system, of which one hour is devoted to interviewing techniques.)

When asked how the nonmanagement people feel about the performance review system, the Personnel Manager said, "We really don't know. There is very little feedback. Occasionally, in an exit interview, a terminating employee will say that his supervisor had not kept him informed as to the adequacy of his performance or about his future potential with the bank."

White Paper

When information on matters of bank-wide interest is to be disseminated, a "White Paper" is used. Each employee receives a personal copy. An average of two White Papers per month is issued. Examples are White Papers No. 81 and 86 (Figures 2 and 3), dealing with the formation of "COMCOM." Other White Papers may deal with such matters as holiday announcements, changing hours of work, etc.

Occasionally a White Paper deals with a policy change. In such cases, supervisors sometimes call their subordinates together to discuss the change and to answer pertinent questions.

---

4. It should be noted that not all officers are supervisors, nor are all supervisors officers.

35. Career Management—The Case of Len White*

Len White's Career

Len White is a vice-president and head of the New Services Development Unit (NSDU) at Metrobank. He has been in his current position for two years, with Metrobank for eight years, and out of college for seventeen years. Reflecting on his career, Len feels that things have progressed well. He earns $80,000 plus bonuses each year, has a budget of $1.3 million, and has the ear of several top managers. Yet the promotion he is interested in—to senior vice-president—still seems out of reach. He is unsure of what he must accomplish to attain his goal.

Len describes his high school and college years as very active. In high school he was involved in many social activities. He participated in sports and ran for student association president but lost. In college he joined a fraternity and played interfraternity sports, but failed to make the two college varsity teams he wanted. Women moved in and out of Len's life until he met Jan in his senior year. They married two years later.

After receiving his undergraduate degree in liberal arts, Len entered an MBA program at a major state university. He majored in marketing and sought employment in companies with good prospects for expansion. Using the University's MBA placement services, Len interviewed with several firms in the consumer package goods industry. He received job offers from two firms and decided to go with CPH, which was the sixth largest in the industry. Len commented on this decision: "I felt CPH would give me the best training and career advancement opportunities. The company had a formalized career ladder for product managers (i.e., the manager responsible for all marketing, sales, and production aspects of a product), paid well, and was prestigious. If you made it in CPH, you could go anywhere in the industry."

Len's simple but clear idea of his short-term goal was to become a product manager. His first job was as an assistant product manager on a new bar soap. This position involved substantial numerical analysis of market and competitive information by product, package size, geographical region, type of distributor, etc., and was the first step in the product manager career path. Assuming acceptable performance in a "number crunching" role, he would be promoted to associate product manager within two years. A second promotion to product manager normally occurred two to three years later. His responsibility would increase with each promotion so that promotion to product manager would give him primary control over a single product. This included product pricing, distribution, packaging, market segmentation, advertising, and product pro-

*Stephen A. Stumpf and Thomas P. Mullen, New York University Schools of Business, adapted from Stephen A. Stumpf and Manuel London, *Managing Careers,* © 1982, Addison-Wesley, Reading, Ma., pp. 15–27. Reprinted with permission. We appreciate the cooperation of the individuals and organizations involved in the case. All names are disguised.

motion. Since one's budget and product were part of a group of related products, his decisions as a product manager would have to fit the product group manager's strategy.

Although Len felt that his early career goals were clear, he reported that initially he knew relatively little about what an assistant product manager actually did. The stereotype Len had was that a product manager would manage a product, develop it by making changes, and coordinate the efforts of subordinates. Hence Len's first few years, although interesting and developmental, did not meet the expectations he had formed as an MBA.

Establishing Himself at CPH

During his first five years, Len's career was managed primarily by CPH; he was seldom consulted on job changes or career interests. After nine months, Len was moved to another product (a fabric softener) within the same product group but under a different product manager. While CPH referred to the move as a developmental rotation, Len was not sure how to interpret it at first: "Was I being transferred because I was good and needed elsewhere, because I needed additional development not available in my current position, or because my immediate superior did not want me any more?" The skills CPH was trying to develop in Len by the transfer were not made clear.

After a two-month adjustment to his new work associates and the duties of the new position, Len reported that analyzing fabric softener data was really no different from working on a bar soap. The fabric softener was somewhat more interesting to Len, given the recent changes in the fabric softener market. More judgments had to be made based on less information, and he was involved in some of those judgments. Len's family situation had also changed—he was the father of a seven-pound newborn boy.

The Advancement Years

During his second year at CPH Len was promoted to associate product manager on the fabric softener. He was transferred ten months later to a new clothes washing detergent, and moved back after a year to a fabric softener as a product manager. While each move was somewhat disruptive to Len's social relationships at work, he met several people, whom he worked with indirectly during this period, who would subsequently affect other career moves. The most notable of these was a superior, Pete Fallon. "I really enjoyed and learned from Pete. He was one of those people who was always getting involved with new things."

After being in the product manager position for a year, Len examined the aspects of various jobs that he liked and disliked. "I liked the feelings of success, the exhilaration of being promoted and accepted, and the career opportunities CPH seemed to offer." However, several concerns were growing: "Did I want to proceed into management which would involve more attention to financial data, accounting reports, and interpersonal relationships, or should I stay with my marketing specialty? How should I proceed from here—just work hard, conform to CPH, innovate, find and nurture political support, and/or be an outstanding contributor?" A third issue related to managing his family relationships in light of the long hours devoted to CPH. He and Jan were expecting another child.

By the end of his third year as a product manager Len realized that the managerial career path was not right for him. He still wanted the higher salary, power, and prestige associated with managing, but not the day-to-day worries, interruptions, coordination hassles, meetings, and continual firefighting. Working on new products was more exciting, seemed to involve less general management, and was more marketing-oriented than working with established products. He felt technically competent in marketing and enjoyed exercising his expertise in new products. Since Len had previously worked with the current group manager for new products, Pete Fallon, it was easy to approach Pete with his career concerns. Several months later when Pete was transferred, he recommended Len as his replacement. Len was subsequently offered the position of group manager for new products. "It was one of the happiest times of my life. My career seemed to be going in a direction that felt good; I enjoyed going to work. My family was settled into a new home. My son was five; my daughter was four months old and she was finally sleeping through the night."

Len's job over the next three years included another promotion to senior group manager for new laundry and cleaning products. His most notable project was developing and analyzing the plans for a new plant to manufacture two new products. The plant would cost $20,000,000 to build, involve hiring 2,000 workers, and be the sole producer of two new products as well as have the flexibility to produce several existing products.

Quite unexpectedly, Len was approached by an executive search firm regarding a position in a smaller competing firm (Cleanit) that would involve the strategic redirection and expansion of its household cleaner line. Len's name was given to the executive search firm by an ex-associate at CPH who was now with Cleanit. "With relatively little investigation of the position, I decided to take it. The salary was better, the challenge was clear and entirely marketing related, and after eleven years with CPH I was beginning to feel the need for change." While the position had potential, the rest of Cleanit was not yet ready for strategic redirection or innovative ideas. When an opportunity at Metrobank presented itself eight months later, Len made another career move.

New Roles at Metrobank

Metrobank had been actively recruiting senior product managers from the consumer package goods firms to meet its goal of becoming a national consumer bank. Metrobank's goals required rapid expansion, new banking services, and greater market penetration. It was looking for an experienced and successful senior product manager to start as a vice-president.

"I probably would not have changed firms so easily during this period if it had involved relocation. But it did not. Besides, I missed working for one of the top firms in the industry. Smaller firms didn't have the resources I needed to do new product development. Since I was only thirty-six, I felt I could risk another move, especially one that promised opportunities for growth and advancement."

The move to Metrobank was a major one in that the organization, its environment, and its products (actually services) were very different from the organizations, environment, and products in the consumer package goods industry. Yet Len agreed with Metrobank that his marketing and new product development expertise would transfer to banking. Having been disappointed with his brief tenure at Cleanit, Len interviewed with four Metrobank executives.

"It was the discussion with Metrobank's president that convinced me. Metrobank was one of the top twenty commercial banks in the U.S. It was embarking on a statewide expansion program that could ultimately double its size, and I had an opportunity to be in the middle of it. I would also be doing the kind of work I wanted to do—new product development and marketing."

During Len's first year at Metrobank he was involved in a new retail banking expansion program; he was learning about marketing financial services by being in the field and talking to branch bank presidents, officers, and consumers. About the middle of the year the legal/regulatory environment changed to permit statewide branch offices. The project quickly moved into the "brick and mortar" stage with twenty-three branches being opened throughout the state during the next few years.

By the end of his first year with Metrobank, an even bigger challenge was presented: the use of minicomputer machines to supplement bank tellers. Len became the lead marketing manager on a task force that might revolutionize branch banking. However, there were technical and marketing challenges that could result in millions of dollars of losses rather than a successful new approach to branch banking: "Could we get consumers to use the machines?" Len organized and implemented marketing research which subsequently suggested that consumers would use machines under certain favorable conditions such as low risk of robbery, provision of receipt, easy access and use, and "idiot-proof" transactions. Once it was reasonably clear that consumers would accept the technological change, it was necessary to get senior management's approval.

Len gave several presentations on the project to senior management (John Snow) and business unit managers in the Retail Banking Unit. After several months of discussion, presentation, financial analysis, and market research, the go-ahead was given: (1) to invest $16 million in bank machines, (2) to redesign branches to permit 24-hour access to machines, and (3) to heavily advertise the new service system.

After more than two years of task force development, the new systems were installed in over 100 branch banks. Len moved into the role of market strategy development specialist for the Retail Banking Unit, Consumer Banking Group (CBG), of Metrobank. After six months Len's role was changed as part of a major reorganization. Len subsequently became Head of Marketing, CBG.

During the development of the machine banking system, Len first met John Snow, head of CBG. When CBG was reorganized, Len began to report directly to Snow at Snow's request. Over the next three years, Metrobank continued its efforts to become a national consumer bank by offering banking services via direct mail (e.g., card products such as VISA and MasterCard, traveler's checks, etc.). Federal regulations prevented branch banking across state lines, hence efforts to become a national bank lacked the physical presence offered by a branch banking system. Len's role as head of group marketing was to provide marketing guidance to the various businesses within CBG on their development of new services.

After three years of working with the CBG businesses with some notable new services successes and failures, Len White suggested to John Snow that "the business units (e.g., Retail Banking, Card Products, Traveler's Checks) just don't know how to develop and integrate new services into their businesses. They are consumed with day-to-day operations; new services get second shift. What is needed is a new services development unit to help institutionalize the new services development process and pass along expertise."

After hearing such suggestions several times, John Snow created the New Services Development Unit (NSDU) as a temporary unit with an expected life of two or three years to get new services developed and implemented throughout CBG. John Snow commented on his decision to create such a unit: "We have been trying to develop new products for several years with only moderate success. Len knew more about new product development than any of the business unit managers or other staff members. The time was right to create a task force to improve our hit record with new products. I might have acted on Len's suggestion earlier except that Len has not always worked effectively with the business unit managers in his role on CBG staff. Sometimes his marketing expertise is perceived to get in the way of running a business. Len does not have 'bottom line' responsibility whereas the business unit managers do. Since it is difficult to determine the cost effectiveness of marketing methods and activities, ideas get suggested that are not easy to evaluate. When a business unit manager rejects marketing ideas or, more typically, stalls action on them, Len has been known to show his frustration. Hence, this new position should give Len some autonomy to get the job done."

During his first two years as head of NSDU, Len and his staff of fourteen banking professionals and six clerical assistants developed four new services. Two were implemented, and two were placed on hold by senior management pending a change in the legal/regulatory environment. Four other new services had been conceptualized and looked favorable based on initial qualitative research on marketability. The NSDU was doing well. However, the latest reorganization of Metrobank and CBG resulted in two layers of management now separating Len from John Snow. John Snow had been promoted and a new layer of management had been created. (See Figure 1.)

The success of NSDU and the Metrobank reorganization stimulated Len's thoughts regarding his career. "Where do I want to go from here? Have I leveled off at age forty-four? Am I beginning to stagnate? Should I redirect my efforts to teaching others and pass my expertise on to my subordinates? What can a staff person do to continue to progress in a line-oriented organization?"

APPENDIX

Metrobank as an Employer

Two years prior to Len's employment at Metrobank, the bank began to design and implement a human resource planning and career development system which would provide: (1) a personnel data base to identify and categorize top talent, (2) a management information system to make use of the data base in filling critical jobs, and (3) a career development program to ensure that the careers of the most talented individuals were being managed effectively.

The need for a personnel inventory, allocation process, and career development program stemmed from rapid growth and market expansion into additional consumer banking services. Managerial jobs at many levels were being created due to the expansion, and there was insufficient talent within the organization to fill the newly created positions. This lack of available talent from within heightened the need for future human resource planning. Dozens of management trainees were hired, many with MBA degrees from top-ranking universities. While the management trainees progressed rapidly to the junior officer level, there was still a gap in managerial talent in middle management.

Len White was hired at the time Metrobank was hiring many middle level managers from outside the banking industry. Based on an analysis of current and future needs, top management identified two areas of expertise that were needed but not currently available within the banking industry: marketing managers and operations managers. The former were recruited from major consumer package goods firms, the latter from manufacturing organizations such as Ford and General Motors.

Metrobank followed the strategy of hiring highly skilled middle managers to reduce their training costs and shorten the amount of time required for a new hire to become effective. The underlying assumption was that it would be more efficient to transfer marketing or operations management skills to banking than to train bankers in marketing or operations management. Given this strategy, it was necessary to develop the new hire's knowledge of banking.

New middle managers and college hires were typically assigned to several projects and rotated through several positions in their first few years to provide developmental experiences. However, the dramatic growth of Metrobank made adhering to historic career paths difficult. The results of this unilateral organizational career management with little regard for individual career plans did not become clear for several years. Many individuals were progressing rapidly; middle management was viewed as effective, and Metrobank was rated as one of the best managed corporations in the United States by *Dun's Review.* While some managers were highly committed to Metrobank, others were not and quietly waited for an opportunity to leave. Turnover among recent college hires was higher than the industry average. This increased the costs of recruitment and selection, and lowered productivity at the junior officer level.

The group within Metrobank of which Len's unit was a member had not begun to utilize the human resource planning and career development systems to any noticeable extent. The pressure of rapid expansion, both geographically and through new product development, had put significant pressure on the group. As a result, any new systems, while recognized as important and useful, were considered too time consuming to investigate fully or implement at this time.

Historically, Metrobank had encouraged an informal but strong mentor/sponsor approach to career planning. It was felt that the better young managers would be identified and coached by more experienced managers while the mediocre and poor managers were treated with benign neglect.

While CBG adhered to this informal policy, several formal human resource functions were also part of the group. CBG, with 200 officer personnel and 2,000 exempt and non-exempt workers, had its own Personnel Office. This office was divided into two departments around functional activities. The two departments are presented below:

Hiring
- recruiting
- compensation
- job analysis

Evaluation and Development
- compensation and benefits
- training and development
- Equal Employment Opportunity (EEO)/ Affirmative Action Planning (AAP)
- performance appraisal

The Hiring Department was the larger of the two and focused primarily on recruiting high potential individuals for entry level and middle management positions. At the entry level they recruited primarily from the top twenty business schools. Upper management believed that you "get what you pay for" and the average starting salary for new recruits was in the upper 20 percent for the industry. A similar policy was used for filling the middle ranks of management during the group's rapid expansion. CBG paid what was necessary to hire the right people to meet their needs.

Job analysis was used primarily by the Hiring Department for middle level positions. Management believed that intelligent new recruits could be molded to particular jobs and the Metrobank culture. As a result, job analysis was not typically used for entry level positions.

The Evaluation and Development Department was considered largely administrative in function. In the compensation area, line managers were given a pool of money three months prior to the annual performance appraisal period from which they drew salary increases for those within their unit. Guidelines for this process were distributed to unit managers but no policy for adhering to the guidelines was enforced.

Training and development was managed internally by a small staff of professionals who worked with the business units to identify programs that were needed. Primary emphasis was on targeting this effort to meet the specific, immediate needs of CBG. Outside consultants were used frequently to augment the internal staff for both designing and implementing these training activities. Programs developed by consultants were owned by Metrobank and considered proprietary.

More generally, the training and development area was expected to pay its own way and therefore needed to generate sufficient cash flow to cover expenses. As a result, each unit sending managers to a program was charged for this service. Rates were comparable to those charged by outside organizations such as the American Management Association (AMA), and managers were free to select between internal training or training at AMA-type institutions.

EEO/AAP activities were largely routine and were administered consistent with Metrobank's corporate-wide Fair Employment Policy. This policy incorporated all existing legislation in this area within a Metrobank-wide Position and Guidelines Statement which was widely distributed throughout the bank. Any major personnel problems or labor disputes were referred to the Metrobank legal department. The centralization of this particular function was done to ensure that the public image of Metrobank was protected.

Performance appraisals were done by each of the units within CBG on an annual basis. Performance appraisal forms—distributed by the Evaluation and Development Department and used by most managers—were frequently modified and augmented by individual units. Organization charts and job descriptions were used with much difficulty because of frequent reorganizations. As one manager said, "Organizational charts are useless. I get a new one at each performance appraisal."

Evaluation of performance was based primarily on one's ability to achieve unit objectives. With the decentralized, profit-center orientation managers were expected to show results within six to nine months. Financial objectives for each unit were identified annually and performance was evaluated against these objectives on a quarterly basis. Judgments by upper management about new managers within a division were made quickly; once formulated they were difficult to change. For cost centers, such as the New Product Development Unit managed by Len White, performance evaluations were judged on the response NSDU received from line managers. Frequently, the careers of cost center managers were made or broken by the evaluations of the line managers who interacted with center.

Managers throughout Metrobank with unsatisfactory performance were generally not fired. A lateral transfer to a less important area was usually arranged. However, the culture was such that lower performing managers frequently left on their own accord. Metrobank was considered an upwardly mobile company and internal competition was heated. As one executive in the Personnel Office noted,

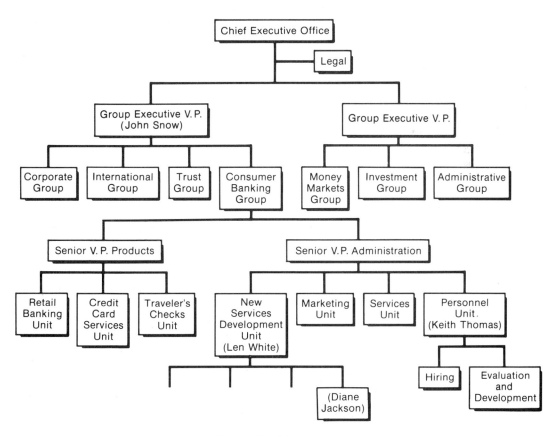

FIGURE 1. Metrobank

"Managers who do not move up quickly realize the opportunities within the bank were very limited." As a result, many managers leave Metrobank each year.

Metrobank recently estimated the cost of management trainee turnover to range from $20,000 to $100,000 *per person* depending on the type of position and amount of formal in-house training required. Given the turnover of high-potential individuals whom Metrobank had hoped not to lose, the cost of replacing management trainees was several million dollars per year.

36.   Career Management—The Case of Diane Jackson*

Diane Jackson's Career

After receiving an undergraduate degree in mathematics, Diane Jackson started work at Metrobank in computer services. She left after one year to get her MBA. She worked as a summer intern the following year in a different Metrobank group. By the time she completed her MBA, she had developed an interest in marketing and received several job offers. She chose Metrobank because she was familiar with the company and felt that Metrobank offered the combination of financial analysis, computer applications, and marketing that she wanted. Her first post-MBA year with the bank involved financial analysis work within the Consumer Banking Group (CBG). She was given an opportunity to work on the minicomputer banking machine task force when the machines were first considered for in-branch use. The assignment "sounded like fun" so she took it. This was Diane's first contact with Len White.

Diane worked on the banking machine task force for nearly two years and was promoted to assistant vice-president in the process. Since it was a task force, it was to be disbanded upon the successful implementation of the systems and services. This meant that task force members needed to find positions in other CBG business units. In her task force work, she developed contacts with officers in the Credit Card Services Unit and they subsequently offered her a position. She was also offered an opportunity to manage a branch within the Retail Banking Unit which she turned down. "I didn't want to manage a branch, or even a group of branches. I figured Retail Banking was probably the way to progress quickly in Metrobank, but I didn't want that job." The position Diane accepted involved new services development work for Credit Card Services (e.g., VISA, MasterCard). Diane again crossed paths with Len White while working in this department. Now Len was head of CBG marketing.

*Thomas P. Mullen and Stephen A. Stumpf, New York University Schools of Business, adapted from Stephen A. Stumpf and Manuel London, *Managing Careers,* © 1982, Addison-Wesley, Reading, Ma., pp. 65–80. Reprinted with permission. All names are disguised.

Diane worked in Credit Card Services for six months before being transferred to the newly created New Services Development Unit (NSDU) headed by Len White. She reported to Len through an intermediate superior who was in charge of two new service concepts. Diane's responsibilities were to develop the service concept, prepare a test market plan, and coordinate marketing efforts with the customer services and systems managers. The NSDU's goal was the quick development of new services which would be handed off to the relevant business units within CBG.

The service concept Diane worked on for a year was one of the NSDU's two implemented successes. The service provided consumers with higher interest on savings than the usual passbook rate. Diane's performance was rewarded by her assuming responsibility for one of the four new service concepts NSDU had defined, but had yet to market. Diane indicated that she felt good about her new role, but really would like to be promoted to the vice-president rank by year's end. This desire was made more salient by unsolicited interest on the part of another organization. She interviewed with a large electrical and appliance manufacturer's credit business for a position as head of new services development. The offer would be a promotion and included a 25 percent increase in salary and "the promise of a line job in eighteen months." "But I didn't want a line job in eighteen months. I like new services development work and want to progress in management along a staff route. I might like to run a business someday, but not by working my way up from the production floor through line positions."

Diane's Discussion with Len

She decided to talk with Len White about her career and met with him several days later. Beginning the conversation, Diane asked Len if she could use him as a sounding board for some career concerns she had. She briefly described her career up until this point including her decision to join the minicomputer task force and her subsequent decisions to join Credit Card Services and then Len's unit, NSDU. She said she was satisfied with her career up until this point but was concerned as to where it was going. Throughout this time she felt that the responsibility for her career development was almost entirely her own. While the bank offered many challenging opportunities and the compensation was high by industry standards, she was not sure if her career had a direction, and even if it did, she was not sure there was a viable career path at Metrobank.

Shortly after she completed her MBA, Diane said she had decided on a three-year career path along a staff functional line that would focus on marketing computer-related services. She also decided she would be an Assistant Vice-President before she turned thirty and was very satisfied when she was promoted at the age of twenty-eight.

More recently however, she had seen many of her associates leaving—some because they were not doing a good job, but others because of the pressure and ambiguous opportunities. "I'm very competitive and I like the pressure, it motivates me. But the fact that I'm not interested in a line job means that there is no standard career path for me to progress along. This makes me think my career opportunities at Metrobank may be limited."

Len responded that her career advancement thus far had not been as haphazard as she might think. In fact she had been identified early in the informal employee tracking system as a high performer. He said one of Metrobank's corporate policies was to challenge new management trainees with special assignments. While the task force position was not part of a formal career development plan, it was considered developmental by CBG management. The offer made to her to manage a branch was also part of CBG's informal career development plan for her. Her decision to turn that offer down shifted future development efforts to her. While the move to the Credit Card Unit was viewed by Diane as continued development, CBG had temporarily abdicated its career management role. Len said that he took up this responsibility again in his offer to Diane to join NSDU and that he subsequently designed a role for her further development in marketing new services.

Despite Diane's concerns, Len knew it was possible to advance in Metrobank to a VP level in a staff role, but was not optimistic about a promotion to senior vice-president. Len indicated that he interacted with a number of high-level people like John Snow and knew a lot about Metrobank. Yet he felt the bank was so decentralized that it was hard to know what career information was really relevant to Diane.

After further discussion and reiteration of these main points, Diane thanked Len for his time and left. She was not sure she felt any better after the conversation and wondered whether Len "had the power to get things to really happen for her."

For Len, the conversation highlighted his concern over Diane's career. "What is the best career pattern for good people like Diane? She has the ability to be a top level manager in Metrobank, but chooses not to take the conventional route of becoming a line manager in a branch bank. Her next promotion to vice-president would reward her high performance and possibly attract other good people into New Services Development. However, it may be difficult for her to move into a line unit as a VP without previous line experience, and without line experience her career path may be blocked. Yet, she has been with Metrobank almost five years, has done an outstanding job, and deserves the promotion."

Personnel's Concerns with Diane

Keith Thomas, the Personnel Director for CBG, had many of the same concerns about Diane that Len did. He had followed Diane's career since she joined CBG as a financial analyst. He had placed her name onto the employee tracking system when she joined the minicomputer task force and had been part of the approval process for her promotion to assistant vice-president.

At the time of her promotion Keith had talked with Diane about moving into a line function at a branch and Diane said she would consider it. After she turned down the move to become a branch manager, Keith had not reviewed her situation again until recently. Len White had contacted him about considering her for promotion to vice-president. Keith had been noncommittal at the time Len mentioned it to him and was feeling less favorable about it as he thought about the implications of such a promotion. In his mind, CBG wanted to encourage their better junior people to get line experience. If Diane was unwilling to do that, he wondered if CBG was the place for her. If CBG was not the place for her, should he contact Corporate Personnel to explore alternative solutions? Since Metrobank was decentralized, this was not as easy or even as appropriate as it might first appear. Each of the seven groups of Metrobank had their own personnel office and transferring between groups was not that common. Another concern was the effect that an internal transfer would have on individuals in situations similar to Diane's. Branch management was not always that popular with many of the bright, young junior managers yet those were exactly the people that CBG wanted out in the branches. How many of these professionals who were currently deciding about a branch manager position would opt for an internal transfer to another group if it became available?

Keith knew he had to sort out his ideas on this pretty quickly. Diane Jackson had called his office earlier that day to ask for an appointment.

37.   The Reporter*

The Reporter recently celebrated its thirteenth year as the student newspaper, at State College. While it has experienced its share of ups and downs, it has always been published on time. In 1983 its staff was awarded the Red Key Student Organization of the Year Award for its outstanding performance and contribution to the college community. On October 20, 1985, *The Reporter* staff failed to print a weekly edition. This was the first time in its history that the paper had not met its deadline.

Background

Until 1964, the campus newspaper's banner read *Exec*. This title epitomized the college founder James D. Atherton's commitment to develop and educate affluent young men into wealthy business executives and leaders in the field.

With the advent of the 1970s, State College underwent drastic changes; it began admitting women into the school. At the same time, the newspaper underwent a major change. Now there are approximately 1,650 full-time undergraduate students pursuing the Bachelor of Science degree in management and about 2,000 graduate students pursuing the Master of Business Administration degree. Of the total enrollment, approximately 1,060 are women.

Traditionally, all student organizations receive operating funds by submitting annual budgets to the Student Government Executive Board. All budgets list the

*Joseph J. Martocchio, New York University. Printed with permission of the author.

This case is based upon a real-life situation. It should serve as the basis for classroom discussion. Its purpose is not to convey what is effective or ineffective management. In this spirit, all proper names, dates, and vital information have been changed.

amount required to conduct operations as well as that necessary to sponsor student-related events. The Government Board must then allocate student activities fees (independent of college administration) as equitably as possible.

In 1973 the *Exec* assumed its current identity *The Reporter*. Previously, the *Exec* had received insufficient operating funds whenever it had printed unfavorable information about student government. In order to operate efficiently and effectively, *The Reporter* had committed itself to accepting funds from the college treasurer directly. Today its management is completely responsible for its operations, future development, and all debts incurred.

Operations

The Reporter, a student newspaper for and by students, links 3,000 individuals on and off campus at all levels of State's hierarchy including students, college staff, administrators, corporation officers, and trustees. The newspaper is published every Thursday during the fall and spring semesters with the exception of vacations and final exam periods. Members of the staff, comprised solely of students and a faculty adviser, are responsible for financial operations and planning, editorial content and policy, production, layout design, and circulation. The staff controls and performs all operations except for printing; printing services are contracted with an offset printer.

Organized along functional lines (Exhibit 1), general operations are overseen by the editor-in-chief. Each associate editor and all managers serve as the "movers" of the organization.

The editor-in-chief is elected by staff members to the post for a one-year period beginning in April; the transition month of May allows the newly elected editor-in-chief and staff members the opportunity to run the paper with the previous staff available to offer advice and support.

A successful candidate for the editor-in-chief position has made significant contributions to the organization by performing exceptionally in any functional area, has impeccable writing skills and command of grammar rules, and has a sincere commitment to task achievement.

Much like the student government president, *The Reporter* editor represents the entire student body. The editor acts as a liaison between the student body and college administration, faculty, and trustees. As part of the position, the editor serves as a member of the Trustee's Committee on Student Affairs which is comprised of both graduate and undergraduate student body presidents, one government-appointed student representative from each school, student judicial court chairperson, Greek Council President, the vice-president for student affairs, a faculty member, and the deans of students and student activities.

The editor's role on this committee is to summarize the issues that affect campus life. While the trustees may be aware of some issues, the editor relates the implication of any given policy or event, and the impact upon students' routines, morale, and attitudes. The editor also provides trustees with input through discussing letters to the editor. Letters, submitted by State community members, express attitudes, values, beliefs, and ways that a situation may be dealt with effectively.

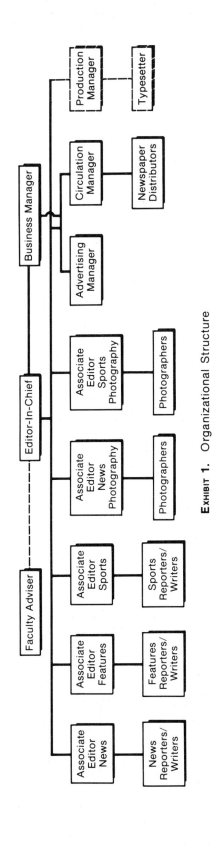

Exhibit 1. Organizational Structure

Serving as a common bond between all persons affiliated with State College, from students to trustees, the newspaper is the student's formal mouthpiece. The newspaper enables students to get readers to know facts and feelings related to student concerns. The newspaper may be likened to a barometer that measures the general atmosphere of the student body.

Organizational Structure

Business Manager

Working closely with the editor is the business manager. Together they monitor the newspaper's financial affairs, allocating funds to support various functions. Only two variable sources of income beyond the student activities fees generate subscription revenue. They are alumni and parent readership, and advertising revenue from local merchants (historically accounting for only 10 percent of operating funds). With approximately 90 percent of the newspaper's circulation confined to the campus, subscription and advertising revenue potential remains relatively low. Insightful planning is essential, otherwise spending more than available would result in the newspaper's shutdown. All debt incurred would be paid with funds from the following year's activities fees.

On the operations side, the business manager establishes the schedule for the collection of accounts receivable and the payment of accounts payable. At the editor's request, the business manager monitors the use of inventory and receives price quotes from various graphic supply houses. By comparing quotes and assessing the organization's needs, the business manager selects the most economical ones.

Finally, this position requires its incumbent to work closely with the college comptroller and treasurer in obtaining funds from the school when needed. Together they determine the optimum means of managing the funds for both short- and long-term requirements.

Associate Editors

Selected by the current editor, the associate editors are responsible for working with the editor frequently. Commitment to task completion, an affinity for writing, and adeptness in organizing people are the minimum requirements for a successful candidate. The news, features, and sports editors all determine their respective strategy, ensuring that each area complements the other style-wise. The associate editors coordinate the number of pages to be used by each.

Individually, each associate editor works with the editor to make certain that the information is objective, well-balanced, and of significance to the readers by answering how, what, why, when, who, and where. Key to any mission is that every story be followed up in subsequent issues, highlighting the impact upon the community, and the implications of both the short-run and the long-run.

Responsible for organizing, developing, and maintaining a staff of peers, each associate editor must establish source contacts from among students, college staff, faculty, and administration. The associate editor then works with each writer, providing support, information, and editorial assistance.

Advertising Manager

The advertising manager generates additional revenue by communicating with local merchants via telephone, letter, or in person. Accounts are won by eliciting a need in the advertiser's minds, communicating to them that a desire exists for the service or product, and convincing them that a handsome return on investments will follow.

Selling is one aspect of the advertising manager's position. Graphic layout is another. While some sponsors submit camera-ready mechanicals, others request that the advertising manager design the ad. Finally, both advertising manager and business manager work together to ensure that payment is received and that additional work is not provided for delinquent accounts.

Circulation Manager

Primary responsibilities of the circulation manager include delivering the mechanical (a mockup of a newspaper issue from which the printer takes photographs for offset printing) to the printer and delivering the printed copies to campus for distribution. With a staff of three or four students, newspapers are placed in students' campus mailboxes, handed to the campus mail center for distribution, to college faculty and administration, and dropped off at various high traffic locations on campus for public reading. For off-campus subscribers, the circulation manager prepares labels extracted from a computer program.

Soliciting for new subscriptions is limited. Feedback indicates that parents and alumni are not interested in day-to-day events on campus. Off-campus subscriptions equal a very small proportion of total circulation. The marginal revenue generated usually covers both fixed and variable expenses, contributing nothing to the newspaper's development.

State's Environment and Its Students

With approximately 30 percent of State's undergraduate students as commuters, the college is classified as a residence campus. Despite its heavy concentration of resident students, the college community, according to former editor (1984–1985) Jack Dolan, is far from cohesive.

> The students at State generally do not get very involved in community activities like the newspaper or government. For the most part, students have off-campus jobs and commitments that they feel are more instrumental to securing a lucrative job after graduation. I've asked many students why they have not gotten involved in community activities. Their feeling is that it is something a person does in high school as a means to present impressive credentials to admission committees of prestigious colleges and universities.

The typical *Reporter* staff member does not fit into the mold which Dolan perceives. Rather, the student displays a greater degree of curiosity and expresses a greater concern about issues affecting the college community as a whole. A staff member tends to possess a higher degree of motivation than others. Additionally, a staff member realizes the benefit of involvement with the newspaper; potential employers generally view extracurricular participation as a predictor of high motivation and a desire to learn varied tasks. The newspaper also provides students with the opportunity to express themselves in such ways as writing, photography, and designing the layout format. *The Reporter* is a learning ground for budding leaders, and allows students to integrate the academic side of management with the realities of running an organization.

Two Cases in Point

1984–1985

Led by Jack Dolan who served as editor during his junior year, *The Reporter* staff was comprised of forty active participants. Upon assuming the role of editor in April 1984, Dolan set out to build the remaining staff of twenty students to a greater size. During the previous year, much of the staff was doubling up in duties performed. For example, during the 1983–1984 administration, Dolan, who served as news editor, also assumed the responsibility for typesetting. Since most viewed this task as dull, volunteers were hard to come by.

Commenting on his decision to enlarge the staff, Dolan stated,

> With the pressure of academics, social concerns, and changing priorities, doubled responsibility just did not allow many of the staff enough room to breathe. In fact, morale suffered because of it. Not only was there a general lack of camaraderie, but the quality of the paper in comparison to previous editions also suffered. Bottom line, the lack of sufficient staffing made working on the paper unappealing. Staying up until 5 A.M. (from noon of the previous day) to produce the mechanical took out all the fun and clouded any benefits to be gained.

Dolan involved himself in every aspect of the newspaper. By working closely with individuals, he sought not only to assist staff members in producing an informative vehicle of communication, but he also discussed the ways in which involvement benefited the individual.

Mindful of the entire staff, Dolan believed that exceptional work by individuals contributed nothing to the entire organization. Teamwork, Dolan felt was imperative. Standards and formats were not determined by any single person. By encouraging communication among each other, generally agreed upon standards and formats were devised. Given the staff members' raw ability and the available equipment with which to work, Dolan often worked in a particular functional area in order to realize realistic goals.

1985–1986

In the spring of 1985, Jean Beene, then a junior, assumed the responsibilities of *The Reporter* editorship. Having served as news editor in 1984–1985, Beene was a writer on the news staff in 1983–1984. A marketing major, Beene felt the role of editor would enable her to test lessons learned in class while accepting a management role in her area of interests.

Except for the news and sports photography editors and business manager, all other management positions were filled by students who had either never worked on the staff or who had worked as reporters/photographers under an associate editor. With the exception of the news and sports photography editor, business manager, advertising manager, and circulation manager, the other associate editors were entering their second year at the college. The 1985–1986 staff totalled twenty volunteers.

With the new staff's first issue just one week away, no attempt had been made to formulate strategies or policies. It was just expected that the functional areas would guess correctly the number of pages to be filled. No meeting had been called to set direction for the associate editors.

As the first issue was in production, the previous editors visited in order to answer any questions the new staff might have had. With production a few hours behind the pace kept during the previous year, Dolan asked Beene, "Jean, I know it is your first issue as editor. Perhaps I can help you out a little so that you (the staff) will not have to stay up all night. Do you mind?"

Beene responded. "Thanks for the offer, Jack. But, it'll be fine. We're new and we're learning." For the remaining few issues before the end of the semester, the staff had produced issues of quality above that of other new staffs in their respective initial periods.

During the summer there had been no contact between the new staff members, except for a note sent by Beene indicating that all associate editors and managers would return to campus three days before new student orientation. Normally, the early return was used by *The Reporter* management to compile an issue for new students that previewed fall sports, student organizations, the orientation program, and key college staff and administrators with whom new students might need to consult. Also included in the note was a time and place for a staffing meeting.

At the staff meeting, Beene welcomed everyone back. She stated that the format for the new issue would be the same as produced during previous years. She asked the editors to make plans for storywriting; the previous year's deadlines would apply. Without further specification, the meeting was adjourned.

As the semester progressed, there was no mention of the traditional *Reporter* open house, designed to have students meet with the management staff, and to afford students the opportunity to learn how they could contribute to the organization. While most reporters from the previous year had graduated, few of the underclass students continued with the paper in the fall of 1985. Contributors to the newspaper plummeted from forty students to twenty students.

Normally a twelve-page paper, eight pages seemed to become the norm (the mechanics of newspaper construction necessitate that an issue be done in increments of four pages). No longer was the production of an issue finished the day before publication at 11 P.M. The average time lapsed to about 3:30 A.M. the day of publication, just a few hours before the printer's 6 A.M. deadline. Students on campus stated that the paper was not as informative as it had been in the past. Clubs no longer sent messages about events and meetings. Traditionally, the newspaper had been the primary vehicle for such communication. The staff members' morale was on the decline.

A Critical Incident

On October 20, *The Reporter* was not published for the first time in its history. At 11 P.M. on its production night, Dolan had gone down to the newspaper's production office at the request of an associate editor. According to Dolan, "The associate editors were quite upset, stating that they were sick of the conditions." Due to understaffing, none of the typesetting had been done (typesetting for an eight-page paper requires about ten hours of labor). After that, layout normally takes four hours. The printer's deadline was only eight hours away.

Beene was determined to put out a paper that week. Even though production was at a standstill, she insisted that they would make it. Everyone knew it was physically impossible. And since the printer runs copy only on Thursday, the outcome was certain. An emergency meeting was held among *The Reporter* staff members.

Given the information presented in the case:

1. What do you expect had happened at the meeting? What considerations (i.e., to staff members, readers) might have been entertained?
2. If you were the editor of *The Reporter,* what would you have done to prevent the situation? As a reality, what would you do now?
3. What are the short- and long-term considerations?

Part VI

Managing Stress, Change, and the Environment in a Context of Social Responsibility and Ethics

Cases Outline

38. St. Luke's Hospital (A)*

Two days after she assumed her duties as director of nurses and of the nursing school of St. Luke's Hospital, Jenny Stewart started on the first of her "get acquainted" rounds. As she turned the knob of the door to the operating room, she heard her name called. The supervisor of the Pediatrics Department approached.

"Won't you let me show you around my department?" Miss Robbins asked. "An operation is in progress, and I think they would prefer that you wouldn't go into the operating room now."

"I know there's an operation going on," the director answered. "That's why I'm going in. You see, I want to observe the methods being used."

Miss Robbins looked uncomfortable to Miss Stewart. "I know that's a very natural desire on your part, but I do hope you will put it off until you are better acquainted. *Please* come with me today and see my department."

Miss Stewart thought the nurse's request rather strange; nevertheless, she looked over the Pediatrics Department and did not return to the operating room. The same afternoon Lois Richards, supervisor of nurses in general surgery, appeared in the doorway of the director's office.

"I understand that you intended to call on us in the operating room this morning," she said.

Miss Stewart looked up from her desk and saw a trim, wide-awake looking woman. "Ah, then you're Miss Richards," Miss Stewart said. "Won't you come in? As a matter of fact, I should like to have dropped in on you this morning but I was sidetracked; so I had to postpone my first visit."

Miss Richards remained in the doorway. "Well, I thought I'd better tell you that you will not need to call on us. When any discussion comes up between the operating room and the nursing office, I come here to settle it."

Miss Stewart was surprised by the flatness of Miss Richards' remark, but she said, "I'm glad to hear that. This is certainly the place for any discussions between department heads to take place. But I shall want to visit you to acquaint myself with the technique used in surgery and with the students in your department."

*From Wendell French, John E. Dittrich, and Robert A. Zawacki, *The Personnel Management Process: Cases on Human Resources Administration.* Copyright © 1978 by Houghton Mifflin Company. Reprinted with permission of the publisher.

"Well, I suppose you can come if you want to, but our surgeons won't like it very much. You see, we feel that our technique isn't open to question; so we hardly need any advice. *I* see that the students do their work well. You needn't have any worries about work in my department."

Miss Stewart smiled. "I can assure you that I'm not worried about the work or the technique used in your department. I just want to get acquainted."

"All right, come ahead, but remember that I told you it would be better if you didn't," Miss Richards said over her shoulder as she disappeared from the doorway.

Miss Stewart felt bewildered. She could not recall anything in her long experience as a nursing instructor and as a director of nursing schools which would have prepared her for what she believed was an antagonistic attitude on the part of the operating room supervisor.

Jenny Stewart's career included graduation from a large midwestern college, graduation from a school of nursing, ten years as teacher in schools of nursing, and seven years as director of schools of nursing. In addition she had spent one summer at the University of Wisconsin, taking courses in anatomy and bacteriology. Before accepting her first position as director of a nursing school, she had taken a course in nursing school administration at the University of Chicago.

As director of nurses and the nursing school at St. Luke's, Miss Stewart was directly responsible to the board of directors, although the superintendent of the hospital was nominally her superior. She planned to carry her serious problems to the superintendent, however, because she believed that her work would be easier and more pleasant. The superintendent of the hospital was Carleton B. Fischer, ex-city editor of the local *Centreville Press*. He had no training in hospital administration, but Miss Stewart considered him cooperative and intelligent. He was fifty years of age, a college graduate, and had been appointed to his position the previous July.

As director of nurses, Miss Stewart was responsible for the proper care and treatment of all patients in the 250-bed hospital.

Her responsibilities as nursing school director included the education of student nurses, the selection and employment of graduate assistants, and the overseeing of nurse instructors. A Nursing School Committee helped her formulate educational policies and advised her on disciplinary matters concerning student nurses.

The director of nurses, Miss Stewart had learned, was expected to take the advice of the Nursing School Committee on vitally important policies. When the committee was of the opinion that any drastic action needed to be taken in the nursing school, it notified the board of directors of its decision. Miss Stewart was an ex officio member of both the Nursing School Committee and the board of directors.

As she sat in her office contemplating what the operating room supervisor had said, Miss Stewart wondered if she had said anything to make Miss Richards angry. She concluded that she had not.

Three days later Miss Stewart visited the operating room while surgery was being performed. She observed carefully the work of the surgeons and was satisfied that what Miss Richards had said about their technique was correct. The surgeons appeared to Miss Stewart not to notice that she was present. She remembered that in former positions the doctors had seemed pleased when she watched them work.

About two weeks later two student nurses from the operating room, Clarice Maltz and June Bader, appeared in Miss Stewart's office. Miss Bader was in tears. Between sobs she blurted out, "Miss Richards kicked me. I used a forceps to take a soiled sponge off the table, but before I reached the sponge rack to hang it up, she kicked me so hard I dropped it. Then she struck my arm with an instrument

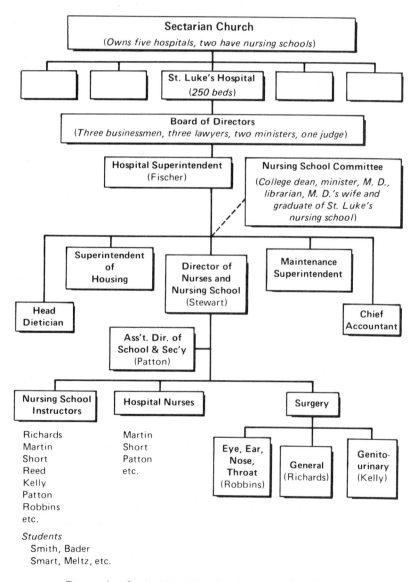

Exhibit 1. St. Luke's Hospital Organization Chart

and screamed in my ear. She said I was a little fool and if I knew anything I would have had the sponge on the rack. When I bent over to pick it up, she kicked me so hard I fell over. Oh, I hurt all over!"

"That's right, Miss Stewart," said Miss Maltz. "I was there when she did it. She kicked her and she hit her."

Miss Stewart, believing that both girls were immature and emotionally upset, thought that imagination and exaggeration must have played a great part in their account of the incident. She thought Miss Maltz's, "That's right, Miss Stewart," rather childish.

She asked both girls to sit down. They talked over the importance of operating room work. She told them that tensions in the operating room developed easily and that the life-and-death responsibility of persons in the room often led them to be irritable at times.

"We understand that," Miss Bader said. "Dr. Tompkins can be very snappy during surgery, but I think he forgets it afterwards."

"We don't like to have our clothing torn by the supervisor, though," Miss Maltz added.

After a fifteen-minute talk the student nurses left the nursing director's office. Miss Stewart decided to check on the conditions of the operating room gowns to ascertain if they would tear easily. Her investigation showed that enough gowns were in good condition. A few which might have torn easily Miss Stewart ordered put to another use.

Miss Martin, a graduate assistant teacher, accosted Miss Stewart in the hall some ten days later. "I hate to confront you with a problem so soon," she said. "You undoubtedly know that for the past four years our directors of nursing have stayed only about one year each. But what you probably don't know is that each one has tried to do something about the way Miss Richards mistreats student nurses. What happens is that the director leaves in a few months and Miss Richards stays on. I think the situation is getting worse. One of the students—Bernice Smith—came to my room last night and showed me bruises on her legs. Miss Richards had kicked her while they were in the operating room. Bernice said that she was going to tell her parents but the other girls talked her out of it. They're afraid to let any outsiders know about the situation for fear that Miss Richards will find out about it and have her "gentleman friend," Dr. Schwartz, make life miserable for them for the rest of their training period. Bernice told me about Virginia Smeck who has scratches from her shoulders to her wrists—the result of Miss Richards' fingernails when something went wrong in the operating room. Bernice asked me not to take her word for it but to see for myself, but I told her that the best thing for me to do, since I knew about all this already, was to tell you about it. You are, after all, the only one whose position gives you the right to do anything about it."

"Yes, you're quite right," Miss Stewart answered.

"I heard that Clarice Maltz and June Bader tried to tell you but that you didn't quite believe them. I realize that you haven't been here long enough to know everything that's going on, so I thought I'd tell you about this myself," said Miss Martin.

"Miss Bader and Miss Maltz did come to see me," Miss Stewart admitted. "But, you see, they were so emotional at the time. . . . Besides, the story they told me just didn't fit into our way of life today—not the American way of life, anyway. I thought that the girls might not understand the intensity of the operating room situation. . . . I still think their story is most unusual to say the least. How about you? Are you convinced that all you've told me is true?"

"You don't live in the nurses' home, Miss Stewart; so you don't know how thin the walls are. For years I've heard that sort of thing discussed. Since Miss Richards hasn't lived in the nurses' home for years, the students discuss her rather freely. I don't know whether or not they realize that anyone else can hear them. You know, your predecessors knew about this situation, but they found themselves in pretty hot water when they inquired into it. I want to tell you how badly I feel about it, though, because I know if you attempt to do anything about it, you will have to leave, too. And you've been here such a short time."

"You can stop worrying about my leaving," said Miss Stewart. "I'm asking you now to tell me anything that you know to be true and are willing to declare to the board of directors."

Miss Martin said, "Oh, I don't want to get mixed up in it at all. But for your own information I'll tell you this: the doctors are back of Miss Richards one hundred percent. They will probably like you in direct proportion to the completeness with which you let Miss Richards alone." She hurried away.

The next day Miss Stewart made it a point to look up Virginia Smeck. The director noticed the scratches. "Why, Miss Smeck, what happened to your arm?" she asked.

"Oh nothing—just a little accident. Excuse me. I've got to hurry to the laundry. Miss Richards sent me for some linen."

Miss Stewart asked Miss Richards to come to her office later that day. The operating room supervisor arrived two hours after the director's request. Miss Richards sat down near Miss Stewart's desk.

"I'm wondering, Miss Richards, if it is difficult here to get students to carry out procedures as taught or if, on the whole, they are quite sincere in their efforts," she began.

"The modern girl is just plain dumb, very careless, and often insubordinate. But don't worry. I don't let them get the best of me."

Said Miss Stewart, "Those are rather harsh words, Miss Richards. What do you mean—insubordinate?"

"Oh, you know very well what it means," Miss Richards replied.

"If there's a question of insubordination, don't you think I should know about it?" asked Miss Stewart.

"I haven't come up against anything yet that I couldn't handle. The students all act the same, but I take care of them."

"But, Miss Richards, if I am to cooperate with you in the handling of students, it seems to me I ought to know a little more about their foibles. What do you mean they all act the same way?"

"Is this kind of talk all you called me down here for?" Miss Richards asked abruptly.

"Something like that," Miss Stewart answered. "You said that you don't let the students get the best of you. Just what do you mean?"

"You take care of the nursing office business and I'll take care of operating room business. See!" Miss Richards replied.

"Are you implying that I should not be interested in what goes on in the operating room?"

"I'm telling you frankly to keep out of what goes on there. Otherwise you'll be sorry. Now I'm busy, and I think I'll go." Miss Richards rose to leave.

Miss Stewart quickly walked to the door and held her hand on the knob. "It's not time for you to go just yet," she said. "I insist upon answers to my questions. As two grown women we should be able to lay our cards on the table and keep levelheaded while we do it."

"Well, just what do you want?" asked the operating room supervisor.

Miss Stewart said, "I'll come directly to the point then. Some very unpleasant stories concerning your treatment of students have been told to me. They are very hard to believe, yet at the present time there is no one but you who can prove whether or not they are true. Did you ever shake, scratch, or kick student nurses in the operating room?"

"Certainly not. I'm warning you to keep out of my business. If you don't, you'll be sorry, I can promise you."

Miss Stewart continued, "If I ever attended to my own business, I'm doing it now. I still hope that you can prove that you do not do that sort of thing."

Miss Richards pushed the director aside and left the office.

Other matters of importance came to the attention of Miss Stewart in the next few days, and she did not have time to think about the affair with Miss Richards.

A week later the nursing director asked Miss Richards to step into a room where they could be alone to talk for a few minutes.

Miss Richards answered, "Our schedule has been heavy today, and our cleaning will take all afternoon. I cannot talk to you today."

Although Miss Stewart tried to find opportunity for another interview, she was never able to find the operating supervisor alone. One of her two graduate assistants was invariably nearby. The nursing director asked her secretary, Miss Patton, about the assistants. Miss Patton, who was also assistant director of the nursing school, told Miss Stewart that Miss Short, the first assistant, was the best graduate assistant on the staff in the school of nursing. Miss Reed, the other assistant, Miss Stewart learned, was also an efficient nurse. Both nurses got along well with Miss Richards.

When the nursing director finally found Miss Richards alone, she asked the supervisor to come into her office. Miss Richards replied: "I do not intend to have time to talk to you."

39. St. Luke's Hospital (B)*

Two days after Miss Richards, the supervisor of nurses in general surgery, had told Miss Stewart that she did not intend to find time to talk with her, Helen Sommers, an alumna of St. Luke's, visited the nursing director at her apartment. In the course of their evening's conversation together, Miss Sommers confirmed what Miss Stewart had learned about Miss Richards.

"I still have some scratch marks on my arm, thanks to Miss Richards," she told Miss Stewart.

The nursing director went to see the superintendent of the hospital the following day. She told him of her concern about the mistreatment of student nurses and waited for his reply.

"I don't doubt that what you say is true, Miss Stewart," he said. "As a matter of fact, I've heard something about this myself from two or three members of the community. I don't mind telling you that the situation has me worried, but frankly I don't know what to do about it. What would you suggest?"

"Well, first of all, I feel directly responsible for all the nurses in the entire Nursing Department. Miss Richards' treatment of student nurses reflects as much on me as it does on the school of nursing. I was thinking that it might be best to take the matter to the Nursing School Committee first. Then . . . well, then perhaps I'll have a better idea of what to do about it."

"I think that would be the thing to do," Mr. Fischer said. "Please keep me posted on what the outcome is. I'm deeply concerned."

Miss Stewart promised to do so and left. That evening she wrote a list of grievances against Miss Richards. In it she included statements made by nursing students, Maltz, Bader, Smith (to Miss Martin), Miss Martin, Miss Sommers, and Superintendent Fischer. Three days later she took the statements, signed by herself, to the bimonthly meeting of the Nursing School Committee which was composed of a retired doctor, a minister, a college dean, a librarian, a graduate of St. Luke's nursing school, and a doctor's wife who was also a registered nurse.

At the meeting Miss Stewart laid before the committee the statements which she had prepared. Although some members of the committee expressed surprise at the disclosure of maltreatment of nursing students by Miss Richards, some committee members, it seemed to Miss Stewart, seemed to know about the state of affairs.

The college dean asked why the situation had not been reported before.

Said Miss Stewart, "I think my short tenure of office and the fact that the last four directors of nursing have occupied the position for a relatively short period of time make the answer to that question rather obvious."

"Something certainly ought to be done if this is true," said the minister, "and from the evidence Miss Stewart has cited, it certainly appears to be true. I think Miss Richards should be made to resign."

*From Wendell French, John E. Dittrich, and Robert A. Zawacki, *The Personnel Management Process: Cases on Human Resources Administration.* Copyright © 1978 by Houghton Mifflin Company. Reprinted with permission of the publisher.

The doctor said, "Let's not be hasty in our judgment, ladies and gentlemen. Our surgeons are very proud of their record of no infections. It seems to me that they would be extremely averse to anything which might lead to Miss Richards' resignation and the possibility of incompetent nursing in general surgery."

"Are our nurses of no consequence as young women, sir?" the minister asked.

"Certainly no one wants to see them mistreated," the doctor rejoined, "but it seems to me that we must not lose sight of the fact that Miss Richards has a reputation as an efficient nurse in surgery."

"Or the fact that nurses are not easily hired these days," rejoined the college dean. "It seems to me . . ."

The nursing school graduate interrupted him. "I wonder if the fact that one of our surgeons, Dr. Schwartz, dates Miss Richards could explain her being allowed to mistreat students without reprimand. I know of certain instances in which nursing students have been mistreated, and I think—in reply to Dean Harmon's question before—that each student has been somewhat hesitant about reporting Miss Richards for fear that certain surgeons might make their lives miserable during the rest of their training."

"But that's foolish," said the doctor.

"Foolish, but possible. I worked in operating rooms, and I've seen that sort of thing so I know it can happen," she answered.

The doctor's wife finally moved that the Nursing School Committee recommend to the board of directors that the director of nurses be given complete support in any measure to stop physical violence in the operating room. The motion was carried unanimously.

Miss Stewart, as an ex officio member of the board of directors, decided to take the recommendation to the next board meeting, the following Monday, but she first talked to Mr. Fischer. He advised her to consult the board. In the meantime Miss Stewart again attempted to talk to Miss Richards. The operating room supervisor told her that she was far too busy to be bothered with trivialities. Miss Stewart waited another day before she tried to interview Miss Richards again. They met in the hall outside the operating room. Miss Stewart said, "I'd like you to drop into my office this afternoon."

Miss Richards' reply was: "Stop bothering me."

On Monday evening Miss Stewart arrived at the directors' conference room early. She watched the various directors as they entered and made mental notes of what she remembered about them from their previous meetings. She nodded to the Reverend William Blakesly when he entered. (He had been chiefly responsible for informing the board of Miss Stewart's qualifications for the position of supervisor.) He had introduced her to Dr. Stephen R. Rauch, an elderly, retired minister, and James B. Davison, a lawyer, two more members of the board. Miss Stewart knew well the chairman of the board, Judge Selwyn C. Roberts of the State Supreme Court, and Thomas L. Alberts, a businessman, whom she had met because of his daily visits to the hopsital to see his daughter who was recovering from an operation. Miss Stewart knew the other members were either lawyers or businessmen who were prominent in the community.

After the usual order of business, Miss Stewart asked for and was granted the floor.

"Gentlemen," she began, "I'm sorry that so soon after our first meeting together I must place a problem before you; nevertheless, a situation has come up with which I am unable to cope, so I've come for some advice. First, I would like to read to you a resolution of recommendation from the Nursing School Committee." She read from a paper: "The Nursing School Committee of St. Luke's Hospital hereby recommends to the board of directors that Miss Jenny Stewart, director of nurses of the hospital, be given complete, unwavering support in any measure to prevent physical violence under the guise of teaching in the operating room."

Miss Stewart awaited comments; when none were forthcoming, she continued:

"I had intended to seek the board's permission to ask Miss Lois Richards, supervisor of nurses in general surgery, to resign her position, but just before I came to this meeting I received her resignation sent through the mail—special delivery. So now you see that Miss Richards has perhaps solved the problem which I am posing for you. Of course, there is one possibility of difficulty: Miss Richards states that her two assistants will leave with her, but I do not accept her statement as final for them."

The members of the board expressed surprise.

"What's this all about?" asked one of the businessmen. "What prompted this resignation?"

In answer Miss Stewart read the report which she had presented to the Nursing School Committee.

"And now you'd like permission to accept Miss Richards' resignation?" Davison, the lawyer, asked.

"That's correct," Miss Stewart answered. "There is no other course open in view of the evidence, is there?" she asked in surprise.

Davison looked at Judge Roberts, who recognized Alberts.

"Now, Miss Stewart, don't you think that you're being a little hasty? I believe we can easily have one of the doctors explain to Miss Richards that she must not continue to mistreat student nurses," said Alberts.

"I'd like to ask you a question, Mr. Alberts," Miss Stewart said. "Do you think that she will listen to a doctor and suddenly mend the ways in which she has been conducting herself for so long? And suppose she decided not to change her attitude, what then?"

The judge answered for Alberts. "It seems to me that we would then know that we had the wrong doctor speak to her. We could easily arrange to have the right man speak to her."

"And in the meantime the students would continue to be kicked and scratched?"

"That is your responsibility," one of the businessmen interjected.

"No, it isn't. For my part I won't be responsible for what goes on in the operating room—I can't be—if Miss Richards is not responsible to me, and right now she's not."

"But you can't avoid your responsibility to the entire hospital. After all, you haven't yet found a way to influence Miss Richards," said elderly Dr. Rauch. "You wouldn't want to remember that you failed in your job because you were unable to make Miss Richards responsible to you."

"Believe me, Dr. Rauch, I would much rather that Miss Richards and I could have settled this. I had not given up really trying until last Friday. I attempted to see Miss Richards twice to talk the matter out—even after my meeting with the Nursing School Committee, but she rebuffed me on both occasions. As a matter of fact, since I began to show interest in the matter of physical violence in the operating room, it seems to have increased. I have no reason to believe that a truce will be called while we wait for doctors to find time to talk this matter over with her. I want to accept her resignation. Of course, I realize that I must have the sanction of this board before I can."

"Have you talked to Mr. Fischer about this?" Davison asked.

"Yes, I have, and he recommended that I bring the problem before the board."

The judge said, "Miss Stewart, you know that Dr. Tompkins, our leading surgeon, is out of town for a few days. Would you not rather we just hold Miss Richards' resignation until you have a chance to talk this situation over with him?"

"No, I wouldn't. Dr. Tompkins does not share any of the responsibility over student nurses with me," Miss Stewart answered.

"But, Miss Stewart, you must remember that Miss Richards has been with us for four years. During that time we have never had any complaints about her techniques in the operating room," one of the lawyers said.

"And after all, the primary purpose of a school of nursing is to teach students to do accurate work," Alberts added. "The results have been excellent for four years; so Miss Richards must have carried out the responsibility of teaching the students an accurate technique. I would hate to think what might have happened to my daughter while she was in the operating room if the nurses, as well as the surgeons, were not doing competent work. Miss Richards must be teaching them something of a very definite value in the operating room."

"I have to agree with Mr. Alberts," said the Reverend Mr. Blakesly. "Miss Stewart, you certainly realize that the lives of patients who go into the operating room must be safeguarded at all costs."

"And I agree with you that every patient must be safeguarded at all costs," said Miss Stewart. "But it seems to me that the real question is: Is physical violence to nursing students a necessary cost?"

A brief silence ensued, then the judge spoke:

"You must realize, Miss Stewart, that you are not only asking the board to decide whether the hospital can get along without a trusted employee or not but that—well, you see—you are so new in your position. . . . It is hard for the board to decide by such an action as you now ask us to take—that you have already proved yourself, er—equal to the situation which confronts us. I say that with no sense of recrimination. As far as I know, the board is completely satisfied with your work . . . and your interest in the hospital is undoubtedly founded upon a sincere desire to do your job well."

Davison said: "No one has mentioned yet the scarcity of nurses today. It might be some time before we can get a capable successor for Miss Richards. In the meantime, Miss Stewart, can we expect that the lives of patients will be safeguarded in the operating room? There is such a shortage of nurses that it might be dangerous to lose Miss Richards at this time."

"I'd like to remind the board that there are two capable nurses who are Miss Richards' assistants in the operating room: Miss Short and Miss Reed. Although both of them are only graduate assistants, I believe that at least one of them should be capable of taking over the responsibilities of operating room supervisor in general surgery. From what I've seen of Miss Short and from what I've heard of her previous record, it seems to me that we would not be inviting trouble if the board would appoint her to the position of supervisor."

"But you said yourself that Miss Richards promised that the two assistants would leave with her," said one of the lawyers.

"And I added that I didn't accept her statement as final for them. . . ."

"But both those girls are only graduate assistants," said Alberts.

"From the tenor of the conversation which I've been hearing around the table," the judge said, "I would surmise that the board is not yet ready to approve the resignation of Miss Richards. . . ."

"I move that we lay on the table this matter of accepting Miss Richards' resignation," said Alberts.

Davison seconded the motion, and it was carried unanimously.

The judge said, "Suppose, Miss Stewart, that you attempt to interview Miss Richards again between now and the next time the board meets. I'd like you to come into the next meeting and report any progress that you've been able to make toward securing her cooperation in this matter. I think I am expressing the feelings of the entire board when I say that we are assured of your deep-rooted interest in the case, and I also want to assure you that the board is completely in sympathy with your attitude toward the—the conduct—in the operating room. You can count on the board to cooperate with you in any further decisions that are made."

The meeting was adjourned, and Miss Stewart left. She walked slowly back to her office, repeating to herself: "And now what can I do?"

40. Midwestern Medical School*

Dr. Randolph Green was the chairman of the Microbiology Department at Midwestern Medical School. In early 1972 he returned from a one-year sabbatical in Sweden, where he had worked at the Tumor Biology Unit of one of the foremost cancer research institutes in the world.

At thirty-eight Dr. Green had traveled quite far in his career. He was considered quite young to be a department chairman at any medical school, and Midwestern was not just *any* school. It was, in fact, the largest regional medical center in the Midwest. Early in his academic career, Dr. Green had discovered a

*Reprinted with permission of Macmillan Publishing Co., Inc. from *Organizational Behavior: Readings and Cases* by Theodore T. Herbert. Copyright © 1976, Theodore T. Herbert. This case was prepared by Roberta P. Marquette under the supervision of Theodore T. Herbert. The case is not intended to reflect either effective or ineffective administrative or technical practices, but was prepared as a basis for class discussion.

basic medical phenomenon and that discovery had ensured his success. By the time the phenomenon was exhausted, he had published twenty articles, been appointed to several study sections of the National Institutes of Health, and had been secured in his position as chairman of the Microbiology Department at Midwestern. For the next ten years, Dr. Green rode on his reputation while he built up one of the better microbiology units in the country. He had over $1 million a year in grant moneys, three laboratories, a full crew of technicians, and several postdoctoral fellows.

During that period everything published from the Microbiology Unit at Midwestern carried Dr. Green's name, but never as first author. It was customary that the provider of funds put his name on everything that went out of the laboratories, even if he had never heard of the work until he saw the paper being readied for mailing. Although this was usually the case in the Micro Unit, most of the postdocs considered it fair enough since the practice was well known, and, after all, without Dr. Green there would be no publications at all.

According to an inside joke, one of the reasons Dr. Green had not done any work in several years was that he was too busy trying to win the Nobel Prize. Despite the fact that the Nobel is supposedly awarded in a totally objective atmosphere, there are accepted ways of "politicking." One way is to go to Sweden a lot, and this Dr. Green did every year, utilizing his grant moneys for financing, and his position as department chairman to obtain released time. The one-year sabbatical in 1971 appeared to many to be part of his big push toward the prize. When he left, he had in his laboratories three very productive postdocs, each of whom was doing very promising work in a major area of fundamental cellular biology.

When he returned from Stockholm, Dr. Green reassembled an office staff which included an editorial assistant. It was this person's job to work for all the members of the microbiology department, doing research, writing and editing papers, proofing galleys, and organizing conferences and workshops. Although all the members of the department utilized the editorial assistant's services, it was clear that first priorities went to Dr. Green and the cellular biology group; for one thing her salary was paid from Dr. Green's grant funds.

The Microbiology Unit was a reasonably good place to work, especially when Dr. Green was out of town, which was most of the time. His presence was always a disturbance. He would get an idea, gather all his technicians, send them scurrying about preparing for a "BIG" experiment, and by the time they got back to say the preparation was done, six chances out of ten he had forgotten all about it. He was fond of telling everyone that he worked best under pressure, but somehow it always seemed to be someone else's pressure. When anyone complained about the constant crisis atmosphere, he would quote Teddy Roosevelt on heat and kitchens.

The editorial assistant was a frequent target for crisis activities. Grant progress reports, new applications, and renewals were always due by a specific date and had to be postmarked by midnight the day before to receive attention. Routinely, Dr. Green would begin dictating these documents around noon the day before mailing, go home at five, and leave Joyce there until midnight getting the document typed, edited, and retyped on the Institute's eight-carbon copy form so that it could be carried around for the necessary signatures and put in the mail the next day.

Joyce didn't like Green, and didn't especially like working for him. She often thought of quitting, but knew that was highly impractical. Midwestern was located in a small college town, and practically the only jobs available were at the university. At the state school, jobs were tightly classified; editorial assistant was the highest rating for which she was eligible, and there were only four other such positions at the University. Chances for transfer ranged from unlikely to impossible. Since she didn't take shorthand (required for a secretary), her next available position was clerk typist I at a cut of $4,000 a year in salary. Joyce was her family's sole support while her husband went to graduate school, and she just couldn't, in good conscience, say goodbye to $4,000 because she didn't like Green and his methods.

One thing that did make the situation more tolerable was the presence of the other people working at the unit. Her personal favorite was Bob Johnson, a young postdoctoral fellow, who was doing work on a particularly difficult problem of keeping phagocytes alive in culture over long periods of time. This problem, while apparently small, would open vast new areas of research when solved. Bob Johnson was extremely bright, but he was not the same kind of researcher as Dr. Green. Bob was patient and methodical, thinking out his programs well in advance, starting up a number of different approaches to the same problem, so that even if most came up dry he would still have at least one avenue to pursue. He enjoyed making fun of Green's research methods. Green tended to putter around waiting for something interesting to happen—the penicillin approach. This was the manner in which he had made his first discovery, and Bob jokingly said that only Green would be naive enough to think that lightning would strike in the same place twice. The approach, called "phenomenology," led to the joke that Green would be in hog-heaven if he found an experiment that made the water turn green every other Thursday, even if he never discovered the cause!

In mid-1974 Bob Johnson began getting some good results, and by August it appeared that he had the problem licked. Everyone was delighted; for Bob it meant his reputation was made, and for the laboratory it meant prestige and the assurance that grant moneys would continue. They had an enormous celebration party, and Dr. Green outlined their strategy to get the maximum mileage out of the research. The paper would appear in the *Journal of Experimental Medicine* (JEM), the best in the field, and to increase interest and exposure, they would put it out in four installments, four months running: first the theory, then the research design, next the methodology, and finally the results.

Joyce and Bob got to work on the papers, and Dr. Green said he would write to the editor of JEM and let him know the paper was coming. Since she usually handled all correspondence regarding publications, Joyce inquired about this letter several days later. Green told her he had given it to his secretary to type because Joyce had been so busy. When she asked the secretary for a copy, the secretary said she couldn't find it. Joyce figured that Dr. Green had forgotten to write the letter, lied because he never admitted a mistake, and that now, reminded, he would take care of the letter. Similar things had happened before, and Joyce thought no more about it.

When the papers were written to their satisfaction, they turned them over to Dr. Green for final editing and approval. This was routine with major papers they sent out of the unit. Dr. Green wrote well and was especially adept at making organizational changes which made complex details flow more logically. But this time, Green "sat" on the paper. Two weeks went by and the paper still hadn't come out of his office. In the meantime Dr. Green had gone off to a conference in New York, and he said he simply hadn't had time to get to it.

The third week passed, and Dr. Green readied to go to England to do a short stint as a guest lecturer at the University of London. That was planned to last three weeks, and neither Joyce nor Bob was able to extract the paper before he left.

While Green was gone, a visitor came to the unit from New York University. He had been in Colorado and had driven the several hundred miles to Midwestern specifically, he said, "to talk further with Dr. Green about *his* research into phagocyte culture." From talking to the visitor it became apparent that Green had gone off to the conference in New York and presented the unpublished paper without giving Bob Johnson any credit at all.

Both Bob and Joyce knew that the longer the paper went unpublished, the more people would associate the work with Dr. Green, and that if they waited long enough people might actually assume that Green had given Bob first author as a gesture of magnanimity.

The next day, while Dr. Green's secretary was at lunch, Joyce went into her files and extracted a copy of the letter to the JEM. Her worst fears were well founded. The letter proceeded as though Dr. Green had done all the research and ended with a comment that he was having one of his postdoctoral fellows do a little more work and when that was completed he would send the paper in.

Joyce knew that something had to be done, but she couldn't decide what. She knew that Dr. Green was wrong, but she wasn't certain that it didn't seem worse to her than it really was because of her dislike for Green and her fondness for Bob Johnson. In addition, Green *was* her boss, and as long as she worked for him she felt she had some type of obligation to him. Quitting would relieve her of that obligation, but would also produce financial disaster. Besides, she rationalized, if she quit, then she would no longer be there to help protect the research fellows from Dr. Green's unfair practices. A new assistant might feel no obligation to pass moral judgments on the activities around him; after all, look at Dr. Green's secretary, who also knew the facts yet did just as she was told.

Whatever the decision, Joyce knew it had to be made before Dr. Green came back and regained total control of the situation.

41. Conflict Management*

Area Manager John H. was surprised and astounded by the conversation he had just heard—if you could call it a conversation! He could hardly believe that two of his key managers could be involved in such a bitter feud. One accused the other of trying to undermine his department by stealing his best people and the other accused in rebuttal that the other manager was simply finding excuses for his bad management. There had been accusation and counteraccusation followed by hot denials and bitter recrimination. He finally decided there was nothing to be gained by further outbursts and sent both men back to their departments. This, he hoped, would give them a cooling off period and himself a chance to try and sort it all out.

It wasn't unusual for Technical Development and Product Engineering to have these differences, but they rarely took on such a heated aspect. John's thoughts turned to Ralph, Manager of Technical Development. He had come highly recommended by the president of another division. He had been very successful in development work and seemed well suited to this assignment. In his six months on the job he had reorganized several sections and initiated new projects. It wasn't spectacular but it appeared competent from all John could see. There had been a few gripes that he was too aloof and reserved, but that was natural in view of the man he had replaced. It always took a little time for these management transitions to settle down. It appeared Ralph was aware of his problem since he had inserted a new manager under him (Frank) who was effective in personal relationships. It was too early to tell how that was working out but it seemed a wise move.

John knew there were problems, however. He had talked with Personnel after the recent Opinion Survey and learned the morale in Ralph's group was down from its usual mark. There seemed to be more employee apathy, more lateness and absences, and more transfer requests. This latter was the most surprising since there were few such requests usually. It was odd to find morale at such a low ebb since the group was well knit and had strong group identity. Personnel had talked informally with a few of the people and their view was (1) the work load was too low and they didn't feel meaningfully utilized and (2) they felt their present management was too distant and reserved.

It was difficult to put these in perspective. From Ralph's viewpoint the low work load was directly traceable to the "game" George was playing. He contended one of George's people would request a "sizing" for a particular job. His people would carefully give cost, technology, and schedule estimates, but then nothing happened. One of his people would call over to find out where the work requisition was and would be told the job had been cancelled by George. His manager would be offered a much smaller job—provided they transferred the people key to the former job request—"to help keep your people busy." When this finally came to Ralph's attention he "hit the roof" and this is what led to the recent confrontation. George's views varied greatly, hence the hot argument.

*This case was prepared by James C. Conant, School of Business Administration and Economics, California State University, and is used here with his permission. Copyright © James C. Conant.

George had been in the department longer than Ralph. He was known as an effective, "hard-nosed" manager who got the job done. He was ambitious and had grown rather rapidly over the last two years. He was adaptable as shown by the fact that he had made the transition from Chemistry to Product Engineering. The Product Engineering Department had a poor reputation prior to George's moving over and he had been instrumental in changing its image to a very positive one. As a result the Department had grown considerably under George. All in all it was a good record.

George contended Ralph was an inefficient manager, with too much fat in his organization, who was unwilling to cut back to a reasonable level. As a result Ralph was pricing himself out of the business. He had to cancel jobs because the costs were prohibitive. George laid some of the blame on the previous manager, Henry, claiming it was Henry's doing that caused the Lab to reach the present ridiculous size. George felt Ralph should reevaluate his situation and curtail the department size and became competitive again. If the cost problem had merit as an argument it could go back to Henry. There was nothing to indicate Ralph's costs were out of line with past history.

George freely admitted to wanting several of Ralph's people. He felt they would be better placed and better utilized in his area, but he hotly denied he had "played any games" to get them. The pressure of the new releases had caused a backlog in his department and he could use expert help.

John wondered why George steadfastly refused to use the Technology group. He was slipping schedules and the overtime costs would eventually overtake the claimed excessive costs of Ralph's group. He wasn't in any serious trouble as yet and might be gambling he could pull his chestnuts out by the transfer of a few key people. If this was his gamble he might be trying to force Ralph's hand.

John decided he had better talk to Henry in order to clarify this matter further. After that was concluded he sorted out the following impressions. Henry had no love for Ralph. He felt it was still his "shop" and Ralph was doing a poor job of taking over. On the other hand Henry supported Ralph's contentions about George. He indicated he had similar problems in the past and had called him on it a number of times. He flatly denied that the group was too large and indicated it would function well if George didn't feel he had to have the managership of all operations necessary to his function. The conversation left John more puzzled than edified.

Well, there it was. All made good points. If George is correct an overhaul is in order and Ralph should get his costs in line. If Ralph is right George must be stopped from disrupting the department and risking full project success for the sake of his own gain. In all probability both have valid points and the problem will be how to respond appropriately to both managers.

Ralph's Viewpoint

Ralph was transferred into this division after several successful projects in Engineering Development. He came highly recommended by the president of another division, under whom he had worked, and was deemed a candidate for higher management in the near future.

There was little doubt about his technical competence. He was informed and innovative. He preferred small groups to large, complex ones, and this was a partial reason for giving him this assignment. Higher growth would depend on his ability to handle larger groups. For this reason the job had been enlarged to encompass additional functions. This meant Ralph had a substantially larger group to manage than his predecessor.

Although Ralph never commented on his reaction to this change in operations for him, he appeared a little overwhelmed by it. He spent considerable time in his office planning and integrating the various functions. He only rarely met with the Lab people and had staff meetings on an irregular basis. It must be emphasized he had been in the job only about six months and still was getting his feet on the ground.

He had never been much of a delegator. Some of this was by temperament and some from the nature of the reward structure. He had been heard to comment: "I do my business in the halls. When I run into the Division President and he asks about my project I can get away with maybe one 'I don't know' and after that I'm known as an 'I don't know guy.'" The result was a tendency to know details that usually are reserved for subordinates. The new job stretched him to the point that he had greater difficulty doing this, but it may account for the inordinate amount of time he spent in his office.

In his approach to others he was direct and confronting. People knew where they stood, and in general their comments indicated they liked this style of managing. He was aware he interacted somewhat stiffly with others and this had occasioned the insertion of Frank at the Lab level. In addition he was planning to change some of the procedures Henry had instituted, and he felt Henry would be an obstacle to these plans. Frank would be a major factor in assuring that the new procedures went as smoothly as possible.

His relationship to Henry was cordial but distant. He had no particular dislike for Henry, but felt the group could be more effectively organized. He was in the process of developing these plans when the problem broke.

His relationship with John, the Director, was essentially OK as far as one could tell. On the whole his "clout" with John was undeveloped, as was his impact on his peers. He seemed to be regarded as an unknown quantity—perhaps something of a threat in view of his reputation.

He was disappointed with the way the meeting turned out. He didn't like shouting matches but he wasn't going to stand by and have George put him or his Lab group down. He was sure they were effective and as soon as he completed some of the new project planning he knew their work load would be more than adequate. He was familiar with people trying the kind of thing George was doing and the only way to avert it was through direct confrontation. He only wished he could better predict John's reaction.

Henry's Viewpoint

Henry was an "old timer" and had been the Lab's Manager for many years. He was affable and outgoing, walking the shop regularly and on a first-name basis with virtually everyone in the Lab. It had been his assignment to create and staff the Lab, and over the several years he managed it he exercised care in the selection and placement of the staff. It had been generally conceded the Lab was staffed with topnotch people.

The Lab group had strong ties with one another. There were a few who had turned down promotions in order to remain with the group. That it was not all one big happy family was indicated by a few dissidents who felt they had been passed over for promotion. On the whole, however, they worked well together and enjoyed a favorable reputation by all concerned.

As Henry had indicated, George had tried to lure some of his better talent away during the recent past. Henry learned of these rather quickly because of his close relationships to the group and he effectively aborted each of these. George had finally given up on this and had gone to outside recruiting for the talent he wanted. This meant a slower indoctrination process for him and slowed down his growth potential. It was Henry who first became aware that George was up to his "old tricks."

He probably should have gone to Ralph with the information about George but he felt at odds with Ralph's methods. He resented the staff role into which he had been put, even though medical advice was the basis for the move. He sensed that Ralph was planning changes and he had not been consulted. When Frank was brought in he felt even more resentful. He regarded his assignment as a "make work" one and did not feel meaningfully utilized. He still felt a strong proprietary interest in the Lab group and would take whatever measures he could to prevent its disruption.

Given a choice of choosing between Ralph or George he would choose Ralph, and eventually this choice had to be made. In his meeting with John he had been fully candid regarding George's tactics and hoped this once John would put a stop to them. He did it more to ensure the Lab remaining intact than because of Ralph. He certainly didn't want to see the Lab destroyed after all the years he'd spent building it to its present state.

George's Viewpoint

George was dynamic, energetic, and technically proficient. He had taken over the Product Engineering group when it was regarded with disfavor and had steadily built into its present respectable state. He had ambition and sought to enlarge his sphere of influence whenever possible. He viewed the situation in this way. "I like this environment. It is highly fluid and I have a lot of freedom to do things the way I believe they should be done. I get reprimanded when I make a mistake— and that's only fair as far as I'm concerned. My attitude is to take over and operate any group I can. If I'm successful it will soon come under my jurisdiction. I keep pushing until I'm told to stop by someone who can make it stick."

This had been George's method of operation as long as he had been a manager. It had paid off handsomely for him, and from the Company's standpoint they had benefited too. His group was well-managed, competently staffed, and morale was at least as good as one could find in the Division. His people were loyal to him and respected his ability. He had considerable "clout" because of his past success and had more than the usual influence with the Director.

He had no personal antipathy for Ralph. He was anxious to secure some of the key Lab people and honestly believed they would be more effective in his organization. He felt this would be better for the Company and would provide the people with greater opportunities for growth. There was some accuracy to the latter, but the former was a matter of opinion.

As he regarded the Lab group he felt they were overstaffed and underutilized. He didn't think Ralph was effective in moving to reorganize the department and felt the people were fair game for his managerial approach.

(It was interesting to this observer that direct methods were never utilized. The ground rules permitted making offers to people in other departments, through promotions, raises, etc. Why George never did was unclear.)

George felt he was an effective manager, better than his peers (possibly including the Director). He felt Ralph was running a country club and that it needed effective management. If possible he wanted to absorb the Lab into his operation, but that would require a restructuring of the organization. Since the Lab served many groups in addition to his, his functions would have to be broadened, an unlikely move at this time.

He was taking a calculated risk in not using the Lab for some of his immediate jobs because he might well get into a last minute "crunch" and, failing to meet schedule, lose some of the ground he had gained. On the other hand if he could secure some key people, he could come in on schedule and be in a position to take over other Lab functions that would arise later. In the meantime it would appear as if the Lab was not as necessary because of the low work load. He, at this time, was the major user of the Lab—although this was not always the case. This depended on the development cycle, which was at a low ebb for other groups, but would probably pick up fairly soon.

All in all George was satisfied with his progress and felt he had a good chance at the Director's job when John was promoted. He wasn't happy about this current situation with Ralph, but felt he could weather it and perhaps make Ralph appear foolish or somewhat less competent. It would be a good time for a put-down, his being new and all. The last meeting with John left him uncertain as to where each stood. He was sure he had not heard the last of the situation.

42. The Case of the Changing Cage*

Part I

The voucher-check filing unit was a work unit in the home office of the Atlantic Insurance Company. The assigned task of the unit was to file checks and vouchers written by the company as they were cashed and returned. This filing was the necessary foundation for the main function of the unit: locating any particular check for examination upon demand. There were usually eight to ten requests for specific checks from as many different departments during the day. One of the most frequent reasons checks were requested from the unit was to determine whether checks in payment of claims against the company had been cashed. Thus efficiency in the unit directly affected customer satisfaction with the company.

---

*Adapted from "Topography and Culture: The Case of the Changing Cage," by Cara E. Richards and Henry F. Dobyns. Reproduced by permission of the Society for Applied Anthropology from *Human Organization,* Vol. 16, No. 1, 1957.

Complaints or inquiries about payments could not be answered with the accuracy and speed conducive to client satisfaction unless the unit could supply the necessary document immediately.

Toward the end of 1952, nine workers manned this unit. There was an assistant (a position equivalent to a foreman in a factory) named Miss Dunn, five other full-time employees, and three part-time workers.

The work area of the unit was well-defined. Walls bounded the unit on three sides. The one exterior wall was pierced by light-admitting north windows. The west interior partition was blank. A door opening into a corridor pierced the south interior partition. The east side of the work area was enclosed by a steel mesh reaching from wall to wall and floor to ceiling. This open metal barrier gave rise to the customary name of the unit—"The Voucher Cage." A sliding door through this mesh gave access from the unit's territory to the work area of the rest of the company's agency audit division, of which it was a part, located on the same floor.

The unit's territory was kept inviolate by locks on both doors, fastened at all times. No one not working within the cage was permitted inside unless his name appeared on a special list in the custody of Miss Dunn. The door through the steel mesh was used generally for departmental business. Messengers and runners from other departments usually came to the corridor door and pressed a buzzer for service.

The steel mesh front was reinforced by a rank of metal filing cases where checks were filed. Lined up just inside the barrier, they hid the unit's workers from the view of workers outside their territory, including the section head responsible for overall supervision of this unit according to the company's formal plan of operation.

Part II

On top of the cabinets which were backed against the steel mesh, one of the male employees in the unit neatly stacked pasteboard boxes in which checks were transported to the cage. They were later reused to hold older checks sent into storage. His intention was less getting these boxes out of the way than increasing the effective height of the sight barrier so the section head could not see into the cage "even when he stood up."

The girls stood at the door of the cage that led into the corridor and talked to the messenger boys. The workers also slipped out this door unnoticed to bring in their customary afternoon snack. Inside the cage, the workers sometimes engaged in a good-natured game of rubber band "snapping."

Workers in the cage possessed good capacity to work together consistently and workers outside the cage often expressed envy of those in it because of the "nice people" and friendly atmosphere there. The unit had no apparent difficulty keeping up with its work load.

Part III

For some time prior to 1952 the controller's department of the company had not been able to meet its own standards of efficient service to clients. Company officials felt the primary cause to be spatial. Various divisions of the controller's department were scattered over the entire twenty-two-story company building. Communication between them required phone calls, messengers, or personal visits, all costing time. The spatial separation had not seemed very important when the company's business volume was smaller prior to World War II. But business had grown tremendously since then, and spatial separation appeared increasingly inefficient.

Finally in November of 1952 company officials began to consolidate the controller's department by relocating two divisions together on one floor. One was the agency audit division, which included the voucher-check filing unit. As soon as the decision to move was made, lower-level supervisors were called in to help with planning. Line workers were not consulted, but were kept informed by the assistants of planning progress. Company officials were concerned about the problem of transporting many tons of equipment and some 200 workers from two locations to another single location without disrupting work flow. So the move was planned to occur over a single weekend, using the most efficient resources available. Assistants were kept busy planning positions for files and desks in the new location.

Desks, files, chairs, and even wastebaskets were numbered prior to the move, and relocated according to a master chart checked on the spot by the assistant. Employees were briefed as to where the new location was and which elevators they should take to reach it. The company successfully transported the paraphernalia of the voucher check filing unit from one floor to another over one weekend. Workers in the cage quit Friday afternoon at the old stand, reported back Monday at the new.

The exterior boundaries of the new cage were still three building walls and the steel mesh, but the new cage possessed only one door—the sliding door through the steel mesh into the work area of the rest of the agency audit division. The territory of the cage had also been reduced in size. An entire bank of filing cabinets had to be left behind in the old location to be taken over by the unit moving there. The new cage was arranged so that there was no longer a row of metal filing cabinets lined up inside the steel mesh obstructing the view into the cage.

Part IV

When the workers in the cage inquired about the removal of the filing cabinets from along the steel mesh fencing, they found that Mr. Burke had insisted that these cabinets be rearranged so his view into the cage would not be obstructed by them. Miss Dunn had tried to retain the cabinets in their prior position, but her efforts had been overridden.

Mr. Burke disapproved of conversation. Since he could see workers conversing in the new cage, he "requested" Miss Dunn to put a stop to all unnecessary talk. Attempts by female clerks to talk to messenger boys brought the wrath of her superior down on Miss Dunn, who was then forced to reprimand the girls.

Mr. Burke also disapproved of an untidy work area, and any boxes or papers which were in sight were a source of annoyance to him. He did not exert supervision directly, but would "request" Miss Dunn to "do something about those boxes." In the new cage, desks had to be completely cleared at the end of the day, in contrast to the work-in-progress files left out in the old cage. Boxes could not accumulate on top of filing cases.

The custom of afternoon snacking also ran into trouble. Lacking a corridor door, the food-bringers had to venture forth and pack back their snack tray through the work area of the rest of their section, bringing a hitherto unique custom to the attention of workers outside the cage. The latter promptly recognized the desirability of afternoon snacks and began agitation for the same privilege. This annoyed the section head, who forbade workers in the cage from continuing this custom.

Part V

Mr. Burke later made a rule which permitted one worker to leave the new cage at a set time every afternoon to bring up food for the rest. This rigidity irked cage personnel, accustomed to snack when the mood struck, or none at all. Having made his concession to the cage force, Mr. Burke was unable to prevent workers outside the cage from doing the same thing. What had once been unique to the workers in the cage was now common practice in the section.

Although Miss Dunn never outwardly expressed anything but compliance and approval of superior directives, she exhibited definite signs of anxiety. All the cage workers reacted against Burke's increased domination. When he imposed his decisions upon the voucher-check filing unit, he became "Old Grandma" to its personnel. The cage workers sneered at him and ridiculed him behind his back. Workers who formerly had obeyed company policy as a matter of course began to find reasons for loafing and obstructing work in the new cage. One of the changes that took place in the behavior of the workers had to do with their game of rubber band sniping. All knew Mr. Burke would disapprove of this game. It became highly clandestine and fraught with dangers. Yet shooting rubber bands *increased.*

Newly arrived checks were put out of sight as soon as possible, filed or not. Workers hid unfiled checks, generally stuffing them into desk drawers or unused file drawers. Since boxes were forbidden, there were fewer unused file drawers than there had been in the old cage. So the day's work was sometimes undone when several clerks hastily shoved vouchers and checks indiscriminately into the same file drawer at the end of the day.

Before a worker in the cage filed incoming checks, she measured with her ruler the thickness in inches of each bundle she filed. At the end of each day she totaled her input and reported to Miss Dunn. All incoming checks were measured upon arrival. Thus Miss Dunn had a rough estimate of unit intake compared with file input. Theoretically she was able to tell at any time how much unfiled material she had on hand and how well the unit was keeping up with its task. Despite this running check, when the annual inventory of unfiled checks on hand in the cage was taken at the beginning of the calendar year 1953, a seriously large backlog of unfiled checks was found. To the surprise and dismay of Miss Dunn, the inventory showed the unit to be far behind schedule, filing more slowly than before the relocation of the cage.

43. Davis Regional Medical Center*

Davis Regional Medical Center is an acute care, general hospital located in Charlesville, a community of 35,000 in the southwestern United States. The organization began in 1950 as a 35-bed facility known as Davis County Hospital. The hospital grew to a capacity of 55 beds after its first three years of operation. Economic growth in the region along with a rapid influx of people resulted in additional expansions and by 1968 the hospital had reached its present capacity of 166 beds.

The population in the region has grown steadily over the last fifteen years. (The population of Davis County was approximately 56,800 in 1960 and 86,600 in 1975.) However, the hospital size has remained unchanged. Approximately 500 people are employed at Davis. The medical staff consists of 75 doctors and dentists. A substantial majority of the medical staff are specialists. Therefore, the hospital offers a wide range of medical services. Current estimates are that the hospital serves 10,000 inpatients and approximately 16,000 outpatients each year.

Regional Medical Center

In 1972, the board of directors of the hospital concluded that it was necessary to undertake a major expansion of the hospital's physical plant if it were to continue to adequately serve residents in and around the Charlesville area. Hospital managers and board members had received numerous complaints concerning overcrowded conditions in the hospital. Beds for patients often were found in the halls and waiting rooms, considerable delays were experienced by new patients registering at the hospital due to the lack of available space, and numerous offices and hallways had become storage points for inventory material and equipment. At one point, hospital administrators were informed by State Health Department officials that if equipment and cartons of supplies were not removed from various hallways, the hospital would not be licensed for the coming year and therefore could not be accredited by the Joint Commission (a national accrediting agency).

The situation had become critical by the time the final decision was made on the expansion. It was decided that a major building effort costing twelve million dollars would be undertaken. The number of beds in the medical facility were to be increased from 166 to 248, and a number of existing services were to be expanded in the new facility. Shortly after the expansion decision was made, the board also changed the name of the hospital from Davis County Hospital to Davis Regional Medical Center. The purpose of this name change was to more accurately reflect the services available and the population served by the growing medical complex. A fundraising drive in Charlesville managed to provide a base of one million dollars with which to begin the expansion. However, a feasibility study completed during the drive suggested that the performance of the hospital

*From Donald D. White and H. William Vroman, *Action in Organizations.* Copyright © 1977 by Holbrook Press, Inc., subsidiary of Allyn and Bacon, Inc., Boston. Reprinted with permission.

(based on past figures) could not financially support the total planned expansion. Therefore, a revised plan was decided upon.

Administrative and Organizational Background

Davis Regional Medical Center, like similar county hospitals in the state, is governed by a seven-member board of directors. State law provided that the board be appointed by the local county judge. As with any political system, appointments are based on a combination of individual qualifications and the political postures of board members. Historically, the board had not provided strong leadership to the hospital. However, recent appointments, together with strong leadership from a new board chairman, had greatly increased the activity and contribution of the board to the operation of the hospital.

The administrator of any county hospital is placed in a unique position of having to respond to political pressures and medical needs of the people whom he serves. In addition, he often finds himself between pressures created by his medical staff, employees, and the public. The toll which these pressures create sometimes is quite high. Such was the case at Davis Regional Medical Center. Within the ten-year period from 1965 to 1975, the hospital had four separate administrators. Three of those administrators along with the one acting administrator served in the position during the last five years.

Reasons for the turnovers were numerous. One administrator, Frederick Harold, was asked to resign after the hospital lost over $250,000 in a period of two years. His replacement, Glen Easton, was charged with the responsibility of putting the hospital back in the black. Within one year Easton had done so. However, during the end of his term as administrator, his decisions affecting patients and employees alike became more and more autocratic and seemingly unrealistic. For example, he once forced an orderly to enter the room of a critically ill patient to collect a dollar-a-day charge for TV service. He had instructed the employee to collect one dollar from each patient each day that the patient was in the room. Acts such as these received considerable attention throughout the community. Later, it was discovered that Easton had leukemia, and he retired from his position as administrator. (A number of his later decisions were attributed, in part, by those around him to his illness.) His replacement was

EXHIBIT 1.   Past Administration at DRMC

Administrator	Years	Reason for Termination
G.B.	1949–53	Under pressure to resign (personal)
B.C.	1953–55	A series of problems both financial and political: asked to resign
H.M. (R.N.)	1955–62	Considered to be a good administrator: resigned under positive circumstances: she may have felt that the job was becoming "Too Big" for her
F.H.	1962–67	Hospital showed a $250,000 loss: was asked to resign
G.E.	1967–71	Illness: under mild pressure to resign
R.W.	1971–74	Was asked to resign
C.B.	1974–present	Currently the DRMC Administrator

Robert Winston who had served as assistant administrator under his predecessor for a period of two years.

The board appointed Winston as administrator of the hospital in 1971. He served in that position until he was asked to resign in 1974. Persons who worked with the hospital during his tenure as administrator (outside consultants and hospital managers) described him as unimaginative and unwilling to put in the necessary work to develop and maintain a strong medical facility. In his final months as administrator, he was on the hospital premises from four to six hours a day. Although reasons for his requested resignation were never made public, personal problems which were believed to interfere with the fulfillment of his administrative responsibilities were cited by the board.

Due to the suddenness with which Winston had been asked to tender his resignation, the board had not yet begun its search for a new administrator. In the interim period of five months Donald Dale, who served as assistant administrator under Winston, was named as acting administrator. He was closely assisted by Larry Engles, the Director of Personnel. The two men worked closely as a team making day-to-day operating decisions.

Dale and Engles were aware of acute employee morale and motivation problems within the medical center. They attributed these problems to the lack of leadership under which the hospital had been operating and employee concerns about what the new administrator would be like. Both recently had attended a seminar for hospital administrators in which the importance of employee attitudes and participation had been a major subject. In particular, they had been impressed by the discussion and illustration of a Management by Objectives (MBO) system designed for health care organizations. They were convinced that such a system would help create greater *esprit de corps* at Davis Regional Medical Center and improve the exchange of ideas and information between department heads within the hospital. Furthermore, the director of personnel believed that supervisory and department head training programs would have to be conducted in order to prepare management personnel throughout the organization for the hoped for MBO-type system.

In July 1974, the director of personnel contacted Dr. John Connors, a university professor and management consultant. It had been Dr. Connors who earlier that year had presented the administrator seminar that Engles and Dale attended. They arranged to meet together and to discuss the present situation at Davis Regional Medical Center. During the next month, the two administrators and Dr. Connors met on numerous occasions and discussed the problems and needs of the hospital.

Both Dale and Engels were emphatic about wanting to develop a more employee-oriented administration. For example, they created a nonsupervisory employee council which met once a month to discuss with the two men problems and conditions throughout the hospital. The intended purpose of this council was to provide a means by which Dale and Engels could enhance two-way communication between the hospital administration and the employees at Davis. Each department elected one person to represent them in the council. Initially, most of the communication was from the top down. However, shortly after the council had been created, a core of employees rose to take leadership of the group. They elected a spokesman and requested that they be permitted to meet once a month without either Dale or Engels present. Thereafter, the employee representatives met twice monthly, once with the administrators and once without them.

Dale and Engels also shared the view that some form of management training should be developed and conducted for department heads and hospital supervisors, whom they saw as the key to hospital effectiveness. There was some hesitancy on the part of Dr. Connors and Mr. Dale to initiate such a program prior to the selection of a new administrator. Both men believed that it might be unfair to saddle a new administrator with a program that he might not favor. The director of personnel, however, felt strongly that the program should be initiated "as soon as possible."

Such a program subsequently was designed by Dr. Connors and agreed upon by the three men. Shortly thereafter, Mr. Dale was informed that a new administrator had been selected by the Board of Directors. The new administrator was scheduled to take over his post at DRMC in approximately four weeks. Mr. Dale told Dr. Connors that his discussions with the new administrator, Mr. Benson, led him to believe that Mr. Benson would be favorable to a management development program. However, both men decided to wait until a formal meeting could be held with Mr. Benson before proceeding with the actual program.

A New Leader for the "Troops"

Arnold Benson came to Davis Hospital from a multi-facility complex in St. Louis, Missouri. He had been selected out of seventy applicants for the position of administrator at Davis County Hospital. Benson was a young man, thirty-three years of age. He held bachelor's and master's degrees in business administration and had considerable experience working in hospital organizations. In his words, "My objective was to become a professional hospital administrator. I realized that since I did not yet have a master's degree in hospital administration I would have to go with a 'back door approach' by working my way up the ranks."

Thus, Benson's first position in a hospital was that of director of purchasing and personnel in a 118-bed facility. He next took the position of assistant administrator in a 156-bed Catholic hospital. In a period of two years, he rose from assistant administrator to associate administrator and finally to that of administrator of the hospital. Finally he became administrator of a 144-bed and a 134-bed multi-hospital complex in St. Louis, Missouri. He remained in the hospital for four years "gaining exposure, experience, and expertise." Prior to his hospital experiences, Mr. Benson had worked for a year and a half on a General Motors assembly line while going to college. He also had spent four years in the Marine Corps, having enlisted when he was seventeen years old.

In the summer of 1974, Arnold Benson began looking for a new position as a hospital administrator. He believed that he had learned a great deal in his present job; however, he was anxious to relocate in a smaller community. The St. Louis Hospital of which he was administrator was located in a predominantly black, low-income, ghetto area. His hospital had been a prime target for numerous union drives (none of which were successful) and he had overseen a major expansion of the hospital facilities. He wanted to relocate in a community of less than 50,000 population somewhere in the southwestern United States. His salary requirements were rather stringent due to his experience in administration. Therefore, he was very pleased when he was selected as the new administrator at Davis Regional.

Benson was a tall athletic-looking man whose mild manners and easygoing Texas drawl tended to hide his "down-to-business" approach to administration. Soon after arriving, he realized that he would be facing many problems inside and outside of the hospital in the next few months. He knew that the most pressing of these was the hospital expansion. Moreover, it was clear to him that the first concern of certain members of the board of directors was the financial position of the hospital.

Financial concerns plagued Mr. Benson from the moment he arrived at Davis Regional Medical Center. During his first weeks on the job, the building program finances consumed almost 50 percent of his time. In addition, two particular decisions, both of which would have a direct impact on hospital employees, had to be made.

The first of these decisions concerned a 10¢ across-the-board pay increase that was due to all hospital employees in January. Mr. Benson had not been told of this promised increase until he had been at the hospital for some time. Immediately upon learning of the proposed increase, he sat down and calculated its impact on his budget. The total cost to the medical center appeared to be well in excess of $200,000. Feeling the need to hold the line on expenses, Mr. Benson decided not to put through the wage increase. In his words, "When I 'came aboard' the board charged me with the financial responsibility of the medical center. If the troops were to get their pay increase in January, it would throw the entire budget out of kilter. I have only been here three weeks, and quite frankly the '75 budget didn't get the attention it deserved." After making this decision, Mr. Benson dictated a memo announcing that while employees at Davis could expect to receive up to a 6 percent increase for the new year, the 10¢ across-the-board increase would not be given. Mr. Benson also stressed that the total financial posture of the hospital would have to be re-evaluated. The memo was posted on the employee bulletin board.

Soon after the memo was posted, a rumor circulated throughout the hospital that the board of directors was about to purchase a new automobile for Mr. Benson. Pictures of Cadillacs and Mark IV Continentals were placed on the bulletin board on an almost daily basis. His memo concerning denial of the pay increase was slashed with a knife and various comments were written on it. (The hospital-owned automobile which Benson actually used was a Ford Galaxie driven by the previous administrator.)

Recognizing the discontent over his decision, Benson met with members of the employee advisory council to discuss the pay question. Several members of the group quoted statistics showing that on the average blue-collar workers throughout the United States were being paid more than were most hospital employees. Mr. Benson replied that he thought it was unfair to quote blue-collar statistics and that he believed the most that a hospital employee at the medical center could look forward to would be to live comfortably. He then asked the members of the advisory council if they would work harder if they received 10¢ per-hour increase. According to Benson, "When all responded negatively, I told them point blank that it appeared that it would be foolish to reward people ten more cents per hour with no increase in productivity." He did go on to tell those present that he would do his best to see to it that they received some pay increases (up to 6 percent based on merit) as soon as the necessary funds became available. In addition, he told them that he hoped to put in effect a new wage and salary administration program in the near future.

The employee council also voiced complaints about other conditions at Davis hospital. Over a period of the next few weeks, Mr. Benson saw to it that many of the problems were dealt with to the group's satisfaction. However, when the last "demand" was met he announced that he believed that there was no longer a need for the advisory group. A question was raised by one of the employees concerning whether or not the group would be permitted to re-form if subsequent problems arose. Mr. Benson replied that it would not be permitted to do so.

Benson was confronted by a second important decision not long after the incident involving the pay increase memo. The hospital had been able to obtain the money necessary for expansion through tax exempt revenue bonds. However, the building program itself did not include much needed parking lots. Arnold Benson, therefore, found it necessary to take his request for an additional $1.3 million to the local banking community. Although the bankers agreed to underwrite the project, the feasibility study on which their decision was based indicated that the parking lots would have to be income-generating entities in their own right. Prior to this time, all parking in hospital lots was provided without charge to the medical staff, employees, and visitors. Now, however, it was clear to Benson that all parties would in the future be required to pay a parking fee.

Although he expected resistance on the issue from the doctors, he was more concerned about the reactions of general employees to the decision. The fact that

EXHIBIT 2. Managerial Personnel on Payroll When Benson Was Hired

| | | Tenure with DRMC | |
| | | Years | Years as |
Name	Department	Employed	Department Head
J.C.	Physical Therapy	25	21
D.T.	Nuclear Medicine	18	6
D.D.	Assistant Administrator	11½	11½
B.G.	Housekeeping	9	2
G.H.	Radiology	8½	8½
K.F.	Nursing	7	2½
L.H.	Dietary	7	7
L.E.	Personnel	5	4
J.H.	E.M.S.	5	1
P.G.	Purchasing	4	1
L.C.	Child Care	4	3
T.M.	Pharmacy	4	2
E.B.	Laboratory	3	2½
D.B.	Medical Records	2½	2½
J.G.	Maintenance	2½	2½
L.P.	Respiratory Therapy	2	2
E.I.	Social Service	1	1
M.R.	Volunteers	1	1
M.K.	Comptroller	1	1

Explanation:
1. Two new departments, EKG and EEG, were added shortly after Benson's arrival. Previously, their functions and personnel were under Nuclear Medicine.
2. Of those department heads listed above, the following persons left DRMC within six months after Benson's arrival: K.F. (resignation requested); L.H. (resigned following demotion); L.E. (resignation requested); P.G. (resigned, but was to have been replaced); E.B. (resigned to take promotion elsewhere); L.P. (resigned to take a similar position elsewhere, was dissatisfied at DRMC).

he had been confronted by this second decision so shortly after his refusal to grant the across-the-board pay increase further aggravated his situation. As far as Benson was concerned, the decision had been made. However, he and Dr. Connors agreed that its announcement should be temporarily postponed.

Management Development

In early January, department heads from throughout the hospital began meeting with Dr. Connors as part of an overall management development program. Those participating met in a series of seven two-hour sessions. The total program took place over a period of approximately one month. (A similar program was conducted for supervisors during the following month.)

According to Mr. Dale, the purpose of the management programs was twofold. He believed that it was necessary to provide those hospital employees in management positions with some form of supervisory training. He also felt that the program would be a good way to single out the department heads and supervisors for "special attention."

The sessions were recommended to the department heads and supervisors by Mr. Benson. However, participation remained voluntary. All but two department heads attended the series of sessions. (Although Mr. Benson and Mr. Dale requested that they be permitted to attend the classes, it was agreed that their presence might inhibit the participation of department heads. Both men were provided with copies of all materials distributed, but neither attended the formal sessions.)

The content of the programs included traditional subjects such as the elements and techniques of supervision. However, emphasis also was placed on achieving improved interpersonal relations between department heads and improving the exchange of information between the departments themselves. (See Exhibit 3.)

One event which took place during the sessions dramatized that a certain amount of distrust and lack of cooperation existed between many department heads throughout the hospital. During one of the early sessions, the participants were asked to complete evaluation forms that were to be used in connection with an exercise known as the Johari Window. The purpose of the exercise was to help the managers see themselves more clearly as others saw them and to help others in the group in a similar manner by providing them with "image feedback" information. The theory behind the exercise together with its purpose was explained to those present. Each manager was asked to write the name of every department head (including him/herself) and to list at least one asset and one liability of that person. Dr. Connors requested that the completed forms be returned to him at the beginning of the next session. The name of the individual providing the "feedback" information was not to be placed on the sheet itself. Dr. Connors explained that he would facilitate the exchange of feedback at the next session by reading the name of a participant followed by the assets and liabilities which were identified by his/her peers.

As he had planned, Dr. Connors began the next session by asking that all feedback sheets be passed in to him. Much to his surprise only about half of the sheets were returned and most of them were insufficiently completed. After a short pause, he asked those present to explain why they had failed to complete

EXHIBIT 3. Outline of Supervisory Development Program, Davis Regional Medical Center

Session[1]	Assignments
1 Introductory Comments and an Icebreaker Supervisory Functions: Models and the Environment Preparing for our Sessions	Case Study
2 The Hospital Organization: Authority, Power and Informal Relationships	Case Study Ch. 15[2]
3 Understanding Ourselves and Others	Case Study
4 Leading and Motivating Employees	Case Study, Film Ch. 1,2
5 Improving Interpersonal and Interdepartmental Communications	Ch. 4, Nominal Grouping Exercise, Role Play
6 Setting Goals and Making Decisions	Case Study, Role Play, Ch. 6,9
7 Evaluating and Handling Employee Conflict	Ch. 11,12, Case Study, Role Play

[1]Sessions—(1 hour and 50 minutes; last 15–20 minutes spent answering questions and dealing with problems on an individual basis.)
[2]Chapters were taken from a hospital supervisory management book selected for the program by Dr. Connors.

the assignment. Following a brief discussion, it was evident that the department heads had decided in another meeting that they would not complete the feedback sheet. Reasons for not wanting to complete the assignment ranged from claims that the participants did not know one another well enough (prior to the management program many of the department heads did not know one another by name, although a "get acquainted" exercise was used in the first session) to fear that the information assembled on each individual would in some way be used against him or her. One woman openly expressed concern that other department heads at the meeting might misuse the information. Another head privately suggested that some of those in attendance thought that Dr. Connors himself might take the information to the administrator. The discussion that followed the failure to hand in the assignment had a cathartic effect on the group. For the first time, many of those in attendance "opened up" and talked about the lack of communication and trust that existed between the department heads and between the department heads and the administrator.

Dr. Connors ended the session by again explaining that the purpose of the exercise was to "improve out understandings of ourselves as well as of those with whom we associate throughout the hospital." After another brief discussion, it was agreed by all that the feedback sheets would be completed and returned at the following session. At that next session, the exercise was completed smoothly. Many of the managers commented afterwards that they believed that the exercise had been beneficial and had helped to open up the group. One department head did comment, however, "To tell you the truth, I think our refusal to complete the feedback sheets helped to break the ice between us. You know, it is the first time we really ever got together and agreed on something."

Subsequent sessions of the department head development program produced numerous positive comments and favorable evaluations of the overall program. Upon completion of the program, each participant received a certificate signed by Mr. Benson and Dr. Connors.

Follow-Up

A few days after the department heads' program was completed, Mr. Benson asked Dr. Connors to meet with him. He began their conference by stating that he was pleased with what he had heard about the sessions and was anxious to ensure that the momentum which had been created would not be lost. He asked Dr. Connors what he thought of bringing all of the department heads together for a weekend retreat at a resort area not far from Charlesville. Dr. Connors was pleased with Mr. Benson's suggestion. He told the administrator that he had seriously considered recommending that such a retreat take place, but was hesitant to do so because of the financial situation at the hospital. Mr. Benson replied that the money for the retreat could be found since he anticipated that the outcome of the retreat would have a positive impact on the operation of the facility.

The following week Mr. Benson told department heads at their weekly meeting on January 31 that the retreat had been scheduled for the weekend of February 14 and 15. He went on to explain that the department heads would gather on Friday morning at the hospital and would drive directly to the resort. All expenses would be paid by the medical center. He told them that he hoped that the meeting would permit a free exchange of ideas.

During the week before the scheduled retreat, Dr. Connors received an invitation from Mr. Benson to meet with the department heads in their meeting on Thursday. Dr. Connors agreed to do so as long as neither Mr. Benson nor Mr. Dale would be present at the meeting.

The meeting itself brought quite a surprise. It was immediately evident to Dr. Connors that the mood of the department heads was not what he had expected. As he walked into the room he heard the men and women present voicing numerous complaints to one another. When they saw Dr. Connors the group immediately quieted down. It was not clear to him whether or not they had been told he would be attending the meeting. Therefore, he explained his presence and told them that he was interested in how things had been going the two or three weeks since their last session. Much to his surprise, the grumbling began immediately. Some of the complaints were minor. However, one complaint in particular took Dr. Connors by surprise. That complaint focused on the upcoming retreat. A few department heads stated that they did not know whether or not they would go to the resort with the rest of the group. One newly married woman stated that it was Valentine's Day and her husband did not want her to leave. Two other heads said they had previous plans to attend a Valentine's Day dance at the Country Club that Friday evening. As discussion continued, it became apparent that the department heads had been told rather than consulted about the retreat. Some expressed displeasure with being "forced" into going to the retreat and using part of their weekend without first being asked their opinion.

Dr. Connors listened carefully and explained to the managers that he himself believed that the retreat was a good idea. He told them about how he had planned on suggesting such an activity to the administrator, but how Mr. Benson had come up with the idea on his own. Moreover, he told them that he believed that they should give Mr. Benson "a chance" during the weekend to see what might come out of the retreat. There were a few supportive comments made by one or two department heads and the meeting broke up.

Dr. Connors left the meeting disturbed. He had not expected to find the level of dissatisfaction which existed among the department heads. As he walked toward the entrance of the hospital he asked himself whether or not he should try to provide any further assistance to Mr. Benson before the group left for the retreat the next morning. He decided to stop in and see the administrator before leaving the hospital.

44.   Why Should My Conscience Bother Me?*

The B. F. Goodrich Co. is what business magazines like to speak of as "a major American corporation." It has operations in a dozen states and as many foreign countries, and of these far-flung facilities, the Goodrich plant at Troy, Ohio, is not the most imposing. It is a small, one-story building, once used to manufacture airplanes. Set in the grassy flatlands of west-central Ohio, it employs only about six hundred people. Nevertheless, it is one of the three largest manufacturers of aircraft wheels and brakes, a leader in a most profitable industry. Goodrich wheels and brakes support such well-known planes as the F111, the C5A, the Boeing 727, the XB70 and many others. Its customers include almost every aircraft manufacturer in the world.

Contracts for aircraft wheels and brakes often run into millions of dollars, and ordinarily a contract with a total value of less than $70,000, though welcome, would not create any special stir of joy in the hearts of Goodrich sales personnel. But purchase order P-23718, issued on June 18, 1967, by the LTV Aerospace Corporation, and ordering 202 brake assemblies for a new Air Force plane at a total price of $69,417, was received by Goodrich with considerable glee. And there was good reason. Some ten years previously, Goodrich had built a brake for LTV that was, to say the least, considerably less than a rousing success. The brake had not lived up to Goodrich's promises, and after experiencing considerable difficulty, LTV had written off Goodrich as a source of brakes. Since that time, Goodrich salesmen had been unable to sell so much as a shot of brake fluid to LTV. So in 1967, when LTV requested bids on wheels and brakes for the new A7D light attack aircraft it proposed to build for the Air Force, Goodrich submitted a bid that was absurdly low, so low that LTV could not, in all prudence, turn it down.

Goodrich had, in industry parlance, "bought into the business." Not only did the company not expect to make a profit on the deal; it was prepared, if necessary, to lose money. For aircraft brakes are not something that can be ordered off the shelf. They are designed for a particular aircraft, and once an aircraft manufacturer buys a brake, he is forced to purchase all replacement parts from the brake

* "Why Should My Conscience Bother Me?" by Kermit Vandivier, from *In The Name of Profit* by Robert L. Heilbroner, copyright © 1972 by Doubleday & Company, Inc. Used by permission of the publisher.

manufacturer. The $70,000 that Goodrich would get for making the brake would be a drop in the bucket when compared with the cost of the linings and other parts the Air Force would have to buy from Goodrich during the lifetime of the aircraft. Furthermore, the company which manufactures brakes for one particular model of an aircraft quite naturally has the inside track to supply other brakes when the planes are updated and improved.

Thus, that first contract, regardless of the money involved, is very important, and Goodrich, when it learned that it had been awarded the A7D contract, was determined that while it may have slammed the door on its own foot ten years before, this time, the second time around, things would be different. The word was soon circulated throughout the plant: "We can't bungle it this time. We've got to give them a good brake, regardless of the cost."

There was another factor which had undoubtedly influenced LTV. All aircraft brakes made today are the disk type, and the bid submitted by Goodrich called for a relatively small brake, one containing four disks and weighting only 106 pounds. The weight of any aircraft part is extremely important. The lighter a part is, the heavier the plane's payload can be. The four-rotor, 106-pound brake promised by Goodrich was about as light as could be expected, and this undoubtedly had helped move LTV to award the contract to Goodrich.

The brake was designed by one of Goodrich's most capable engineers, John Warren. A tall, lanky blond and a graduate of Purdue, Warren had come from the Chrysler Corporation seven years before and had become adept at aircraft brake design. The happy-go-lucky manner he usually maintained belied a temper which exploded whenever anyone ventured to offer any criticism of his work, no matter how small. On these occasions, Warren would turn red in the face, often throwing or slamming something and then stalking from the scene. As his coworkers learned the consequences of criticizing him, they did so less and less readily, and when he submitted his preliminary design for the A7D brake, it was accepted without question.

Warren was named project engineer for the A7D, and he, in turn, assigned the task of producing the final production design to a newcomer to the Goodrich engineering stable, Searle Lawson. Just turned twenty-six, Lawson had been out of the Northrup Institute of Technology only one year when he came to Goodrich in January 1967. Like Warren, he had worked for a while in the automotive industry, but his engineering degree was in aeronautical and astronautical sciences, and when the opportunity came to enter his special field, via Goodrich, he took it. At the Troy plant, Lawson had been assigned to various "paper projects" to break him in, and after several months spent reviewing statistics and old brake designs, he was beginning to fret at the lack of challenge. When told he was being assigned to his first "real" project, he was elated and immediately plunged into his work.

The major portion of the design had already been completed by Warren, and major assemblies for the brake had already been ordered from Goodrich suppliers. Naturally, however, before Goodrich could start making the brakes on a production basis, much testing would have to be done. Lawson would have to determine the best materials to use for the linings and discover what minor adjustments in the design would have to be made.

Then, after the preliminary testing and after the brake was judged ready for production, one whole brake assembly would undergo a series of grueling, simulated braking stops and other severe trials called qualification tests. These tests are required by the military, which gives very detailed specifications on how they are to be conducted, the criteria for failure, and so on. They are performed in the Goodrich plant's test laboratory, where huge machines called dynamometers can simulate the weight and speed of almost any aircraft. After the brakes pass the laboratory tests, they are approved for production, but before the brakes are accepted for use in military service, they must undergo further extensive flight tests.

Searle Lawson was well aware that much work had to be done before the A7D brake could go into production, and he knew that LTV had set the last two weeks in June 1968 as the starting dates for flight tests. So he decided to begin testing immediately. Goodrich's supliers had not yet delivered the brake housing and other parts, but the brake disks had arrived and, using the housing from a brake similar in size and weight to the A7D brake, Lawson built a prototype. The prototype was installed in a test wheel and placed on one of the big dynamometers in the plant's test laboratory. The dynamometer was adjusted to simulate the weight of the A7D and Lawson began a series of tests, "landing" the wheel and brake at the A7D's landing speed, and braking it to a stop. The main purpose of these preliminary tests was to learn what temperatures would develop within the brake during the simulated stops and to evaluate the lining materials tentatively selected for use.

During a normal aircraft landing the temperatures inside the brake may reach 1000 degrees, and occasionally a bit higher. During Lawson's first simulated landings, the temperature of his prototype brake reached 1500 degrees. The brake glowed a bright cherry-red and threw off incandescent particles of metal and lining material as the temperature reached its peak. After a few such stops, the brake was dismantled and the linings were found to be almost completely disintegrated. Lawson chalked this first failure up to chance and, ordering new lining materials, tried again.

The second attempt was a repeat of the first. The brake became extremely hot, causing the lining materials to crumble into dust.

After the third such failure, Lawson, inexperienced though he was, knew that the fault lay not in defective parts of unsuitable lining material but in the basic design of the brake itself. Ignoring Warren's original computations, Lawson made his own, and it didn't take him long to discover where the trouble lay—the brake was too small. There simply was not enough surface area on the disks to stop the aircraft without generating the excessive heat that caused the linings to fail.

The answer to the problem was obvious but far from simple—the four-disk brake would have to be scrapped, and a new design, using five disks, would have to be developed. The implications were not lost on Lawson. Such a step would require the junking of all the four-disk brake subassemblies, many of which had now begun to arrive from the various suppliers. It would also mean several weeks of preliminary design and testing and many more weeks of waiting while the suppliers made and delivered the new subassemblies.

Yet, several weeks had already gone by since LTV's order had arrived, and the date for delivery of the first production brakes for flight testing was only a few months away.

Although project engineer John Warren had more or less turned the A7D over to Lawson, he knew of the difficulties Lawson had been experiencing. He had assured the young engineer that the problem revolved around getting the right kind of lining material. Once that was found, he said, the difficulties would end.

Despite the evidence of the abortive tests and Lawson's careful computations, Warren rejected the suggestion that the four-disk brake was too light for the job. Warren knew that his superior had already told LTV, in rather glowing terms, that the preliminary tests on the A7D brake were very successful. Indeed, Warren's superiors weren't aware at this time of the troubles on the brake. It would have been difficult for Warren to admit not only that he had made a serious error in his calculations and original design but that his mistakes had been caught by a green kid, barely out of college.

Warren's reaction to a five-disk brake was not unexpected by Lawson, and, seeing that the four-disk brake was not to be abandoned so easily, he took his calculations and dismal test results one step up the corporate ladder.

At Goodrich, the man who supervises the engineers working on projects slated for production is called, predictably, the projects manager. The job was held by a short, chubby and bald man named Robert Sink. A man truly devoted to his work, Sink was as likely to be found at his desk at ten o'clock on Sunday night as ten o'clock on Monday morning. His outside interests consisted mainly of tinkering on a Model-A Ford and an occasional game of golf. Some fifteen years before, Sink had begun working at Goodrich as a lowly draftsman. Slowly, he worked his way up. Despite his geniality, Sink was neither respected nor liked by the majority of the engineers, and his appointment as their supervisor did not improve their feelings about him. They thought he had only gone to high school. It quite naturally rankled those who had gone through years of college and acquired impressive specialties such as thermodynamics and astronautics to be commanded by a man whom they considered their intellectual inferior. But, though Sink had no college training, he had something even more useful: a fine working knowledge of company politics.

Puffing upon a Meerschaum pipe, Sink listened gravely as young Lawson confided his fears about the four-disk brake. Then he examined Lawson's calculations and the results of the abortive tests. Despite the fact that he was not a qualified engineer, in the strictest sense of the word, it must certainly have been obvious to Sink that Lawson's calculations were correct and that a four-disk brake would never have worked on the A7D.

But other things of equal importance were also obvious. First, to concede that Lawson's calculations were correct would also mean conceding that Warren's calculations were incorrect. As projects manager, he not only was responsible for Warren's activities, but, in admitting that Warren had erred, he would have to admit that he had erred in trusting Warren's judgment. It also meant that, as projects manager, it would be he who would have to explain the whole messy situation to the Goodrich hierarchy, not only at Troy but possibly on the corporate level at Goodrich's Akron offices. And, having taken Warren's judgment of the four-disk brake at face value (he was forced to do this since, not being an engineer, he was unable to exercise any engineering judgment of his own), he had assured LTV, not once but several times, that about all there was left to do on the brake was pack it in a crate and ship it out the back door.

There's really no problem at all, he told Lawson. After all, Warren was an experienced engineer, and if he said the brake would work, it would work. Just keep on testing and probably, maybe even on the very next try, it'll work out just fine.

Lawson was far from convinced, but without the support of his superiors there was little he could do except keep on testing. By now, housings for the four-disk brake had begun to arrive at the plant, and Lawson was able to build up a production model of the brake and begin the formal qualification tests demanded by the military.

The first qualification attempts went exactly as the tests on the prototype had. Terrific heat developed within the brakes and, after a few, short, simulated stops, the linings crumbled. A new type of lining material was ordered and once again an attempt to qualify the brake was made. Again, failure.

Experts were called in from lining manufacturers, and new lining "mixes" were tried, always with the same result. Failure.

It was now the last week in March 1968, and flight tests were scheduled to begin in seventy days. Twelve separate attempts had been made to formally qualify the brake, and all had failed. It was no longer possible for anyone to ignore the glaring truth that the brake was a dismal failure and that nothing short of a major design change could ever make it work.

In the engineering department, panic set in. A glum-faced Lawson prowled the test laboratory dejectedly. Occasionally, Warren would witness some simulated stop on the brake and, after it was completed, troop silently back to his desk. Sink, too, showed an unusual interest in the trials, and he and Warren would converse in low tones while poring over the results of the latest tests. Even the most inexperienced of the lab technicians and the men who operated the testing equipment knew they had a "bad" brake on their hands, and there was some grumbling about "wasting time on a brake that won't work."

New menaces appeared. An engineering team from LTV arrived at the plant to get a good look at the brake in action. Luckily, they stayed only a few days, and Goodrich engineers managed to cover the true situation without too much difficulty.

On April 4, the thirteenth attempt at qualification was begun. This time no attempt was made to conduct the tests by the methods and techniques spelled out in the military specifications. Regardless of how it had to be done, the brake was to be "nursed" through the required fifty simulated stops.

Fans were set up to provide special cooling. Instead of maintaining pressure on the brake until the test wheel had come to a complete stop, the pressure was reduced when the wheel had decelerated to around 15 mph, allowing it to "coast" to a stop. After each stop, the brake was disassembled and carefully cleaned, and after some of the stops, internal brake parts were machined in order to remove warp and other disfigurations caused by the high heat.

By these and other methods, all clearly contrary to the techniques established by the military specifications, the brake was coaxed through the fifty stops. But even using these methods, the brake could not meet all the requirements. On one stop the wheel rolled for a distance of 16,000 feet, nearly three miles, before the brake could bring it to a stop. The normal distance required for such a stop was around 3,500 feet.

On April 11, the day the thirteenth test was completed, I became personally involved in the A7D situation.

I had worked in the Goodrich test laboratory for five years, starting first as an instrumentation engineer, then later becoming a data analyst and technical writer. As part of my duties, I analyzed the reams and reams of instrumentation data that came from the many testing machines in the laboratory, then transcribed it to a more usable form for the engineering department. And when a new-type brake had successfully completed the required qualification tests, I would issue a formal qualification report.

Qualification reports were an accumulation of all the data and test logs compiled by the test technicians during the qualification tests, and were documentary proof that a brake had met all the requirements established by the military specifications and was therefore presumed safe for flight testing. Before actual flight tests were conducted on a brake, qualification reports had to be delivered to the customer and to various government officials.

On April 11, I was looking over the data from the latest A7D test, and I noticed that many irregularities in testing methods had been noted on the test logs.

Technically, of course, there was nothing wrong with conducting tests in any manner desired, so long as the test was for research purposes only. But qualification test methods are clearly delineated by the military, and I knew that this test had been a formal qualification attempt. One particular notation on the test logs caught my eye. For some of the stops, the instrument which recorded the brake pressure had been deliberately miscalibrated so that, while the brake pressure used during the stops was recorded as 1000 psi (the maximum pressure that would be available on the A7D aircraft), the pressure had actually been 1100 psi!

I showed the test logs to the test lab supervisor, Ralph Gretzinger, who said he had learned from the technician who had miscalibrated the instrument that he had been asked to do so by Lawson. Lawson, said Gretzinger, readily admitted asking for the miscalibration saying he had been told to do so by Sink.

I asked Gretzinger why anyone would want to miscalibrate the data-recording instruments.

"Why? I'll tell you why," he snorted. "That brake is a failure. It's way too small for the job, and they're not ever going to get it to work. They're getting desperate, and instead of scrapping the damned thing and starting over, they figure they can horse around down here in the lab and qualify it that way."

An expert engineer, Gretzinger had been responsible for several innovations in brake design. It was he who had invented the unique brake system used on the famous XB70. A graduate of Georgia Tech, he was a stickler for detail and he had some very firm ideas about honesty and ethics. "If you want to find out what's going on," said Gretzinger, "ask Lawson, he'll tell you."

Curious, I did ask Lawson the next time he came into the lab. He seemed eager to discuss the A7D and give me the history of his months of frustrating efforts to get Warren and Sink to change the brake design. "I just can't believe this is really happening," said Lawson, shaking his head slowly. "This isn't engineering, at least not what I thought it would be. Back in school, I thought that when you were an engineer, you tried to do your best, no matter what it cost. But this is something else."

He sat across the desk from me, his chin propped in his hand. "Just wait," he warned. "You'll get a chance to see what I'm talking about. You're going to get in the act, too, because I've already had the word that we're going to make one more attempt to qualify the brake, and that's it. Win or lose, we're going to issue a qualification report!"

I reminded him that a qualification report could be issued only after a brake had successfully met all military requirements and, therefore, unless the next qualification attempt was a success, no report would be issued.

"You'll find out," retorted Lawson. "I was already told that regardless of what the brake does on test, it's going to be qualified." He said he had been told in those exact words at a conference with Sink and Russell Van Horn.

This was the first indication that Sink had brought his boss, Van Horn, into the mess. Although Van Horn, as manager of the design engineering section, was responsible for the entire department, he was not necessarily familiar with all phases of every project, and it was not uncommon for those under him to exercise the what-he-doesn't-know-won't-hurt-him philosophy. If he was aware of the full extent of the A7D situation, it meant that matters had truly reached a desperate stage—that Sink had decided not only to call for help but was looking toward that moment when blame must be borne and, if possible, shared.

Also, if Van Horn had said, "regardless what the brake does on test, it's going to be qualified," then it could only mean that, if necessary, a false qualification report would be issued! I discussed this possibility with Gretzinger, and he assured me that under no circumstances would such a report ever be issued.

"If they want a qualification report, we'll write them one, but we'll tell it just like it is," he declared emphatically. "No false data or false reports are going to come out of this lab."

On May 2, 1968, the fourteenth and final attempt to qualify the brake was begun. Although the same improper methods used to nurse the brake through the previous tests were employed, it soon became obvious that this too would end in failure.

When the tests were about half completed, Lawson asked if I would start preparing the various engineering curves and graphic displays which were normally incorporated in a qualification report. "It looks as though you'll be writing a qualification report shortly," he said.

I flatly refused to have anything to do with the matter and immediately told Gretzinger what I had been asked to do. He was furious and repeated his previous declaration that under no circumstances would any false data or other matter be issued from the lab.

"I'm going to get this settled right now, once and for all," he declared. "I'm going to see Line [Russell Line, manager of the Goodrich Technical Services Section, of which the test lab was a part] and find out just how far this thing is going to go!" He stormed out of the room.

In about an hour, he returned and called me to his desk. He sat silently for a few moments, then muttered, half to himself, "I wonder what the hell they'd do if I just quit?" I didn't answer and I didn't ask him what he meant. I knew. He had been beaten down. He had reached the point when the decision had to be made. Defy them now while there was still time—or knuckle under, sell out.

"You know," he went on uncertainly, looking down at his desk, "I've always believed that ethics and integrity were every bit as important as theorems and formulas, and never once has anything happened to change my beliefs. Now this. . . . Hell, I've got two sons I've got to put through school and I just. . . ." His voice trailed off.

He sat for a few more minutes, then, looking over the top of his glasses, said hoarsely, "Well, it looks like we're licked. The way it stands now, we're to go ahead and prepare the data and other things for the graphic presentation in the report, and when were finished, someone upstairs will actually write the report.

"After all," he continued, "we're just drawing some curves, and what happens to them after they leave here, well, we're not responsible for that."

He was trying to persuade himself that as long as we were concerned with only one part of the puzzle and didn't see the completed picture, we really weren't doing anything wrong. He didn't believe what he was saying, and he knew I didn't believe it either. It was an embarrassing and shameful moment for both of us.

I wasn't at all satisfied with the situation and decided that I too would discuss the matter with Russell Line, the senior executive in our section.

Tall, powerfully built, his teeth flashing white, his face tanned to a coffee-brown by a daily stint with a sun lamp, Line looked and acted every inch the executive. He was a crossword-puzzle enthusiast and an ardent golfer, and though he had lived in Troy only a short time, he had been accepted into the Troy Country Club and made an official of the golf committee. He had been transferred from the Akron offices some two years previously, and an air of mystery surrounded him. Some office gossips figured he had been sent to Troy as the result of some sort of demotion. Others speculated that since the present general manager of Troy plant was due shortly for retirement, Line had been transferred to Troy to assume that job and was merely occupying his present position to "get the feel of things." Whatever the case, he commanded great respect and had come to be well-liked by those of us who worked under him.

He listened sympathetically while I explained how I felt about the A7D situation, and when I had finished, he asked me what I wanted him to do about it. I said that as employees of the Goodrich Company we had a responsibility to protect the company and its reputation if at all possible. I said I was certain that officers on the corporate level would never knowingly allow such tactics as had been employed on the A7D.

"I agree with you," he remarked, "but I still want to know what you want me to do about it."

I suggested that in all probability the chief engineer at the Troy plant, H.C. "Bud" Sunderman, was unaware of the A7D problem and that he, Line, should tell him what was going on."

Line laughed, good-humoredly. "Sure, I could, but I'm not going to. Bud probably already knows about this thing anyway, and if he doesn't I'm sure not going to be the one to tell him."

"But why?"

"Because it's none of my business, and it's none of yours. I learned a long time ago not to worry about things over which I had no control. I have no control over this."

I wasn't satisfied with this answer, and I asked him if his conscience wouldn't bother him if, say, during flight tests on the brake something should happen resulting in death or injury to the test pilot.

"Look," he said, becoming somewhat exasperated, "I just told you I have no control over this thing. Why should my conscience bother me?"

His voice took on a quiet, soothing tone as he continued. "You're just getting all upset over this thing for nothing. I just do as I'm told, and I'd advise you to do the same."

He had made his decision, and now I had to make mine.

I made no attempt to rationalize what I had been asked to do. It made no difference who would falsify which part of the report or whether the actual falsification would be by misleading numbers or misleading words. Whether by acts of commission or omission, all of us who contributed to the fraud would be guilty. The only question left for me to decide was whether or not I would become a party to the fraud.

Before coming to Goodrich in 1963, I had held a variety of jobs, each a little more pleasant, a little more rewarding than the last. At forty-two, with seven children, I had decided that the Goodrich Company would probably be my "home" for the rest of my working life. The job paid well, it was pleasant and challenging, and the future looked reasonably bright. My wife had bought a home and we were ready to settle down into a comfortable, middle-age, middle-class rut. If I refused to take part in the A7D fraud, I would have to either resign or be fired. The report would be written by someone anyway, but I would have the satisfaction of knowing I had had no part in the matter. But bills aren't paid with personal satisfaction, nor house payments with ethical principles. I made my decision. The next morning, I telephoned Lawson and told him I was ready to begin on the qualification report.

In a few minutes, he was at my desk, ready to begin. Before we started, I asked him, "Do you realize what we are going to do?"

"Yeah," he replied bitterly, "we're going to screw LTV. And speaking of screwing," he continued, "I know now how a whore feels, because that's exactly what I've become, an engineering whore. I've sold myself. It's all I can do to look at myself in the mirror when I shave. I make me sick."

I was surprised at his vehemence. It was obvious that he too had done his share of soul-searching and didn't like what he had found. Somehow, though, the air seemed clearer after his outburst, and we began working on the report.

I had written dozens of qualification reports, and I knew what a "good" one looked like. Resorting to the actual test data only on occasion, Lawson and I proceeded to prepare page after page of elaborate, detailed engineering curves, charts, and test logs, which purported to show what had happened during the formal qualification tests. Where temperatures were too high, we deliberately chopped them down a few hundred degrees, and where they were too low, we raised them to a value that would appear reasonable to the LTV and military engineers. Brake pressure, torque values, distances, times—everything of consequence was tailored to fit the occasion.

Occasionally, we would find that some test either hadn't been performed at all or had been conducted improperly. On those occasions, we "conducted" the test—successfully, of course—on paper.

For nearly a month we worked on the graphic presentation that would be a part of the report. Meanwhile, the fourteenth and final qualification attempt had been completed, and the brake, not unexpectedly, had failed again.

During that month, Lawson and I talked of little else except the enormity of what we were doing. The more involved we became in our work, the more apparent became our own culpability. We discussed such things as the Nuremberg trials and how they related to our guilt and complicity in the A7D situation. Lawson often expressed his opinion that the brake was downright dangerous and that, once on flight test, "anything is liable to happen."

I saw his boss, John Warren, at least twice during that month and needled him about what we were doing. He didn't take the jibes too kindly but managed to laugh the situation off as "one of those things." One day I remarked that what we were doing amounted to fraud, and he pulled out an engineering handbook and turned to a section on laws as they related to the engineering profession.

He read the definition of fraud aloud, then said, "Well, technically I don't think what we're doing can be called fraud. I'll admit it's not right, but it's just one of those things. We're just kinda caught in the middle. About all I can tell you is, Do like I'm doing. Make copies of everything and put them in your SYA file."

"What's an 'SYA' file?" I asked.

"That's a 'save your ass' file." He laughed.

Although I hadn't known it was called that, I had been keeping an SYA file since the beginning of the A7D fiasco. I had made a copy of every scrap of paper connected even remotely with the A7D and had even had copies of 16mm movies that had been made during some of the simulated stops. Lawson, too, had an SYA file, and we both maintained them for one reason: Should the true state of events on the A7D ever be questioned, we wanted to have access to a complete set of factual data. We were afraid that should the question ever come up, the test data might accidentally be "lost."

We finished our work on the graphic portion of the report around the first of June. Altogether, we had prepared nearly two hundred pages of data, containing dozens of deliberate falsifications and misrepresentations. I delivered the data to Gretzinger, who said he had been instructed to deliver it personally to the chief engineer, Bud Sunderman, who in turn would assign someone in the engineering department to complete the written portion of the report. He gather the bundle of data and left the office. Within minutes, he was back with the data, his face white with anger.

"That damned Sink's beat me to it." he said furiously. "He's already talked to Bud about this, and now Sunderman says no one in the engineering department has time to write the report. He wants us to do it, and I told him we couldn't."

The words had barely left his mouth when Russell Line burst in the door. "What the hell's all the fuss about this damned report?" he demanded loudly.

Patiently, Gretzinger explained. "There's no fuss. Sunderman just told me that we'd have to write the report down here, and I said we couldn't. Russ," he went on, "I've told you before that we weren't going to write the report. I made my position clear on that a long time ago."

Line shut him up with a wave of his hand and, turning to me, bellowed, "I'm getting sick and tired of hearing about this damned report. Now, write the goddam thing and shut up about it!" He slammed out of the office.

Gretzinger and I just sat for a few seconds looking at each other. Then he spoke.

"Well, I guess he's made it pretty clear, hasn't he? We can either write the thing or quit. You know, what we could have done was quit a long time ago. Now, it's too late."

Somehow, I wasn't at all surprised at this turn of events, and it didn't really make that much difference. As far as I was concerned, we were all up to our necks in the thing anyway, and writing the narrative portion of the report couldn't make me any more guilty than I already felt myself to be.

Still, Line's order came as something of a shock. All the time Lawson and I were working on the report, I felt deep down, that somewhere, somehow, something would come along and the whole thing would blow over. But Russell Line had crushed that hope. The report was actually going to be issued. Intelligent, law-abiding officials of B. F. Goodrich, one of the oldest and most respected of American corporations, were actually going to deliver to a customer a product that was known to be defective and dangerous and which could very possibly cause death or serious injury.

Within two days, I had completed the narrative, or written, portion of the report. As a final sop to my own self-respect, in the conclusion of the report I wrote, "The B. F. Goodrich P/N 2-1162-3 brake assembly does not meet the intent or the requirements of the applicable specification documents and therefore is not qualified."

This was a meaningless gesture, since I knew that this would certainly be changed when the report went through the final typing process. Sure enough, when the report was published, the negative conclusion had been made positive.

One final and significant incident occurred just before publication.

Qualification reports always bear the signature of the person who has prepared them. I refused to sign the report, as did Lawson. Warren was later asked to sign the report. He replied that he would "when I receive a signed statement from Bob Sink ordering me to sign it."

The engineering secretary who was delegated the responsibility of "dogging" the report through publication, told me later that after I, Lawson, and Warren had all refused to sign the report, she had asked Sink if he would sign. He replied, "On something of this nature, I don't think a signature is really needed."

On June 5, 1968, the report was officially published and copies were delivered in person to the Air Force and LTV. Within a week, flight tests were begun at Edwards Air Force Base in California. Searle Lawson was sent to California as Goodrich's representative. Within approximately two weeks, he returned because some rather unusual incidents during the tests had caused them to be canceled.

His face was grim as he related stories of several near crashes during landings—caused by brake troubles. He told me about one incident in which, upon landing, one brake was literally welded together by the intense heat developed during the test stop. The wheel locked, and the plane skidded for nearly 1,500 feet before coming to a halt. The plane was jacked up and the wheel removed. The fused parts within the brake had to be prided apart.

Lawson had returned to Troy from California that same day, and that evening, he and others of the Goodrich engineering department left for Dallas for a high-level conference with LTV.

That evening I left work early and went to see my attorney. After I told him the story, he advised that, while I was probably not actually guilty of fraud, I was certainly part of a conspiracy to defraud. He advised me to go to the Federal Bureau of Investigation and offered to arrange an appointment. The following week he took me to the Dayton office of the FBI, and after I had been warned that I would not be immune from prosecution, I disclosed the A7D matter to one of the agents. The agent told me to say nothing about the episode to anyone and to report any further incident to him. He said he would forward the story to his superiors in Washington.

A few days later, Lawson returned from the conference in Dallas and said that the Air Force, which had previously approved the qualification report, had suddenly rescinded that approval and was demanding to see some of the raw test data taken during the tests. I gathered that the FBI had passed the word.

Omitting any reference to the FBI, I told Lawson I had been to an attorney and that we were probably guilty of conspiracy.

"Can you get me an appointment with your attorney?" he asked. Within a week he had been to the FBI and told them of his part in the mess. He too was advised to say nothing but to keep on the job reporting any new development.

Naturally, with the rescinding of Air Force approval and the demand to see raw test data, Goodrich officials were in a panic. A conference was called for July 27, a Saturday morning affair at which Lawson, Sink, Warren, and myself were present. We met in a tiny conference room in the deserted engineering department. Lawson and I, by now openly hostile to Warren and Sink, ranged ourselves on one side of the conference table while Warren sat on the other side. Sink, chairing the meeting, paced slowly in front of a blackboard, puffing furiously on a pipe.

The meeting was called, Sink began, "to see where we stand on the A7D." What we were going to do, he said, was to "level" with LTV and tell them the "whole truth" about the A7D. "After all," he said, "they're in this thing with us, and they have the right to know how matters stand."

"In other words," I asked, "we're going to tell them the truth?"

"That's right," he replied. "We're going to level with them and let them handle the ball from there."

"There's one thing I don't quite understand," I interjected. "Isn't it going to be pretty hard for us to admit to them that we've lied?"

"Now, wait a minute," he said angrily. "Let's don't go off half-cocked on this thing. It's not a matter of lying. We've just interpreted the information the way we felt it should be."

"I don't know what you call it," I replied, "but to me it's lying, and it's going to be damned hard to confess to them that we've been lying all along."

He became very agitated at this and repeated his "We're not lying," adding, "I don't like this sort of talk."

I dropped the matter at this point, and he began discussing the various discrepancies in the report.

We broke for lunch, and afterward, I came back to the plant to find Sink sitting alone at his desk, waiting to resume the meeting. He called me over and said he wanted to apologize for his outburst that morning. "This thing has kind of gotten me down," he confessed, "and I think you've got the wrong picture. I don't think you really understand everything about this."

Perhaps so, I conceded, but it seemed to me that if we had already told LTV one thing and then had to tell them another, changing our story completely, we would have to admit we were lying.

"No," he explained patiently, "we're not really lying. All we were doing was interpreting the figures the way we knew they should be. We were just exercising engineering license."

During the afternoon session, we marked some forty-three discrepant points in the report: forty-three points that LTV would surely spot as occasions where we had exercised "engineering license."

After Sink listed those points on the blackboard, we discussed each one individually. As each point came up, Sink would explain that it was probably "too minor to bother about," or that perhaps it "wouldn't be wise to open that can of worms," or that maybe this was a point that "LTV just wouldn't understand." When the meeting was over, it had been decided that only three points were "worth mentioning."

Similar conferences were held during August and September, and the summer was punctuated with frequent treks between Dallas and Troy, and demands by the Air Force to see the raw test data. Tempers were short and matters seemed to grow worse.

Finally, early in October 1968, Lawson submitted his resignation, to take effect on October 25. On October 18, I submitted my own resignation to take effect on November 1. In my resignation, addressed to Russell Line, I cited the A7D report and stated: "As you are aware, this report contained numerous deliberate and willful misrepresentations which, according to legal counsel, constitute fraud and expose both myself and others to criminal charges of conspiracy to defraud. . . . The events of the past seven months have created an atmosphere of deceit and distrust in which it is impossible to work. . . ."

On October 25, I received a sharp summons to the office of Bud Sunderman. As chief engineer at the Troy plant, Sunderman was responsible for the entire engineering division. Tall and graying, impeccably dressed at all times, he was capable of producing a dazzling smile or a hearty chuckle or immobilizing his face into marble hardness, as the occasion required.

I faced the marble hardness when I reached his office. He motioned me to a chair. "I have your resignation here," he snapped, "and I must say you have made some rather shocking, I might even say irresponsible, charges. This is very serious."

Before I could reply, he was demanding an explanation. "I want to know exactly what fraud is in connection with the A7D and how you can dare accuse this company of such a thing!"

I started to tell some of the things that had happened during the testing, but he shut me off saying, "There's nothing wrong with anything we've done here. You aren't aware of all the things that have been going on behind the scenes. If you had known the true situation, you would never have made these charges." He said that in view of my apparent "disloyalty" he had decided to accept my resignation "right now," and said it would be better for all concerned if I left the plant immediately. As I got up to leave he asked me if I intended to "carry this thing further."

I answered simply, "Yes," to which he replied, "Suit yourself." Within twenty minutes, I had cleaned out my desk and left. Forty-eight hours later, the B. F. Goodrich Company recalled the qualification report and the four-disk brake, announcing that it would replace the brake with a new, improved, five-disk brake at no cost to LTV.

Ten months later, on August 13, 1969, I was the chief government witness at a hearing conducted before Senator William Proxmire's Economy in Government Subcommittee of the Congress's Joint Economic Committee. I related the A7D story to the committee, and my testimony was supported by Searle Lawson, who followed me to the witness stand. Air Force officers also testified, as well as a four-man team from the General Accounting Office, which had conducted an investigation of the A7D brake at the request of Senator Proxmire. Both Air Force and GAO investigators declared that the brake was dangerous and had not been tested properly.

Testifying for Goodrich was R. G. Jeter, vice-president and general counsel of the company, from the Akron headquarters. Representing the Troy plant was Robert Sink. These two denied any wrongdoing on the part of the Goodrich

Company, despite expert testimony to the contrary by Air Force and GAO officials. Sink was quick to deny any connection with the writing of the report or of directing any falsifications, claiming to be on the west coast at the time. John Warren was the man who supervised its writing, said Sink.

As for me, I was dismissed as a high-school graduate with no technical training, while Sink testified that Lawson was a young, inexperienced engineer. "We tried to give him guidance," Sink testified, "but he preferred to have his own convictions."

About changing the data and figures in the report, Sink said: "When you take data from several different sources, you have to rationalize among those data what is the true story. This is part of your engineering knowhow." He admitted that changes had been made in the data, "but only to make them more consistent with the overall picture of the data that is available."

Jeter pooh-poohed the suggestion that anything improper occurred, saying: "We have thirty-odd engineers at this plant . . . and I say to you that is incredible that these men would stand idly by and see reports changed or falsified. . . . I mean you just do not have to do that working for anybody. . . . Just nobody does that."

The four-hour hearing adjourned with no real conclusion reached by the committee. But the following day the Department of Defense made sweeping changes in its inspection, testing, and reporting procedures. A spokesman for the DOD said the changes were a result of the Goodrich episode.

45. Just a Few Votes More*

She was gone now, but he would not soon forget her parting words.

"Frankly, I don't know what I'll do," she had said. "I just don't know if I can accept the presidency of the alumni association after this—this incident."

He had calmed her, promising a swift resolution of the problem.

"Tomorrow morning—" he had said. "I'll talk to Peters and Graves and get back to you tomorrow morning."

Now he was alone, staring out the windows at the quad below, watching the students as they crisscrossed the lawn on their way to classes. President Mathews glanced at his watch, then called his secretary into the room.

"Doris, get John Peters and Bill Graves on the phone; tell them to be here at two o'clock without fail."

"Yes, sir. Can I tell them what the meeting is about?"

"Oh, I think they'll know, Doris."

"All right." She turned and left the room, pulling the door shut behind her.

Yes, he thought, I'm sure they'll know.

*Educational Record, Winter 1981. Copyright © American Council on Education, Washington, D.C. Used by permission.

President Mathews talked with Peters first. John Peters had been hired just two years before on the recommendation of Graves, the vice-president for institutional advancement. Peters was a personable young man, bright, eager, full of energy. Even Mathews had to admit that the alumni director was one of the best he had ever worked with—which made this particular conversation all the more difficult.

"John," he began, "I've just had a talk with Mary Chambers about certain irregularities in the alumni board election. She claims you tampered with the election results. Is that true?"

The blood seemed to drain from Peters' face, and when he began to speak, his lips trembled.

"Well," he said, "I wouldn't exactly call it *tampering.*"

"No? What would you call it then? She says you changed votes, John."

Peters squirmed in his chair, shifting his weight from one hip to the other.

"Yes, but I explained that to her. It was only a few votes out of thousands, and some of them were ambiguous anyway. Besides, we ended up with a new board that's more representative of the alumni constituency—geographically, by class, by sex, you name it."

He paused, hoping for some positive sign from Mathews, but the president just stared down at him, forcing him to avert his eyes.

"Look," he continued, "I did it for the good of the college."

Mathews grunted and shook his head.

"Oh, come now, John," he said. "For the good of the college?" The sarcasm was not lost on Peters.

"All right," said Peters, "I may have made an error in judgment. I told her that. I guess I was just too eager to have a board that represented the real interests of the alumni for once. And it was so close; I didn't see what harm it would do."

"No harm? John, what you did was wrong. And now we're sitting on a powder keg. Chambers has threatened to resign."

Peters looked up, startled.

"But—"

"And I'm not going to let that happen, John, not if I can help it. Do you understand?"

"Yes, but—"

"That's all for now, John. I'll talk to you again about this tomorrow." He turned and walked to the window, his back to Peters.

Peters got up and started for the door.

"And Peters—"

"Yes, sir?"

"Ask Bill Graves to come in."

Peters nodded and left the room. Moments later, Bill Graves, Peters' supervisor, came in. Mathews motioned him to sit down.

"Bill, we have a big problem."

"Yes, by the look on John's face just now, I thought we did. Is it the Chambers thing?"

"Yes, she's upset—and rightly so—about the alumni board election. But you know all about that, don't you, Bill? She says she talked to you about it."

"Yes, this morning. Stormed into my office—quite upset."

Mathews stood up, walked around to the front of the desk, and looked down at Graves.

"She claims you were aware of Peters' actions, and condoned them. Is that true?"

"After the fact, yes, but the point is—"

"The point is we've tampered with a free election, and we've got to rectify that situation, Bill." He leaned back against the desk, folding his arms across his chest.

Graves shook his head. "But I don't see how," he said. "The election results have already been announced to all the candidates; appointment letters have gone out. And, really, when you think about it, what harm has been done?"

Mathews thrust his hands into his pockets and began pacing back and forth in front of the desk.

"Not you, too, Bill? We did it *for the good of the college,* is that what you're going to say?"

"I'm only saying there's nothing we *can* do now. And Peters is such a good man—surely we can't risk losing him over a small matter like this. The best thing we can do is just forget it."

"You may forget it, Bill, and Peters may forget it, but Mary Chambers isn't going to forget it—she's threatened to resign over this, did you know that?—and I certainly can't forget it, either."

"But what choice do you have? You can't let the board or the alumni or the public get wind of this. And firing Peters would be cutting off your nose to spite your face. So I would—"

Mathews cut him off in mid-sentence.

"I know what you're saying. You're saying *be practical, ignore the moral questions just this once.* Well, I'm not so sure I can do that, or that I have to."

"What will you do, then?"

Mathews walked back to his chair and sat down.

"I told Chambers I'd get back to her tomorrow morning, I'll think it over tonight and let you know tomorrow."

Next morning, President Mathews met with Mary Chambers.

"I've given this matter a great deal of thought," he began, "and I hope you'll agree with the decision I've come to. Here's what I propose to do. . . ."

What would you do? Why?

46. The Road to Hell*

John Baker, chief engineer of the Caribbean Bauxite Company of Barracania in the West Indies, was making his final preparations to leave the island. His promotion to production manager of Keso Mining Corporation near Winnipeg—one of Continental Ore's fast-expanding Canadian enterprises—had been announced a month before, and now everything had been tidied up except the last vital

*This case was prepared by Mr. Gareth Evans for Shell-BP Development Company of Nigeria, Ltd. Reproduced here by permission.

interview with his successor—the able young Barracanian, Matthew Rennalls. It was vital that this interview be a success and that Rennalls should leave his office uplifted and encouraged to face the challenge of his new job. A touch on the bell would have brought Rennalls walking into the room, but Baker delayed the moment and gazed thoughtfully through the window considering just exactly what he was going to say and, more particularly, how he was going to say it.

John Baker, an English expatriate, was forty-five years old and had served his twenty-three years with Continental Ore in many different places: in the Far East; in several countries of Africa and Europe; and, for the last two years, in the West Indies. He hadn't cared much for his previous assignment in Hamburg and was delighted when the West Indian appointment came through. Climate was not the only attraction. Baker had always preferred working overseas (in what were termed the developing countries) because he felt he had an innate knack—better than most other expatriates working for Continental Ore—of knowing just how to get on with regional staff. Twenty-four hours in Barracania, however, soon made him realize that he would need all of this "innate knack" if he was to deal effectively with the problems in this field that now awaited him.

At his first interview with Hutchins, the production manager, the whole problem of Rennalls and his future was discussed. There and then it was made quite clear to Baker that one of his most important tasks would be the "grooming" of Rennalls as his successor. Hutchins had pointed out that not only was Rennalls one of the brightest Barracanian prospects on the staff of Caribbean Bauxite (at London University he had taken first-class honors in the B.S. engineering degree) but, being the son of the Minister of Finance and Economic Planning, he also had no small political pull.

The company had been particularly pleased when Rennalls decided to work for them rather than for the government in which his father had such a prominent post. They ascribed his action to the effect of their vigorous and liberal regionalization program which since World War II had produced eighteen Barracanians at mid-management level and had given Caribbean Bauxite a good lead in this respect over other international concerns operating in Barracania. The success of this timely regionalization policy had led to excellent relations with the government—a relationship which had been given added importance when Barracania, three years later, became independent. This occasion had encouraged a critical and challenging attitude towards the role foreign interests would have to play in the new Barracania. Hutchins had therefore little difficulty in convincing Baker that the successful career development of Rennalls was of the first importance.

The interview with Hutchins was now two years old; and Baker, leaning back in his office chair, reviewed just how successful he had been in the "grooming" of Rennalls. What aspects of the latter's character had helped and what had hindered? What about his own personality? How had that helped or hindered? The first item to go on the credit side would, without question, be the ability of Rennalls to master the technical aspects of his job. From the start he had shown keenness and enthusiasm and had often impressed Baker with his ability in tackling new assignments and the constructive comments he invariably made in departmental discussions. He was popular with all ranks of Barracanian staff and had an ease of manner which stood him in good stead when dealing with his expatriate seniors. These were all assets, but what about the debit side?

First and foremost, there was his racial consciousness. His four years at London University had accentuated this feeling and made him sensitive to any sign of condescension on the part of expatriates. It may have been to give expression to this sentiment that as soon as he returned home from London he threw himself into politics on behalf of the United Action Party who were later to win the preindependence elections and provide the country with its first Prime Minister.

The ambitions of Rennalls—and he certainly was ambitious—did not however, lie in politics for, staunch nationalist as he was, he saw that he could serve himself and his country best—for was not bauxite responsible for nearly half the value of Barracania's export trade?—by putting his engineering talent to the best use possible. On this account, Hutchins found that he had an unexpectedly easy task in persuading Rennalls to give up his political work before entering the production department as an assistant engineer.

It was, Baker knew, Rennalls' well-repressed sense of race consciousness which had prevented their relationship from being as close as it should have been. On the surface, nothing could have seemed more agreeable. Formality between the two men was at a minimum; Baker was delighted to find that his assistant shared his own peculiar "shaggy-dog" sense of humor so that jokes were continually being exchanged; they entertained each other at their houses and often played tennis together—and yet the barrier remained invisible, indefinable, but ever present. The existence of this "screen" between them was a constant source of frustration to Baker since it indicated a weakness which he was loath to accept. If successful with all other nationalities, why not with Rennalls?

But at least he had managed to "break through" to Rennalls more successfully than any other expatriate. In fact, it was the young Barracanian's attitude—sometimes overbearing, sometimes cynical—toward other company expatriates that had been one of the subjects Baker had raised last year when he discussed Rennalls' staff report with him. He knew too that he would have to raise the same subject again in the forthcoming interview because Jackson, the senior draftsman, had complained only yesterday about the rudeness of Rennalls. With this thought in mind, Baker leaned forward and spoke into the intercom. "Would you come in, Matt, please? I'd like a word with you," and later, "Do sit down," proffering the box, "Have a cigarette." He paused while he held out his lighter and then went on.

"As you know, Matt, I'll be off to Canada in a few days' time; and before I go, I thought it would be useful if we could have a final chat together. It is indeed with some deference that I suggest I can be of help. You will shortly be sitting in this chair doing the job I am now doing; but I, on the other hand, am ten years older, so perhaps you can accept the idea that I may be able to give you the benefit of my longer experience."

Baker saw Rennalls stiffen slightly in his chair as he made this point, so added in explanation, "You and I have attended enough company courses to remember those repeated requests by the personnel manager to tell people how they are getting on as often as the convenient moment arises, and not just the automatic 'once a year' when, by regulation, staff reports have to be discussed."

Rennalls nodded his agreement, so Baker went on, "I shall always remember the last job performance discussion I had with my previous boss back in Germany. He used what he called the "plus and minus" technique. His firm belief was that when a senior, by discussion, seeks to improve the work performance of his staff, his prime objective should be to make sure that the latter leaves the interview encouraged and inspired to improve. Any criticism must, therefore, be constructive and helpful. He said that one very good way to encourage a man— and I fully agree with him—is to tell him about his good points—the plus factors—as well as his weak ones—the minus factors—so I thought, Matt, it would be a good idea to run our discussion along these lines."

Rennalls offered no comment, so Baker continued: "Let me say, therefore, right away, that as far as your own work performance is concerned, the plus far outweighs the minus. I have, for instance, been most impressed with the way you have adapted your considerable theoretical knowledge to master the practical techniques of your job—that ingenious method you used to get air down to the fifth-shift level is a sufficient case in point—and at departmental meetings I have invariably found your comments well taken and helpful. In fact, you will be interested to know that only last week I reported to Mr. Hutchins that from the technical point of view, he could not wish for a more able man to succeed to the position of chief engineer."

"That's very good indeed of you, John," cut in Rennalls with a smile of thanks. "My only worry now is how to live up to such a high recommendation."

"Of that I am quite sure," returned Baker, "especially if you can overcome the minus factor which I would like now to discuss with you. It is one which I have talked about before, so I'll come straight to the point. I have noticed that you are more friendly and get on better with your fellow Barracanians than you do with Europeans. In point of fact, I had a complaint only yesterday from Mr. Jackson, who said you had been rude to him—and not for the first time, either.

"There is, Matt, I am sure, no need for me to tell you how necessary it will be for you to get on well with expatriates, because until the company has trained up sufficient men of your caliber, Europeans are bound to occupy senior positions here in Barracania. All this is vital to your future interests, so can I help you in any way?"

While Baker was speaking on this theme, Rennalls had sat tensed in his chair, and it was some seconds before he replied. "It is quite extraordinary, isn't it, how one can convey an impression to others so at variance with what one intends? I can only assure you once again that my disputes with Jackson—and you may remember also Godson—have had nothing at all to do with the color of their skins. I promise you that if a Barracanian had behaved in an equally peremptory manner I would have reacted in precisely the same way. And again, if I may say it within these four walls, I am sure I am not the only one who has found Jackson and Godson difficult. I could mention the names of several expatriates who have felt the same. However, I am really sorry to have created this impression of not being able to get on with Europeans—it is an entirely false one—and I quite realize that I must do all I can to correct it as quickly as possible. On your last point, regarding Europeans holding senior positions in the company for some time to come, I quite accept the situation. I know that Caribbean Bauxite—as they have been doing for many years now—will promote Barracanians as soon as their experience warrants it. And, finally, I would like to assure you, John—and my father thinks the same too—that I am very happy in my work here and hope to stay with the company for many years to come."

Rennalls had spoken earnestly and, although not convinced by what he had heard, Baker did not think he could pursue the matter further except to say, "All right, Matt, my impression *may* be wrong, but I would like to remind you about the truth of that old saying, 'What is important is not what is true but what is believed.' Let it rest at that."

But suddenly Baker knew that he didn't want to "let it rest at that." He was disappointed once again at not being able to "break through" to Rennalls and having yet again to listen to his bland denial that there was any racial prejudice in his makeup. Baker, who had intended ending the interview at this point, decided to try another tack.

"To return for a moment to the 'plus and minus technique' I was telling you about just now, there is another plus factor I forgot to mention. I would like to congratulate you not only on the caliber of your work, but also on the ability you have shown in overcoming a challenge which I, as a European, have never had to meet.

"Continental Ore is, as you know, a typical commercial enterprise— admittedly a big one—which is a product of the economic and social environment of the United States and Western Europe. My ancestors have all been brought up in this environment for the past two or three hundred years, and I have, therefore, been able to live in a world in which commerce (as we know it today) has been part and parcel of my being. It has not been something revolutionary and new which has suddenly entered my life. In your case," went on Baker, "the situation is different because you and your forebears have only had some 50 or 60 years' experience in this commercial environment. You have had to face the challenge of bridging the gap between 50 and 200 or 300 years. Again, Matt, let me congratulate you—and people like you—once again on having so successfully overcome this particular hurdle. It is for this very reason that I think the outlook for Barracania—and particularly Caribbean Bauxite—is so bright."

Rennalls had listened intently, and when Baker finished, replied, "Well, once again, John, I have to thank you for what you have said, and, for my part, I can only say that it is gratifying to know that my own personal effort has been so much appreciated. I hope that more people will soon come to think as you do."

There was a pause, and for a moment Baker thought hopefully that he was about to achieve his long-awaited "breakthrough," but Rennalls merely smiled back. The barrier remained unbreached. There remained some five minutes' cheerful conversation about the contrast between the Caribbean and Canadian climate and whether the West Indies had any hope of beating England in the Fifth Test before Baker drew the interview to a close. Although he was as far as ever from knowing the real Rennalls, he was nevertheless glad that the interview had run along in this friendly manner and, particularly, that it had ended on such a cheerful note.

This feeling, however, lasted only until the following morning. Baker had some farewells to make, so he arrived at the office considerably later than usual. He had no sooner sat down at his desk than his secretary walked into the room with a worried frown on her face. Her words came fast. "When I arrived this morning I found Mr. Rennalls already waiting at my door. He seemed very angry and told me in quite a peremptory manner that he had a vital letter to dictate which must be sent off without any delay. He was so worked up that he couldn't keep still and kept pacing about the room, which is most unlike him. He wouldn't even wait to read what he had dictated. Just signed the page where he thought the letter would end. It has been distributed, and your copy is in your 'in tray.'"

Puzzled and feeling vaguely uneasy, Baker opened the "Confidential" envelope and read the following letter:

From: Assistant Engineer
To: The Chief Engineer, Caribbean Bauxite Limited

14th August, 1967

ASSESSMENT OF INTERVIEW BETWEEN MESSRS. BAKER AND RENNALLS

It has always been my practice to respect the advice given me by seniors; so after our interview, I decided to give careful thought once again to its main points and so make sure that I had understood all that had been said. As I promised you at the time, I had every intention of putting your advice to the best effect.

It was not, therefore, until I had sat down quietly in my home yesterday evening to consider the interview objectively that its main purpose became clear. Only then did the full enormity of what you said dawn on me. The more I thought about it, the more convinced I was that I had hit upon the real truth—and the more furious I became. With a facility in the English language which I—a poor Barracanian—cannot hope to match, you had the audacity to insult me (and through me every Barracanian worth his salt) by claiming that our knowledge of modern living is only a paltry 50 years old whilst your goes back 200 to 300 years. As if your materialistic commercial environment could possibly be compared with the spiritual values of our culture. I'll have you know that if much of what I saw in London is representative of your most boasted culture, I hope fervently that it will never come to Barracania. By what right do you have the effrontery to condescend to us? At heart, all you Europeans think us barbarians, or, as you say amongst yourselves, we are "just down from the trees."

Far into the night I discussed this matter with my father, and he is as disgusted as I. He agrees with me that any company whose senior staff think as you do is no place for any Barracanian proud of his culture and race—so much for all the company "claptrap" and specious propaganda about regionalization and Barracania for the Barracanians.

I feel ashamed and betrayed. Please accept this letter as my resignation which I wish to become effective immediately.

c.c. Production manager
    Managing director

Part VII

Effective Managing

Cases Outline

- Robertson Rubber Products, Inc. (RRPI)
- C Company (I and II)
- Lee Department Store

47. Robertson Rubber Products, Inc. (RRPI) *

Many people see the man who owns his own business as "having it made." To them, he is his own boss, and can come and go as he pleases. There are not set hours in which he must report for or stay at work. He can tell people what to do, and they had better do it if they want their jobs. They also believe that he is making bushels of money.

In reality, small, independent, owner-managed businesses are not the panacea commonly thought. The following case illustrates the growth and development of one such firm, Robertson Rubber Products, Inc. (RRPI), by its present owner-manager, Mr. Fred Engle. To all who want to be their own bosses, it would be wise to reflect a moment on the pros and cons of owning that "dream venture."

Early Company History

In 1893, Isaiah Robertson founded the company that still bears his name. Mr. Robertson perceived an opportunity to serve industrial customers with a limited line of rubber products as a manufacturer's representative. His son-in-law joined the firm in 1915; the business began to prosper, directing its activities to the "after-market" rubber products customer.

In 1930, Mr. Robertson hired an experienced rubber products salesman, who convinced him that great opportunities were available in "jobbing" operations.

World War II saw a greatly increased demand for rubber products of all kinds, and the firm expanded operations by adding a manufacturing job shop to produce those small specialty items that large rubber manufacturers were not interested in producing. The company developed a reputation as the place to go with a problem that larger firms considered to be of too limited potential volume to warrant the tooling expenses incurred. When the war ended, Robertson Rubber Products had annual sales of nearly $1 million, and had found its niche between the little company that lacked RRPI's skills and the big company that was not interested in the volume of job that Robertson manufactured.

*This case was prepared by Donald W. Scotton, Chairman, Departments of Marketing and General Administration, and Jeffrey C. Susbauer, Department of Management and Labor, The Cleveland State University. Copyright © Donald W. Scotton and Jeffrey C. Susbauer. Reprinted by permission.

Market and Competitive Environment

At present, Robertson sales are generated 30 percent from jobbing, 30 percent from manufacturing, and 40 percent from distributing. Of these, the manufacturing operations are the most profitable, while distributing has the least margin. Intense distributor and jobber competition exists in the market area currently served by the company, which is generally confined to the state of Missouri.

Manufacturing competition is less intense, since the manufacture of rubber products is a specialized business requiring considerable skill and expertise. Most smaller rubber firms do not have the skills or resources to manufacture, and therefore elect to stay out of this facet of the business. RRPI concentrates on specialized, shop type operations with relatively frequent low volume runs. The well-equipped shop area of the Robertson plant contains almost no special-purpose machinery.

Larger manufacturers cannot compete with Robertson's expertise and overhead rates, and are generally uninterested in attracting the types of jobs Robertson performs. Some competition does exist within the market area served by RRPI from other small rubber products manufacturing concerns, but the impact of over twenty-five years of experience in this field has contributed to a solid list of satisfied customers. Opportunities generally exist for further manufacturing, jobbing, and distribution expansion of the enterprise without expanding the market territory boundaries.

Mr. Fred Engle

Mr. Fred Engle held a variety of jobs after graduating from Purdue University in 1937, with B.S. and M.S. degrees in Metallurgical Engineering. Among other occupations, he had been a mining engineer and an assistant production manager for a medium-sized corporation prior to serving as a major in the U.S. Army during World War II.

Shortly after the war, he came back to work for RRPI. He was to go on to become the next president of the firm. One major factor leading to this position was the fact that he married the boss's daughter, but it was by no means his only asset.

When Mr. Engle assumed control of the company in 1949, it had gone through several changes. From its early stages of being strictly a distributor, it had diversified into manufacturing, jobbing, and distribution. His major contribution to the continuation of this diversification was to change the primary direction of the firm from the after-market to the "Original Equipment Manufacturer (OEM)" market. The firm continues to supply the after-market to this day; over 1,500 items for this portion of RRPI's business are stocked.

Mr. Engle felt that the company could best develop through the use of the manufacturing facilities. He apparently made the proper decision, because the firm has grown from about $1 million in annual sales when he became president, to nearly $3.5 million in sales in 1972. In addition, Mr. Engle has made major modifications to the structure of the firm internally during his twenty-four-year tenure as owner-manager.

Present Organization Structure

The Robertson organization, currently housed in a satisfactory two-story building downtown in a large mid-central city, employs forty-eight people, including Mr. Engle. Mr. Engle and his wife own 90 percent of the stock of the concern. A simplified organization chart is shown in Exhibit 1.

Mr. Engle feels that his company is relatively unique, and that this is a direct result of his planning and operating philosophy. He noted that most small, closely held, owner-managed firms do not really provide for the succession of the enterprise in the event of the death or retirement of the owner-manager. (It is not unusual for such firms to simply dissolve when the principal owner-manager retires or dies.)

The board of directors of the firm includes Mr. Engle and his wife. One longtime employee, who is also a stockholder, is the only other inside director of the firm. Mr. Engle has placed several outside directors on this body to advise him and serve as devil's advocates to his plans and whims, including other businessmen, the dean of the local college of business administration, an economist, and a lawyer. Mr. Engle believes that if his board does not thwart at least one of his ideas at each session, they are not doing their jobs. It should be noted that Mr. Engle is free to accept or reject the advice of the board, given his ownership position.

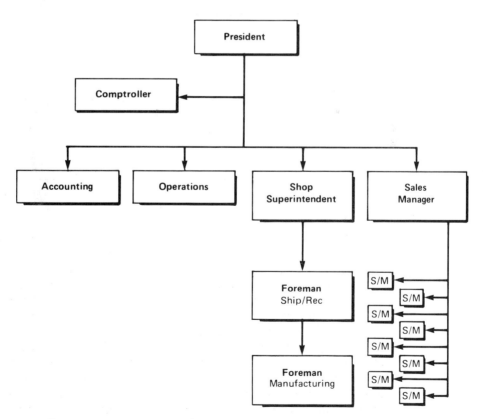

Exhibit 1. Organization Chart, Robertson Rubber Products, Inc. (RRPI)

Financial and Fiscal Controls

Though his formal academic background was obtained in engineering, Mr. Engle considers sound financial control systems essential to the success of his firm. He hired a staff comptroller for the corporation in 1964 to ensure that he was receiving timely information upon which to make decisions and gauge the performance and direction of the firm. It has proven to be a wise decision, in his estimation.

As Mr. Engle explained:

> The large firm can make many mistakes, but it is insulated from the shock effect of those errors. In the small firm, a major mistake can have catastrophic effects because there are few buffers, checks, and balances. At the same time, a properly responsive control system can provide me with the means of finding out about the mistake, and the small size of my operations pays the dividend of being able to respond more quickly than the large firm can.

Employee Relations: Philosophy

Until 1971, the company did not differ from many small firms. It was run in a paternalistic fashion, with fairly lax work rules, no unionization, and a "happy family" atmosphere. Mr. Engle became concerned that perhaps the family was *too* happy when he noticed his cost of overhead and manufacturing labor rising in relation to previous year's performance.

His corrective action—replacing the manufacturing operations foreman with a more hard-nosed supervisor—produced the reverse effect anticipated. He had hoped the new foreman would make people more conscious of the need to be productive and improve the manufacturing margin. Instead, the new foreman managed to alienate the hourly employees; they, in turn, sought a union to represent them as their bargaining agent.

Like most managers, Mr. Engle viewed this unionization attempt with uncertainty; he dragged his feet as long as he could and mounted a countercampaign. Finally, when he could not legally postpone recognition further, the union became the workers' representative in his shop.

After the shock had worn off, he reflected on what was accomplished by unionization:

> Prior to 1971, there were no strict rules that were really enforced. Everyone in this company had the right to come to me and complain about their problems. I had to figure out all the wage rates, merit increases, percentages of profit sharing for each employee. We had an inhouse grievance system, but it always included my negotiation with the worker and the foreman. When the union came in, I suddenly found out that I no longer had to perform most of these functions. The labor contract set the wage rates, fringe benefits package, and laid out procedures for handling disputes. Strangely, the two workers who most agitated for union recognition were not backed by the union when we fired them shortly after the union took over for infractions of the work rules. All of a sudden, the union became the enforcer, and made the employees "toe the line." Also, in exchange for a $.15 per hour raise, we negotiated the end of merit increases and profit

sharing for the hourly workers. There are several of the hourly workers that now wish they did not have to pay the initiation dues to the union and those monthly dues. The union also makes sure that production quotas are achieved.

Salaried and Officer Personnel

Of the forty-eight people employed by Robertson Rubber Products, thirty-one are included in these categories. Salaried personnel (twenty-eight) are distributed among the accounting, operations, and sales functions of the business. All of these people share in any profits the company makes each year.

For thirty years, Robertson has had an employee bonus plan keyed to profitability. In these thirty years, only in 1971 has the company failed to distribute some portion of profit to these employees. In recent years, this distribution has ranged from a high of 24 percent of pre-tax profit to a low (excluding 1971) of 10 percent of the profits.

Prior to Mr. Engle's ascendancy to the presidency, profit sharing was the only fringe benefit the company had for employees. Mr. Engle believed that:

> . . . in order to retain those good employees and attract competent new ones, there had to be a better fringe package. Therefore, over the years, I have added additional fringes of full hospitalization, a group life insurance policy, and a sickness and accident policy to what the employees could receive from the company. Of course, they have been covered by Social Security for many years.

Under the charter of the company, as amended, Mr. Engle is required to pay a minimum of 5 percent of profits before taxes into the company profit-sharing fund. This is a deferred compensation to employees covered. It takes three years of continuous employment, full time, to be eligible for any benefits, and the employees' rights to the noncontributions fund becomes fully vested after thirteen years of continuous employment.

Compensation in the company is perhaps unique when compared to similar practices in government and large private corporations. Mr. Engle commented:

> We have several salesmen who work for the firm who have not grossed less than $30,000 for years. Their compensation is geared to their productivity on a commission basis. As a consequence, there are a handful of individuals in this company that earn more than I do. I think this is healthy, and I encourage it. After all, the more they sell, the more worth I have in the company. But you don't find this condition in your run-of-the-mill, Fortune 500 firm.

The "Comfort Stage"

One of Mr. Engle's problems is the fact that he has been owner-manager of this company for over twenty years. He has guided its growth and development from a corporation doing slightly less than $1 million annual sales to one doing in excess of $3.5 million—a growth rate compounded over 10 percent annually. It currently takes about $25,000 in additional working capital to generate growth at the rate previously obtained. He has reached what he describes as the "comfort stage"—a position where he obtains sufficient remuneration from the company to support his material needs and desires. Increasingly in the past few years, he has been able to do what he wants, within limits, and still keep the company on an even keel. In recent months, for example, he has felt sufficiently comfortable about the competency of his subordinates that he has been able to take off a week at a time to pursue his golfing in various places around the country.

> What do I do now? I've mastered the job. What directions should the company pursue? The corporation is perfectly capable of expanding market territories, if desired. Present accounts can be maintained and new ones can be acquired through normal business expansion without excessive efforts on my part. Should I take more remuneration from the business? Should I sink more into the venture, even at this mature stage? Should I retire, turn the firm over to someone else with more need to succeed at this point?
>
> I have felt no great need to expand this company at more than the inflationary rate—about 5 percent a year. If we are to get ahead of the game that we currently play in this economy, it must expand at more than this rate, yet I am very comfortable at the 5 percent pace, and can live very adequately on that kind of expansion. My goals are no longer driven by the need to achieve that kind of success, and these may be incompatible with my employees' needs—particularly the newer ones. At the same time, I am still in charge, the one who makes the ultimate decisions upon which the company sinks or swims. I think the corporation has done right by me. The weight of the decision-making will not really pass out of my hands until I relinquish the reins of control. Unfortunately, although the invitation is open, my son-in-law is not interested in joining the firm, and I have some hard decisions to make. I am not independently wealthy, yet my ambition is somewhat less urgent than it was ten, fifteen, or twenty years ago.

As Mr. Engle told the case writer this story, he turned to an article in that morning's *Wall Street Journal* that described a small company in South Dakota that also was suffering problems similar to his firm's.

> Here, this is exactly my dilemma—the locale is different, but the problems are still the same. These people [in the article] have been successful, but they can't interest their children in following in their footsteps. I've still got some years before I would have to retire, but if I wanted to step down tomorrow, the business would have no one step into my shoes.

48. C Company (I) *

Assignment

After reading the following problem, develop a list of interview questions that will be useful in conducting an assessment of company practices.

Problem

You are a team of management consultants hired to assess the current management practices in the corporate offices and the Research and Development Division of a large, heavy equipment Manufacturing Company. The product line of the company is limited to industrial motors such as those used in overhead cranes, heavy moving equipment, road building equipment, and motors to power large trucks. The company designs and makes both gas and diesel engines. Approximately 200 professional and/or managerial employees are located in the corporate offices, and 200 in the R & D division. You plan to interview a select sample of 50 to 75 employees at various levels in the organization, from eleven departments. The sample will be selected with the aid of the Personnel Vice-President and is intended to include employees at various age levels, with various years of tenure with the company, and with various perspectives and educational backgrounds.

Specifically, the management is interested in having you develop questions which, when asked, could render answers to the following questions:

1. How should the company corporate offices and R & D divisions be organized, i.e., should it have a classical, organic, a mix of two, or some other kind of structure?
2. What are the kinds of policies and practices that will
   * most likely motivate employees?
   * most likely attract and retain employees?
   * most likely develop employee ability to improve job performance?
3. What style of leadership should the company be attempting to select and develop for the management of its corporate offices and R & D Divisions?

Group Discussion Assignment

Since this is a planning session for the consulting team, the problem is to develop a list of interview questions that will be used to guide team members in the investigation.

---

*This case was prepared by Robert J. House, University of Toronto, and John R. Rizzo, Western Michigan University, and is used here with their permission.

Assumptions

You are to assume there is no universal "best way" to manage, and that the organizational structure, leader style, and motivational strategy of the company will depend on what you find in the interviews. Assume that after conducting the interviews you will have another planning meeting to develop recommendations for the company management. The problem before you is to develop the key questions to be answered in the investigation.

C Company (II)

Problem

After reading the following interview findings, prepare notes to answer the following questions:

1. What are the appropriate organizational structures and leadership style for this company?
2. How should the company go about making the necessary changes?

Discuss this question thoroughly and be prepared to defend your position to the class.

Assumption

Assume that as a result of your investigation your team has been able to agree on the following description of the client company.

Interview Findings

The following description of the company is based on actual interviews with seventy-five members of a large heavy equipment manufacturing company. The interviewees included nine vice-presidents of the corporation and sixty-six others who the personnel vice-president selected on the basis of criteria suggested by the consultant. The personnel vice-president was requested to select persons in all divisions who (a) represented a wide variety of experience, perspective, age, and training, and (b) would be willing to give frank opinions concerning their perceptions of the organizational climate, the leadership styles of superiors, their satisfactions and dissatisfactions, and any problems they were experiencing in carrying out their responsibilities. Of the seventy-five interviewees approximately forty were in supervisory or managerial positions. The remainder were in engineering or corporate staff groups such as finance, marketing research, or personnel. The interviewees were generally very cooperative and willing to share their perceptions and feelings in the interviews. Approximately twelve interviewees appeared to be unwilling to share feelings, and restricted their comments to descriptive rather than evaluative statements. The results of the interviews are reported here.

In general, the interviews revealed an organization seeking to excel and grow, offering its members opportunity and challenge in the endeavor. Yet many employees were experiencing a marked degree of frustration, tension, and stress.

More specifically, interviewees described an organization highly motivated toward the maintenance of a large share of a growing and increasingly competitive market. Within this framework, there existed opportunity for individual success and contribution. It was reported that higher management dealt with problems openly and fairly, and treated recommendations from below with thoroughness and objectivity. The interviewees' statements also suggested that the firm appeared remarkably free of political maneuvering.

However, the organization was not without significant problems. The manner in which the foregoing attributes manifested themselves created substantial personal and organizational strains. For example, there was an emphasis on short-run productivity and activity designed to meet day-to-day problems. The emphasis on the immediate was perceived to occur at the expense of long-range projects and of creative efforts designed to both prevent the day-to-day "firefighting" and to enable continued growth and market penetration. Communication often consisted of ambiguous changing and inconsistent directions frequently coming from different sources several levels above one's immediate superior. Cases of alleged unwarranted or unexplained change, incompatible goals, and the like, were frequently reported. Cases of exasperation and cross-pressure on individuals seemed commonplace. Downward communication was highly work-oriented and impersonal. The rationale and intent of directions often went unexplained and frequently took the form of requests for information or productivity which required individuals to work toward seemingly uncoordinated, short-run efforts. Upward communication consisted of progress reports, responses to inquiries, and requests for approval. The latter was viewed duplicative, delaying, and representative of failure to delegate. Many signatures were required for approval of expenditures budgeted earlier. There was a lack of philosophy, policy, or stable objectives to guide work. Minor reorganizations were almost commonplace, and major reorganizations were not uncommon. These conditions prevented the development of cooperative and coordinative team efforts.

At the individual level, there existed little in the way of orientation upon employment or systematic training and development efforts. New employees had to rely on their own sensitivities to obtain a "feel" for both company needs and the definition of an acceptable contribution. High rewards for outstanding performances were promised to individuals early in their careers, but to attain them a visible and outstanding contribution was expected within the first two years of employment.

One form of evidence that the firm sought exceptional individual achievement existed in its recruitment practices. Approximately eight years prior to the time of the study, the company recruited a number of top students from prominent midwestern graduate business schools. Four years later, the recruiting effort was redirected to prominent Ivy League and California schools. In many cases these new employees were given upper-middle management and staff positions of considerable responsibility, or placed as assistants to key top officers. Several assistants became vice-presidents of the firm. This recruiting practice resulted in frustration and resentment among those already in the firm, for newly recruited groups filled positions and assumed responsibilities which might have served as rewards for others. Consequently, longer tenured employees perceived the reward system as emphasizing educational credentials rather than service and experience. This contributed to turnover in the "forgotten" groups. There were also frequent incidents of new top recruits leaving due to lack of receptivity to their ideas, or having to fill unchallenging positions.

The foregoing was coupled with a narrow-based reward system consisting primarily of economic (pay, bonus) and status (promotion) recognitions.

This situation was exacerbated by several other related conditions. The criteria used to evaluate performance were perceived as ambiguous, and sometimes inconsistent. And peer competition (though not malicious) was reported as very high. Appraisal took place behind closed doors, and feed-back on performance usually occurred after the reward had been determined and approved at levels far above the immediate superior. Although the members of top management were generally viewed as sincere in their intent, and dealt with *operational* problems openly, *personnel* decisions were dealt with secretly and management was viewed as "past and blame oriented," seeking to find who was responsible for errors rather than treating errors as learning experiences to be avoided in the future.

Hence, individuals were surrounded with cues of success and failure, sensed the importance of achievement in an aggressive and energetic firm, yet were left ambiguous regarding evaluation in a blame-oriented climate. Supportiveness, coaching, feedback, and mutual confidence necessary for cooperative team efforts were lacking. These conditions created a great deal of uncertainty, tension, and strain for many individuals. They constitute, basically, a stress climate. In summary, the characteristics of the organization suggested by the interviews were:

- Aggressive, achievement-oriented firm
- Well-intended, sincere top management
- Open, fair receptivity and resolution of problems
- Low political and malicious behavior, open discussion
- Emphasis on short-run productivity and innovation
- Downward task-oriented communication
- Changing, conflicting, or ambiguous directives
- Lack of clear policies or philosophy
- Individual motivation to achieve and succeed
- Ambiguous criteria used in personnel decisions
- Blame orientation
- Low feedback, coaching, team efforts
- Limited base of rewards
- Uncertainty, tension, stress

Technological Environmental Description

Having described the internal structural and interpersonal characteristics of the organization, we now turn to the primary technology and the external environment of the organization.

The company designs, assembles, and markets its own products, the major product being a heavy industrial capital goods item that is assembled in the main domestic plant from parts manufactured there, in other plants, or by suppliers. Annual sales of the company had increased over the last five years from $175,000,000 to $330,000,000. At the time of the interviews the company employed 14,500 employees.

The industry in which the company operates is one in which technological advancements are infrequent. There have been no fundamentally new products introduced in the industry in the last ten years. However, the existing products and manufacturing processes of the industry change continually as a result of product and process modification. Such change is change in degree rather than kind, however, reflecting incremental advances in technology rather than major breakthroughs into fundamentally new products. Competition, increasing in the industry, is based primarily on cost reduction, marketing service, improvement in existing product capabilities, increases in product life, and ability to meet customer demands for delivery and customization of fixtures.

Products are produced in response to customer orders in lots ranging from a few to several thousand. The major components of the product are almost always standard parts but even these are numberous. Furthermore, each order has a different combination of fixtures, and occasionally minor parts will be manufactured specifically to meet customer requirements. Hence, although an assembly line exists, it must be highly responsive in meeting varied orders.

Although the firm varied the basic product greatly, there seemed to exist marked opportunity to systematization and standardization of production and assembly. Evidence for this lies in the fact that there existed in the firm strong differences of opinion regarding standardization versus responsiveness to all customer demands for modifications. Many felt that much more was possible in the way of standardization and reduction in order variances, while others felt that responsiveness and a job-shop operation were major strengths of the firm.

Description of Task Structures

The tasks of the majority of the employees were semi-structured since they were almost all engaged in somewhat repetitive, analytic work (such as product engineering, personnel, marketing, and financial analysis).

Immediate superiors neither completely lacked position power nor had the complete power over the career welfare of their subordinates. The employees in the organization units studied were all classified as professional or managerial employees, and the majority of them possessed educational credentials or technical skills that are in high demand in American industry. Consequently, dependence on either their immediate supervisors or the company for career welfare and employment security was minimal.

49. Lee Department Store*

The Place

The offices of the Lee Department Store are in eastern Ohio. The store is located in a town of 40,000 persons where it has been established for some fifty years.

Main Characters

John Lee. He is the president and treasurer, having inherited the presidency upon the death of his father nine years ago. He and his mother control 90 percent of the capital stock of the department store. He was more or less forced into the presidency upon the death of his father, inasmuch as he was the only son. Lee's ambition is to be a portrait painter, and he has been trained for this. As a result, he seems more interested in painting than in the success of the store. By far the major part of his time is spent on portraits which he paints for friends. Nevertheless, Lee does take an interest in the store to the extent that he frequently makes personnel and work changes which he thinks will improve the immediate situation. These changes are of the "spur-of-the-moment" type rather than carefully analyzed to determine the effects or repercussions on the entire workforce. John Lee's manner with the employees is quite forceful. He indicates he is the boss and accepts no arguments.

Albert Abbot. Now chief accountant and office manager, Abbot has been with the Lee Company for nineteen years, since his graduation from high school. He has gradually been given additional duties since his employment, until he became chief accountant and office manager seven years ago. Abbot has an extremely easygoing nature, giving no orders or supervision unless specifically requested to do so. His manner is such that he seems to assume more and more duties without complaint.

Bill Brown. Hired by John Lee six months ago, Bill is twenty-six years of age, and just released from the Air Force, where he had been a supply officer. A few days after his release, Bill and his wife visited the campus of his alma mater, where he graduated with a major in accounting before entering the Air Force for three years. John Lee was attending his class reunion at his college, and, through an old friend, met Bill. This acquaintance led Lee to offer Bill a job as accountant in the office of the Lee Department Store. Though Bill hesitated to take the job offer because he felt he would like to visit the store and meet the employees with whom he was to work, Lee made an attractive offer and seemed to want an immediate acceptance, so Bill did accept before Lee left the class reunion. When Bill accepted the offer, Lee said, "I haven't talked this idea over with my chief accountant, but I am sure it will work out fine."

---

*From *Human Behavior at Work* by Keith Davis, Copyright © 1972 by McGraw-Hill, Inc. Used with permission of McGraw-Hill Book Company.

Office Staff.   In the office staff are approximately fifteen girls and older women. The older office employees have been with the Lee Department Store all their working lives—for a period of about twenty years. They have been working with Albert Abbot, with whom most of them went to high school, for the seven years he has been chief accountant and office manager. Most of the office girls are unmarried. They get along very well together, often planning parties and picnics during office hours. They often see each other after office hours, particularly in their church organization, because nearly all of them belong to the same church. Abbot also is a member of this church. Because of their length of service, their chumminess in the office, and their comparative freedom in their jobs, the girls are satisfied with somewhat less than the going wages in the community.

The Situation

The general offices of the Lee Department Store are located on two different floors: the rear of the second floor and the rear of the third floor. This is necessary because of the layout of sales space in the store. The credit department (three older women), cashiers (two younger girls), and Abbot are located on the rear of the second floor. The general accounting offices (eight older women, three younger girls), and the administrative offices, and Lee are located on the rear of the third floor.

John Lee, upon returning from his college reunion, discussed Bill's arrival with most of his office staff. Lee arranged to have a desk for Bill in the office on the third floor. This enabled Bill to be near the employees and the general accounting records with which his main assignment dealt. Bill Brown's principal job was to assist Albert Abbot in the preparation of daily, weekly, and monthly accounting reports. Lee, as well as the general manager and department managers, felt that the reports which were being presented to them by Abbot were of no value as a control of operations, because they were received one to four months after the end date of the period covered. To this Abbot agreed but felt he was too busy with everyday assignments to improve this situation.

On Bill Brown's first day at the store he was taken on a tour of the store and offices by Lee and was introduced to most of the employees, including Abbot, whom Bill was to assist. John Lee introduced Bill to the office employees and department managers, with the comment, "Bill is going to assist us in the accounting office. Now we'll be getting the reports out on time."

Bill spent most of his first day talking with employees with whom he was to work and talking with Lee regarding types of information he felt that he and the department managers needed. The employees were very cordial, and Bill looked forward to working in this friendly work atmosphere. That evening Lee and his wife took Bill and his wife to dinner at a local restaurant as a welcome and wedding present. During the evening, Lee frequently talked enthusiastically about the portrait work he was doing. Bill felt quite flattered when Lee said, "Bill, I feel as though I can stay away from the office a good deal more now that I know the reports for our managers will be coming out on time."

Bill spent most of the first week with Abbot learning the various accounting procedures. Bill found him very cordial and willing to help at any time upon being asked. Throughout the next few months he and Bill became quite friendly.

On many occasions, as the months passed, they would get together with their wives for an evening of bridge.

Bill respected Abbot's judgment and found him very helpful. Frequently Abbot would say, "Bill, you've sure helped me by taking the pressure for those reports off my mind. John, occasionally, when he wasn't worrying about his painting, really put the heat on."

As Bill got into the routine of his duties, he found that they required him to work very closely with most of the women in the two offices, because nearly all of them performed some phase of bookkeeping. Using the statistical and accounting data prepared by these women, Bill prepared his reports for John Lee and the department managers. Bill was in daily contact with nine of the older women employees (eight on the third floor and one on the second floor) and three of the younger girl employees (two on the third floor and one on the second floor).

Bill worked at his job intensively, because he wanted to succeed in his first civilian job. Within two months he was able to have reports on the desks of the store managers (Lee and Miller) and the department managers in a time interval that was satisfactory to them. Bill was frequently called into top-level departmental sales meetings to discuss reports he had prepared. Since Bill's desk was located on the third floor, it was convenient for Lee or Miller, the vice-president and general manager, to call Bill in a loud voice, with a comment such as, "Bill, will you come in here and help us out with these reports?"

Bill felt he was doing a good job at the company, but he did have many minor problems. Below are three representative experiences, in the order of their occurrence, which Bill had during his first six months of work.

1. Upon asking for data from one of the older women, Bill was told, "What's the hurry? Albert never seemed to bother us with asking for this information. We always gave it to him when we were ready." In reply to this, Bill attempted to explain the value of the reports and the need for their promptness. It seemed to Bill that explanation only encouraged here to delay the information a while longer.

2. One of the younger girls in the third-floor office came to Bill and complained that errors were made by the clerks on particular sales tickets, receiving invoices, and packing slips. The girls frequently brought errors of this type to Bill's attention. As was his usual practice, he spoke tactfully and courteously to the clerks and other store employees who made the errors. He pointed out their mistakes and how they affected the information that was needed. Bill heard by the grapevine that the employees he had corrected often complained that he was trying to "run the store."

3. Miller told Bill to instruct the girls in the third-floor and second-floor offices not to stay out for coffee so long in the morning. Their practice was to take a few minutes each morning to go across the street for coffee. (Abbot and Bill never went out for coffee.) This practice had existed for a number of years, without objection by management. Often they stayed longer than seemed reasonable to Miller. In response to Miller's instructions, Bill said to the women in the offices, "Mr. Miller asked me to ask you not to stay out so long for coffee in the morning." He said this to all the women as a group on each floor one afternoon as they were getting ready to go home.

Bill sometimes noticed resentment among the older office women, therefore he tried to be especially nice to them. He attempted to be tactful and courteous in his requests for data. He tried to be helpful with any requests they made of him. Nevertheless, the older women office employees by their actions, manner, and words made Bill feel uncomfortable and out of place.

One morning, about six months after Bill's employment, Lee called Bill into his office. Lee had not worked regularly at the store for weeks because he was busy with a portrait. He said to Bill, "Bill, I wish you would do two things for me as sort of a special assignment. One, revise our outdated accounting expense code system. We need to be able to expand our classifications of expenses. The older code is far out-of-date, as we have used it for some twenty years. This will make it necessary that the office employees memorize a new code system, but I don't think that will be too much for them. And then, as project number two, I wish you would prepare a job analysis on each of the girls in the office. Miller suggested you do this. It has never been done before, so I think it might prove to our advantage to know just what each of the girls is doing. Prepare one for the girls on the second-floor office, too, will you? Take your time on these projects; just work them in with your regular duties. Oh, by the way, tell Albert you are doing this for me." Bill agreed that he would try to do both of these assignments.

As Bill returned to his desk, and as Lee left the office to go home to work on his portrait, Bill pondered how he would go about his new assignments.